Library of Congress Cataloging-in-Publication Data

Schaffel, Kenneth, 1953–1988.
   The emerging shield: the Air Force and the evolution of continental air defense, 1945–1960 / Kenneth Schaffel.
      356p. 24¾cm. — (General histories)
      Includes bibliographical references.
      ISBN 0-912799-60-9. — ISBN 0-912799-61-7 (pbk.)
      1. United States—Air defenses, Military—History. 2. United States, Air Force. Air Defense Command—History. I. United States. Air Force. Office of Air Force History. II. Title. III. Series.
UG733.S33 1990
358.4′145′0973—dc20   90-347   CIP

Foreword

American concerns over air defense of the continental United States were at their most grave in the 1950s. The descent into cold war in the late 1940s, the confrontation of two hostile political systems in distant Korea, and the Soviet development of atomic weapons earlier than expected by American military experts came together to stimulate popular pressures for a shield against manned bombers reaching the American heartland from the North Pole. The effect on the newly independent Air Force was significant—it required that the Air Force modify its weapons inventory, just as the service had settled on a strong strategic nuclear offensive force to deter an enemy attack. The new requirements for strategic defense threatened to compete heavily for resources with the Strategic Air Command, itself undergoing a buildup and the introduction of new airplanes and a ballistic missile force.

The Air Force nevertheless soon realized that the prospect of an attack by bombers armed with nuclear weapons was real. At least a rudimentary defense system, one capable of growing in strength and sophistication as demands dictated, would be needed to persuade the Soviets that an attack might not succeed. The postwar Air Defense Command, an administrative and planning backwater compared to the Strategic Air Command, suddenly assumed far greater significance, absorbing a larger portion of the defense budget.

The expansion of the air defense effort after the mid-1950s had an impact on service roles, forcing the Air Force to consider issues it had not addressed in the past. An effective guided missile defense in the latter part of the decade brought the U.S. Army into the Continental Air Defense Command. Continental implications of the defense problem went beyond dividing responsibilities for tracking and destroying incoming attackers. A wide range of international political issues attended the emplacement of a defensive warning system, for much of its construction had to be on Canadian soil. Even here, the Air Force willingly proceeded, convinced that early warnings of an attack received from the net deployed in arctic regions would improve the survivability of the SAC force that would launch the counterblow.

The Office of Air Force History is proud to publish this history as a memorial to a dear friend and valued colleague, the late Capt. Kenneth Schaffel, USAF. Captain Schaffel joined the office in early 1982 as a second lieutenant just out of the Officer Training and Air Weapons Controller Schools. He took a manuscript that had been partially completed by two other authors, reorganized it, rewrote sections, completed the research, drafted new chapters, and put the whole of it into publishable form. He was indefatigable in his effort and succeeded magnificently in providing, for the service whose uniform he wore, a comprehensive study of the evolution of North American air defense. In 1985, he was assigned to Headquarters Space Command as an intelligence officer. Tragically, the Air Force lost a dedicated and talented officer when Captain Schaffel died in an accident in August 1988. This volume is his legacy to the historical profession, and to the nation he served so well.

RICHARD H. KOHN
Chief, Office of Air Force History

Preface

In the 1950s, the United States Air Force led the way in building continental air defenses to protect the nation against bomber attack. By the end of that decade, the United States and Canada deployed a warning network of ground-based radars extending from the United States' southern borders to the arctic tundra, a fleet of airborne early-warning planes, naval radar picket ships, radar platforms (the Texas Towers) fastened to the ocean floor in the Atlantic Ocean, and a civilian corps of ground observers. Once warning of approaching enemy bombers had been received, the military forces of the United States and Canada were prepared to unleash against the invader an arsenal of weapons that included fighter-interceptors equipped with lethal air-to-air missiles, antiaircraft artillery, and short- and long-range surface-to-air missiles, some nuclear tipped. The whole system was coordinated through a technologically advanced, computer-oriented command and control system, the first of its kind ever deployed.

The story of the rise of air defense in the United States after World War II is complex, and this volume does not presume to be a complete history of the subject. It focuses on the U.S. Air Force's predominant role in defense of the continental United States against manned bomber attacks. Although the U.S. Army, the U.S. Navy, and the Canadian Air Force contributed resources to the mission, the U.S. Air Force had primary responsibility for research, development, and deployment of most of the systems and weapons. The outstanding exception was antiaircraft artillery, the province of the U.S. Army. In some respects, the Army can be said to have fielded a complementary air defense system separate from that of the Air Force. This book, however, examines the Army's part in the mission only as it concerns roles and missions controversies with the Air Force.

The volume begins with the U.S. Army Air Service's involvement with air defense in World War I and traces the story through to the late 1950s and early 1960s. At that time, the intercontinental ballistic missile supplanted the bomber as the most dangerous long-range threat to North America, precipitating a dramatic decline in bomber defenses over the next two decades. A number of important themes emerge: the development of technology, particularly for command, control, and communications systems; roles and missions debates; interpretations and analysis of the threat; and Air Force theories and approaches to offensive and defensive strategic warfare. The last is by far the most pervasive theme.

In the period covered by this volume, the Air Force consistently held true to its belief that "the best defense is a good offense," despite the rise of air defense as a national priority. For most of history, military organizations have favored offensive strategies, for taking the offense is a way of planning and structuring the battle. Assuming the initiative by striking the first blow offers clear benefits as opposed to waiting and reacting defensively. The offense is usually viewed by military organizations as a positive force to achieve victory, whereas defense seems to seek only a negative goal—that of preservation.*

The characteristics of air warfare made an offensive strategy especially appealing to the Air Force. From the first aerial attacks in World War I, most air theorists thought the airplane was the supreme offensive weapon, particularly because of its speed and agility.† The benefits afforded the defense on the ground in the forms of terrain, fortifications, and popular support seemed to lose all relevancy in the air battle. World War I suggested that an effective air defense required coordination of a wide array of antiaircraft elements. First, it would be necessary to receive early warning of approaching aircraft. Next, the enemy's planes would have to be continuously tracked as they neared their target, with some method to indicate the direction, height, speed, and size of the oncoming force. Devices would be required to identify friend from foe and to inform pilots of the enemy's whereabouts. Finally, a commander on the ground would have to assess this information and control the interception of the attacking force by friendly fighters. If everything worked as hoped, well-planned and organized bomber attacks would still probably achieve success by avoiding or breaking through the defenses and by hitting their targets. As airmen viewed the situation, the best that could realistically be expected for air defense was *limited* success, and it was questionable if such success was worth the effort and expense involved.

Advantages of the offense seemed plain to airmen from many nations in World War I and in subsequent years. For U.S. air officers, the offense also was compelling as part of the American legacy. Although a new and distinct combat arm, the Air Force inherited a tradition advocating the destruction of an enemy's armed forces by the most direct means available. In his treatment, *The American Way of War,* military historian Russell F. Weigley has argued convincingly that, although the United States has usually followed a defensive grand national strategy, in

---

*Reasons why military organizations favor offensive strategies are explained in the following: Jack Snyder's "Civil-Military Relations and the Cult of the Offensive, 1914 and 1984" [*International Security* 9, no. 1 (summer 1984):120], George H. Quester's *Offense and Defense in the International System* [(New York, 1977), pp 1–12], and Barry R. Posen's *The Sources of Military Doctrine: France, Britain, and Germany Between Two Wars* [(Ithaca, N.Y., 1984), pp 47–51].

†The characteristics setting the air battle apart from other forms of warfare are described well in Bernard Brodie's still valuable *Strategy in the Missile Age* [(Princeton, N.J., 1959), pp 177–80].

wartime it has strived for complete victory. This policy allowed U.S. combat forces, at least before the Korean War, to pursue total victory. The postwar duality of the awesome strategic (atomic) power unleashed by the Air Force's B–29s against Japan and of President Truman's charge, made to Congress on December 9, 1945, that the United States would maintain "in constant and immediate readiness" a strong deterrent force could thus seem to epitomize the "American way of war" as described by Weigley. This marriage of strategic power and of nuclear readiness was unprecedented in twentieth century American military history.

In some respects, the Air Force doctrine for strategic warfare followed the views of the great Prussian military philosopher, Carl von Clausewitz. Clausewitz's masterwork, *On War,* held that parrying a blow could serve a useful purpose, but that in itself such action went against the very nature of warfare, which is not mere endurance. To be truly effective, Clausewitz thought, defense must eventually revert to offense for "the defensive form of war is not a simple shield, but a shield made up of well-directed blows." Also, after meeting an attack, Clausewitz advocated that a military force be prepared to launch a counterattack, as unleashing the "Sword of Vengeance" was the "greatest moment of defense." For the Air Force, the Strategic Air Command constituted its "Sword of Vengeance."

In the following pages, the author will attempt to explain the dichotomy between the Air Force's reliance on the strategic offense as the cornerstone of its strategy and its mandate to provide, for a time, an adequate continental air defense. This volume describes the effort to create such a system while still relying, for basic strategy, on deterrence and a retaliatory force primed to assume the offensive.

Kenneth Schaffel

Acknowledgments

The late Capt. Kenneth Schaffel, author of this fine work on continental air defense, was killed in an accident in Colorado Springs in August 1988, prior to his having had the opportunity to write his acknowledgments. Captain Schaffel, however, had made clear his debt to the late Thomas A. Sturm, a historian in the Office of Air Force History, who began the research and writing for this book in the 1970s. Before retirement, Mr. Sturm had accomplished a great deal of research and written a number of draft chapters. When Captain Schaffel was assigned to the Office of Air Force History, he contacted Mr. Sturm, and the two formed a fast friendship. Dr. H. O. Malone, formerly a historian in the Office of Air Force History and now command historian for the U.S. Army Training and Doctrine Command, also contributed to the project before Captain Schaffel arrived at the history office. Also useful to Captain Schaffel was a monograph done by Mr. Clyde R. Littlefield, Office of Air Force History, on the semiautomatic ground environment (SAGE) system.

Captain Schaffel was indebted to the following members of the final panel that reviewed the manuscript: Dr. Richard H. Kohn, Col. John F. Shiner, Mr. Herman S. Wolk, Dr. B. F. Cooling, and Mr. Jacob Neufeld, all of the Office of Air Force History; Prof. Allan R. Millett, The Ohio State University; Prof. Joseph T. Jockel, St. Lawrence University, then serving temporarily in the Office of Canadian Affairs, U.S. State Department; Mr. DeWitt S. Copp, USAF Historical Advisory Committee; and Maj. Owen Jensen, USAF. Dr. Haskell Monroe, University of Missouri-Columbia, forwarded helpful comments.

Also helpful were these historians in the Office of Air Force History who participated in Captain Schaffel's seminars: Maj. John Kreis, Dr. Eduard Mark, Lt. Col. Vance Mitchell, Dr. Walton Moody, Mr. Bernard Nalty, Col. John Schlight, Dr. Wayne Thompson, Mr. Warren Trest, and Dr. George Watson.

Captain Schaffel would also have thanked the dedicated people at the National Archives and the Manuscript Division, Library of Congress, who helped him greatly with his research.

In the Editorial Branch, Office of Air Force History, Ms. Vanessa D. Allen began the editing of the manuscript, and Mrs. Barbara Wittig then took over the brunt of the editing, guiding the book to completion. Dr. Alfred Beck, Chief, Editorial Branch, also helped the manuscript through the editorial process.

ACKNOWLEDGMENTS

Contributing from the Graphics Branch, 1100th Resource Management Group, Air Force District of Washington, were Mrs. Susan Linders, who oversaw the graphics production; Mr. Bruce John, who prepared the maps; and Mrs. Tracy Weeks Miller, who prepared the charts.

Contents

Photographs

Charts

Maps

Tables

Chapter 1

Genesis of the Air Defense Mission

The history of air defense begins with the use of manned flight for military purposes. On June 5, 1783, the Montgolfier brothers, Jacques Etienne and Joseph-Michel, demonstrated the first public ascension of their hot-air balloon; less than eleven years later, the French constructed the first military balloon, *L'Entreprenant*. In April 1794 the French Army formed a balloon company. The next month it began reconnaissance operations over Austrian lines. General Jean Baptiste Jourdan, who had approved the formation of the balloon company, was impressed with information he received concerning enemy movements. Austrians, confused by this new element in warfare, took defensive action on June 13, 1794. They used two seventeen-pound howitzers to fire at the balloons. Although their shooting was ineffective, the Austrians opened the first chapter in the history of air defense.[1]

Ground forces tried to thwart reconnaissance balloons throughout the nineteenth century. During the American Civil War, Union and Confederate batteries directed guns at balloons attempting free flight over enemy lines.[2] During the 1870 Siege of Paris, Germans incorporated the first modern antiballoon defenses, and Krupp, the great arms manufacturer, produced a twenty-five-millimeter rifle mounted on a pedestal and light cart. These guns were only marginally successful by day, and the French managed to neutralize them completely by launching their balloons at night. The guns soon left service, and balloons became more or less standard equipment in armies, mostly serving as experimental models instead of as practical devices.[3]

Early in the twentieth century, airplanes and airships began to replace balloons as the premier aeronautical instruments of war. By the beginning of World War I in 1914, airplanes and airships had largely displaced balloons as reconnaissance vehicles. Pilots and observers of the newly formed national air services noted and reported the formations and movements of mass armies and directed friendly fire upon enemy positions. They soon discovered that airplanes could be used for more deadly missions than mere scouting and surveillance.

The role of aircraft in battle became more sinister when airmen armed their machines with guns and bombs, and used them to harass and even to destroy enemy scouts. In the summer of 1915, the Germans introduced the Fokker *Eindecker*, a monoplane equipped with a fixed gun. Designed by the Dutchman Anthony Fokker, this gun was aimed by pointing the aircraft itself. The pilot, using synchronized gearing of the gun and the propeller, fired streams of machinegun bullets through the propeller. With this advantage, the Fokker became "the hired killer of the air with no secondary purpose." [4]

On the ground, the machinegun helped establish the ascendancy of defensive warfare; its use in airplanes promoted the ascendancy of offensive warfare, in the opinion of some military commanders. To defeat the *Eindecker*, Britain and France encouraged the development of even more lethal aircraft, capable of penetrating enemy lines and attacking both air and ground forces. Achieving a technical advantage in aircraft, they planned to take the fight to the enemy. Maj. Gen. Hugh Trenchard, Commander of the Royal Flying Corps squadrons stationed in France, scorned the very notion of "standing on the defensive in the skies." In three-dimensional warfare, he thought, there was little choice involved in employing offensive or defensive tactics. With no place to hide and unable to construct fortifications, pilots had to remain the aggressors or face almost certain destruction.[5] In 1916, when Britain and France temporarily assumed a technological edge in fighter aircraft, Trenchard claimed that the principles of air power had not changed since the Wright Brothers first flew thirteen years before: "The aeroplane is not a defence against the aeroplane. But the opinion of those most competent to judge is that the aeroplane as a weapon of attack cannot be too highly estimated." [6]

Despite Trenchard's strong words, he was at times forced to avoid forays beyond Allied lines in order to parry thrusts by the enemy. The Royal Flying Corps, flying aircraft inferior to German models, suffered heavy losses in men and equipment when they ventured behind enemy lines; the Allied air forces faced not only superior pursuit planes but fire from antiaircraft artillery and machineguns on the ground as well. To counter this situation, the British and French supplemented their fighters with antiaircraft fire on those occasions when German air commanders ordered missions over British and French-controlled territory.

The semantics of air combat, as World War I demonstrated, could be extremely confusing. Labeling dogfights of the period as either offensive or defensive can be deceptive. An aircraft could employ a set of basic tactics for defensive purposes on one day and contribute to the air offensive by using similar tactics the next. The tactical air war over the Western Front was certainly a nebulous theater in which to separate offensive and defensive strategies. In any case, the arena in which air defenses were first pitted against a strategic attack* took place not on the Western Front but in the so-called First Battle of Britain, when German bombs tested the fledgling air defenses of Great Britain.

As early as 1908, parliamentary committees began investigating Britain's ability to resist attack from airplanes or airships. Although a general awareness existed among politicians, defense officials, and military officers of the threat that Germany's growing fleet of Zeppelins posed to Britain, no important action occurred before the war to provide air defense. The danger posed by the new air weapon was still obscure,[7] and most British, when they thought about air attack at all, equated it with fantasies like those described in H. G. Wells's futuristic novels.[8]

When the war began, Britain had no air units specially designated for home defense, and the Army's entire Royal Flying Corps was posted to France. Responsibility for air defense thus fell to the Admiralty, which controlled seaplanes, while the Royal Garrison Artillery supplied most of the heavy guns placed on British territory. On September 3, 1914, Winston Churchill, as State Secretary of the Admiralty, assumed responsibility for the air defense of Britain, a task he performed with characteristic force and energy. Churchill began by composing the first carefully considered expression of air defense theory. In this memorandum, he offered pragmatic suggestions for the combined employment of pursuit planes, sound detectors, searchlights, observers, and antiaircraft artillery. Most important, he emphasized that it would be imperative to destroy an enemy's attacking aircraft or airships as far away from the target as possible.[9] This could be performed by long-range interceptors acting strictly in a defensive role or by bomb-loaded pursuit planes attacking enemy airship sheds or airdromes. Shortly after Churchill issued his memorandum, Royal Naval Air Service biplanes armed with four twenty-pound bombs raided German airship bases. One Zeppelin was destroyed.[10]

German bomb-equipped airships began to attack Great Britain in force beginning in 1915. Britain's first response, related to Churchill's proposal for destroying enemy air vehicles far from their targets, was known as forward air defense. This offensive form of defense used friendly craft to destroy Zeppelin airships in their assembly plants or on the ground before they could be launched from Belgian airfields. Attacks by British naval planes, launched from established airfields near the French port of Dunkirk, enjoyed some success, even forcing Germany to abandon its own air fields in Belgium. Unfortunately, the British failed to bring German airship construction to a halt: the Germans simply constructed more Zeppelin sheds in parts of occupied France that Allied aircraft could not reach. When the airships continued raids against Britain,

---

* An operation designed to destroy an enemy's will to fight or its capacity for war.

3

government and military authorities realized more and better means would have to be invested in defeating airships in friendly skies. As historian Barry D. Powers noted, "It proved not to be true that the best defence was a strong offence with respect to the airship threat, even though this was the position taken by the most outspoken air power advocates." [11] However, the philosophy that the best defense was a good offense took root in the minds of airmen from all nations in World War I. The concept of "forward air defense," although not always termed as such, would continue to influence air power theorists long after the war's end.

On June 7, 1915, a British naval pilot, Sublieutenant R. A. J. Warneford, became the first aviator to destroy an airship in flight. Warneford maneuvered his Morane-Saulnier Bullet monoplane, armed only with gravity weapons, above the airship and dropped small firebombs, sending the leviathan to the ground in flames over Ghent, Belgium. [12] To be effective against German airships—slow, vulnerable, and filled with thousands of cubic feet of highly explosive gas—the British needed to develop incendiary ammunitions. When British air defense units received explosive and incendiary bullets for their Lewis machineguns in spring 1916, the dirigible's days were numbered. [13] By midsummer the German Army air service, after suffering heavy losses, discontinued airship raids. Forays by lighter-than-air craft of the German Navy persisted until war's end, but their destructive effect thereafter was negligible.

German airship raids took a toll on the British war effort. By the end of 1916, Zeppelin attacks had killed 500 civilians and caused some 17,000 military personnel to be diverted to the air defense of Britain. The failure of the airships to cause greater destruction apparently resulted less from the effectiveness of British air defenses than from innate deficiencies in the Zeppelins. Pilots merely took advantage of these handicaps to shoot down the craft. [14] No sooner had the airships been driven away than a more serious threat appeared over Britain.

After 1916, the long-range bomber replaced the airship in the German Army air arm. Although carrying a smaller bombload than the Zeppelins, bombers were faster and more difficult to intercept than dirigibles. On the Eastern Front, Russia's Igor Sikorsky premiered the 4-engine *Ilya Mourometz*, proving the durability of the heavily defended bomber. Meanwhile, by 1916 Germany had ready powerful, twin-engine bombers built by *Gothaer Waggonfabrik*. The more advanced models, as fast as contemporary pursuit planes, could remain in the air up to 6 hours. Armed with 3 defensive machineguns and up to 1,100 pounds of bombs, the Gothas later joined with larger bombers, the so-called *Riesenflugzeug* (Giant aircraft) in Germany's long-range arsenal. [15]

The first intensive German bomber raid on Britain on May 25, 1917, killed or wounded 286 people in Folkestone and Shorncliffe. A second

4

raid on London on June 13 killed or wounded 594 people.[16] The Germans planned to attack key industrial sites and airfields. Unfortunately, poor weather and unsophisticated bombing methods forced them to scatter their bombs over wide areas, causing civilian deaths and heavy property damage.

Like the earlier Zeppelin raids, the German bomber campaign forced the British to divert men and resources from the Western Front to home defense, in response to a public outcry demanding protection in the wake of the first destructive attacks. Trenchard and General Sir Douglas Haig, British Army Commander on the Western Front, objected strenuously. The war ministry, which had assumed responsibility for air defense from the admiralty in 1916, however, transferred from France experienced Royal Flying Corps squadrons equipped primarily with Sopwith Camels and SE–5s.[17]

The British at first seemed mesmerized by the large German bombers. Soon, however, the addition of quality pursuit planes, along with unseasonal storms and the coming of winter, enabled them to consolidate and build upon the air defense system devised earlier in response to the airship danger.[18] In July 1917, Great Britain established the London Air Defense Area (LADA), under the command of Maj. Gen. Edward B. Ashmore, an experienced artillery expert and pilot. By the summer of 1918 Ashmore had turned LADA into a centralized intelligence and command network. All the various air defense components then at hand—gun stations, searchlight batteries, pursuit units, barrage balloon screens, inland and coastal observer posts, and fire and police units— maintained contact with Ashmore's headquarters. Dispersed subcontrol stations telephoned Ashmore's central control to warn of aircraft flying over Britain. While the general watched from a raised gallery, plotters traced the course of every plane identified by observers on a large-scale map. Situated in the gallery directly in front of him were switches enabing him to talk to any of his subordinates at the subcontrols. He needed only to turn his head to speak with an air force commander who transmitted messages to the pursuit planes' airfield at Biggin Hill by way of a direct line.[19]

Based on a sound general concept, in operation the LADA network nevertheless experienced difficulties. For example, before takeoff, observers and plotters could supply pilots with only approximate indications of a raider's location. This limited information appeared sufficient when the enemy flew a slow-moving airship, but when the enemy flew a speedier, elusive bomber, more accurate and timely information was required. Though a ground-to-air wireless radio system would have been a godsend, these devices were not ready for general use until a month after the last bomber raid, in June 1918. In the meantime, several methods tracked the enemy's location. One of these involved the laying out of

5

white arrows pointing along the ground in the general direction of sighted bombers. This expedient met with little success; airborne pilots virtually had to seek out the enemy on their own.[20]

For all its technical difficulties, LADA functioned efficiently enough to force the Germans to change their tactics. Coordinated efforts allowed British antiaircraft artillery gunners to hold fire when their pursuit planes were in the area. Daytime combined operations took a rising toll of Gothas and Giants. German losses in day operations caused them to bomb almost exclusively at night. Still they had little success. These World War I bombers lacked range, proper navigational aids, and suitable bombsights. They could not fly under less than ideal weather conditions. These factors as much as the British defenses eventually contributed to thwarting Germany's bombardment effort.[21]

Overall, British air defenses performed credibly in opposing equally unsophisticated German bombers. They developed a complex network around London consisting of 266 antiaircraft artillery guns; 271 pursuit aircraft, barrage balloons, and observer and listening posts; and a direct-line communications net. In sum, this elementary system bore a striking resemblance to the defenses the Royal Air Force's Fighter Command would deploy in 1940, with the outstanding exception of radar. In their postwar analyses of the First Battle of Britain, airpower theorists on both sides of the Atlantic were more impressed with the German air offensive, attributing its decline near the end of the war to the general collapse in Germany's fortunes. (Trenchard, in fact, planned in the closing stages of the war a similar, though more deadly, bomber offensive against Germany that was forestalled by the November 1918 armistice.) Especially impressive, German bomber raids simply bypassed the bulk of Britain's pursuit plane strength on the Western Front, much as German submarines avoided Britain's Grand Fleet in the North Sea. Trenchard and his adherents also pointed out that air defense had proved a terribly expensive operation in terms of tying down pursuit planes, antiaircraft artillery, and other resources. Although the outcome of the first large-scale strategic offensive/defensive air campaign had produced no clear-cut victor, advocates for the bomber attributed this to technical inadequacies in the bomber that could be easily overcome. The emergence of air defenses, meanwhile, was usually played down or ignored, and the likelihood of significant improvements was not seriously considered.[22]

The United States and Air Defense: The Early Years

The American military experience in the Great War was shorter and less instructive than most of the other major participants. Unlike Britain,

America never had to face the threat of air attack. Nevertheless, some Americans recognized the danger airships and airplanes posed in the hands of a foreign aggressor. The distinguished scientist Alexander Graham Bell, in an April 1916 address before the Navy League of the United States, warned that the nation might eventually be the victim of airship raids. Bell vividly described the destruction and chaos that would ensue as bombs rained down upon the nation's great cities. The famous inventor argued that steps should be taken immediately to create a formidable air force, capable of shooting invaders out of the sky.[23]

Bell's warning failed to stimulate the establishment of home air defense forces. Government officials, military officers, and the public assumed that, protected by ocean barriers, the nation was virtually invulnerable to air bombardment. This judgment proved sound, and the need for air defenses never became an issue. In Europe, meanwhile, American airmen's experience with air defense was limited basically to theater operations. For example, Brig. Gen. William "Billy" Mitchell employed observers and pursuit planes on alert at ground stations during the large-scale offensive at St. Mihiel.[24] Such operations had little similarity with the strategic defense of an entire nation.

After the war, military aviators came home to a nation whose people and leaders desired a return to traditional American isolationism. Congress reduced military and naval forces drastically from wartime force levels to a peacetime force designed for defensive missions. The Navy remained the first line of defense against foreign invaders, while the Army protected territorial possessions serving as barriers against enemies who might elude the fleet and attempt to make coastal inroads. The Air Service, organizationally a part of the Army,* did not have a dominant mission, one that clearly determined the direction of war. It assisted ground troops by conducting observation missions, fending off enemy aircraft, and dropping bombs and strafing enemy positions. It shared off-shore reconnaissance duties with the Navy (which, adding to the confusion, had its own air branch and prescribed missions including, for example, convoy operations and attacks on enemy submarines). Yet, brash, war-experienced air officers struggled to gain greater autonomy, eventually to become a separate service like the British Royal Air Force. These airmen knew that to realize their goal they had to postulate an airpower philosophy stressing the airplane's unique capabilities as a war-winning weapon.[25]

Billy Mitchell led the fight for a separate Air Service in the first half of the 1920s. Like Hugh Trenchard, whom he had met during the war, Mitchell believed the bomber was destined to become the dominant

---

* The Army air arm was administered originally by the Signal Corps. The Air Service was organized as a branch of the Army Expeditionary Forces in 1917. It was not until June 4, 1920, that the Office of the Chief of the Air Service was established.

force in warfare. Trenchard's trademark was the relentless air offensive. He advocated using the morale effect of the airplane to defeat the enemy—"this can only be done by attacking and continuing to attack." [26] Mitchell's fervent advocacy of air power gained him the reputation of a stormy petrel, yet he could also be pragmatic. Before his court martial and subsequent resignation from the Army in 1926, Mitchell usually attempted to merge his theories into the framework of orthodox U.S. defense policy. That policy concerned itself principally with the defense of the continental United States and its possessions, such as the Philippines, Hawaii, and the Panama Canal. Since sea power, including the newly devised aircraft carrier, posed the greatest threat to the mainland and outlying territories, Mitchell agitated his opponents and inspired his disciples when, during the early 1920s, he demonstrated in a series of tests that aerial bombing could sink modern warships. [27]

Mitchell and his adherents, officers such as William T. Sherman and Thomas DeWitt Milling (theorists on the proper use of the air weapon), [28] suggested how aircraft could be employed defensively to protect America's shores against troop-carrying warships and aircraft carriers. The airplane could spot approaching battleships and carriers and sink or cripple them before they could mount a threat. Moreover, U.S. aircraft could also conceivably perform preemptive operations, annihilating any hostile air bases that an enemy might establish in the Western Hemisphere. Because airmen usually labeled such actions as air defense measures, confusion arose over what constituted *offense* rather than *defense.*

Convinced of the unique role of the airplane as a weapon against warships in national defense, Mitchell and some of his more optimistic supporters believed that the air force could function most effectively as a separate service. Certainly, capability to defend the nation's coasts was important and it dovetailed perfectly with the nation's defensive military posture, but leading lawmakers, officers of the Navy and ground forces, and even some airmen remained skeptical that the airplane's contribution to coast defense warranted independence to the Air Service. Still, Mitchell's bombing exhibitions sparked intense debate on the issue and helped earn the air arm additional recognition in 1926 with the creation of the Air Corps and the establishment of the Office of the Assistant Secretary of War for Air under F. Trubee Davison. [29]

Defining the Mission

The mission of defense as applied to military aircraft was a topic of heated controversy. Throughout the 1920s and much of the next decade, the Army air arm and the Navy argued over the terms of the coastal defense mission. How far could the Army's planes venture over the water before they trespassed into areas of naval responsibility? Similarly, how far inshore could the Navy operate? In January 1931, Army Chief of Staff General Douglas MacArthur and Chief of Naval Operations Admiral William V. Pratt concluded an agreement prescribing distinct missions for the air arms of both services. Naval aviation would be based on carriers used to help the fleet defeat a hostile force at sea.[30] The Navy would remain the first line of defense, but, as MacArthur pointed out, the Army and its air arm were responsible for "defending the coasts both in the homelands and in the overseas possessions."[31]

Early in 1933, following extensive studies by the War Department General Staff and the Office of the Chief of the Air Corps, a Chief of Staff letter, "Employment of Army Aviation in Coast Defense," further delineated intramural responsibilities. Army aviation's coastal defense mission was defined as the "conduct of air operations over the sea in direct defense of the coast."[32] Assigned a finite role in national defense, many Air Corps officers pressed even harder for independence. MacArthur was equally determined to deny complete independence to the Air Corps, but he later endorsed an Air Corps reorganization reflecting the coastal defense mission and approved the formation of General Headquarters (GHQ) Air Force, a combat arm capable of, among other things, rapid concentration for coastal defense.[33]

Simply defining the air defense mission was not sufficient to establish its importance. Two official committees convened to examine future roles of military aviation. The Drum Board in October 1933 and the Baker Board in July 1934 minimized the threat of air attack against the United States. The Baker Board emphasized that defense of the nation would require a joint effort among the service branches.[34] War Department planning to protect the coasts against air attack was, therefore, not an exclusive responsibility of the Air Corps.[35] In fact, a War Department directive of May 1935 decreed that the principal role in the mission—close-in defense—lay with the Coast Artillery's antiaircraft artillery forces, supplemented as required by pursuit aviation and aircraft warning services.[36]

Development of Air Defense Doctrine and Tactics

The War Department directive of May 1935 limited the Army's air arm in overall air defense planning. It specified that GHQ Air Force, established in March 1935, would coordinate with field army commanders to provide pursuit units for air defense.[37] GHQ Air Force had responsibility not only for sending long-range aircraft to destroy approaching hostiles but also for considering the role of pursuit aircraft in air defense. Army aviation had earlier had a similar focus, even if airmen preferred to emphasize the offensive form of air defense.

In the late 1920s and early 1930s, air doctrine governing the defense of the United States took shape at the Air Corps Tactical School (ACTS) on Maxwell Field, Montgomery, Alabama. Most of the students were lieutenants and captains. They studied the range of options for employment of air power, including the use of pursuit planes in air superiority, ground support, and air defense. Most found particular interest in the ideas of Billy Mitchell, Hugh Trenchard, and the Italian theorist, Giulio Douhet,[38] who, to one degree or another, advocated the bomber as the epitome of air power. Douhet, perhaps, presented the case for the bomber most forcefully and in the most partisan style.

Douhet assumed that the airplane potentially possessed such great advantages of speed and altitude that it could destroy targets on land or sea while it remained unscathed. He foresaw the development of an indomitable battle plane, a bomber so heavily armed that it could fight its way through swarms of defensive aircraft to reach its target. Douhet could not predict that technical progress would strengthen air defenses sufficiently to challenge his "Battle Plane."[39] The grandiose assessments of the power of the bomber offered by Douhet, and to a lesser extent by Mitchell and others, did not gain general acceptance in the 1920s. The equipment of that era simply belied their claims.

A typical American bomber of the 1920s, the Martin MB-2, had limited range, a service ceiling of a mere 7,000 feet, and a maximum speed of only 98 miles per hour. Contemporary pursuit planes easily outperformed it. But as the 1920s gave way to the 1930s, bombers began to achieve new standards of proficiency. In the United States the Boeing B-9, purchased in limited numbers, and the Martin B-10, the standard Army bomber of the period, advanced bomber capability. The B-10 had a service ceiling of 24,000 feet and a top speed of 213 miles per hour. The aircraft could carry more than a ton of high explosives, twice the bombload of the MB-2.[40]

No longer could the pursuit plane outpace the bomber. Standard pursuit aircraft like the Curtiss P-6 or the Boeing P-12 were no match for the Martin in terms of speed and range. Indeed, except for the occasional substitution of an air-cooled engine for the more common liquid-cooled models, all the air arm's pursuit planes resembled the Curtiss racer of 1922, a biplane that achieved an average speed of 205.8 miles per hour.[41] The problem with pursuit aircraft was not the engine, for horsepower and efficiency improved steadily; it was the failure to reduce aerodynamic drag that slowed the craft. Whereas the bomber could retract its landing gear into an engine nacelle, the pursuit plane was handicapped with a slim fuselage and wings that required external bracing.

Neither the fuselage nor the wings could accommodate the necessary mechanism for retractable gear. As late as 1932 when Boeing developed an all-metal monoplane, the P–26 Peashooter, the new pursuit plane remained burdened with fixed landing gear, externally braced wings, and an open cockpit.[42] As the bomber became more formidable, its presence became dominant. In 1926 there had been one bomber to every four pursuit aircraft in the Air Corps aircraft inventory; by 1937 there were eleven bombers to every nine pursuit planes, and the Air Corps had already taken possession of thirteen B–17 four-engine bombers.[43]

The bomber gained a technological advantage over the pursuit plane and began to dominate Air Corps doctrine, in part because of competition among the various aircraft companies. Douglas, Boeing, and Martin in particular built long-range aircraft for commercial purposes. Many of the technical developments used in these aircraft could be transferred to bombers. Aircraft designers found it more difficult to incorporate these innovations into pursuit aircraft primarily because a pursuit plane's smaller size created engineering problems.[44]

To defeat bombers, the smaller, more maneuverable pursuit planes required a substantial speed advantage over their larger opponents. Air Corps exercises conducted in the late 1920s and early 1930s indicated that pursuit planes were no match for current bombers. In the Ohio maneuvers of 1929, outclassed interceptors gave little or no trouble to penetrating bombers, inspiring Maj. Walter H. Frank, ACTS Assistant Commandant, to declare "that an air force is principally an offensive weapon rather than a defensive one."[45]

Frank's view gained widespread acceptance in the Air Corps as the 1930s progressed. Young officers at ACTS, although willing to acknowledge a debt to Mitchell, Trenchard, and Douhet, devised a concept of warfare that dwarfed anything suggested by the early bomber apostles in terms of theory and sophistication—strategic precision daylight bombing. Among the outstanding airmen who contributed their talents to the development of this concept were Donald Wilson, Laurence S. Kuter, Haywood S. Hansell, Harold L. George, and Kenneth N. Walker. Wilson and a brilliant major, Muir S. Fairchild, began research to identify those interdependent segments of a modern industrialized economy that might be vulnerable to precision bombing, presaging the collapse of an enemy's political structure. A watershed occurred in 1935 when Boeing produced its model 299, the prototype of the B–17. For many Air Corps officers, the B–17 could finally translate theory into reality.[46]

It seemed to many airmen that precision bombing created the critical role that would justify an independent Air Force. Yet, as bombardment theory and equipment developed and matured, the Air Corps also examined other aspects of air combat, including the use of pursuit planes in tactical air support and air defense operations. Although progress occurred faster for bomber development, aircraft companies cooperated with the Air Corps to produce pursuit aircraft capable of performing specialized missions. In addition, the Air Corps continually conceptualized and developed tactics for pursuit planes in different combat roles. One of these roles involved bomber defense.

In 1930 the Air Corps experimented with the use of an air defense early-warning system in exercises conducted at Aberdeen, Maryland. The rudimentary warning service consisted of ground observers who used radios or telephones to relay aircraft sightings to a central control unit.[47] Although inconclusive, the results of the war games seemed to shed at least some doubt on Major Frank's completely gloomy assessment of the value of defensive air forces made the previous year during the Ohio exercises. Prospects for the development of the warning system encouraged the Air Corps to continue testing it.

From May 15 to 27, 1933, at Fort Knox, Kentucky, joint air-ground exercises tested antiaircraft artillery operating with and without the cooperation of pursuit planes. The exercise further investigated the use of a distant intelligence net working in tandem with Air Corps defense units. Claire L. Chennault, an outspoken, grizzled forty-two-year-old captain and outstanding pilot, the future leader of the renowned Flying Tigers, participated in the exercise. A pursuit instructor in ACTS, his parochial and uncompromising advocacy of pursuit planes matched that of those who declared the bomber as the ultimate aerial weapon.

As at the Aberdeen exercises three years earlier, the deployment of an early-warning system at Fort Knox produced mixed reviews. Chennault, nevertheless, drew a number of important lessons from the tests and came away convinced that efficient air defense could become a reality. He believed that pursuit aircraft could not be expected to maintain defensive patrols during periods of possible attack, since these procedures wasted fuel and drained the energy and morale of pilots. Instead, machines and pilots should stand by on the ground, ready to take off after previously established observation points had determined the altitude, general course, and probable objective of an approaching enemy formation. Advance warning would enable pursuit planes to meet the enemy far from the intended targets and destroy him. Although Chennault realized any system that relied primarily on ground observers to relay information could not work fast enough to be fully efficient, he believed advances in technology, both in aircraft and communications, would minimize delays and misunderstandings.[48]

By the time of the Fort Knox exercises, pursuit aircraft engineering and radio telephony were being improved. The Air Corps began to respond to requests from commanders in the field, like the one from Lt. Col. Henry H. Arnold, commander of March Field, California, to secure equipment capable of satisfying other needs.[49] Though Arnold fervently advocated the strategic bomber, he and other airmen remained disturbed by years of neglect in the pursuit branch. Aircraft companies soon found themselves being encouraged to use new technology to improve not only bombers but all other types of military aircraft as well. Pursuit engines increased in power, and, when equipped with superchargers, could develop even greater power at high altitudes. The general adoption of the monoplane configuration reduced drag, as did the presence of retractable landing gear and enclosed cockpits. Simultaneously, radio communication improved enormously, permitting reliable air-to-air and ground-to-air communication. The Consolidated P–30, ordered in 1934, featured a controllable pitch propeller, retractable landing gear, and cockpit heating, essential for chasing bombers in sustained operations at high altitudes.

When the Air Corps purchased 77 Seversky P–35s in June 1936, standard features included retractable landing gear, all-metal construction, and enclosed cockpits. Before World War II, the United States developed several advanced pursuit planes, including the Curtiss P–36 Hawk and P–40 Warhawk, the Bell P–39 Airacobra, and the Lockheed P–38 Lightning. Although only the Lightning was designed specifically as an interceptor, all could function in air defense.[50] These superior aircraft coupled with their advanced communications led to improved pursuit tactics, in which formation leaders could coordinate attacks even when their formations were widely separated. In terms of air defense, directors on the ground were better prepared to receive information from forward observers and to direct pursuit planes to an approaching enemy.[51]

Gordon P. Saville

Although most Air Corps members recognized a need to improve pursuit performance as part of an early-warning defense system, theorists in ACTS and their superiors throughout the Air Corps considered the offensive clearly superior. Astute American airmen realized that investing every aviation resource in offensive means was impracticable; it would represent a politically impossible position in a country that emphasized a grand national defensive strategy. Americans would certainly demand defense, and not only the offensive type of air defense that the Air Corps preferred. To earn credibility and advance its goal of independence, the Air Corps would have to provide direct pursuit defense of the continental United States.

Air Corps willingness to perform air defense was not motivated entirely by selfish, political goals. Exercises seemed to indicate that defense could complicate an adversary's plans and achieve some limited success in active operations. Also, the Air Corps and the Army's Coast Artillery had become rivals for dominance in the mission. While it seemed obvious to air officers that the pursuit plane's extensive range and mobility made it the preeminent air defense weapon, not all artillery officers agreed. One went so far as to suggest that the principal purpose of antiaircraft artillery should be to release aviation from all defensive duties and to concentrate on offensive action.[52]

The concept of air defense, while far from completely neglected in the Air Corps, failed to stimulate a level of intellectual curiosity in ACTS students on a par with the more glamorous theory of precision strategic bombardment. Chennault proved to be an exception, as shown by his interest in the testing programs at Aberdeen and Fort Knox. His major concern, however, was the use of the pursuit plane in the offensive air superiority role. In 1935, he was replaced by the officer who would, when permitted, devote almost all his thought and energies to air defense—Capt. Gordon P. Saville. In the process, Saville would become the Air Force's air defense authority, the driving force behind most of the programs implemented until his retirement in 1951.

Saville, born in Macon, Georgia, in 1902, was the son of a Regular Army officer. His older brother had graduated from West Point, but the younger Saville rejected an appointment to the United States Naval Academy because the discipline of a midshipman's life did not attract him. He wished to fly airplanes and was willing to subject himself to military life if given the chance to fly. Thus, after studying engineering at Antioch College and the Universities of Washington and California, he became a flying cadet in 1926. He graduated and received a regular commission in the Air Corps the next year.

After commissioning, Saville served in a number of pursuit aircraft units, where he developed his skills as a pilot. In one assignment, he worked for Lt. Col. Benjamin D. Foulois, future Chief of the Air Corps, as a squadron executive officer at Mitchel Field, New York. Foulois, recognizing exceptional abilities in the young officer, helped him a few years later gain entrance to ACTS; Saville graduated first in the class of 1933–1934.

During his tours at ACTS, first as a student and later as an instructor, Saville participated in the wide-ranging debates during which Air Corps officers expressed and developed their ideas. As his knowledge of pursuit aircraft increased, he became intrigued with air defense. He became immersed in his work, yet he avoided the quarrels that had embroiled Chennault with the champions of the bomber. Unlike Chennault, he did not dispute the dominance of the bomber as an *offensive* weapon. He focused solely on the *defensive* functions of pursuit aircraft. After pondering the results of several war games, Saville decided that air de-

Capt. Gordon Saville

fense in which pursuit planes played the primary role, possessed the potential to disrupt seriously the bomber offensive, although some bombers would always penetrate the defenses and hit their targets.[53]

Warning and control, key words in air defense operations, were and remain the core of a functioning system. Air Corps exercises beginning in the late 1920s and early 1930s demonstrated the feasibility of an early-warning network in defensive pursuit operations. In the same period, airmen began testing methods to intercept enemy aircraft by using ground radio to direct pursuit planes to their prey. The first extensive test of the control element coupled with early warning did not occur until December 1935 when the Army's combat air arm, GHQ Air Force, assembled in Florida under its commander, Brig. Gen. Frank M. Andrews. Offensive forces in the exercise included Martin B–10 and B–12 bombers and Curtiss A–12 attack planes. Defensive forces, Boeing P–26 pursuit planes, were assigned to the 2d Wing, commanded by Brig. Gen. Henry Conger Pratt.

Saville knew he was taking a risk. In his system, the ground control officer commanded the pursuit formation from takeoff to interception, a procedure that violated the current American air command and control practices. Leaders routinely led their pursuit formations when airborne,

15

an arrangement originating in World War I when air combat formation developed. At that time, the leader usually communicated with his formation through prearranged signals. Later, radio advisories of sightings of enemy aircraft by ground observers or by observation planes brought no change to the formation leader's responsibility for finding and attacking the enemy. Saville proposed to shift command from the cockpit to the ground, a move likely to arouse strong opposition.[54]

While testing Saville's proposal, Col. Ralph Royce, commander of a pursuit squadron, became especially incensed after receiving orders from the ground dividing his formation and sending aircraft off in different directions to intercept approaching bombers. During the postmission critique, Royce persistently objected to orders from the ground and demanded to know who had invented this system that presumed to tell him how to deploy his forces. Captain Saville, in charge of the ground operation, found himself in an uncomfortable position confronted by an angry senior officer. General Pratt completely supported Saville. He informed Royce that the orders were his, thus temporarily ending the argument. For the remainder of the exercises, pursuit leaders understood that General Pratt sanctioned, though he did not directly transmit, any orders that passed through their headsets.[55]

In the overall postexercise critique, held December 12, Pratt insisted that in the future, instructions radioed from the ground that aided pursuit interception constituted commands rather than advice. Ground controllers would exercise *air command*, not *air liaison*. Controllers, Pratt reasoned, had information not available to the pursuit leaders and were therefore in a superior position to direct aerial interceptions. "The entire system," he concluded, "is predicated on ground control at all times. When that command is interrupted or assumed by others—the system is immediately susceptible to failure."[56]

In the Florida exercises of 1935, Captain Saville helped advance American air defense procedures a major step beyond the simple concept of early warning. Without electronic aids, Saville's methods resembled those used by General Ashmore in LADA during World War I. While Saville benefited from quicker communications and two-way radio, the ground controller still played something of a guessing game in calculating an approaching bomber's height, speed, and destination on the basis of reports transmitted by ground observers and observation aircraft. Another element was needed before so-called ground-controlled interception (GCI) would become a reliable command and control system. Radar, the missing piece in the puzzle, had just then been tested in air operations in Great Britain, but it would not become known to most Air Corps officers for years to come. In the meantime, although the World War I mindset of some pilots caused them to resist GCI, the record supports Saville's view that those Air Corps leaders who attended the 1935 maneuvers, including acting Brig. Gen. Henry H. Arnold, were impressed by GCI and encouraged its development in succeeding years.[57]

Warning and control exercises further proved their worth in joint exercises conducted by GHQ Air Force and Army Coast Artillery between 1936 and 1938. In May 1937, during an exercise at Muroc Lake, California, the military prevailed upon the Southern California Edison Company, as well as the San Joaquin Light and Power Company, to cooperate in early-warning portions of the exercises by donating communications and electrical equipment and by allowing their civilian employees to volunteer as observers.[58]

Another operation, the joint antiaircraft artillery–Air Corps exercises conducted at Fort Bragg, North Carolina, in 1938, performed the most intensive testing of U.S. early-warning and combined air defense forces held before the outbreak of World War II. The exercise used the new 4-engine B–17, the less fearsome B–10 and B–18 bombers, and, as principal interceptor, the P–35. The Army's standard antiaircraft equipment included searchlights, sound detectors, communications devices, and guns. The 3-inch gun could hit targets at 20,000 feet, firing 25 aimed shots per minute. An intermediate 37-mm gun and a short-range .50-caliber machinegun supplemented the 3-inch piece.

At the time of the Fort Bragg maneuvers, the Coast Artillery was undergoing important changes. Its traditional harbor defense mission was being rapidly superseded by antiaircraft responsibilities, but it was, as yet, as unprepared as the Air Corps to offer substantial protection for the American mainland. In fact, the Army sent all regular antiaircraft units east of the Mississippi to Fort Bragg, and they could not protect a circular area one mile in diameter.[59] The Coast Artillery, like the Air Corps and all other branches of the U.S. military, suffered to a degree from parsimonious peacetime defense spending.

The relatively meager resources available did not prevent air and ground commanders from studying new ways to use their defense forces when under attack. Most airmen viewed the pursuit plane as the principal agent of active defense. Interceptors guided by radio communications could disperse quickly and defend multiple objectives. While these aircraft provided the first line of defense, antiaircraft batteries stationed around key targets supplied a type of last-ditch defense. One of the key advantages of antiaircraft artillery included the capability to fire on short notice (five minutes or less), forcing attacking aircraft to drop their bombs at higher altitudes, thus decreasing bombing accuracy.

In public statements, Air Corps and Coast Artillery commanders graciously admitted that air defense would only work as a combined operation. The Fort Bragg maneuvers, however, indicated problems in joint operations, especially in the effective coordination of guns and planes in air defense. During the maneuvers, some artillerists complained about strict hold-fire orders when friendly aircraft operated in their vicinity. The gunners also claimed that the period between sighting the enemy and launching fighters had been too long for successful GCI. Some airmen interpreted this as pointing up the futility of pursuit defense and the value of artillery. Speaking for the Air Corps, Muir Fairchild protested that it served little purpose to defend fixed military installations, the basic use for antiaircraft artillery, while "leaving the whole of our country from Miami, Florida, to Portland, Maine, and from New York to Chicago . . . the barest shadow of a defense." [60] Fairchild's case seemed obvious to airmen: the pursuit plane's flexibility rendered it the most potent weapon in the air defense arsenal. At Fort Bragg, civilians once again manned the aircraft warning systems. As at Lake Muroc the previous year, the military commanders generally liked their performance. Nonetheless, closer cooperation between primary air defense elements—pursuit planes, early-warning observers, ground control stations, and antiaircraft artillery—was plainly required. The Air Corps believed that all air defense components should come under one commander, preferably an airman operating from a control center. Unconvinced of the total dominance of pursuit planes in air defense, or the superior capabilities of air officers for running a total system, the Coast Artillery refused to acquiesce to the arrangement suggested by the Air Corps. [61]

By the late 1930s, even the most diehard bomber zealot realized pursuit planes could serve important offensive and defensive functions. ACTS devised limited objectives for air defense. By imposing even minimum limitations on the bomber, air defense became "economical." The presence of an air defense network meant that bombers would at least have to sacrifice range and bombload to carry guns, ammunition, armor, and self-sealing fuel tanks. Moreover, the attackers would be forced to fly at high altitudes, not only decreasing bombing accuracy but requiring supercharged engines with a resulting weight penalty. Indeed, an air defense system might be successful enough in daylight to force the enemy to bomb by night, taxing navigational skills and further decreasing accuracy. [62]

Air Corps leaders supported the limited air defense objectives. General Andrews, skeptical at first, came to believe that pursuit planes could intercept hostile aircraft if supplied timely warning. [63] Lt. Col. Carl A. Spaatz, Chief of the Plans Division in the Office of the Chief of the Air Corps and a future Air Force Chief of Staff, recommended to General Arnold that doctrine be modified to read that it was "impossible to stop a determined air offensive, but defensive pursuit could inflict heavy damage on the attackers and make their success expensive." [64] Arnold himself told Maj. Gen. Delos C. Emmons, Andrews's replacement as head of GHQ Air Force, that he believed pursuit planes could, at times, shoot down bombers flying in formation. [65]

On the eve of the Second World War, key Air Corps doctrine stressed the employment of strategic bombers launching precision attacks in daylight, aimed at an enemy's vital military and economic strongpoints. Although they would have liked the assurance of escort pursuit planes, most American airmen thought the bombers could successfully perform their missions deploying in defensive formations. Exercises seemed to indicate that not all the attacking bombers would be able to penetrate the defenses and that casualties would not be prohibitive.

As for air defense, Air Corps leaders staunchly agreed with Capt. Harold L. George who, in congressional testimony in 1935, declared, "The best defense against air attack is an offensive against the places from which the attack originates. . . ." [66] Though the Air Corps blurred the distinction between what constituted air defense and what constituted preemptive attack, practical considerations necessitated preparations to defend mainland targets with pursuit planes coordinating with antiaircraft artillery. Most air arm leaders believed that such an approach could provide limited defenses, although they had little confidence it would repulse a well-organized bomber attack; thus they refused to adjust Air Corps offensive plans. Unfortunately, American airmen knew little about the developing technology that would soon transform air warfare and dramatically improve prospects for successful air defense: radar.

Chapter 2

Air Defense in World War II

By the end of the 1930s, Arnold, Spaatz, Andrews, and others acknowledged that limited air defense was economical and could hinder, if not defeat, a determined air offensive. Most U.S. bombers could evade or fight their way through enemy defenses, even if unaccompanied by escort pursuit planes, and could bomb their targets. As long as commanders accepted some losses, Air Corps planners believed that the clear advantage remained with offensive forces. However, the tactics and strategies of air combat constantly changed as technology rapidly advanced. Because the Air Corps failed to understand how to apply radar to military purposes, U.S. strategic offensive and defensive capabilities were not fully operational on the eve of World War II.

In the late 1930s, scientists from around the world, including the United States, knew that radio energy of very high frequency is reflected instead of absorbed by an object in its path.[1] In uncomplicated terms, radar, by means of reflected radio waves, detects with the speed of light distant objects in the sky, on the land, or on the sea. It can "see" in much the same manner as the eye sees by means of light waves. Moreover, radar can determine an object's range, since the speed of its radio waves is a constant factor.[2] To use this technology for operational purposes, scientists had to develop and refine several crucial components.[3]*

Although no nation monopolized radar developments before World War II, the British first adapted them to military operations. The independent Royal Air Force emphasized strategic bombing as ardently as the U.S. Army Air Corps; yet, for many reasons, British politicians took the lead to supply the nation with a radar-oriented air defense system.

---

* To use radar in practical operations, scientists had to develop a transmitter to emit pulses of energy in a sharply defined directional beam. Because this allowed lapses between emissions, the receiver could register the energy reflected from the target. Scientists had to develop further a device known as a cathode ray tube, already in existence in experimental television sets, and an oscilloscope, which could show on the tube the shadow images, or blips, created as the aircraft reflected back to the source the radio energy beamed out. Measuring the time lapse between the emitted pulse and the return signal (echo) would give a good estimate of the altitude and range of the aircraft. Finally, the cavity magnetron tube, capable of developing great power at very short wavelengths, would make the whole instrument feasible as a military device.

Unlike the United States, Britain faced the menace of the German *Luftwaffe*, which grew by leaps and bounds in the mid-1930s under Nazi control. Because of geography, Britain could not afford to procrastinate over ways to meet the threat. Despite the protests of most Royal Air Force commanders (with the notable exception of Air Chief Marshal Sir Hugh Dowding, head of Fighter Command), the nation's civilian leadership made air defense a major priority. This system concept fit in well with Britain's overall national defensive strategy, which was based on the conviction of scientists and their supporters in government that radar technology could provide the mainstay in an efficient air defense system.[4]

In the United States, no perception of a distinct threat existed. Therefore, no urgency was associated with the development of radar for military purposes. This did not mean that military applications were completely unknown or ignored. Both the Army and Navy had been testing radar techniques since the early 1920s. By 1935 scientists at the Naval Research Laboratory had used radio-pulse ranging to explore the ionosphere. In 1938 the Air Corps believed it possible for the Signal Corps to devise, in the near future, an early-warning radar with a range of 120 miles. Still, U.S. military and political officials did not make air defense a priority, and insufficient funding for research and poor methods of technical interchange between the services resulted. When the Battle of Britain began in the summer of 1940, American radar had just emerged from its developmental stage.[5]

At ACTS, the fountainhead of American air theory and doctrine, instructors and students knew little about radar's implications for air warfare. The concept was rarely mentioned in lectures, and, when it was discussed, details were almost nonexistent. For example, in early 1940 an instructor, lecturing on important foreign developments in air defense, only vaguely referred to the rumor of detection stations being constructed in Britain.[6] Arnold and his chief assistants in Washington apparently kept radar a closely guarded secret, disseminating little important information to the field.

After the war, Maj. Gen. Haywood S. Hansell, Jr., an outspoken advocate of the strategic bomber, remarked that the "Air Corps ignorance of radar development was probably a fortunate ignorance." He reasoned that if American air planners had understood the full significance of radar for strengthening air defenses, they might have decided that losses in planes and lives would outweigh the damage to enemy industry. This would have been unfortunate, Hansell concluded, because ACTS confidence in strategic bombing subsequently proved correct, despite radar.[7] A postwar comment by Maj. Gen. Muir S. Fairchild addressed the same topic from a different perspective:

> The one place where we were badly off the track was in
> our conception of the effectiveness of the defensive force.
> At that time radar was so secret that even the [ACTS] in-
> structors were unaware of what it could accomplish and we
> were forbidden to mention its existence or even to intimate
> that any such thing as radar was possible. This secrecy, of
> course, resulted in a distortion of our instruction because of
> the great effect that radar has in permitting interceptions to
> be made. Without radar or early warning systems the effec-
> tiveness of the air defense presents a completely different
> picture. [8]

Suffering from this glaring gap in its technological arsenal as the
European powers moved toward war in the summer of 1939, the Air
Corps nevertheless benefited with the increased funding of the late 1930s
and hurried to improve its readiness for combat. Continental air defense
received increased attention as part of the overall effort. One small,
though important, indication of the heightened focus on air defense took
place in July when Captain Saville, recently graduated from the Army's
Command and Staff College and building a reputation for air defense expertise, joined the Plans Division in the Office of the Chief of the Air
Corps. [9]

The start of war in Europe in September 1939 stimulated Maj. Gen.
Henry H. Arnold's staff to discuss the possibility of giving the Air Corps
unchallenged dominance in coastal defense. Saville and other staff members perceived the *Luftwaffe* as a potential threat to American security; it
was not impossible that the Germans could attack with small aircraft carried by submarines. [10] These officers also thought Germany might establish bases close enough to launch one-way bombardment missions against
the continental United States. [11] A Japanese attack from the Pacific
seemed less likely at this time.

General Arnold agreed with his staff's general conviction that the
development of defensive aviation in the United States had been permitted to lag. In November 1939, on the recommendation of Saville, he suggested that the War Department set up a general air defense test sector
in Maj. Gen. Hugh A. Drum's First Army Area in the east. The sector,
under Air Corps command, would set the precedent for expansion into
the other three Army areas if it became necessary. [12]

On September 1, 1939, the day war began, General George C. Marshall, an officer on good terms with Arnold (they had served together in
the Philippines in 1914) and considered to be friendly to Air Corps interests, became Army Chief of Staff. Among other things, Marshall would
decide which Army component would be responsible for air defense. He
agreed to create an air defense organization headed by an Air Corps officer; however, he did not place the new command under unequivocal Air
Corps control. He specifically assigned the organization to First Army in

General George C. Marshall

order to retain "unity of command" for all Army defense preparations in the field army areas. He insisted that the command remain small and be restricted to studying and field testing air defense techniques and equipment.[13]

The First Air Defense Command, 1940–1941

Brig. Gen. James E. Chaney, a former Executive Officer and Chief of Plans for the Chief of the Air Corps from July 1934 to July 1938, led the new Air Defense Command (ADC) activated February 26, 1940, at Mitchel Field, New York. The command's mission was to employ and test various air defense systems. It also formulated air defense doctrine and submitted its recommendations to the Office of the Chief of the Air Corps. ADC headquarters consisted of six officers and thirteen enlisted men with Lt. Col. William E. Kepner as Executive Officer. A former Marine, World War I National Guard infantryman, and record-setting balloonist, Kepner had been commander of all defensive aviation in the 1938 Fort Bragg exercises. Captain Saville transferred to the command to serve as Plans and Training Officer.

General Chaney, who had little background in air defense, made Saville his unofficial air defense coordinator. For Saville the task was a dream come true. At last, he could develop, refine, and put into practice

Maj. Gen. James E. Chaney

the principles of coordinated air defense he had worked out in ACTS and as a member of the Air Corps Board.[14]*

Saville and the other overworked individuals who launched ADC faced a number of inconveniences. They were expected to map out an air defense system for the northeastern part of the United States, while toiling in cramped, cold offices heated by kerosene stoves. Housing for enlisted personnel was extremely poor, and morale was low. It was a credit to the few assigned to ADC that so much important work was accomplished.[15]

The small command had two subordinate Army Signal Corps units assigned directly, created by Chief Signal Officer Maj. Gen. Joseph O. Mauborgne. ADC controlled neither pursuit nor antiaircraft artillery units—none could be spared because of steadily increasing Army war emergency authorizations. It could only test the Army's ability to furnish fixed air defenses without interfering with the primary goal of maintaining utmost mobility in all combat arms. As a result, ADC used civilian volunteers to act as aircraft observers and to operate telephone and plotting tables in information centers. It trained its volunteers and then tested their ability to put the warning service into operation during an emergency. Only after months of such preparatory work were pursuit planes

---

* Saville served full time on the Air Corps Board during his assignment in ACTS. The board considered wide-ranging doctrinal issues and made recommendations to the Chief of the Air Corps.

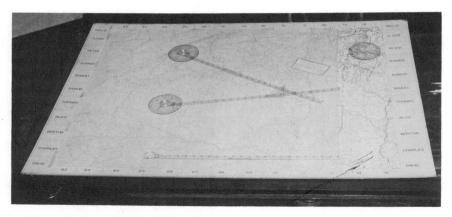

Plotting board used in Watertown maneuvers, August 1940

and mobile artillery placed under ADC control. Laying the foundation, ADC arranged for suitably located air and artillery stations, for pilots trained in controller techniques, and for enlisted airmen to install and operate radio for GCI.[16]

By 1940, the Signal Corps had assumed a major air defense role. At the urging of General Arnold, Chief of the Air Corps, personnel at the Signal Corps research and development facility at Fort Monmouth, New Jersey, had worked on the development and production of the so-called SCR–270 and SCR–271 mobile and fixed early-warning detectors. Both had major weaknesses. They possessed only crude early-warning capability and could only approximate the direction and distance of approaching planes. Furthermore, they could not report altitude nor could they detect low-flying objects. They were hard to adjust, often showed blind lanes, and were subject to enemy jamming (using countertransmissions or confusion reflectors).[17]

General Mauborgne organized signal units in early 1940 to handle communications throughout aircraft warning services. More significantly, he established information centers to supervise collection and processing of aircraft warning data. By May of that year, each commanding general of the four continental field armies had been tasked with setting up an aircraft warning service. These units were not designed to be stationary. In fact, the urgency for early warning of air attack in the Panama Canal Zone prompted General Marshall to send the first such signal units there.[18]

ADC planned to bring its test sector into operation by January 1941. While a pursuit instructor in ACTS, Saville had proposed setting up an air defense laboratory on the coastal frontier section of First Army Area. Because he considered the east coast the most vulnerable part of the nation, Saville reasoned that a successful test of the system would justify permanently integrating the region's air defenses under a single commander. The experiment would serve as a training ground for the cadres required to institute identical systems in the other three army areas. [19]

Plans for the test sector exercise were interrupted when General Drum directed Chaney and his staff to provide air defense support during First Army maneuvers in northern New York state. Chaney, Kepner, and Saville jumped at this opportunity to prove the command's worth. They established a combined information and control center in the Watertown National Guard Armory and called some twenty Reserve officers to active duty to assist with controller and other duties. The aircraft warning service now had two new components—two SCR–270 radar stations and a large group of volunteer observers. Civilian employees of telephone companies and government agencies had participated in previous early-warning exercises, notably those at Lake Muroc and Fort Bragg, but this exercise represented the first use of local civilians recruited from all walks of life. Pursuit planes from Selfridge Field, Michigan, and Langley Field, Virginia, deployed onto air fields in Syracuse and Utica, New York. Air defense preparations for the maneuvers were finally completed when the Coast Artillery furnished three regiments of antiaircraft artillery under the command of Brig. Gen. William Ottman, who established his headquarters in Richville, New York. [20]

The Army maneuvers lasted from August 19 to 23, 1940. Aircraft warning data flowed efficiently into the Watertown center, enabling Air Corps personnel to launch pursuit aircraft on ground alert and to direct them to the interception points. Though the use of radar made the system more sophisticated than Saville's 1935 GCI experiment in Florida, observers still made low-level sightings and supplemented the unreliable American radar sets. To coordinate pursuit and antiaircraft artillery operations, Generals Chaney and Ottman exchanged liaison officers and formulated rules of engagement. For example, pursuit pilots could not enter areas covered by antiaircraft artillery defenses except on orders from the Watertown command center. When access was needed, the artillery liaison officer at Watertown advised the Richville center. In this way Chaney and Ottman sought to prevent the guns from firing on friendly aircraft while allowing artillerymen maximum freedom to fire. All subsequent air defense exercises and operations followed these rules. [21]

During the exercise, pursuit planes intercepted attackers long before they reached their targets. This unified air defense pleased Drum, Chaney, and Ottman. Chaney reported that his success "astonished" the maneuver umpires, but he cautioned against complacency. The raids, he said, were limited by ADC rules and took place in a relatively small geographical area. The ADC staff also believed it had insufficient resources,

Information center *(above)* **and Air Defense Headquarters** *(below),*
Syracuse, New York, during Watertown maneuvers, August 1940

in either personnel or equipment, for use in the exercise. Nevertheless,
the generals returned in high spirits to Mitchel Field to resume work on
the test-sector exercise set for January 1941.[22]

The Battle of Britain entered its most crucial stages during the
weeks following the First Army war games. The Royal Air Force victory was attributable to a number of factors, among them the success of
British radar and GCI systems and procedures. In early September 1940,
as the battle entered its final phase, the British shared highly classified
information with the United States. The renowned scientist Sir Henry
Tizard and his delegation introduced American Army officers to the
mysteries of British electronic equipment.[23] At the same time, American
officers observed British defense procedures first-hand. General Arnold
traveled to England and was especially impressed with British scientific

accomplishments. In just one afternoon he received "detailed inside information about what air defense really meant—something we in the United States had been getting piecemeal." [24]

In October 1940, Chaney and Saville flew to England to study Fighter Command's techniques and equipment. Like Arnold, they understood that radar was crucial to Britain's ability to retain control of the air. Saville also knew that, while an air defense net similar to Britain's had been devised and tested in the United States, the necessary electronic equipment required to make America's defense system truly workable was not yet available. [25]

Based on their observations in Britain, Chaney and Saville offered a number of important recommendations for improving air defenses. Backed by General Arnold, they requested installation of fixed early-warning radars of the British type as well as installation of airborne intercept radar. With airborne radar, although still rudimentary, Royal Air Force interceptor pilots could pinpoint attacking aircraft at night and during adverse weather conditions, after ground controllers had directed them to the general vicinity of the raiders. Chaney and Saville also asked for an improved version of British IFF (identification, friend or foe) equipment, which was installed on Royal Air Force aircraft and responded automatically to queries from ground radar stations. They wanted to install the same VHF (very high frequency) radio communication in American air defenses as that employed by the Royal Air Force's Fighter Command to scramble, control, and recover its interceptors. The Signal Corps was urged to duplicate GCI radar that Britain had begun to develop and which displayed on a scope the position of an aircraft. Finally, Chaney and Saville asked for lightweight radar, similar to British equipment, for use by mobile air defense task forces. [26]

Although the Chief Signal Officer resented the Air Corps implication that all British radar achievements transcended those of the Signal Corps, Mauborgne and his staff went to work to obtain British equipment and to contract it to American and Canadian firms for copy and manufacture. The Massachusetts Institute of Technology (MIT), destined to play a critical role in future air defense developments, established the soon to be famous Radiation Laboratory to design and develop microwave (very short electromagnetic wave) radar equipment, expected to give long-range coverage and high resolution. The Signal Corps also pressed ahead with the refinement and manufacture of its own designs. [27]

In January 1941 ADC brought its test sector into operation on schedule. Just as the December 1935 GHQ Air Force exercise in Florida had marked the beginning of the use of GCI in the United States, the test sector signaled the start of meaningful large-scale air defense operations.

The ADC staff divided the sector into two parts for effective command and control. A temporary information center set up in a National Guard Armory in Boston controlled the northern area; the southern area included the ADC information center housed in leased space in the Bell Telephone Company in downtown New York. This facility became the first permanent information center. The Army engaged an architectural engineering firm to design it according to ADC specifications. Capt. William Talbot, Commander of ADC 2d Operations Company (Aircraft Warning), supervised construction and the installation of equipment. The center quickly became Drum's and Chaney's showplace, serving as the prototype for all future centers.[28]

Testing lasted from January 21 to 24. The ADC staff hoped to develop doctrine rather than to organize permanently any or all of the northeast area. The two information centers received data from 700 observer posts staffed by more than 10,000 civilian volunteers. Recruited by the ADC staff with the assistance of patriotic and civic organizations, volunteers were deployed with the help of the Bell Telephone Company. In another innovation, ADC used filter centers between ground observers and the information centers to winnow out duplicate aircraft sighting reports. Throughout the exercise, Chaney gave his plans officer, Saville, a free hand to test all aspects of the air defense procedures Saville had developed in ACTS.[29]

The tests proved generally satisfactory, despite some problems. Although civilian observers performed with a fair degree of efficiency, ADC concluded that a visual and audio observer system, no matter how well organized and trained, remained inadequate to supply information for interception at night and under poor visibility. The power of the three available SCR–270 radar sets was insufficient to cover the seaward approaches to the test sector, underscoring Chaney's and Saville's contention that American electronic equipment was not well enough developed to serve as an integral element in air defense systems.[30]

In fall 1940, several organizational developments also occurred that affected the Air Corps. Initial studies in the Office of the Chief of the Air Corps indicated that the air defense of the United States should be based on strategic air areas instead of on a single command agency or army and corps area. In January 1941 four subordinate Air Districts commenced operations under GHQ Air Force—Northeast, Northwest, Southeast, and Southwest—to decentralize training. Previously, in November 1940, an Army General Headquarters/GHQ had activated, and GHQ Air Force moved from control by the Chief of the Air Corps, General Arnold. As a component of the field forces, GHQ Air Force came now under the direct command of the Chief of Staff, General Marshall. This move did not undermine Arnold's authority over GHQ Air Force, for late in October 1940 Marshall had designated Arnold to be

Filter board staffed by civilians in New York City during the January 1941 Air Defense Command tests

Acting Deputy Chief of Staff for Air.[31] In his new role, Arnold proposed during Army General Staff discussions on War Department reorganization in the winter of 1940–1941 that the Air Corps assume sole responsibility for planning air defenses and begin installing the equipment and assigning the units in all four air districts. His recommendation was accepted as part of a broader War Department reorganization.[32]

Meanwhile, Maj. Gen. Lesley J. McNair, GHQ Army Chief of Staff, advocated the division of the United States into four regional commands, distinct from the field armies.[33] On March 17, 1941, the War Department accepted most of McNair's ideas and divided the continental United States into four defense commands—Northeastern, Central, Southern, and Western—with the field army commanders serving as unified defense commanders.[34] The March 17 order also replaced the four air districts with four air forces, subordinate to GHQ Air Force. Instead of establishing an air defense command within each air district, as the Air Corps proposed, each numbered air force received an interceptor command. The defense commands had no authority over the four air forces, and responsibility for the awkwardly expressed "aviation and air defense portions of defense plans for the Defense Commands" remained with the Commanding General of GHQ Air Force, Lt. Gen. Delos C.

Emmons.[35] This ensued because on February 28, 1941, Marshall had approved Arnold's request to let the air arm assume responsibility for peacetime air defense of the United States.[36] Air Corps officers mistakenly believed that the same arrangement would prevail in wartime.

Major differences characterized the projected interceptor commands from ADC. Whereas ADC was a small planning and test headquarters with only two signal units assigned, interceptor commands would have their own organic pursuit units and mobile aircraft warning services. The interceptor commands also had operational control of antiaircraft artillery, barrage balloons, and searchlight units attached by Army GHQ. Each of the four regional air defense organizations would develop plans for aircraft warning services in their respective areas, following doctrine and practices developed largely by Saville and the ADC staff.[37]

Planning for the regional commands began during a training course that Saville organized from March 25 to April 12, 1941, on Mitchel Field for some sixty officers selected to hold key command or staff positions in the new interceptor commands. He and the teaching staff gave detailed briefings on the experiences and techniques of ADC, after which the students drew up plans for air defense in each interceptor command area. In each area there would be an interceptor command center to supervise the operations of regional information centers. These regions, in turn, would run GCI operations through pursuit aircraft control centers, facilities similar to those employed in Britain by Fighter Command. These pursuit aircraft control centers would be provided with new electronic equipment run by pursuit aircraft control squadrons (modern weapons controllers). During previous exercises, pilots on loan from pursuit squadrons (or pilot reservists) had performed controller duties. Now, the pursuit aircraft control squadrons would provide most of the officers needed for that operation. Chaney had concluded that, provided the chief controller was a rated (flying) officer, nonpilots could perform the controller function. Plans to create controller squadrons did not, therefore, threaten to diminish the already seriously restricted number of pursuit pilots.[38]

As the officer now responsible for the air defense of the United States, General Emmons established in his headquarters at Bolling Field in Washington, D.C., an air defense section under the direction of Col. David McL. Crawford. In Emmons's view, the first goal of the four air forces and their interceptor commands was to prepare for air defense of the coastal areas. Planning and installing aircraft warning services were important components of that task and, as a Signal Corps officer, Crawford could make a significant contribution.[39]

In spring 1941, a target date of August 1 was set for achieving air defense readiness, only a short interval for locating and installing radar stations along both coasts to provide early warning of approaching enemy aircraft. Thousands of civilian observers had to be recruited and trained for tracking the movement of aircraft over land areas, information and filter centers had to be readied to receive and screen sighting reports from observer and radar stations, and provisions had to be made to enable pursuit controllers to communicate with interceptor and artillery units. With so much to accomplish in such little time, achieving a completely operational system proved impossible by the target date.[40]

Meanwhile, more organizational changes involving the Air Corps were under way. On June 20, 1941, the Army Air Forces (AAF) was created with Arnold, as Major General, becoming Chief, AAF, directly under the Army Chief of Staff. Maj. Gen. George H. Brett, made Chief of the Air Corps, was subordinate to Arnold. GHQ Air Force, under Emmons, as Lieutenant General, was redesignated as Air Force Combat Command and realigned to a position under Arnold's jurisdiction, an unusual situation that lasted until the attack on Pearl Harbor.[41]

Peacetime air defense of the United States now rested in the AAF. Although the question of who would command air defenses in wartime remained unsettled, the AAF proceeded to create an integrated operational air defense system. The success of that undertaking occurred only through the hard work and cooperation of the many Coast Artillery and Signal Corps officers assigned to the staffs of the interceptor commands, numbered air forces, and Air Force Combat Command.[42]

Despite the formation of interceptor commands in each of the numbered air forces, Emmons had at first planned to keep ADC intact as a planning, inspection, and test agency, but the shortage of trained personnel made his designs impractical. ADC was inactivated on June 2, 1941, and its staff and signal companies were assigned to I Interceptor Command located with its parent First Air Force on Mitchel Field.[43]

As the international situation became increasingly critical for the United States during summer and fall 1941, severe shortages of equipment required for a unified air defense persisted. These included pursuit aircraft, antiaircraft artillery, barrage balloons,* radar and radio equipment, and trained personnel. Air defense commanders agreed that first priority should be given to acquiring early-warning radar and to training men to maintain it, as well as to recruiting civilians to staff filter and information centers. When Marshall decided that Chief Signal Officer

---

* Barrage balloons had been deployed in the First World War and were still considered by some commanders as useful supplementary air defense resources. Balloons denied air space to hostile aircraft both by physical obstruction and by their psychological effect on pilots. The balloons lessened the danger of dive bombing, forcing pilots to stay at higher altitudes where they could be more easily detected. Also, the balloons were especially effective under conditions of poor visibility. On the other hand, the balloons tended to break away in storms, creating a hazard by trailing their still-attached cables; used dangerous hydrogen gas; could menace friendly pilots; and could advertise the location of targets they were supposed to defend.

Moored barrage balloon of the type used by the 4th Antiaircraft Artillery Command on the U.S. west coast

Mauborgne was not moving fast enough to provide American air defense equipment equal to that of the British, he replaced him with Deputy Chief Signal Officer Maj. Gen. Dawson Olmstead.[44]

Olmstead took immediate action. The Fort Monmouth Signal Center expanded its aircraft warning training program and prepared to open a similar large facility in Florida. The AAF also set out to open a "finishing school" for radar operators at Drew Field, Florida. In addition, both MIT and Harvard University began special courses in electronics for air, signal, and artillery officers. Finally, the Signal Corps commissioned nearly 300 young engineers and physicists from civilian life, made them members of the Electronics Training Group, and sent them to Britain to study radar operations in Fighter Command.[45] This and other related programs gave the AAF the communications-electronics expertise it needed for the air defense system, but not until many months after America entered the war.

Pursuit-interception preparation also proceeded slowly. New aircraft capable of fair-weather interception arrived in increasing numbers, but they had many maintenance and flight problems. As for night and all-weather interceptors, the AAF made little progress. Engineers and draftsmen began work on the design of a night fighter, eventually produced as the Northrop P-61. Until this plane appeared, the AAF fit rudimentary airborne intercept radar into Douglas A-20 attack bombers, converting them to P-70s for interim use as night fighters. Until radar-equipped night fighters appeared, pilots had to seek out nocturnal raiders by silhouetting them against the sky or by using moonlight or the illumination of antiaircraft searchlights.[46]

Antiaircraft artillery searchlights in the Los Angeles region, circa 1940

In each interceptor group, pursuit aircraft control squadrons provided interceptor directors and supplied communication specialists. Personnel, equipment, and training facilities for these new units, like almost everything else, remained scarce. Through prodigious effort, three interceptor commands exercised their defense systems in fall 1941; another, the IV Interceptor Command responsible for the California coastal area, had its stations and forces in place for exercises by December 7, 1941. In the absence of proposed pursuit aircraft control centers, whose designs and locations remained to be decided, regional information centers performed GCI, as had been done under the old ADC. Pursuit aircraft group commanders took charge of the information centers during exercises, with mixed results. The exercises revealed that the new interceptor commands understood how they were to perform their missions even if, for the moment, they lacked the means to do it well.[47]

After the inactivation of ADC, Maj. Gordon Saville served as executive officer to Brig. Gen. John C. McDonnell, head of I Interceptor Command, the focal point of U.S. air defense operations during summer and fall 1941. In that period, Saville prepared a manuscript titled "Air Defense Doctrine" in which he outlined the fundamental principles of air defense, organizational structure of interceptor units, and techniques for making air defense estimates and plans. This draft manual soon became the authoritative air defense handbook of the AAF.[48]

A year before Saville composed his study, a group of AAF officers led by Col. William Kepner, ADC Executive Officer, studied and reported on various air defense problems. Kepner admitted that the term air defense had never been defined adequately. He and his group concluded that air defense "excludes counter air force and similar *offensive* [emphasis added] operations which contribute to security rather than air defense." [49]

This definition was a beginning. By October 1941 Saville could define air defense more precisely as the direct defense against enemy air operations. Counter–air force operations, including the bombing of enemy airdromes and ground and naval forces to deny an opponent air bases, were not within the scope of his definition. He considered active air defense, in broad terms, as "the organization and the action designed to interdict enemy air movement within a predetermined air space." [50] Active air defense, as opposed to passive air defense (i.e., civil defense measures), could be divided into two categories: local and general. Local air defense provided active defense for a specific objective or narrowly defined locality. Local defense used antiaircraft artillery and barrage balloons, with pursuit planes less frequently used as basic weapons. Pursuit aircraft became the principal weapon in general air defense when a larger area embracing a greater number of potential targets was defended. Local defenses such as antiaircraft artillery were used only as auxiliaries in general air defense. [51]

When Saville prepared his air defense manual in 1941, most of the terms and theories he presented were known since the time of the German bombing of Britain in World War I. Saville had, in fact, promulgated many of the same themes during his years in ACTS. "Air Defense Doctrine" was nevertheless significant because it codified all the major principles of active air defense, unambiguously, into one clear, concise manual.

By the end of 1941, the old ADC cadre at Mitchel Field had broken up to form the nuclei of new regional aircraft warning units and to operate early-warning units for task forces sent to Newfoundland and Iceland. General Chaney headed the U.S. Army delegation observer team in London; Colonel Kepner commanded one of the new tactical air support organizations; and Major Saville returned to Britain to get the most recent information on late technological developments that might benefit American air defense. Soon, Saville could use that information.

Air Defense in Wartime

On the morning of Sunday, December 7, 1941, Maj. Kenneth P. Bergquist, Operations Officer for the 14th Pursuit Wing in Hawaii, awoke to the crash of exploding bombs. Once he realized the islands were actually under attack, he quickly dressed and, after a series of adventures evading machinegun bullets from strafing Japanese airplanes, drove past burning Pearl Harbor, the great naval base on Oahu. He arrived at the Fighter Control Center located at Fort Shafter, east of Pearl Harbor, the information and weapons direction locus for the air defense of Hawaii.[52]

Unfortunately, Bergquist could not take effective action. Procedures for coordinating radar, pursuit planes, and antiaircraft artillery in the air defense battle were only being worked out in the weeks before the attack. In addition, actions taken earlier on the orders of Lt. Gen. Walter C. Short, Army Commander in Hawaii, had practically ensured that air defense elements would be paralyzed in the event of air attack. Short's major concern had been sabotage, so he ordered antiaircraft artillery ammunition boxed and most of Hawaii's P–36 and P–40 defensive pursuit planes concentrated on Wheeler Field, north of Pearl Harbor. Thus when the Japanese attacked, Army antiaircraft artillery delayed its response, and many of the rows of pursuit planes became sitting ducks. Most of the pursuit aircraft that succeeded in becoming airborne (with no direction from the control center) were destroyed before they could reach altitude.

The first requirement for successful air defense—early warning—had failed. The Navy, solely responsible for distant reconnaissance, was understrength in patrol craft and had failed to identify the approaching naval armada. The Army had available 6 operational SCR–270 mobile radars with ranges from 75 to 125 miles seaward, but a shortage of spare parts and an inadequate power supply rendered them good only for supplying 3 or 4 hours a day of training. On the morning of the attack, the Opana Mobile Radar Station on the northern tip of Oahu was operating. The two privates on duty picked up the blips representing the attacking force on their radarscopes and called the information center. The only officer on duty at the time, Navy Lt. Kermit Tyler, believed the blips indicated a scheduled flight of B–17s flying from California to the Philippines by way of Hawaii. Tyler had no way to verify his assumption because he did not have use of the desperately needed IFF equipment. He failed to call Bergquist, whose first notice of attack was the bombing that awakened him from a sound Sunday morning sleep.[53]

Bergquist, who would later hold many important air defense posts overseas and in the United States, was a West Point graduate originally commissioned in the Field Artillery. After earning his wings and transferring to the Air Corps, he received an assignment to Langley Field, Virginia. There he became one of the few officers actively involved in early experiments in GCI techniques. He went to Hawaii in mid-1939 for duty as Operations and Intelligence Officer for the 18th Air Base and Pursuit Group. In June 1940 he moved to the 14th Pursuit Wing, predecessor of the VII Fighter Command.[54]

Bergquist worked diligently in Hawaii, but not until he attended Saville's school on Mitchel Field in spring 1941 did he learn what air defense meant. The young major heard of developments in the Royal Air Force's struggle against the *Luftwaffe* and *for the first time* discovered how radar was revolutionizing air defense. He returned to the islands eager to apply these lessons to the problem of coordinating Hawaii's air defenses. According to Brig. Gen. Howard C. Davidson, Commander of the 14th Pursuit Wing (the Hawaiian Air Force was commanded by Maj. Gen. Frederick L. Martin), Bergquist tore into his work, building the Control Center almost single-handedly. When the major returned to Hawaii from Mitchel, said Davidson, "he was a great help to us [but] we hardly knew what he was talking about." [55]

Indeed, as events transpired, it was simply too late to disseminate knowledge and fully integrate the technology and operational procedures required to make air defense effective in Hawaii. Bergquist and his Army and Navy counterparts responsible for air defense had tried valiantly to implement twenty-four-hour-a-day air raid warning and control in the months and weeks before December 7, apparently with little urging or encouragement from their superiors. According to the most thorough chronicler of the surprise attack, Gordon W. Prange:

> No attitude on the part of Washington, no lack of equipment or funds can explain or excuse the failure to establish at least approach lanes or a reporting system to account for planes in Hawaiian skies. All that such procedures required was an appreciation of the value of incoming aircraft identification and fighter direction—abundantly demonstrated in the Battle of Britain—plus a little initiative and cooperation. But unfortunately those qualities, equally costless and priceless, appear to have been missing.[56]

Prange perhaps underestimates the difficulties involved, but the system doubtlessly could have been built had Hawaii's commanders recognized the requirement earlier. Thus, it would not be accurate to say the air defense system failed because no coordinated plan of action existed. In the words of the official Air Force historian, "In the circumstances, it was virtually impossible to put up anything approaching an effective air defense." [57]

After World War II, the psychological backlash of Pearl Harbor left Americans determined to deter a similar disaster. Instead of building elaborate air defense systems, American military planning depended on atomic monopoly. Spurred by the proliferation of strategic offensive weapons, the developing military configuration became anchored on the concept of deterrence. America would field sufficient air defenses to ride out an attack, but the linchpin of the military arsenal would be the retaliatory capability invested in the Strategic Air Command.

All that lay ahead. In the last days of 1941, Americans for the first time seemed to have good reason to fear air attacks against the mainland. Before Pearl Harbor, many believed the Navy strong enough to prevent enemy aircraft carriers or plane-carrying submarines from staging air raids against the east or the west coast. But the surprise attack in the Pacific altered the public mood drastically, for the assault had served as a model for future attacks in addition to destroying much of America's naval strength there. Rumors soon circulated that German submarines carrying light attack planes lurked off the east coast and that Germany might seize the French aircraft carrier the *Bearn* anchored in the West Indies. The public's apprehension rose when President Franklin D. Roosevelt warned the nation on December 9 that an enemy air attack upon either coast was a possibility. [58]

The AAF responded quickly to the perceived challenge. In the first hours after Pearl Harbor, the four interceptor commands in the continental United States activated their aircraft warning services. In one of his last acts as Commander of Air Force Combat Command, General Emmons deployed pursuit units to coastal airbases, and as in the exercises conducted a few months earlier, pursuit aircraft group commanders used regional information centers as their control centers. General McNair, head of GHQ Army and later the Army Ground Forces (AGF) commander, placed mobile antiaircraft artillery units under the direction of interceptor commands. [59]

Chaos prevailed initially on air defense stations, but soon the system began to function as planned with a firmly established chain of command. General Arnold acted to prevent that chain from being interrupted. Pointing to the possibility of air attacks on either coast as the only immediate threat to the mainland, Arnold proposed that the AAF be awarded primary responsibility for guarding against this threat. He suggested that the AAF receive command of shore-based Navy and Marine aircraft for air defense to ensure unity of command. [60]

Marshall did not agree with these requests although he did not intend to deprive airmen of top command, as indicated by his appointments of General Andrews over all Army forces in Panama and of General Emmons in Hawaii after Pearl Harbor. For unity of command, as the Chief of Staff interpreted it, Army combat commanders, including AAF officers, had to take their orders exclusively from him and the General Staff. The unity of command imposed therefore was not what Arnold had intended. On December 11, 1941, Marshall activated an Eastern Theater of Operations under General Drum and, on December 20, a Western Theater under Lt. Gen. John L. DeWitt. The theater commanders reported to Army General Headquarters. First and Second Air Forces were assigned to Drum while Third and Fourth Air Forces went to DeWitt.

Meanwhile, Maj. Gen. Millard Harmon replaced General Emmons as Commander of Air Force Combat Command. Harmon protested to Arnold, newly promoted to lieutenant general, about the "dangerous experiment [that] nullifies a large portion of the output of the Air Force for the past six years in preparation for war. . . ." [61] Arnold concurred, and apparently persuaded Marshall and McNair that the current command arrangements for the air forces were faulty. On December 31, 1941, Marshall returned control of Second and Third Air Forces to Air Force Combat Command, reduced Drum's theater to the geographical limits of Eastern Defense Command, and exempted specified units in his theater from his jurisdiction.

Before Marshall transferred Second Air Force back to the AAF, General DeWitt made IV Interceptor Command responsible for all Western Defense Command air defense regions from the borders of Canada to Mexico. Five regional headquarters operated from information centers in Seattle, Portland, San Francisco, Los Angeles, and San Diego. Across the continent, Drum took similar action in February 1942, ordering I Interceptor Command to manage the control centers Third Air Force had been installing in the southern Atlantic coastal regions. Thus I Interceptor Command had nine information centers: Boston, New York, Philadelphia, Wilmington, Norfolk, Charleston, Jacksonville, Tampa, and Miami. [62]

A significant feature of the wartime defense structure concerned the deployment of antiaircraft artillery. The Coast Artillery Corps had resisted all proposals to assign antiaircraft artillery forces to interceptor commands. The AAF protested, but the issue remained unresolved when the United States went to war. To meet the now staggering demands for guns at home and abroad, Marshall formed the Antiaircraft Artillery Command in March 1942 to create and train new units. Drum and DeWitt, meanwhile, decided to keep their artillery units organizationally separate from the interceptor commands. The artillery commanders on the east and west coasts, Maj. Gen. Sanderford Jarman and Maj. Gen. Fulton Q. C. Gardner, respectively, reported to Drum and DeWitt with the same authority and rank as the interceptor commanders. At the same time, Jarman and Gardner operated their own warning services consisting of their own troops and civilian volunteers. In a very real sense, therefore, two separate air defense systems operated during most of the war. [63]

Command and control for air defense was only one of many problems complicating the existence of Army GHQ. Arnold and the Air Staff (which, with the AAF, had been formally established in June 1941), meanwhile, led a campaign to reorganize the War Department. The resultant major realignment in March 1942 abolished the Office of the Chief of the Air Corps and the Air Force Combat Command. The AAF became coequal to the Army Ground Forces (replacing Army GHQ) and the Services of Supply (later Army Service Forces). Arnold became Commanding General of the AAF. [64] These changes were expected to provide the air arm with a greater degree of autonomy and a more decisive role when it believed it could make important contributions on the basis of its expertise, including contributions to air defense.

A few months before Pearl Harbor, Arnold had brought Brig. Gen. Muir S. Fairchild from ACTS to Washington as Assistant Chief of the Air Corps. In the March 1942 reorganization, Arnold made Fairchild Director of Military Requirements, an agency with subordinate directorates that included Bombardment, Ground Support, and Air Defense. The Air Defense Directorate, replacing the Air Defense Section of Headquarters Air Force Combat Command, was designed to ensure balanced assignments of men and materiel to air defense forces and to train key personnel. No sooner did Fairchild arrive in Washington than he decided he needed his old friend from ACTS, Gordon Saville, close at hand for his expertise in air defense. Fairchild arranged to have Saville brought home from Britain where he was studying Royal Air Force air defense operations, promoted him to lieutenant colonel, and gave him a free hand to coordinate home air defense matters.[65] Thus began a brilliant partnership that would, in time, drive the air defense developments in the United States.

Upon his return to the United States, Saville accompanied Sir Robert Watson-Watt, noted British air defense technician, on an inspection of west coast air defenses. Watson-Watt found that the principal mobile radar used for aircraft alert, the SCR–270, contained several major defects. Most important it could not discriminate between friendly and unfriendly aircraft. To alleviate this design problem in future air defense components, Watson-Watt suggested giving civilians with outstanding scientific credentials more responsibility for devising and implementing air defense systems. Although the United States had already begun doing this, Saville agreed to press the issue in Washington. He also arranged to use experienced air defense personnel as instructors in an operational training unit at Orlando, Florida, rather than sending them to overseas stations to meet the demand for trained air defense personnel. Saville took these actions because Fairchild, in the wake of the creation of the new AAF, had selected him Director of Air Defense in his Military Requirements Division.[66]

Now a full colonel, Saville assembled a staff of highly competent officers from the AAF, antiaircraft artillery, and the Signal Corps for his Washington office and, later, for the AAF School of Applied Tactics in Orlando. War-experienced Royal Air Force officers also offered advice. The prewar plan whereby interceptor commands furnished the training to convert airmen, Signal Corps personnel, and artillerymen into members of a unified air defense team fell casualty to the demands of war, complicating Saville's job. It was the Directorate of Air Defense who had to pick up the pieces and see that new plans were implemented.[67]

Maj. Gen. Muir S. Fairchild

The defense structure that emerged in late 1941 and early 1942 differed extensively from that of the prewar period. Southern Defense Command and Third Air Force committed considerable resources in the early months of the war to institute a Gulf Coast warning system, but no full-fledged air defenses ever developed there. The same was true with the Central Defense Command in the Sault Ste. Marie area. Only the two coastal areas, east and west, proceeded with defense preparations on a large scale corresponding to the perceived threat.[68]

By May 1942 the AAF began to deemphasize home air defense in all areas. This became apparent when Arnold directed the two coastal air defense forces to create pursuit aircraft units specifically for overseas duty. In a related development, Arnold oficially changed the name of the pursuit category of aircraft to that of fighter, symbolizing, among other things, that AAF interceptor pilots would train to conduct multiple duties. He also changed the name of the interceptor commands to fighter commands for the same reason, and the Air Defense Operational Training Unit became the Fighter Command School. He and his staff now believed that the threat of air attack against the mainland had drastically diminished. Requirements for fixed coastal air defenses became secondary to those for mobile ones, that is, defenses that could be sent to an overseas theater.[69]

Knowing the consequences of unpreparedness for the Army and Navy at Pearl Harbor, defense commanders in the continental United States wanted to avoid being caught by surprise and fought to obtain as much manpower and equipment as they could. Military and civilian officials in Washington appreciated the consequences of even a small-scale attack by enemy carriers or submarine-based aircraft against mainland targets, but they had to weigh the possibility of this occurring against the requirement to train units for warfare overseas. Consequently, as the perception of the risk of air attack diminished in the latter half of 1942, an unstated policy of calculated risk developed among Washington defense planners with respect to American air defense.[70]

In the first weeks after Pearl Harbor, Drum and DeWitt maintained entire fighter groups on air defense alert, which crippled training for other missions such as close air support of ground troops or the attainment of air superiority. By spring 1942, Arnold and the numbered air force commanders had lowered the alert requirement. Still, the newly designated fighter groups needed more freedom from air defense responsibilities to enhance their capabilities.[71]

Saville, now a brigadier general, helped resolve this issue in November 1942 by consolidating air defense forces in so-called air defense wings in key information centers on the east and west coasts. The wings, each headed by a brigadier general, had a headquarters consisting of AAF, Signal Corps, and Antiaircraft Artillery Command officers and enlisted men. Subordinate to the wings were signal companies that operated radar stations and managed communications for wing aircraft and warning services. The Fighter Commands, I and IV, commanded the fighter wings while Drum's and DeWitt's antiaircraft artillery commanders remained in absolute control of their gun units, which they allocated to the wings for air defense duty. Most important, fighter allocations were kept to a minimum, allowing increased aircraft in overseas combat theaters. In short, coastal air defense consisted of eight air defense wing areas and six surveillance regions. This remained the basic air defense organization until 1944 when the AAF began to dissolve it.[72]

By May 1943, Arnold strenuously called for additional decreases in the air defense establishment despite Saville's belief that the force should be maintained for at least psychological purposes.[73] In rejecting that argument, Arnold stated: "I can't see any excuse for maintaining these establishments just to meet the fears of a lot of people who are carried away by a feeling that something may happen. We are hard at war now, and the people of the United States have got to admit it."[74]

Not surprisingly, Arnold's view prevailed, and by 1943 air defense had lost its status as a directorate in the Air Staff. By the end of that year, the Air Staff judged the possibility of an air attack against the continental United States negligible, and practice air raid alerts ceased.[75]

Brig. Gen. Gordon P. Saville

Arnold decided that Saville's talents would be better used in command of the XII Tactical Air Command, preparing for the invasion of southern France. Air defense of the United States after the immediate post–Pearl Harbor shock had become, in the absence of imminent threat, the lowest priority mission for the AAF.

The air defense system, built up in the wake of the outbreak of war in Europe and reinforced after Pearl Harbor, was never tested in actual combat operations. The Japanese launched bomb-carrying free-flight balloons beginning in November 1944, but they did little damage. In all, Japanese balloon bombs killed six members of a picnic group near Bly, Oregon on May 5, 1945; ignited two small brushfires; and caused a momentary loss of power at the plutonium production plant in Hanford, Oregon.[76]

Various combat theaters around the world benefited from the air defense doctrine, organization, and equipment developed to ensure America's defense against air attack. Fighter Command School, activated in Orlando, Florida in mid-1942, trained officers designated for key air defense duties at home and abroad in the use and maintenance of equipment as well as in all aspects of air defense operations. The school, redesignated the AAF School of Applied Tactics in December 1942, under

Saville's command also drew up specifications for ground and airborne radar devices needed for mobile air defense. Personnel in the three air defense wings sent to North Africa in early 1943 and the three additional wings sent to Britain later that year trained in the school or under officers who previously trained there. A steady flow of officers moving from combat theaters through the school kept instructors abreast of fast-changing overseas requirements. [77]

The IX Air Defense Command, formed by the Commander of the Ninth Air Force, Maj. Gen. Hoyt S. Vandenberg, provided an outstanding example of stateside air defense training proving beneficial to the combat effort abroad. The organization performed superbly in furnishing air defense of rear areas after the Normandy landings in 1944. [78] The air defense system and doctrine established and developed in the prewar and early wartime eras was thus put to good use, although not for the purpose intended. The air defense net established in the United States also formed the basis on which planning began during the middle of the war for postwar defense. The likely emergence of a new and more powerful threat gave a sense of importance to that task.

Chapter 3

Planning for Air Defense in the Postwar Era

As the AAF dismantled the air defense systems built in the early years of World War II, it lay the foundations for postwar air defense planning. These preparations were part of the effort made by the Air Staff in anticipating an independent air force. War Department Field Service Regulation, Field Manual (FM) 100–20, "Command and Employment of Air Power," issued July 21, 1943, recognized the AAF as coequal to the AGF in combat theaters, and specified three principal air force missions: strategic, tactical, and air defense.[1]

General Arnold established two major postwar planning offices in AAF Headquarters, including the Special Projects Office, headed by Col. F. Trubee Davison, the first Assistant Secretary of War for Air from 1926 to 1932. Also created was the Post War Division, led briefly by Brig. Gen. Pierpont M. Hamilton, a World War II Medal of Honor recipient, who was soon replaced by Col. Reuben C. Moffat. Moffat worked directly under Maj. Gen. Laurence S. Kuter, Assistant Chief of Air Staff, Plans. An experienced test pilot, Moffat had served in numerous operational assignments, and Kuter relied on his good judgment. While the Special Projects Office was concerned largely with demobilization planning, the Post War Division concentrated on postwar force planning.[2]

The planners assumed that the postwar air force, whether it remained a part of the Army or became a separate service, would command all elements of air defense. The Chief of Staff, General George C. Marshall, seemed to confirm this view in August 1944 when he reassigned responsibility for research and production of electronic equipment used by the AAF from the Signal Corps to the air arm. Personnel and resources from the Signal Corps transferred to the AAF late in 1944. From then on, the AAF gradually assumed responsibility for electronic equipment used in domestic and overseas air defense systems.[3] By July 1945, the Signal Corps had, with the concurrence of the War Department, stepped out of the postwar air defense planning picture. The AAF emerged with sole responsibility for training, deploying, equipping, and operating the fighter force and the radar on which it depended for warning and control.[4]

Members of the postwar Air Staff were equally determined to control antiaircraft artillery for air defense operations. To ensure unity of command in an attacked area, FM 100–20 specified that all elements of an air defense system, including antiaircraft artillery, be under the overall command of an AAF officer.[5] The assignment of the 4th Antiaircraft Artillery Command to Fourth Air Force on the west coast, and the success of IX Air Defense Command in France, confirmed the validity of the doctrine for the Kuter-Moffat planning group. Early in 1944, the planners proposed that postwar air defenses should include an antiaircraft artillery contingent of 140,000 men. Although the General Staff failed to respond immediately, the planners felt confident the proposal would eventually be accepted. Support for this position came from field commanders and General Henry H. Arnold's staff. Lt. Gen. Carl Spaatz, Commander of the United States Strategic Air Forces in Europe, advised Arnold in late 1944:

> the development of all weapons for coordinated defense should be pushed. Antiaircraft artillery is making strides in effectiveness. . . . All measures for defense should be coordinated under our control, including radar and counter radar, interceptors . . . as well as antiaircraft artillery in order that we can get behind research and development in the field.[6]

Maj. Gen. Homer R. Oldfield, an artillery officer assigned temporarily to the Air Staff, strongly advocated this view. He considered the issue to be a command problem, pointing out that

> to divorce antiaircraft artillery from the [air defense] team and to place it on a cooperative basis not only violates the principle of unity of effort and economy of force, but endangers the success of the air defense mission.[7]

Because of this stance, AAF leaders began to reconsider the status of nonrated (nonflying) officers in the postwar Air Force. Before World War II, Air Corps officers necessarily performed a wide variety of nonflying duties, but the overwhelming majority considered themselves pilots first and foremost. In fact, the Air Corps Act of 1926 codified this way of thinking by limiting nonpilot permanent officer personnel to ten percent of the Air Corps. Wartime contingencies, however, underscored the need for capable officers with specialties in such fields as maintenance and logistics, many of whom entered the AAF directly from civilian occupations and would be lost to the service once the war ended. Postwar planners realized that an independent air force required highly qualified individuals possessing many technical skills in addition to the ability to pilot airplanes and perform other flying-related duties. General

Arnold was especially committed to integrating nonrated officers, such as artillerymen, into the AAF. He insisted that his planners consider steps to create career paths for these officers that would give them equal opportunity to command air defense operations and to be promoted to general officer rank.[8] Arnold's views were reflected in a memo from his deputy, Lt. Gen. Barney M. Giles, a few months before the conclusion of the war in Europe:

> The phase during which exclusive pilot management was essential is drawing to a close. . . . Regulations limiting the responsibilities of non-rated personnel must be changed. Every opportunity must be given to skills and abilities needed for a well rounded, flexible organization if the United States is to maintain its air leadership.[9]

Wartime planning for integration of antiaircraft artillery into the area air defense organizations culminated in a policy proposal drafted by Oldfield and Maj. Gen. Lauris Norstad, Kuter's successor as Assistant Chief of Air Staff, Plans. Arnold signed the proposal and sent it to the War Department General Staff shortly before the Japanese surrendered. The AAF had proved in war its ability to "assume the responsibility for large air defense operations, including the administration and employment of antiaircraft artillery," said Arnold. Accordingly, he believed it essential to assign artillerymen at once to the AAF:

> Air defense [will be] the first of several missions of the post-war military establishment and the mechanism set up for air defense will bear, initially, almost the entire burden of our national safety. Defense against air attack, if it is to be efficient and conform to the principles of economy of force involves the security of vital areas rather than the protection of individual objectives within these areas. Security of a vital area requires the closest cooperation between the three elements of air defense—fighter aviation, aircraft warning service and antiaircraft artillery. This can only be assured under a unified command. Harmonized operations, necessary now while AAA [antiaircraft artillery] is of limited range, will be doubly needed as the development of AA [antiaircraft] guided missles greatly increases the range of AA fire and the difficulty of coordinating it with the movement of our own piloted aircraft.[10]

By emphasizing vital areas instead of individual objectives, Arnold, perhaps unconsciously, reflected the impact of Gordon Saville's thinking on air defense doctrine. Significantly, Arnold also recognized the future use of guided missiles in air defense operations and the importance of their control by an air force commander in a unified defense setup.

Maj. Gen. Earle E. Partridge, Assistant Chief of Air Staff, Operations, Commitments and Requirements, one of the outstanding younger wartime leaders, further clarified how nonrated officers would be regarded in the postwar air forces. Aware that ground forces officers were concerned about the treatment they would receive should they become part of the air forces, Partridge assured them that plans were being developed to make antiaircraft artillery units a cohesive part of the unified air defense team and not a separate corps. Like Arnold, Partridge emphasized that artillery officers would be given opportunities to advance to general officer grades. Although artillery officers would not have direct command of flying units, they would be granted "adequate staff position recognition," including a position on the Air Staff such as General Oldfield had during the war.[11] Despite Arnold's and Partridge's assurances, ground officers remained apprehensive about transferring to the air forces. In any case, the General Staff did not immediately address the issue, and the postwar status of antiaircraft artillery officers remained uncertain.

Establishment of the Air Defense Command

In the last months of the war, General of the Army Henry H. Arnold instituted in the AAF several important changes designed, in part, to form a planning base for an independent postwar air force.[12] Foremost among these changes was the establishment of Headquarters Continental Air Forces at Bolling Field, Washington, D.C., on December 15, 1944.[13] The four numbered air forces in the United States were assigned to the new command. As with Twentieth Air Force in the Pacific, Arnold reserved personal command of the Continental Air Forces, appointing Maj. Gen. St. Clair Streett as his deputy. From this time forward, Arnold had three planning agencies for postwar planning—the Post War Division and the Special Projects Office in the Air Staff, and Streett's headquarters at Bolling Field—in addition to his own Personal Advisory Council composed of the AAF's most promising young officers, who rotated between combat and staff duty.[14]

While Streett and his staff recognized the need to plan and organize continental air defense for the postwar period, they believed some priorities were more urgent. They were determined to establish, without delay, a strategic strike force capable of operating worldwide. Designated tactical units, moreover, were to train with ground forces and the Navy, and combat units and crews were to prepare for deployment overseas.[15] In Streett's view, the urgency of these tasks overshadowed those of air defense preparations.

The Continental Air Forces staff planned for a postwar air force large enough to complete increasingly difficult and important missions. But late in 1944, General Marshall, convinced that the American public

General of the Army, Henry H. Arnold

would not support peacetime forces anywhere near the size contemplated by Air Staff and General Staff planners, directed the staffs to consider less ambitious estimates of postwar requirements. Following Marshall's instructions, the General Staff concluded that the postwar Army could not exceed 275,000 men. More concretely, the Army could afford to maintain only 5 divisions and 16 air groups,[16] far from the Air Staff's wish for 105 groups.

The General Staff added a new step to the postwar planning equation late in the spring of 1945. Army planning groups thereafter proposed interim force levels and organizational structures for the first three years after war's end and permanent plans for the period beyond. Meanwhile, General Kuter left the Air Staff for an assignment in the Pacific and Lt. Gen. Ira C. Eaker returned from his Mediterranean command to become Chief of the Air Staff and deputy to Arnold. Eaker faced the dilemma of clarifying what constituted *interim* rather than *permanent* planning as the AAF began to lay the groundwork for a postwar air force. He had to measure carefully the known mission requirements against Marshall's standard of avoiding unrealistic demands.[17]

Meanwhile, the General Staff's estimate of an interim postwar Army had risen to 500,000. An interim plan designed by Eaker and his staff, however, projected a need above that figure for the AAF alone. Before the disparity between the two projections could be reconciled, the war in the Pacific ended. President Harry S. Truman directed the Joint Chiefs of Staff (JCS) to decide on "the overall peacetime requirements of the Armed Services" and to submit a well-developed plan for his consid-

51

eration.[18] General Marshall immediately established a special committee under Brig. Gen. William W. Bessell, Jr., to prepare a force plan based on 500,000 men and another under Lt. Gen. Alexander M. Patch to examine the organization of the War Department (neither Bessell nor Patch was an airman).[19]

By October 1945, Bessell had prepared a proposal to allocate 165,000 men to the postwar air forces, a level sufficient for about 22 air groups.[20] In contrast, General Eaker and General Spaatz, who had begun to act in Arnold's stead in September 1945 (he did not officially replace Arnold until February 1946), believed the air forces could not operate effectively with less than 400,000 men and 70 groups of reduced strength.[21] The figure of 400,000 men did not include antiaircraft artillery personnel. The Patch Board would decide whether that contingent of the Army would come under control of the air forces.

Air planners advocated expanding the projected personnel allocations for air forces to include artillerymen. But the report of the Patch Board, submitted in mid-October 1945, rejected the Air Staff's proposals. While the board recognized the coequality of air and ground elements within the War Department, it steadfastly upheld the continued subordination of both to one chief of staff, recommending that antiaircraft artillery should remain with the ground forces.[22] Airmen, upset by Patch's recommendations, protested only mildly rather than risk jeopardizing current progress on the question of a separate air force. That restraint paid dividends in December 1945 after General Dwight D. Eisenhower succeeded Marshall as Army Chief of Staff. Sympathetic to the air arm's aspirations, Eisenhower approved the 70-group, 400,000-man program.[23]

Airmen hoped he would also reverse the unfavorable Patch Board findings. Early in December 1945 the new Chief of Staff reconvened the board under the chairmanship of the former Ninth Army Commander, Lt. Gen. William H. Simpson, who replaced the recently deceased Patch. Released January 18, 1946, Simpson's report proved a major disappointment to the airmen. Simpson endorsed Patch's recommendation that antiaircraft artillery should remain an integral part of the ground forces,[24] and Eisenhower refused to override the board's decision. In late January, he directed War Department Assistant Deputy Chief of Staff Brig. Gen. Henry I. Hodes to convene a meeting of General Staff, Air Staff, and Army Ground Forces officers to convert the proposals of the Simpson Board into a definite plan of action.[25]

It is an understatement to say that the Air Staff planners were upset with the results of the Simpson Board study and Eisenhower's subsequent approval of its provisions. Yet the Chief of Staff had not forsaken the airmen; instead he encouraged them to prepare for the formation of a separate air force, a goal he supported as ardently as they did. Eisenhower enjoined the airmen to work cooperatively with the General Staff

General Carl Spaatz

until legislation could be passed to realize their objective. Spaatz, whose professional abilities Eisenhower respected tremendously as a result of their wartime collaboration in North Africa and Europe, quietly accepted the Chief of Staff's assurances. In the meantime, Eisenhower guaranteed Spaatz that he would continue to serve as a member of the JCS. Further, the wartime post of Assistant Secretary of War for Air, filled in January 1946 by W. Stuart Symington, would continue.[26] These steps were designed to ensure adequate air force representation in military councils.

With Eisenhower's backing, Spaatz and the AAF could proceed to consider future mission requirements. In late March 1946, Spaatz reorganized the AAF, disestablishing the Continental Air Forces and apportioning its functions and resources among three new operational commands.[27] Reflecting AAF traditions and wartime doctrinal lessons, Strategic Air Command, under General George C. Kenney, was headquartered at Bolling Field; Lt. Gen. Elwood R. Quesada commanded Tactical Air Command at Langley Field in Virginia; and Air Defense Command came under the command of Lt. Gen. George E. Stratemeyer, with headquarters at Mitchel Field, New York (the home of the wartime ADC).[28] Spaatz and other AAF spokesmen publicly referred to these changes as functional, implying they had constructed a major AAF command to conduct each of the air missions recognized in FM 100–20.[29]

The hardworking, genial Stratemeyer was Arnold's Chief Executive Officer from April 1941 to January 1942 and subsequently served with

53

distinction in the China-Burma-India theater.[30] Six numbered air forces (First, Second, Fourth, Tenth, Eleventh, and Fourteenth) were assigned to Stratemeyer's ADC. By July, the air forces had been given area responsibilities corresponding to those of six newly restructured continental armies under the command of General Jacob L. Devers. Stratemeyer not only was concerned with air defense responsibilities but also was burdened with organizing, operating, and maintaining the Air Reserve and Air National Guard.[31] To perform these missions, Stratemeyer had only two percent of the AAF's manpower.

From spring 1945 until mid-1946, the 243-group AAF of World War II dwindled to 54 understrength groups, 21 of which were fighter groups. Eliminating intermediate headquarters and assigning a heavy workload of missions to fighter groups allowed the AAF to meet its overseas obligations with minimum manpower. At home the air forces had few resources. All General Spaatz and his staff could do was to decide how to apportion the planned 70 groups to each of the overseas air forces and the stateside operational commands as the AAF rebuilt. Kenney's Strategic Air Command (SAC) received the bombardment groups of Second Air Force and two of the four fighter groups still operational in the United States; Quesada's Tactical Air Command (TAC) received the personnel and equipment of Third Air Force and the other two fighter groups; and Stratemeyer's ADC received remnants of First and Fourth Air Forces, their fighter groups having been assigned to SAC. Plainly, the AAF gave priority to SAC and TAC at the expense of ADC.

Spaatz's actions were carefully considered. Although he planned to retire at war's end, he promised Arnold he would manage the AAF until a separate air force could be established. He wanted to rebuild as quickly as possible the combat-ready capability of the AAF, shattered by the impact of rapid demobilization.[32]

The creation of SAC and TAC offered Spaatz greater immediate prospect of meeting his objective. The missions of these commands required and permitted the immediate development of a combat capability, but ADC was another matter. During the war, General Arnold had stated that air defense would be the most important priority for the postwar military establishment because "the mechanism for air defense will bear . . . almost the entire burden of our national safety." War Department actions governing the creation of ADC had not granted it the means, structure, or clear authority to begin air defense activity in any meaningful sense. When Arnold expressed his views about the importance of the postwar air defense mission, he did not know that the United States would possess an immediate postwar atomic monopoly. Because of this capability, the risk of air attack seemed small, and Spaatz and his staff believed they had time to deal with the problem of air de-

Maj. Gen. George E. Stratemeyer

fense should the need arise. So while Kenney and Quesada began to rebuild and develop operational capabilities in their respective strategic and tactical spheres of responsibility, Stratemeyer went to work on his Air Reserve and administrative functions. He also attempted to help the Air Staff define more precisely his command's present and future duties. [33]

Meanwhile, the Air Staff began the uncertain task of planning the initial disposition of the 70 projected groups. Although the AAF had an approved goal of 400,000 men, too few to support 70 groups, Spaatz approved activation of all of them. He believed that establishing the full complement of groups, even if understrength, would improve prospects of obtaining additional personnel in the future. [34]

In this reallocation, the Air Staff assigned the 425th Night Fighter Squadron to ADC. This unit, 1 of 7 wartime night-fighter squadrons scheduled for retention in the peacetime air forces, still flew the P–61, although plans called for it to reequip with P–82s in 1947. The squadron would then assist in developing all-weather interception tactics in preparation for receiving jet interceptors. Stratemeyer assigned the 425th to March Field, California, where the Fourth Air Force retained some 300 radar and communication specialists.[35] In addition, Spaatz assured Stratemeyer that ADC would receive reinforcements in manpower and equipment as soon as possible. Plans called for ADC to activate one aircraft control and warning group and to expand the night-fighter squadron to an operational all-weather group.[36] Such promises of limited expansion could hardly hope to satisfy ADC commanders. But for Spaatz and the Air Staff, they accurately reflected the postwar military situation of air defense having a low priority.

As was true at the end of World War I, at the conclusion of World War II most Americans were anxious to forget about war and return to normal life as quickly as possible. They could do this secure in the knowledge that only the United States possessed atomic weapons. Sole possession of "the bomb" also influenced the thinking of military planners who approached the issue of continental air defense with no sense of urgency. Although the general agreement was that the Soviet Union represented the most likely future adversary, a 1946 AAF intelligence analysis predicted that the Soviets would, for the foreseeable future, remain a land power, and their air forces would be "tactical in design." [37]

In fact, after World War II, the Soviet dictator Josef Stalin had assigned his military forces three major tasks. The most important was to consolidate the Red Army's powerful position in eastern Europe and keep alive the threat of a Soviet drive to the Atlantic. Thus began what many western observers came to perceive as the Soviet Union's Hostage Europe policy. The overwhelming strength of the Red Army would balance the U.S. atomic monopoly and deter America from attacking the Soviet Union with atomic weapons. Stalin's second directive, also partly in response to American nuclear superiority, was to build effective air defenses as soon as possible. Finally, he wanted the Soviet Union to have its own nuclear capability.[38]

The successful completion of the last task would have required the development of a long-range carrier vehicle, able to reach the United States and, preferably, return to a base in the Soviet Union. Western analysts thought this would be difficult since the Soviets had emerged from World War II with little experience in strategic air operations. Their experience was limited even though bomber development had achieved some importance before the war. Then, the Soviets could boast of a small but extremely talented group of bomber designers, led by the brilliant Andrei W. Tupolev who developed the four-engine TB–3, the mainstay of Soviet bombers in the 1930s. Although the Soviets had among their ranks proponents of independent bomber operations in the tradition of Douhet, Mitchell, and Trenchard, the dominant ground forces officers of the Red Army never permitted the bomber designers to develop and disseminate their ideas. Furthermore, most advocates for independent strategic air operations were executed in Stalin's wholesale purges of 1937–1938, as were most of the leading ground forces commanders (Stalin apparently did not take sides in a doctrinal dispute when ordering who was to be murdered).[39]

In World War II, although most Soviet bombers formed an independent long-range aviation command (*dal 'nebombardirovochnaya aviatsiya,* or DBA) under the direct control of the Supreme High Command (Stavka), their most important mission supported the ground forces. Very infrequently did DBA—composed mainly of TB–3s, some lend-lease American B–25s, and twin-engined I1–4s—direct its strikes against targets behind the frontlines, such as German industrial sites. Only 0.2 percent of all Soviet Air Force sorties were in fact designated as independent air operations. Probably because of its predominately tactical mission, DBA lost its independent status in 1944, and most of its bombers were assigned to tactical air units. At the end of the war, the Soviet Union could not compare with the United States in terms of technology and experience in strategic air operations.[40]

After the war, in public pronouncements Stalin played down the U.S. atomic monopoly and dominance in strategic aircraft. He asserted that atomic bombs and long-range bombers did not mitigate the importance of "permanent operating factors," all of which he related to ground warfare. Despite this sanguine facade, Stalin was actually determined to develop atomic weapons and wed them to long-range aircraft. The Soviets had achieved what became a tremendous technological coup in August and November 1944 when three U.S. B–29s force-landed in Soviet territory after completing missions over Japan. Two of the B–29s were eventually dismantled and reproduced by the Soviets as the Tu–4 medium-range bomber, expected to be able to reach the United States on one-way missions.[41]

When the Russians would pose a serious threat, however, was debatable. U.S. military and civilian authorities were well aware of Soviet efforts to build a strategic bomber force because the Soviets had, not very circumspectly, attempted to purchase B–29 tires, wheels, and brake assemblies in the United States in 1946.[42] No matter how soon the Soviets perfected a bomber that could attack the United States, most military and civilian intelligence estimates predicted that the Soviet Union would not possess an atomic capability until at least 1952. Still, most military leaders advocated preliminary investigations and preparations to meet whatever threat eventually materialized. Accordingly, in the fall of 1945, the JCS accepted the probability of future air operations occurring across the North Atlantic and polar regions, the shortest distance between the two powers.[43] Accepting the concept of enemy bombers approaching the American heartland by these routes, it seemed logical that American retaliatory strikes would follow over the same air lanes. Based on this reasoning, in February 1946 General Spaatz set as a priority the deployment of the air defense portion of the seventy groups in "the areas essential to the security of the polar approaches, namely the North Atlantic and Alaska. . . ." [44]

The so-called polar concept triggered a host of activities destined to affect the future of air defense developments in North America. It led, for example, to an agreement between the United States and Canada to retain the wartime Permanent Joint Board on Defense. The two nations also propitiated their close World War II defense ties by agreeing to establish, under the Joint Board, a new Military Cooperation Committee. [45] By early 1946, the Committee had started work on an actual plan for defending the United States and Canada against air attack across the polar regions. The AAF planned, in cooperation with the Royal Canadian Air Force, to establish bases and command channels for offensive and defensive operations along air routes that led across Newfoundland directly into the critically important eastern Canada and northeastern U.S. industrial zones. The United States also opened negotiations with Denmark for military stations in Greenland and with Iceland for similar concessions in that country. Finally, the polar concept induced General Spaatz to grant priority to Alaska over the continental United States for air resources. In fall 1946, he told his commanders that "development of the Arctic front is our primary operational objective." [46] *

The huge materiel and personnel demands inherent in the polar concept prevented Spaatz and Stratemeyer from proceeding seriously with the limited domestic air defense preparations foreseen by the 1946 reorganization. That reorganization, with six ADC numbered air forces covering the entire area of the United States, involved the dispersal of air defense forces throughout the length and breadth of the country. The polar concept, on the other hand, required that air defense means be concentrated largely outside the nation. As General Stratemeyer informed his commanders in July 1946, it appeared as though the Royal Canadian Air Force would garrison air defenses installed in Canada, and the AAF would garrison those in Alaska, Greenland, Iceland, and the United

---

* The polar concept, of course, hardly applied only to AAF plans for air defense. Because the AAF's most powerful bomber at the time, the B–29, lacked the range to hit Soviet targets from the continental United States, Spaatz envisioned forward basing areas in the far north. But SAC encountered apparently insurmountable difficulties operating under arctic conditions. In July 1947, SAC Deputy Commander Maj. Gen. Clements McMullen remarked in frustration while attempting to find a suitable operating base in northern Canada: "I have practically shed my polar concept." The AAF eventually opted in the late 1940s to deploy most of its strategic strength on forward bases in Europe and the Far East [Harry R. Borowski, *A Hollow Threat: Strategic Air Power and Containment Before Korea* (Westport, Conn., 1982), pp 77–88].

States. In time, ADC's role would probably be concentrated on vital areas of the west coast and in the northeast. The air defense of Alaska, Greenland, and adjacent areas would come under the jurisdiction of separate commands.[47]

Early Planning Efforts

General Spaatz, had he been free to do so, would have combed the AAF worldwide to locate and reassign to Alaskan Air Command the skilled aircraft warning specialists needed there. However, JCS agreements required the AAF to maintain operational air defense systems as well in the Philippines, Okinawa, Guam, Japan, Korea, and Germany.[48] The small number of specialists trained in air defense operations remained therefore scattered throughout the world. Although a training program for aircraft warning experts had been started, it was not expected to increase in manpower until 1948. In the interim, Spaatz turned to ADC to provide trained personnel for Alaska.[49]

In November 1946, acting on Spaatz's instructions, Stratemeyer deployed his single P–61 night-fighter squadron from California to McChord Field, near Tacoma, Washington. Spaatz also authorized Stratemeyer to activate the day interceptor fighter group assigned ADC in the seventy-group program and base it at Dow Field, Maine. Stratemeyer's orders were to establish an air defense training squadron at McChord and a jet aircraft training operation at Dow. ADC was programmed to retrain the P–61 fighter unit into a two-squadron all-weather group. By March 1947, more personnel and P–47 aircraft had been transferred to Dow, and preparations soon began for conversion to P–84 Thunderjets.[50] On the west coast, the 425th Night Fighter Squadron, which had come to McChord with only one P–61 aircraft, soon received additional planes and personnel to maintain them.[51] On both the east and west coasts units strove to achieve operational capability. In the west an aircraft control and warning group activated on May 21, 1947, and airmen were given the chance to learn one or more of the many air defense skills so sorely needed in Alaska and other commands worldwide.[52]

ADC moved promptly to realize the training system advocated by Spaatz for air defense requirements in Alaska. Simultaneously, Stratemeyer and his staff of young, combat-experienced officers at Mitchel Field continued planning the operational air defenses for the continental United States. Strictly a paper exercise at the time, their plans proposed a far different course and role for ADC from the one imposed by higher headquarters. The ADC staff had begun its work with futile requests to

P–61 Black Widow, the United States' first night fighter

the Air Staff for clarification on the command's mission. In March 1946, Spaatz had hastily and informally issued SAC, TAC, and ADC interim mission statements. Stratemeyer was charged with organizing and administering a thus far nonexistent entity, the integrated air defense system of the continental United States. The program included training active duty units as well as those of the Air National Guard and the Air Reserve in the most advanced methods of air defense operations.[53]

The interim mission statement said nothing about the extent of ADC's responsibility in the event of an air attack against the United States. Yet Spaatz, during congressional budget hearings in 1946, stated that there must be only *one* commander responsible for the air defense of the United States. This would provide unity of command and ensure proper organization to prevent another surprise like the one at Pearl Harbor. Spaatz also stated his intention that ADC should eventually staff radar stations around the clock.[54] When the ADC staff pressed the Air Staff to explain how, under the seventy-group limitation, the command would obtain the means to install and maintain radar systems, the answer emerged that fighter aircraft and aircraft control and warning units of the Air National Guard would provide the "primary elements of this system."[55]

This news could hardly have been reassuring to ADC officers, for, although the War Department had determined to develop the National Guard into a combat-ready reserve, almost no action had been taken in that direction so far. Spaatz, however, told Stratemeyer that he would eventually have emergency command of all AAF resources with air defense capabilities. In addition, Spaatz promised at the opportune moment to unify ADC command responsibilities, not a simple task; he would have to solicit authority through the JCS for Stratemeyer to take charge of Army antiaircraft artillery and Navy shore- and harbor-based fighter, radar warning, and antiaircraft artillery forces in an emergency.[56]

ADC was well aware that Spaatz's guarantees were based on a weak foundation. In June 1946, the Army Ground Forces again made clear its intention to maintain control of antiaircraft artillery operations. The Navy was equally uncooperative in having its air defense forces come under ADC control in an emergency. Meanwhile, the Air National Guard had been only recently organized and remained understaffed and inadequately equipped. The Air Reserve, for similar reasons, was unprepared to assume air defense duties as well.[57]

With the fluctuating air defense situation, some air defense staff believed, by early 1947, that AAF Headquarters' failure to delegate responsibility clearly and to share the risk was an attempt to make ADC the scapegoat should a surprise air attack occur.[58] The staff believed this, though a bolt-from-the-blue air attack on the United States at the time was extremely unlikely. Many of the air defense staff recalled their shock and bewilderment after the Japanese attack on Pearl Harbor. They also remembered that the Pearl Harbor attack destroyed the careers of the principal commanders responsible for its defense. Subsequent events proved, however, that the Air Staff, with its many pressing duties in a period of reduced defense spending, ignored air defense less than it used the limited means at its disposal to build up the strategic striking force, considered by airmen the nation's most potent deterrent and war-waging instrument.[59]

Stratemeyer urged his staff to work to the best of their abilities with the resources available to them. He fully realized the less than crucial importance of his command, as interpreted by the Air Staff. He strove to improve the capability of ADC and planned to provide the nation, eventually, with staunch air defenses. Working with an unclear charter, Stratemeyer and his staff and subordinate commanders began negotiations in summer 1946 with other AAF commands, the Air National Guard, and the Army antiaircraft artillery forces to use their personnel in an emergency. The ADC staff also prepared and submitted to the Air Staff its ideas on how to proceed with home air defense in the near and long terms. Thus ADC plans conflicted with the Air Staff's intention of using the command merely as a source of trained personnel for Alaskan and overseas use. Stratemeyer's staff believed that if ADC was to be held responsible for the air defense of the United States, then specific programs should be developed to provide it with the means to assume that duty; otherwise, the command should be specifically reconstituted as an advanced training organization.[60]

Stratemeyer issued his proposal to establish some air defense for the United States on October 18, 1946. He planned to concentrate his forces, as they became available, in the northeast or the northwest United States. This, he believed, would permit him to make the best use of the forces available to him for training. ADC would also be in a position to develop an air defense in being, that is, an operational system in at least one of the areas most susceptible to air attack by way of the polar routes. [61]

Following the submission on October 18 of this so-called Air Defense Plan (Short Term) 1946–1947, Stratemeyer traveled to Washington on October 23 to outline his requirements for air defense in a personal presentation. His audience included Assistant Secretary of War for Air Symington, Spaatz, and members of the Air Staff. During his presentation, the ADC chief emphasized the need for careful consideration by government officials of continental air defense problems. It was urgent, according to Stratemeyer, that a decision be made quickly regarding allocation of funds and resources for air defense. All who listened to his plea seemed concerned, and for a brief period after his visit a flurry of activity occurred at AAF Headquarters on the air defense issue. This soon dissipated, however, as Spaatz and the Air Staff focused on what they considered more pressing matters, especially the drive for an independent air force. [62]

Although the response from the Pentagon was not encouraging, Stratemeyer persisted in having his staff prepare and submit plans. In late November 1946, he forwarded to Spaatz a plan for establishing an air defense in being. Basically, the plan called for a gradual buildup in the components of air defense networks and personnel to manage them. Stratemeyer believed such an expansion would produce, by mid-1948, a defense system that would "give a reasonable chance of interception and destruction of minor air raids . . . in the most vital areas of the country." These defenses, he said, "would prevent the unopposed destruction by hostile forces on the opening of hostilities of those areas . . . most necessary to the industrial and military mobilization." Further, such forces could be eventually expanded to provide total air defense coverage for the United States. Stratemeyer's plan indicated the minimum forces necessary to initiate an interim continental defense against nonnuclear attack. [63]

ADC received no indication from AAF Headquarters that its short-term, or air defense in being, plan was given careful consideration. The air defense staff nonetheless began a five-month effort to produce a comprehensive long-range air defense plan under the direction of Stratemeyer's plans chief, Col. John B. Carey, one of the AAF's most knowledgeable officers in air defense. The air defense plan (long term), submitted on April 8, 1947, outlined the ultimate requirements to provide air defense against a "well prepared and major attack by air." On the basis of Air Staff intelligence that predictably identified the Soviet Union as the only foreseeable enemy, Carey and his staff concluded that it would be 1955 before the Soviets could develop the means (match a fleet of long-range bombers with atomic weapons) to deliver an attack. They warned that if the Air Staff and government authorities decided to build an air defense system, at least two years would probably be required, starting from the nucleus proposed in the plan of November 1946.[64]

The long-term plan proposed that ADC have 38 control and warning groups, 34 all-weather fighter groups, about 300 antiaircraft artillery battalions, and 83 guided-missile groups, requiring 700,000 people for implementation. For more effective command of such a large organization, the plan recommended moving ADC Headquarters from Mitchel Field to a more central location, such as Kansas City, and accommodating it in a protected command center. Carey also proposed reorganizing the command into four air forces with subordinate defense wings. Headquarters at each echelon would operate from centers hardened to protect against air attack.[65] Carey greatly overestimated the personnel needed to implement future air defense systems. Nevertheless, as an indication of the richness and vision of his plan, many of his ideas for the command, control, and protection of air defense forces were implemented in much the same form as he envisioned.

The long-term plan concentrated on air defense of the continental United States. It noted that additional forces had to be arranged for an Arctic theater to defend Alaska, Canada, Newfoundland, Greenland, and Iceland. Some means had to be found to establish a peripheral early-warning zone comprised of radar stations, Navy radar picket vessels, and airborne search radar. These elements would be located across northern Canada and Alaska, west to Hawaii, and from Greenland to Puerto Rico.[66]

Stratemeyer admitted to Spaatz that ADC's proposals might seem large to "those of us who have been scratching to get the few people required for the seventy group program," but he added they were very small considering the vast area to be defended. Consequently, he hoped to proceed along the lines of his November 1946 plan to create an air defense in being. He would start with a small system in the northeastern part of the United States and gradually install additional networks in other critical areas if and when ADC received additional forces. This would remain ADC's goal until 1953 when, if current threat estimates proved valid, the long-range plan would be implemented.[67]

Stratemeyer recognized that some alternative might emerge. Technological developments could conceivably result in a radar system capable of warning and control at ranges beyond 1,000 miles. The defender would need only a few surveillance and control units, not an expensive and widespread network. Given this advantage, plus an in-place defense system based on an updated air defense doctrine, the air forces might

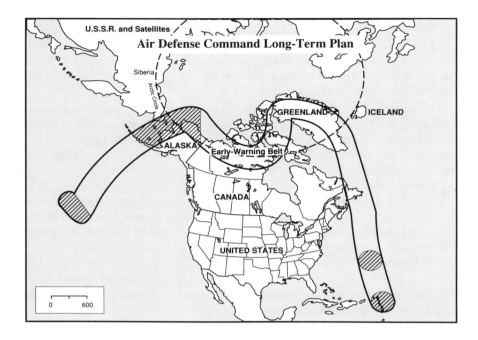

"avoid the unending expenditures of present defense measures." In the next eight years, progress in the tools of air defense and the methods of their employment would render the expensive World War II systems, on which ADC planning was based, unnecessary. Still, warned Stratemeyer, the longer air defense research and development was delayed, the less chance the United States would have for discovering and using advanced technology. Before the new defensive array was operational, a potential enemy's actions might necessitate large-scale air defense preparations on the older World War II model.[68] Stratemeyer's ideas seemed perfectly logical, but they brought to the fore what had become and continued to be a grave dilemma: With only limited resources, how much could the AAF afford to invest in air defense at the expense of what it considered to be more urgent priorities?

Under the circumstances, the answer could not satisfy ADC. For the moment, the Air Staff could not endorse the ideas championed by Stratemeyer "with any implication that the means required for implementation [could] be provided."[69] The Air Staff sympathized with the air defense chief's contention that he was being held responsible for preventing a surprise air attack on the United States without being supplied the means to accomplish his mission.

Because ADC could perform only as a training and administrative agent of the AAF, the Air Staff considered revising its mission statement to include only air defense planning. But Air Staff officers agreed that this would have been tantamount to announcing that the AAF was unable to provide air defense, doubtlessly damaging prospects for an independent air force. Considerable controversy on overall policies and programs affecting air defense thus prevailed from fall 1946 into summer 1947 in AAF Headquarters.[70]

Some solace may have been provided to ADC staff members in knowing that, while no positive action occurred regarding their proposals, air defense was at last becoming a subject of serious debate among Air Staff officers. Stratemeyer's ideas had precipitated an exchange between the Assistant Chief of Air Staff for Plans and the Assistant Chief of Air Staff for Operations, Commitments, and Requirements, Maj. Gen. Otto P. Weyland and General Partridge.

Partridge, a 1924 graduate of the U.S. Military Academy, had briefly commanded the New York Air Defense Wing in 1943. He was experienced in fighter and bomber operations and would greatly influence future U.S. air defense activities. In spring 1947 he argued that the Soviets would soon possess "weapons greatly exceeding World War II types in range, speed, and lethal attack." He denigrated ADC requests to the Air Staff for establishing operational systems hinged on World War II–type equipment. Complying with these requests would be, he believed, "a diversion of our crumbling resources to sustain . . . bow and arrow systems" and an indefensible waste of funds that should be targeted for research and development of equipment needed to counter the future threat. Partridge suggested all currently existing fixed operational systems be eliminated and only "nuclei aircraft control and warning systems" be supported for the foreseeable future. He believed enough air defense equipment could be stockpiled to outfit small task force units that might be needed to reinforce threatened areas. Further, new production of present-generation radars should be confined to just that needed for supporting such limited operations. Money saved in this process, he concluded, could be channeled into research and development of future systems.[71]

General Weyland, Assistant Chief of Air Staff for Plans, had earned his reputation as head of the XIX Tactical Air Command, which gained fame for its classic air support of General George Patton's Third Army campaign in France in 1944. Weyland also was well versed in air defense tactics, having commanded the 16th Pursuit Group in Panama shortly after Pearl Harbor. He largely agreed with his colleague's logic, but he posed other considerations he thought Partridge had overlooked. He focused particularly on the psychological and political implications of the air defense issue. Stating he was as anxious as anyone on the Air Staff to avoid wasting scarce funds, Weyland pointed out that the AAF was trying to persuade the American people that one of its chief missions was

Brig. Gen. Earle E. Partridge

the air defense of the United States. Since mere acceptance of this responsibility no longer seemed enough, he argued that the airmen actually had to provide some visible measures of defense. Therefore, he believed that at least a skeleton air defense system had to be maintained, even if it meant using outdated equipment and scarce personnel. As plans director, he was confident that new developments and techniques could be formulated and tested within the interim skeleton system. At the very least, claimed Weyland, these actions would assure the public that the AAF was making every effort to establish and maintain a "practical and effective air defense system." [72] Weyland's views thus concurred more with Stratemeyer's than with Partridge's. The ADC Commander and the Air Staff plans chief agreed on the need both to begin research programs in technologies applicable to future air defense systems, and to install temporary systems using World War II equipment. Partridge, however, agreed that development of future systems required research, but he believed that establishing temporary defenses using outdated equipment made little sense.

A few months after this exchange of views, General Spaatz asked a panel of officers to formulate a statement on AAF air defense policy. This Air Staff group reported in August 1947 that the AAF certainly could not plan to provide adequate air defense for the entire United States. To do so, they believed, would endanger the national economy and "leave little room for the air offensive," a move that "would be disastrous since real security lay in offensive capability." They thus recommended air defense "be provided only around these areas vital to our war effort . . . areas determined at the highest level [and which contain] targets of political, economic, industrial, and military importance." [73] Examined carefully, this statement merely rephrased the position Stratemeyer advocated over the past year. Almost everyone agreed, therefore, that the AAF had to establish a minimum operational air defense system in the United States, if not for strategic then for psychological and political reasons. The big questions remained, When? and On what scale?

The Radar Fence Plan

Late in 1946, General Partridge had pointed out that under the seventy-group program the AAF would have insufficient forces to meet essential air defense requirements; air defense needs had been projected not only by ADC, but also by Alaskan Air Command and other commands with air defense responsibilities. [74] This situation did not greatly disturb Partridge because he believed the immediate threat of air attack against the United States was minimal. Assistant Secretary of War for Air Stuart Symington found that conclusion unacceptable. He knew some opponents of a separate air force argued that airmen were incapable of performing the many nonoperational tasks necessary for raising, equipping, and training forces or that they would not concern themselves with any aspect of air power other than offensive operations. Symington, sensitive to such criticism, was anxious to demonstrate that the AAF could manage its affairs as well as the land and naval components. He asked Spaatz, in drawing up the AAF budget requests, to "carefully consider the military need for an adequate air defense system for the United States, with an emphasis on our polar frontiers." [75]

Spaatz turned for help to his scientific advisor, Dr. Theodore von Karman. He asked the scientist, active since World War II in planning future AAF scientific and technological requirements, to find a solution to the problem of creating an air defense system that would be not only adequate for immediate needs but also flexible enough to adapt to technical advances. [76] Von Karman believed this large order exceeded the capacity of the AAF Scientific Advisory Board. He suggested, and Spaatz agreed, that the job be given to Douglas Aircraft Company's research and development (RAND) * project. RAND officials put a group to

---

* The RAND project was established in May 1946 as a virtually autonomous department of the Douglas Company. In 1948, the independent and nonprofit RAND Corporation came into being. Although the bulk of its funding came from the Air Force, RAND

work on the problem in early 1947 and by July had issued a preliminary report. Their appraisal recommended against a large investment of funds in the near future for obsolete air defense equipment intended to protect against the highly improbable prospect of an air attack. Such an investment might, RAND warned, foster a dangerous "Maginot Line" complacency among the American people. Nevertheless, RAND agreed with almost everyone who possessed any knowledge of the problem that it was necessary to have a certain amount of air defense, although failing to stipulate how much was enough.[77] In response to the RAND study, the Air Staff urged that minimum requirements for air defense of the United States be determined and that needed forces be brought into being. To do so would enable the AAF to avoid dissipating its strength in the face of multiple air attacks and hampering its ability to launch counterattacks on a foe. Once a minimum air defense was established, other resources could be dedicated exclusively to offensive action.[78]

Spaatz was anxious to determine what that much talked-about concept—minimum air defense—actually entailed. He asked the head of Air Proving Ground Command, Maj. Gen. Carl A. Brandt, to develop a program for establishing a test operation at Eglin Field, Florida. The program would be designed "to estimate the air defense capabilities of modern radar equipment against modern aircraft and air operations." Spaatz informed Brandt that the development of an air defense system for the United States would cost enormous sums of money for equipment, construction, and manpower. The results of such a test, therefore, could have a decisive influence on the nature and extent of the program ultimately initiated.[79] Even before Spaatz decided on the test program, the question of air defense requirements seemed to acquire new implications.

In mid-June 1947, newly appointed Atomic Energy Commission (AEC) Chairman David E. Lilienthal asked Secretary of War Robert Patterson for a review of emergency military protection at vital facilities of the AEC. The purpose of the review was to ensure that all precautions had been taken to safeguard important installations against enemy action or other incidents beyond the capability of civilian security forces to handle.[80] Patterson agreed that it was crucial to provide protection for AEC facilities, even more so than political or industrial centers. He turned the matter over to the War Department General Staff for further study.[81]

As Deputy Chief of Staff for Operations in the Air Staff, General Norstad was assigned to study the problem. His previous assignment had been Assistant Chief of the Air Staff for Plans. An experienced staff offi-

---

was permitted a wide breadth of research independence while studying matters crucial to the Air Force and national security.

cer, from winter to spring 1947 he teamed with Admiral Forrest P. Sherman to draft legislation for what was to become the National Security Act. Norstad was well informed concerning Stratemeyer's proposals for current and future air defense requirements. Further, he possessed an intimate familiarity with overall available AAF resources. [82]

Having solicited the concurrence of Spaatz and General Jacob Devers, commander of the Army Ground Forces, Norstad advised the War Department not to implement a crash program allocating scarce air defense resources for the express purpose of guarding AEC facilities. Norstad thought the War Department should postpone action until the AAF had devised a comprehensive air defense plan for the nation. In planning for active air defense of the United States, however, Norstad promised that the AAF would pay particular attention to the protection of AEC sites. [83]

Less than a month later, on July 16, 1947, Congress passed the National Security Act authorizing the establishment of an independent United States Air Force. The Air Force was to "be organized, trained, and equipped for prompt offensive and defensive air operations." President Truman's Executive Order of July 26 implementing the statute emphasized the Air Force's responsibility to "provide means for coordination of air defense among the services." [84] Meanwhile, on July 18, Truman appointed the Air Policy Commission under the chairmanship of Philadelphia attorney Thomas K. Finletter to develop an integrated national air policy. [85] Soon afterward, military and civilian leaders of the Air Force were invited to appear before the Finletter Commission to explain what the Air Force would require to perform its duties and how such resources should be employed.

The emergence of the Air Force as a separate service, together with Secretary of the Air Force Symington's appeals and the upcoming Finletter Commission hearings, finally persuaded Air Force leaders they could no longer afford to delay preparing a plan to defend U.S. airspace. Having at last achieved its dream of independence, the Air Force moved to reevaluate its attitude toward air defense. Formerly, the Air Staff had shared in the War Department's responsibility for guarding the nation against air attack. The General Staff prescribed the air defense organizational structure and issued the basic mission directives. Now, at least in terms of fighters and radar systems, the Air Force had to demonstrate its resolve and ability to have operational air defenses in place.

A major obligation for developing an air defense plan devolved on the Air Force Communications Directorate headed by Maj. Gen. Francis L. Ankenbrandt. General Vandenberg, who had succeeded General Eaker on his retirement as second in command of the air forces on September 1, invested Ankenbrandt with the task of preparing the aircraft control and warning portion of the plan. While planning was the primary

W. Stuart Symington, after serving as Assistant Secretary of War for Air, becomes Secretary of the Air Force. Administering the oath is Chief Justice Fred Vinson. Others in the photograph are, *left* to *right*, Secretary of the Army Kenneth C. Royall, Secretary of National Defense James V. Forrestal, and Secretary of the Navy John Sullivan.

duty of the Air Staff directorate of plans and operations, the job at hand called for the technical expertise that only Ankenbrandt's staff possessed. The heart of the matter, as always in air defense operations, remained warning and control. Ankenbrandt's staff was composed of officers well qualified to deal with this problem. Skilled in electronics and communications, many had served under General Saville on the early wartime air defense staff. These officers offered Vandenberg his best prospect for the rapid development of a plan for radar control and warning.[86]

Ankenbrandt's goal was to design a system that would "prove a strong deterrent to enemy air attack with conventional bombers by providing the best air defense system available today." The system would constitute tangible proof to the nation that the Air Force was serious about defending the United States against air attack.[87] The report, prepared by Ankenbrandt and his communications officers, was called the Radar Fence Plan (code named Project SUPREMACY). If the Air Force received funds to begin at once, the plan forecast a radar warning and control system in operation by 1953. The system would consist of 411 radar stations and 18 control centers in the continental United States serviced around the clock by 25,000 regular U.S. Air Force personnel and nearly 14,000 Air National Guard radar specialists. The plan allowed for a total expenditure of $600 million over a 5-year period. Construction and purchase of radar and other equipment would account for $388 million,[88] while the remainder, as Vandenberg noted, would cover expansion or modifications.[89]

The Radar Fence Plan clashed markedly with the advice offered by RAND. RAND had advised against investing heavily in a modern air defense system, fearing such action could instill a Maginot Line temperament within the national consciousness and could take resources from the strategic forces. Ankenbrandt and his staff, on the other hand, believed that the Air Force could best serve and win the confidence of the nation by providing an air defense system that incorporated the most advanced methods and technology available.* Anxious to display its abilities to perform a variety of missions, the new Air Force, temporarily at least, supported Ankenbrandt's view.

A few weeks after the formal separation of the Air Force from the Army, Ankenbrandt and his staff conducted extensive briefings on the Radar Fence Plan for a wide audience of listeners from the Air Force, the JCS, and the Office of the Secretary of Defense (created by the National Security Act as part of the National Military Establishment). The briefings were well received. Stratemeyer and his staff in particular believed the plan provided the minimum coverage for strategic areas.[90] On November 21, 1947, Air Force Chief of Staff Spaatz approved the Radar Fence Plan and directed the Air Staff to seek funds for its implementation.[91] Accompanied by Lt. Gen. Edwin W. Rawlings, Air Comptroller, Ankenbrandt met with Bureau of the Budget representatives to discuss how to secure funds so that work on the first stage of the program could begin at once. Officials in the Budget Bureau dashed Air Force hopes for quick action by insisting that funds for construction could only come from supplemental appropriations approved by Congress. Without such enabling legislation and the concurrence of the two senior services, the Budget Bureau could take no action on the plan. Rawlings therefore prepared the necessary paperwork and submitted it in early 1948 to the Army and Navy for review.[92] That put the plan in an indefinite "hold." This cumbersome procedure was necessary because the Air Force had yet to be invested with unambiguous primary responsibility for continental air defense.

---

* Ankenbrandt generally opposed installing older equipment in the system. He described the capabilities of World War II radar equipment as follows: "They have an optimum coverage against conventional bombers of approximately 150 miles at 20,000 feet. They provide inefficient coverage above 30,000 feet and zero coverage above 35,000 feet. Their low angle coverage is limited by the horizon to approximately 35 miles at 1,000 feet and correspondingly shorter ranges at lower altitudes. Their performance in controlling friendly jet interceptors is poor. These deficiencies in World War II types are undoubtedly known to all nations since basic techniques have been completely declassified and are widely published. Specifically, Russian information on radar is considered completely abreast of the art because of the acquisition of German radar scientists and equipment, and their acquisition of allied lend lease radar equipment in quantity" [Memo, Ankenbrandt to Spaatz, Oct 22, 1947, Spaatz Papers, Box 263, LC].

Air defense operations consisted, as always, of four major components: detection, identification, interception, and destruction. Radar stations and control systems figured prominently in detection, identification, and interception, but they could not themselves cause destruction. Ankenbrandt stressed in his briefings that the Radar Fence Plan did "not in itself provide air defense." Air Force leaders preparing to appear before the Finletter Commission had to become familiar with Stratemeyer's ideas for a complete system incorporating the "trip wire" formed by the Radar Fence. A total air defense network would only be complete with advanced aircraft and weapons systems, operated and serviced by qualified personnel. Although most of the potential witnesses had a reasonably good understanding of Stratemeyer's problems and his proposed solutions, most realized that no subject was as obfuscated by semantic difficulties as air defense. This posed a potential problem because both Symington and Spaatz were determined that every officer appearing before the commission would speak with one voice on whatever aspects of Air Force policy the panel members chose to probe. In Symington's view, if Air Force officers underestimated the importance of the air defense mission, they would become subject to the criticism that the Air Force was simply interested in "attempting to prove that the main way to win a war is through strategic bombing." [93]

The generals were anxious to prove to the Finletter Commission that they were using all the limited means at their disposal to provide a semblance of air defense. Under the circumstances, ADC suddenly became subject to much attention from Headquarters USAF. In mid-October 1947, Vandenberg went to Mitchel Field to discuss the situation with Stratemeyer, and then invited him to Washington where, on October 23, he briefed major Air Force leaders. His audience included Symington, Spaatz, and key members of the Air Staff, including Norstad, just assigned as Air Force Deputy Chief of Staff for Operations after his tour on the War Department General Staff. This meeting proved an important event in the story of postwar air defense. Vandenberg achieved success in clearing the way for Stratemeyer to initiate actual air defense operations.

Stratemeyer emphasized in his briefings the proposals his operations staff had made in their long-range plan. He believed that ADC Headquarters should be moved inland; the organizational structure should be reduced to four, rather than six, numbered air forces; and these intermediate headquarters should be transferred to more suitable locations. At all levels, headquarters needed to be provided command posts, situated near administrative headquarters, and to be designed to withstand attack by all foreseeable weapons. Of primary importance, Stratemeyer pleaded, ADC should be freed of all missions not related directly to air defense and the administration and training of Air Reserve forces. Symington and Spaatz agreed with Stratemeyer's proposals, and Vandenberg informed Stratemeyer in November that the Air Staff was implementing his proposals for reorganization.[94] At best, ADC had been a training, planning, and administrative agency, but decisions emanating from the Washington meeting paved the way for transforming Stratemeyer's organization into an operational command.[95] Experimental air defense groups and systems soon appeared on the east and west coasts.

One casualty of the new plans for ADC was the air defense project Spaatz had assigned to General Brandt at the Air Proving Ground. Shortly after the Washington meeting, Spaatz rescinded his instructions to Brandt. Since Spaatz first conceived of the test project, it was increasingly apparent that worldwide shortages of trained aircraft control and warning personnel would prevent "accomplishment of any but the most vital air defense missions."[96] Spaatz nonetheless wanted to find a sound basis for guiding systems planning, development, and procurement. One alternative would have been to subject air defense problems to seminar-type discussions in the Air War College. But as Spaatz realized, Air Force officers were, for the most part, too limited in their knowledge of strategic air defense to meet the rigorous demands of such an approach. The only reasonable alternative, he believed, was to "establish a few tactical systems whose primary function would be to defend certain vital areas of the United States." These units would also act as an air defense proving ground for carrying out a test program.[97]

Attempts to Come to Terms with the Mission

In appearances before the Finletter Commission, Air Force leaders stated the first mission of their service, in preparing for the defense of the United States, was to meet a surprise attack with an instantaneous counterthrust of both offensive and defensive forces.[98] Vandenberg explained in testimony before the House Appropriations Committee that the Air Force's primary task was allotting sufficient long-range bomber and reconnaissance forces to the "immediate counter air offensive." Just as important was defending the United States and its outlying bases from air attack. From these bases, the retaliatory attack would be launched. For this purpose, Vandenberg estimated the Air Force would need to deploy twenty-five fighter groups.[99] Vandenberg did not intend that SAC and TAC be shorn of their fighter escort and fighter bomber groups or that the forces be converted to air interceptor duty under ADC. Instead, he meant that all fighter groups function effectively in defensive as well as offensive roles. Spaatz elaborated on this theme in testimony a few days later. Although it was necessary for fighter aircraft to be under one air defense commander, it was not essential that fighter units be attached to air defense organizations at all times. During World War II, Spaatz moved units from strategic to tactical operations, as long as the various units were trained to perform different functions.[100]

Stratemeyer presumably possessed, under provisions of his interim mission statement, authority to call on the tactical forces of all Air Force commands, or even other services, during an emergency. But when he attempted to exercise his prerogative, he encountered unyielding opposition. Other military commanders simply refused to cooperate. Either they believed their own forces too poorly manned and equipped to accomplish their primary missions, not to mention assuming secondary air defense responsibilities, or they questioned Stratemeyer's authority. So while Stratemeyer welcomed the new emphasis on placing all Air Force fighter groups at the disposal of ADC in an emergency, he wanted assurance that his fellow field commanders understood the concept. At the end of 1947, Headquarters USAF complied. The Air Staff issued ADC its first formal mission directive, replacing the interim statement of March 1946. The new directive proclaimed unequivocally that Stratemeyer was empowered to "train and direct operationally those units of the regular national defense establishment assigned or attached as part of a defense force in being." Additionally, the directive made clear what should have been obvious: "the chief mission of the Air Defense Command is the preparation for and execution of defense operations against air attack on the continental United States."[101]

The Air Force also sought to clarify and strengthen ADC's authority with respect to the use of Air National Guard units in an emergency. In fall 1945, the War Department decided to establish and maintain the Guard as a combat-ready force, capable of immediately expanding regular land and air forces whenever war threatened.[102] The Air National Guard fighter units represented, as AAF Headquarters proclaimed, ADC's most promising potential source of fighter-interceptors for emergency air defense.

Stratemeyer, unfortunately, had endless problems, some of his own making, with the Air National Guard program.[103] In 1946, he had made several unsuccessful attempts to influence policy toward greater control of the Air Guard by regular forces, particularly control by his own command. Before Stratemeyer's campaign to acquire these units, Air Force leaders had assured the National Guard Bureau they had no intention of assuming direct control of the Air Guard during peacetime. Spaatz now admitted to Stratemeyer that he had been mistaken about employment of all air reserve forces in permanent support of the air defense mission. Such forces, said Spaatz, constituted a total Air Force reserve and were to be used in an emergency to support the Air Force in a variety of missions.[104] Spaatz also amended the ADC mission statement. In April 1946,

Stratemeyer had written the Chief of the National Guard Bureau to explain that, as air defense commander, his mandate involved ensuring the effectiveness of the Air National Guard, and organizing and administering the Guard in its "federally reorganized status." [105] Air Guard officials apparently interpreted this as an infringement on their autonomy. Spaatz told Stratemeyer that, in the future, ADC would have to check with higher headquarters before issuing declarations or instructions of any type to National Guard officials. [106]

After this episode, Stratemeyer carefully avoided embarrassing Headquarters USAF on Air Guard matters. He continued, however, to speak his mind in confidential letters to Spaatz when he felt state authorities were hampering his attempts to organize units. [107] Many Air Force leaders, especially General Partridge, who favored removing the Air Guard from control by the National Guard Bureau gave him their support. [108] When he briefed the Air Force leadership in October 1947, he claimed that for the Air Guard to be of any value to him, his command would require first call on the services of all fighter and radar squadrons. Once ADC's need for their services had passed, he agreed that the squadrons could return to other duties. Furthermore, he wanted operational control of Air Guard forces in peacetime for training purposes. [109]

By October 1947, Spaatz agreed it was time to support Stratemeyer completely on this issue. Spaatz secured National Guard Bureau concurrence for ADC to train Air Guard tactical units and to "be prepared to direct them operationally as part of a force in being." [110] In subsequent correspondence, Spaatz told Stratemeyer the Air Guard would comprise his primary source of air defense units. Also, in case of war or a national emergency, all Air Guard units would initially be available to ADC. [111]

These developments—the Radar Fence Plan, the decision to begin operational air defense with existing means, and the authority for using Air National Guard units—were greeted with enthusiasm on Mitchel Field. For nearly two years, ADC had borne responsibility for air defense, but without forces or clear authority to accomplish that task. Now, at the end of 1947, Stratemeyer was gratified to perceive a change. As he told his subordinate commanders, he was happy to report that at Headquarters USAF an "ever-increasing importance [was] being placed on requirements for air defense of the continental United States." [112]

The Finletter Report, released on January 1, 1948, generally pleased Symington, Spaatz, and Vandenberg. The commission's findings formed the basis of the Air Force position during JCS discussions on roles and missions in the national military establishment. The commission recommended the nation adopt a new strategic policy built around air power. It also proposed that the seventy-group program remain the goal of the new, separate U.S. Air Force, attaching an urgency to its swift completion. The panel members warned that this minimum force had to be equipped with modern aircraft and staffed, trained, deployed, and otherwise made ready to deal "with a possible atomic attack on the country by January 1, 1953." After that date, the United States would require a considerably stronger Air Force to ensure security, because intelligence sources reported that Soviet long-range bomber programs were making considerable progress. [113]

Although the Finletter Commission left the decision on how to distribute the seventy groups to the Air Force, it insisted the Air Force by 1953 "possess the complicated defensive equipment of modern electronics and modern defensive fighter planes and ground defensive weapons." Commission members, while recognizing the need for a radar early-warning system, cautioned against the extraordinary expense of such a system, if constructed, to provide total coverage. The Finletter Commission, in this regard, expressed fears similar to those expressed by RAND. A continuous coverage system, they believed, might tend to "divert us—as the Maginot Line diverted France—from the best defense against an atomic attack, the counter-offensive striking force in being. [114] Civilian defense planners seemingly accepted the Air Force contention that the best defense was a potent offense while almost everyone who studied the matter agreed that some yet-to-be-defined minimal air defense was needed to limit damage, assure the public, and provide the early warning necessary to launch strategic bombers in a retaliatory response. The Air Force, meanwhile, had proved its willingness to provide such a minimal defense. Whether the Radar Fence Plan would supply satisfactory air defense coverage or whether its scale would prove too costly remained unresolved.

Active Operations Begin

In the weeks before the release of the Finletter Report, ADC worked hard to execute the decision made in Washington to begin operational air defense on the east and west coasts. In the west, Fourth Air Force redeployed its single operational fighter unit from McChord Field, Washington, to Hamilton Field, California, late in November 1947. The squadron had over 300 officers and enlisted men as well as 13 Northrop P–61 Black Widow aircraft. The Black Widow, the first American aircraft designed for a night-fighting role, was rapidly becoming obsolete. The Air Force was anxious to replace it with the North American P–82 (later redesignated the F–82) Twin Mustang, which was two P–51 fuselages joined by single wing and stabilizer sections between them. Because development on converting the P–82 into an all-weather interceptor lagged, at the end of 1947 the P-61 remained the Air Force's only night, all-weather fighter aircraft.[115]

P-61 aircrews trained in air defense procedures on McChord with the 505th Aircraft Control and Warning Group, which would become instrumental in operational defense. As its training program expanded and its technicians gained proficiency, the unit became an important source of operational data for officers responsible for managing or implementing the Radar Fence Plan. Visitors from throughout the Air Force converged on McChord to observe and learn about the practical aspects of aircraft control and warning procedures. Here airmen, who later rose to key maintenance and controller positions in the worldwide air defense operations, received introduction to their skills.[116]

On the east coast, training proceeded similarly. As with Fourth Air Force in the west, plans to replace the 52d All Weather Fighter Group's P-61s with P-82s collapsed when the Twin Mustang production program encountered engine problems. Stratemeyer had additional Black Widows removed from storage and sent to the Air Force Depot Facility in Mobile, Alabama, for restoration and modification. Then, early in 1948, P-61s began to be issued to the designated squadrons.[117]

In the midst of initial efforts to begin operations, ADC officers involved in these projects were summoned to the Pentagon in January 1948 to meet with Air Staff representatives. The meeting was called to plan an air war game for May 1948, billed as the largest peacetime exercise ever conducted by the Air Force. The exercise plan designated SAC to furnish the Red, or strike, force, while ADC would deploy the Blue force in defense of the eastern seaboard from Maine to Virginia. TAC and Air National Guard units would also participate. Headquarters USAF was uncertain if it could obtain sufficient funds to complete the exercise on the scale desired. If so, ADC would be allowed to move the 505th Warning and Control Group to the east coast for the war games. The 505th trained intensely throughout the first months of 1948 in anticipation of a move order.[118] The 505th's exceptional state of preparedness, however, made it the most likely candidate for another assignment even before it received orders to the east coast.

After moving from the west coast to participate in the war games, the 505th was expected to remain in the east. ADC planned to concentrate its meager radar warning and control resources in the northeastern United States pending approval and funding of the Radar Fence Plan, but its plans were abruptly and drastically altered late in March 1948. With no advance warning, Headquarters USAF directed that an emergency air defense system be established to operate around the clock in Alaska and the Pacific Northwest. Shortly after, First Air Force in the east was ordered to put its fighter units on alert. The usefulness of this move was uncertain since First Air Force did not yet control the serv-

P–82 Twin Mustang, designed for tactical versatility

ices of the 505th and thus lacked any type of radar warning and control capability.[119]

These events began Thursday, March 25, when Spaatz suddenly informed the Air Staff that he wanted Alaskan air defenses "augmented" immediately.[120] The following day, a top secret message over his signature went to the Alaskan Air Command directing it to "place existing radar warning [units] on continuously operating basis by 4 April."[121] On March 27, a similar directive instructed Stratemeyer to activate immediately a functioning air defense system for the protection of Seattle and the atomic energy plant in Hanford, Washington.[122] That same day, officers from Stratemeyer's staff met in the Pentagon with staff members from SAC and TAC as well as with representatives of the Air Transport Command. Arrangements were made to airlift radar teams from TAC's only radar unit to Alaska for emergency duty. SAC simultaneously began preparations to send one of its two P–51 Mustang fighter groups to Alaska and the other to the Pacific Northwest for emergency air defense duty.[123]

Spaatz initiated emergency air defense measures in March 1948 for a number of reasons. First, it is clear that, contrary to the views presented by the Central Intelligence Agency (CIA) (established in 1947 under the provisions of the National Security Act) and by the intelligence divisions of the Army and Navy, Air Force intelligence believed the United States in danger of a surprise attack from the Soviet Union. Warnings from overseas commanders reinforced such feelings. Lt. Gen. Ennis C. Whitehead, Air Force Commander in the Far East, for example, began late in 1947 to report "strange incidents and excursions" over Japan. Correlating these suspicious flights with simultaneous bellicose actions of the Soviet Union in Berlin and elsewhere, Whitehead told Spaatz of his concern over the "grave danger of war with the USSR within a few months."[124] In Berlin itself, Lt. Gen. Lucius D. Clay, American Military Governor of Germany, submitted an equally bleak estimate of Soviet intentions just two weeks after the Communist coup in Czechoslovokia. Clay had believed earlier that war would not break out for at least ten years, but now he sensed a change in Soviet attitude that led him to conclude war "could come with dramatic suddenness." [125] In the middle of March, President Truman told Congress what the military already took much for granted, that the Soviet Union was the enemy of the United States.

In this crisis atmosphere Secretary of Defense James V. Forrestal and the JCS held their celebrated "roles and missions" conference in Key West, Florida, from March 11 to 14, 1948. Though the conference proved indecisive on many crucial issues, the decisions reached may have provided further rationale for the Air Force directive on emergency deployment of air defense forces.

In Key West, the JCS confirmed the principle upon which the Air Force already based its planning: continental air defense was primarily a function of the U.S. Air Force.[126] The conferees also endorsed the Finletter Commission's report emphasizing the need to begin installing air defenses to ensure a minimum system that would be in place by 1953. Although the system would incorporate the resources of all three services in an emergency, the JCS gave the Air Force primary responsibility and prerogative to write doctrine and make arrangements for such cooperation.[127] The JCS also established the Continental United States Defense Planning Group within the Joint Staff organization to explore the question of who would command overall air defenses in case of war.[128] Whether the Key West participants discussed the Radar Fence Plan, including the problem of acquiring personnel for duty in the proposed radar systems, is uncertain. In any event, the JCS decided to lower the requirement for Panama Canal Zone defenses to free radar specialists posted there for duty in the United States. From these personnel, Headquarters USAF eventually gained the manpower needed to operate an emergency air defense network in the First Air Force area.[129]

In addition to the high-level concern over the possibility of a Soviet air attack and the confirmation in Key West of the Air Force's primary responsibility for the air defense mission, a third factor contributed to the activation of an air defense emergency in March 1948. The Air Staff viewed the initiation of emergency operations as a first step in the implementation of the Radar Fence Plan. Once established, much of the system created during the emergency would be retained; the Air Force would then seek funds to expand and improve the system. As Stratemeyer later expressed it, ADC was now authorized to establish, within its means, "actual defenses."[130] He hoped that funding for both the seventy-group Air Force and the Radar Fence Plan would soon increase those means significantly.

In areas designated air defense emergency zones, personnel worked around the clock to establish working systems. Despite the airmen's herculean efforts, obstacles proved overwhelming. On the west coast, for example, when an echelon of SAC's 27th Fighter Group arrived on McChord Field to operate in tandem with the 505th control and warning group, it was discovered that the P–51 pilots had been trained exclusively in escort missions and had never before flown air intercepts. In vain, the 505th began a crash training program in ground-controlled interception procedures.[131]

Countless difficulties of varying complexity arose in all the emergency defense areas. Commanders and their men were tireless in their efforts, but air defense forces were generally disorganized and inadequately manned, trained, and equipped. Fortunately, in mid-April, the Air Staff informed Stratemeyer that the crisis had passed, and it ended the emergency.

When the emergency operations had ceased, General Hoyt S. Vandenberg had, for practical purposes, succeeded Spaatz as Chief of Staff (he officially succeeded Spaatz on April 30, 1948). The nephew of Senator Arthur Vandenberg and a graduate of West Point, the new Air Force Chief was handsome, suave, and intelligent. Prior to becoming Vice Chief of Staff, under General Spaatz, Vandenberg in 1946 and 1947 had been head of the Central Intelligence Group of the War Department General Staff and, subsequently, Director of the Central Intelligence Agency in the Office of the Secretary of War. Vandenberg came to his position with a broad background and knowledge in all aspects of air force operations. Most of his energy would be initially directed, however, in making SAC the powerful deterrent force it was intended to be. The new Vice Chief of Staff, General Muir S. Fairchild, would have to decide precisely how to retrain and develop the limited air defense systems begun during the emergency. His problem would have been considerably less had the Radar Fence Plan been fully approved and funded. The draft legislation the Air Force submitted to the other services for concurrence in February 1948 had been stalled; the Army had responded promptly and favorably but the Navy, as of mid-April, had no decision.[132] As time was quickly running out in the funding deliberations for fiscal year 1949, Stratemeyer pressed Headquarters USAF for detailed instructions on how he should proceed to develop operational air defenses.

Assuming his post in the midst of this turmoil and uncertainty, Fairchild vowed to provide a continuity of purpose for the Air Force's air defense mission. Having just launched the Air Force's postwar military education program as Air University commander, Fairchild's concern was less with inculcating a Maginot Line consciousness among Americans by establishing a too-strong air defense network than it was with the fact that, at the moment, the nation had no effective air defenses. After considering the situation, Fairchild decided to concentrate air defense planning under a general officer experienced in all aspects of the subject and unburdened with other duties. He knew exactly whom to choose—Maj. Gen. Gordon Saville.[133]

Chapter 4

Saville Takes Charge

Generals Hoyt S. Vandenberg and Muir S. Fairchild took the helm during a testing period in the young history of the U.S. Air Force. America's possession of the atomic bomb did not deter the Soviet Union from its aggressive policy in Europe, highlighted by the Communist coup in Czechoslovakia in February 1948. In a speech before Congress on March 17, President Harry S. Truman castigated the "ruthless course" pursued by the Soviets, stating, "There are times in world history when it is far wiser to act than to hesitate." He suggested the temporary reinstitution of selective service and, without the public's knowledge, advanced development of the hydrogen bomb.[1]

As for the Air Force, it first looked to SAC to meet the threat posed by the Soviet Union. Sadly, although the Air Force portrayed the command as the nation's premier instrument of deterrence and war fighting, SAC was at the time, according to a historian of the postwar period, a hollow threat. Americans, generally unaware of SAC's unpreparedness for war, would have been shocked, as was President Truman, to learn of the meager stockpile in the atomic weapons arsenal. Worsening matters, SAC crews were understaffed and ill prepared for combat missions, bombers did not possess the range to attack the Soviet Union and to return to the United States, and plans to attack key Soviet military and industrial sites were sketchy at best because of inadequate intelligence about the sites and the difficulties of including such widely scattered targets in a coherent targeting scheme. SAC's situation only began to improve slowly when Vandenberg appointed General Curtis E. LeMay to lead the command in October 1948.[2]

Meanwhile, ADC was less ready than SAC for combat. The alert of March 1948 found air defense forces totally unprepared. Radars and fighter aircraft were few, and those available were obsolete. Trained radar operators, ground controllers, and pilots were scarce, often poorly trained in air defense operations. The result of the alert assumed as much significance for ADC as it had for SAC, since the Soviets' actions indicated they were not intimidated by the American atomic bomb. Air Force intelligence reports now predicted the Soviets could have their bomb within a year. In addition, a Soviet defector, Col. G. A. Tokayev, stated they were working to improve the performance of their B–29 copy, the Tu–4.[3] Although the Bull could not yet be refueled in flight and thus could only undertake one-way missions against the continental United States, Air Staff officers believed the Soviets would not hesitate to sacrifice bomber crews in making such an attack. This information worried Fairchild. He thought if war between the superpowers broke out, the Soviets would likely launch the opening salvo, and Americans would expect the Air Force to resist an attack before sending off retaliatory assaults.* Believing no time should be lost in creating a functioning air defense system, Fairchild decided to call on Gordon Saville, the preeminent Air Force air defense authority, to initiate the process.

"Thank God Santy is where he is!", Saville exclaimed on learning of Fairchild's ascent to the office of Air Force Vice Chief of Staff. At this time Saville served in Rio de Janeiro as Chief of the Air Section of the Joint Brazil–United States Military Commission. Recently promoted to major general, Saville had not been involved directly in air defense activities since 1943 when the United States had started to dismantle the air defense organizations and networks in place since the beginning of the war. He then transferred to the Mediterranean theater, where he distinguished himself as the head of XII Tactical Air Command in the Allied invasion of southern France. Saville served in other tactical air assignments during and immediately after the war. He later became Deputy Commander of the Air Transport Command and was assigned to Brazil. He obtained valuable experience during these diverse and important assignments, although air defense remained his professional passion. That the Air Force leadership believed it could spare him from air defense responsibilities reflects the meager importance awarded the concept at the time. Fairchild decided to change all that. Almost seven years earlier, after Pearl Harbor, as Director of Military Requirements, Fairchild had brought Saville to the Pentagon to be responsible for air defense matters. Now, in what he recognized as another crisis, Fairchild again ordered Saville to Washington. Together they would establish the groundwork for a modern continental air defense system.[4]

The Vice Chief of Staff and his air defense expert made an unlikely team. Saville was, simply, a maverick. Brash and brutally blunt, he thought he understood more about air defense than anyone in the Air

---

* Striking the first blow in an atomic conflict had obvious advantages, and as historian David A. Rosenberg has pointed out, the JCS believed in 1945 that the United States should be prepared "to strike the first blow if necessary . . . when it becomes evident that the forces of aggression are being arrayed against us." Such an attack would have to be authorized by the President after consultations with his cabinet. The proposal was finally dropped by the JCS on August 7, 1950, because it was "highly questionable as to constitutionality" [David A. Rosenberg, "The Origins of Overkill: Nuclear Weapons and American Strategy, 1945–1960," *International Security* 20, no. 4 (spring 1983): 17].

Tu–4 Bull, the Soviets' four-engine midwing bomber, similar to the U.S. Air Force's B–29 Superfortress.

Force, and he did not hesitate to inform his superiors of their ignorance on the subject. Col. Bruce K. Holloway, who would later become Air Force Vice Chief of Staff and Commander of SAC, served for a time as Saville's deputy. Working with him was, as Holloway later recalled,

> kind of like living with a bomb . . . he was a real goer, a dynamo, a tremendous salesman, three jumps ahead of most other Air Force officers in operational and technical know-how. . . . He was a highly intelligent guy, innovative and very articulate . . . a lot of people didn't trust him, they were jealous of him.[5]

Like Saville, "Santy" Fairchild was short and rather heavyset; in contrast to the flamboyant Saville, Fairchild's nature was quiet and circumspect. He flew combat missions in World War I, and after the war he became a test pilot and served in several engineering assignments. He also attended the various Army service schools, including ACTS where he served as instructor. He spent World War II in Washington in various staff jobs, notably the Joint Strategic Survey Committee. Composed of three officers, one each from the Army, Navy, and Army Air Forces, the committee advised the JCS on a wide range of military policy. As one of the "elder statesmen,"[6] Fairchild performed his duty admirably although he would have preferred a combat assignment. To his disappointment, however, poor health and his reputation as a superb staff officer conspired to keep him at his desk in the Pentagon. His successes were not unnoticed by his superiors, nor did a lack of combat experience hinder his career. In 1946 he became the first Commanding General of Air University and, in May 1948, Vice Chief of Staff.[7]

Fairchild's most distinctive professional quality appeared to be his penetrating, analytical intellect. In the words of Saville:

> If there was a conference going on, and people [were] talking and debating, it was very probable that during that conference sometime Santy would make a speech of about twenty words, and that ended it. He was sitting there and listening and making up his mind. . . . And when he spoke, everybody listened. And when they got through listening and thinking about it for just a minute . . . they kind of looked at each other—like we are kind of stupid, aren't we.[8]

Fairchild and Saville shared mutual respect, a strong belief in the flexibility of air power, and the devotion to prepare the Air Force to meet many contingencies. They did not dispute SAC's primacy but argued for a more equitable distribution of resources. On these premises, they resolved to move forward in homeland air defense. Assured of Fairchild's support, the feisty Saville planned to forego working through channels and to expedite an air defense buildup.

Saville arrived in Washington in June 1948, eager to learn the exact nature of his duties and to go to work. His assignment, unique in Air Force history, was to ADC Headquarters where he would act as Special Projects Officer. He could have located in Washington, since he received an appointment to the Air Staff, but he constantly shuttled between Long Island, New York, and Washington. On Mitchel Field he formally reported to Maj. Gen. Howard M. Turner, ADC Vice Commander; on the Air Staff he served as head of a new Air Defense Division and reported directly to Maj. Gen. Samuel E. Anderson, Director of Plans and Operations in Norstad's Office of Deputy Chief of Staff for Operations. In practice, Saville had ready access to and only answered to Fairchild.[9]

Saville quickly assembled a large staff on Mitchel Field and a smaller staff in the Pentagon. In ADC Headquarters, air defense planners moved from Stratemeyer's regular staff to Saville's office. The ADC chief, selfless and determined to do whatever was necessary to improve the nation's air defense position, acknowledged Saville's expertise and cooperated completely in this new arrangement. Meanwhile, officers who had been working for Ankenbrandt on the Radar Fence Plan now joined Saville's department in the Air Staff. Saville filled both staffs with officers who had worked for him on the wartime air defenses. With the organizational shake-ups completed and the staffs assembled, he began to make a complete survey of the postwar air defense situation and to decide how to proceed.

For the moment, the situation remained bleak. Saville conducted his survey against the background of war games held in the Pacific Northwest from April 28 to May 10, 1948. The exercise, the first large-scale postwar test of U.S. Air Force offensive-defensive capabilities, had been postponed in March because of the air defense emergency. When completed in May, the exercise confirmed Fairchild's worst fears.

The 505th Aircraft Control and Warning Group and F–61s deployed to McChord from Mitchel and Hamilton air bases participated in the exercise. TAC contributed to the defending forces by dispatching a squadron of Lockheed F–80 Shooting Star jets to Spokane. SAC assumed the attacking role with B–29 bombers.[10]

When the war games ended, all agreed the air defenses were inadequate. In simple terms, had the B–29s been enemy aircraft, the northwest would have been hard hit. The F–80 day fighters lacked range and were not equipped with electronic equipment necessary to take off and intercept B–29s when the Superfortresses attacked under cover of bad weather. Black Widows fared no better. The World War II–vintage F–61s, referred to as all-weather aircraft, did not have the speed to close with the bombers (the B–29 was also considered obsolete by the Air Force) or the deicing equipment required for bad weather operations. Compounding the problems, a lack of qualified ground control intercept officers forced enlisted personnel to act as controllers in addition to performing their radio operation and maintenance duties. Too few radars deployed and, moreover, those that did were out of date.[11]

Revision of the Radar Fence Plan

After the inauspicious northwest exercises, Saville began his task by examining the status of the Radar Fence Plan, devised largely by Ankenbrandt and his communications staff. If Congress approved funding, the plan would provide within five to eight years an aircraft warning system that relied to a great extent on World War II–type radars designed to operate against slow, propeller-driven aircraft. The radars would doubtlessly have problems acquiring and tracking the contemporary jet aircraft and jet bombers then being developed. The radars also would be of little use in identifying jet or piston planes approaching from below 5,000 feet.[12]

Despite all the Radar Fence Plan's drawbacks, Saville could have accepted it because Ankenbrandt's scheme provided a trained cadre and a basic radar net for future improvements and expansion. If and when better radars became available, an air defense system framework would be established and ready to accept them. Meanwhile, the older radars could provide training and might be useful in detecting a conventional bombing raid, the likeliest threat at the time.

The plan got no support in Congress. The bill's supporters had problems even getting it introduced. Bureau of the Budget officials recom-

P–80 Shooting Star, the United States' first aircraft with a jet propulsion gas turbine engine (*above*). B–29, the United States' first aircraft with a fire control system (*below*).

mended to Secretary of Defense Forrestal on May 24, 1948, that the objectives and costs of the bill be reconsidered. Budget officials considered them too high in relation to other military requirements of equal or greater priority. In arriving at this conclusion budget officials had been influenced by Dr. Vannevar Bush and his Research and Development Board (established in June 1946 by the Secretaries of War and the Navy to coordinate military research and development programs), which concluded construction of a radar system using obsolete equipment made little sense. Pursuing this logic, the Bureau of the Budget claimed that the Radar Fence Plan failed to coordinate all present and future air defense requirements. Bureau officials questioned, for instance, the benefit of the plan if Canada did not construct a complementary system to track aircraft approaching over the polar routes, or if the Air Force proceeded to build the radar fence and had no trained personnel to operate the stations.[13]

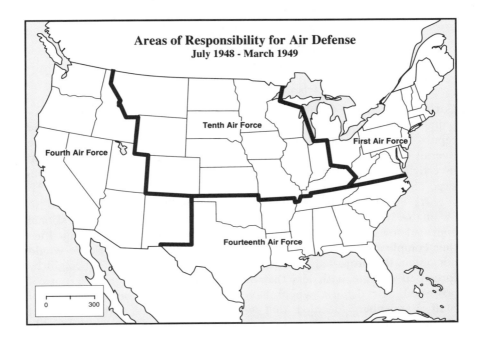

Areas of Responsibility for Air Defense
July 1948 - March 1949

Tenth Air Force

First Air Force

Fourth Air Force

Fourteenth Air Force

0   300

These were valid concerns. Under Secretary of the Air Force Arthur S. Barrows informed Forrestal that he agreed the Air Force had not calculated the needs and total estimated cost of air defense for the years ahead. He also spoke of unspecified actions under way that would eventually clarify Air Force plans for continental air defense. Regardless, Barrows believed the Air Force had to implement the "basic element" (the radar fence) immediately to ensure the nation possessed an "effective defense system against such enemy air attack as could be launched in the next five to eight years." [14]

Despite intense opposition, Barrows and Secretary Symington continued to press sympathetic congressmen to sponsor the bill. Their efforts were apparently rewarded when the bill was introduced in the Senate on May 27 and in the House of Representatives on June 2. But on June 3, President Truman directed Forrestal to "defer making heavy, forward commitments until we have an opportunity to insure a balanced program and to avoid building structures which cannot be supported on a sound basis in subsequent years." [15]

On July 1, Forrestal asked the JCS to reassess the Radar Fence Plan in this new light. The study, he said, would involve

> a fine sense of judgment. . . . On the one hand there are
> questions of economy involved in spending a substantial

> amount of money on radar which now is not completely effective and which will probably be obsolete in a few years, and on the other hand there is the obvious fact that the use of the present types of radar would give us at least some protection against a surprise attack during the years in which superior types are being developed.

Forrestal asked the Chiefs to complete the study and provide their recommendations to him before October 1948. Specifically, he wanted the report to evaluate the Radar Fence Plan by considering its role in the overall defense program. Forrestal believed it particularly important to investigate possible modifications in the plan that might achieve "the desired objectives at lower cost." [16]

As events developed, Fairchild and Saville were too hurried to await the JCS final report. It appeared to them that final congressional approval for the Radar Fence Plan would be too long in coming. Further complicating the matter were indications that the Air Force would not obtain the projected strength of seventy groups by 1950; it might be forced to operate with less than the fifty-nine understrength groups it possessed. Air defense would have fewer resources because Chief of Staff Vandenberg decided that worsening relations with the Soviet Union required the Air Force to bring SAC to peak efficiency as quickly as possible. Fairchild and Saville did not dispute the Chief's reasoning, yet they recognized an urgent need to have an air defense system that could be expanded and modernized. Therefore, Fairchild asked Saville to prepare an Air Force position on air defense that Vandenberg could present "with confidence and authority" to congressmen and government officials. As Saville expressed it, Fairchild directed him to "do the job in a sensible and economical way" and present a plan that "showed how much of our resources that we have now can divert to air defense without crippling us." So while the Radar Fence Plan was not officially dead, Saville proceeded to develop a less expensive plan, more likely to be approved. [17]

Accordingly, Saville's staffs on Mitchel Field and in the Pentagon reviewed everything the Air Force had accomplished, or failed to accomplish, with respect to air defense since World War II. Their studies produced three general conclusions. Most obvious, the Air Force could not discharge its air defense responsibilities by continued waiting. Second, the Radar Fence Plan would have to be replaced in light of delays already encountered, limited funding for fiscal year 1949, and anticipated 1950 budget limitations. Despite these handicaps, they concluded that the establishment of a limited air defense in being required immediate action, pending final approval of any overall program for air defense. [18]

In the course of the planning effort, officers chosen by Saville assumed projects from General Stratemeyer's staff officers in ADC Head-

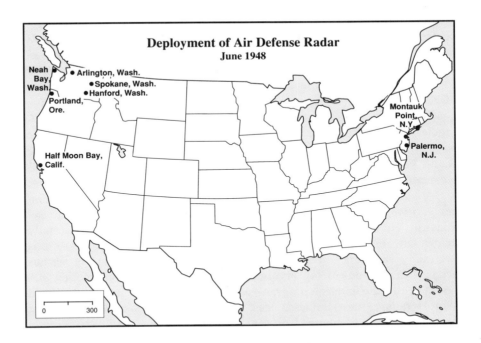

Deployment of Air Defense Radar
June 1948

quarters. Although Stratemeyer cooperated with this arrangement, many officers on the ADC staff were dismayed. They believed the Air Staff was giving only cursory attention to their well-developed proposals. Now, when the Air Staff appeared ready at last to devote more serious attention to air defense, the ADC officers' services were not used. Saville made enemies not only on Mitchel Field but in the Pentagon as well, where he upset higher-ranking officers by sending his plans and reports straight to Fairchild and Vandenberg without going through the chain of command. Despite leaving a trail of bruised egos in his wake, Saville claimed, "I wasn't going to stand in line and wait. Time was pressing here." He was only able to work in this unusual manner because of Fairchild's sponsorship.[19]

After working long hours for nearly two months, Saville presented Vandenberg and Fairchild with a proposed solution to the radar control and warning problem. Totally aware of the need for more trained personnel and a quantitative and qualitative improvement in air defense fighter units, Saville initially concentrated all his energies on the radar systems. Other air defense components could be added once the basic element, the radars, functioned.

Saville recommended that the Air Force, at a cost of $116 million in fiscal years 1949 and 1950, install 75 radar stations and 10 control centers in the continental United States, with 10 radar stations and 1 control center in Alaska. Most stations would be equipped with World War II microwave early-warning radars, old but usable. A few chosen in strategically important areas would receive new and better radars, at a cost of $30 million. Over half the $116 million would be spent on construction of the radar sites. By comparison, the Radar Fence Plan would have consisted of 411 radar stations and 18 control centers, staffed by 25,000 regulars at a cost of some $600 million over 5 years. Saville left open the possibility that his interim plan would constitute the first phase of the Radar Fence Plan or any other air defense plan that might finally be implemented. [20]

Vandenberg and Fairchild approved Saville's plan, and on September 9, 1948, Saville presented his ideas to Secretaries Forrestal and Symington. He stated that the few current radar installations were totally inadequate; in fact, the overall picture for continental air defense was "certainly shocking." The radar situation appeared particularly serious because of the long delay involved in developing and constructing stations. While the interim program would, for the most part, use World War II radars, these could at least provide high-level coverage against propeller-driven bombers. For low-altitude sightings, Saville suggested augmenting the civilian Ground Observer Corps until superior radars could be developed. Saville admitted that his interim plan was not intended to provide the United States with an invulnerable air defense system; it would, however, afford the foundation for a stronger system that could be reinforced and improved. It was, in any case, "a great deal better than nothing." Summing up, Saville reminded Forrestal and Symington that "this matter is one of great urgency and requires immediate action. Nothing can be found in the world situation, in the attitude of the people, or in any other field which would justify continued delay. We *must* get on with it." [21]

During his presentation, Saville noted that the older radars he proposed installing could serve in "model systems," where air defense theories and tactics could be tested. His military superiors and distinguished and influential scientists, Dr. Vannevar Bush, for one, supported his view. Although Bush favored pressing forward on future air defense needs, "and not on any major procurement of current equipment that would materially divert effort," he could understand the logic of model air defenses. He recommended to Vandenberg that the Air Force establish a system "for the emergency and operational test evaluation of the various elements" of air defense. [22]

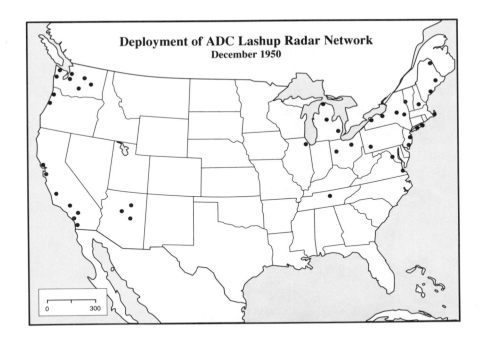

Deployment of ADC Lashup Radar Network
December 1950

Charles A. Lindbergh, then an Air Force Reserve colonel, also supported the model air defense idea.* Lindbergh accepted Vandenberg's invitation to serve an active duty tour as his special consultant, investigating technical and operational matters affecting the U.S. Air Force. In assessing the needs of SAC, Lindbergh concluded that, for the bomber force to develop into a truly powerful striking force, it needed to train against adequate air defenses. (The Soviets had already begun efforts to improve their air defenses.) He told Vandenberg that present Air Force equipment and air defense forces were incapable of approximating wartime conditions in the performance of training exercises. Lindbergh therefore advocated model networks, stating that "the need for a training area of this kind is so vital that immediate steps should be taken to set it up." Forrestal conceded the requirement and approved the diversion of funds. [23]

In the meantime, the Air Force designated $554,000 to begin work on permanent radar stations. As Saville pointed out, the first tasks would be to select locations for 85 radar stations in the continental United

---

* Lindbergh made the first flight across the Atlantic in 1927. During World War II, he served as a technical representative with Lt. Gen. George C. Kenney in the Pacific theater. His tour as special consultant to Vandenberg was only one of a number of special assignments he undertook for the post–World War II Air Force. Lindbergh was rewarded with a reserve brigadier general commission in 1954.

AN/CPS–5 search radar,
the basic unit of the Lashup
system

States, lease property, prepare engineering blueprints, and arrange with the Army Corps of Engineers to construct the stations. Approximately $152,000 would remain for the immediate installation, on government-owned property in the northeast, of a temporary radar system that might be used as a model system. To differentiate this from the anticipated permanent system, planners described the model system as the Lashup project. "Lashup" soon became synonymous with all temporary radar systems established in the United States. As Saville explained, Lashup enabled the Air Force to "provide the best possible air defense for the least possible cost, beginning immediately and lasting until our permanent system can be implemented." [24]

While Saville formulated his interim plan, the JCS evaluated the Radar Fence Plan. In fall 1948 Forrestal had instructed the Chiefs to re-examine the plan in light of the changes proposed by Saville. The Chiefs were generally pleased with Saville's ideas, especially with the cost reductions, and on October 20 they recommended to Forrestal that the interim plan be submitted to Congress. In doing so, the Chiefs stated that it was essential for the nation to have an effective air defense system in place by 1953, and meeting that goal was "second only to the capability to launch an immediate and effective counterattack." [25]

On December 30, 1948, Maj. Gen. Samuel Anderson, Saville's immediate superior on the Air Staff, formalized the goals for Lashup in a letter to General Stratemeyer. While the permanent system was being constructed, Anderson directed ADC to complete Lashup networks in the northeast and the northwest and in the Albuquerque, New Mexico, area. The systems would consist of a total of twenty-four radar stations plus control centers. All stations would be equipped with World War II heavy radars obtained from Air Force depots; they were tentatively scheduled to be operational by March 15, 1949. To allow the stations and control centers to achieve this status according to schedule, the Air Force planned to divert funds from less pressing priorities. Additional monies would be required, however, to implement the remaining provisions in the interim plan. In that regard, Fairchild and Saville prepared to take their case before Congress in spring 1949. [26]

Establishment of the Continental Air Command

Fairchild's intention that Saville present details of the interim plan to Congress before taking charge of the air defense buildup created a problem concerning Saville's future position and status. Saville temporarily held positions on both the ADC staff and the Air Staff, but Fairchild wanted a sharper definition of Saville's responsibilities before Saville made his congressional appearance.

After numerous high-level Air Staff discussions, in most of which Fairchild participated, the Air Force created the Continental Air Command (CONAC), combining the resources of ADC and TAC. Two developments contributed preponderantly to the reorganization. First, President Truman decided in late 1948 to keep a sharp rein on defense spending. For the Air Force this meant operating at a strength of forty-eight groups for the foreseeable future. Under the circumstances, Vandenberg and Fairchild agreed that SAC, still far below the minimum desired combat capability, would receive priority for personnel, bases, funds, and weapons. That decision was not expected to impede progress in air defense too much because Saville's interim plan had substantially reduced targeted funds; however, the decision meant that TAC would be strapped for resources. The Air Force could not possibly reinforce TAC under the forty-eight-group restriction and still meet the requirements of the strategic forces. All that could be done was to retain a nucleus for future tactical air increases if and when the occasion demanded.[27]

In the second development influencing the establishment of CONAC, President Truman decided to strengthen the reserves to compensate for the reduction in the Regular forces. Truman instructed the JCS to provide adequate means for prompt and effective employment of reserves in an emergency. This order presented a problem for the Air Force because Stratemeyer had recently instituted a four–air force alignment he thought best for air defense procedures in the United States. That alignment, unfortunately, was not conducive to coordination of reserve affairs with the six army areas in the nation, and another reorganization was required.[28]

It was against this background that CONAC appeared. The Air Force, determined to alleviate problems caused by decreased defense spending, made the best use of the means at hand. Under provisions of the reorganization, the air defense and tactical air missions combined under one command. Reduced in status and made subordinate, ADC and TAC had operational headquarters under CONAC and its new chief, General Stratemeyer. The Air Force could now assign the combined resources of both units to either ADC or TAC, according to need.

The creation of CONAC solved Fairchild's problem of finding a suitable position for Saville, who assumed command of the new ADC located on Mitchel Field and staffed largely by members of his former planning groups. Meanwhile, TAC released its two air forces, with their assigned combat and administrative units, to Stratemeyer's direct command. A former TAC fighter group assumed air defense as its primary responsibility, as did three fighter groups transferred from SAC to Stratemeyer's command.[29]

To solve the reserve forces problem, the Air Force reverted to a six–air force arrangement in the United States, which helped to coordinate affairs with an equal number of army areas and to improve overall management. Saville received operational control of the individual air forces' air defense groups, and he, not the appointed commanders of the six continental air forces, became responsible for air defense in peacetime and during actual attack. The air force commanders would be expected, however, to organize, supply, and administer the groups. Thus Saville could address operational and planning considerations, free of administrative duties. While the origin of this unconventional arrangement is uncertain, it appears to have been sponsored by Fairchild and influenced strongly by Saville. The new setup for ADC resembled too closely that of the 1940–1941 air defense headquarters to have been totally coincidental. To perform its tasks, the first ADC possessed no tactical forces; it relied on the operational control of aircraft, equipment, and personnel belonging to other organizations. The designers of the new ADC assumed that the same procedure could work again.[30]

The steps taken in December 1948 by the Air Force to establish a functioning air defense network were important. Under Stratemeyer's supervision, CONAC allowed Saville generous authority as head of ADC. A logical command and control alignment for air defense now existed. Further, the interim plan served as a realistic blueprint for the establishment of radar systems, and the new organization increased the number of interceptor units. The Headquarters USAF order of December 1948 that Lashup systems be operational by mid-March 1949 set a clear first goal for CONAC. The order allowed Stratemeyer and Saville to call for all the support they considered necessary from other Air Force commands to perform the air defense mission.

Taking the Case to Congress

The Air Force wanted to install radar control and warning systems on the east and west coasts to serve as model systems as quickly as possible. In June 1949, the First Air Force tested the northeastern Lashup system. Although commanders were troubled by inadequate radar and aircraft and incompletely trained personnel, they were relieved to be training, at last, under what approached realistic conditions.[31]

The September 1949 exercises were more comprehensive in the northeast. This time civilian observers participated in the warning system. Officers planning the deployment of permanent radar stations knew they would need civilians to provide unbroken coverage around the areas selected for protection early in the program, during the First Augmentation. Although the basic radar component projected in the First Augmentation, the AN/CPS–6B, served both search and height-finding functions, it could not identify enemy aircraft flying below approximately 5,000 feet. To compensate for this deficiency, Saville's interim plan called for ground observers used "as local adjuncts to each radar to provide a measure of low coverage." In time, if necessary and funds permitted, unmanned low-altitude radars might be developed. They would be placed between and forward of the permanent stations to substitute for or to complement civilian observers. For the present, Saville viewed observers as "the only practicable low cover answer for any system by 1952." [32]

For the September exercises, state civil defense agencies, formed at the request of Saville's staff, recruited successfully for the operation. The Air Force selected the observer post locations and set up filter centers to evaluate information received from the ground observers before reported enemy sightings were transmitted to the control center. As it had during World War II, the Bell Telephone Company provided lines between observer and filter centers and between Lashup stations and control centers. When the exercise ended, commanders agreed that the civilian observers performed as well as their brief training allowed.[33]

Before the northeast exercises, Congress approved Saville's interim program, and President Truman signed the bill on March 21, 1949. Testimony presented before congressional armed services committees by Saville and Fairchild proved instrumental. Fairchild declared the early-warning system essential to the nation's safety. He warned that without it the country could face an attack that "could result in disaster on a nation-wide scale and surely would result in unnecessary death and destruction throughout our country should we be attacked in the future."[34]

Testifying before the armed services committees of both houses, Saville urged the installation of a radar system immediately, even though it would not incorporate the most advanced equipment. Saville admitted that "with respect to the future we cannot speak with certainty. We know that we will require new and better radar equipment as it becomes available—in much the same way we need new and modern aircraft. Our equipment will develop and change."[35]

Although Congress passed the measure without debate, the lawmakers had not awakened to the pressing need for progressive air defense. Saville's plan appealed to them because it reduced sharply the costs estimated for completion of the original Radar Fence Plan. Saville had carefully followed Fairchild's instructions, devising a program "on the cheap" and ordering his staff to adhere to the KISS ("keep it simple, stupid") principle.[36] He presented to Congress an inexpensive plan, insufficient by itself but likely to be approved and to serve as a suitable foundation for later expansion. His success meant that, although actual allocations for the program were delayed, a start had at last been made.

Fighter Aircraft for Air Defense

During the course of his congressional testimony, Saville noted that the Air Force required more efficient aircraft to perform its air defense mission effectively. From the moment Fairchild assigned him his task, Saville concentrated on the radar problem, knowing any inadequate component could ruin an air defense network. While Saville worked on the radar systems, his deputy, Col. Bruce K. Holloway, an experienced fighter pilot, examined the needs of the interceptor force. The foremost need was for an all-weather night interceptor.

In 1949, the all-weather fighter groups on the east and west coasts began to receive F–82 Twin Mustangs, expected to replace the F–61 and serve as a stopgap all-weather fighter until a superior airplane could be developed. It soon became obvious that the F–82s were no improvement over the obsolete F–61s. The Twin Mustang performed miserably at night and during inclement weather. Furthermore, the complex technology required to produce a fast plane burdened by heavy electronic equipment and carrying a pilot and a radar operator had not been developed for the F–82. The aircraft experienced extreme difficulty attaining and operating above 25,000 feet, below the ceiling of SAC's B–29s and B–50s (an improved B–29) and, presumably, the Soviet Union's Tu–4, its most advanced bomber. For the moment, Saville and his staff had no option but to make do with the F–82 while stepping up the search for its replacement. [37]

The F–82's dismal showing came as no surprise to Holloway as he investigated the Air Force stance on fighter-interceptors, present and future. The veteran fighter commander, Maj. Gen. William Kepner, head of the Air Proving Ground on Eglin Air Force Base, Florida, since August 1948, had joined Holloway in his study, and, together, they instituted performance tests on currently available interceptors. They found the "fighter element," in planning for a minimum air defense system, "in the poorest shape." The Twin Mustangs along with the day jet fighter F–80 and the F–84s currently in use were, according to Holloway, "practically worthless" for air defense. Having concluded this, Holloway had to determine the types of fighters required for air defense and whether the Air Force had projects under way to provide them in a reasonable time. [38]

Holloway discussed this matter with Saville, and they decided that the minimum requirement for an air defense fighter would be for the aircraft to "take off on a runway when the ceiling was zero-zero [no visibility], go and make the interception and get back on the runway." They thought that advancements in technology would produce an interceptor "whose pilot only had to take the aircraft off, maintain proper tailpipe temperatures, and land the aircraft." For other procedures, "the interception will be controlled from the ground by radar which will automatically guide the aircraft to the target; the interceptor's radars and computers will make the final interception, fire the weapons, and the aircraft will be returned to the airdrome automatically." [39]

When informed of these seemingly visionary ideas, Fairchild appointed several officers to study them further. Major Generals Kenneth B. Wolfe and Franklin O. Carroll of the Air Materiel Command headed the group that included Maj. Gen. Carl Brandt, former Chief of the Air Proving Ground, and Colonel Holloway. They first studied the capabili-

F–89 Scorpion. An "interim" fighter, this model resulted from the Air Force's request for a plane equipped with ground-controlled radar capable of finding, intercepting, and attacking enemy targets.

ties of the large, heavily armed, two-place jet all-weather interceptors then being developed: the Curtiss F–87 and the Northrop F–89.[40]

Meeting on Muroc Field, California, in October 1948, the group watched both aircraft perform. It decided that the Air Force should purchase only the F–89. Brandt and Holloway, so disappointed with the performance of both airplanes, suggested the service not accept either. They agreed that the Air Force initiate a design competition for a completely new fighter that would be ready by 1954 and would feature technology to meet performance standards specified by Saville and Holloway. Fairchild directed the Air Staff on October 14, 1948, to halt manufacture of the F–87 and to put the "best of a poor lot," the F–89, into production as soon as possible, along with the Lockheed two-seat, radar-equipped F–94 (derived from the conversion of the Air Force's first operational jet fighter, the P–80 Shooting Star, into a two-seat trainer). The Air Force expected to receive these interim fighters no later than mid-1950.[41]

Saville and Holloway soon proposed another solution to the interim interceptor problem. The North American Company suggested their new F–86 fighter could be modified into a one-man, all-weather interceptor. Disagreeing with some Air Force officers who believed a pilot could not simultaneously fly a plane and operate sophisticated electronic equipment, Saville and Holloway advised the Air Force to support North American's proposal. They argued their case before a board of officers, directed by General Joseph T. McNarney, tasked to "review and make

F–86 Sabre. This fighter was modified into a one-man, all-weather interceptor to serve as an "interim" fighter.

recommendations for changes, if necessary, in the composition of the 48 group program, Aircraft Production Program, and the Research and Development Program of the USAF." Saville and Holloway presented a convincing argument, and in July 1949, acting on the board's recommendation, Symington authorized the Air Materiel Command to spend $7 million to convert the F–86 into an interceptor. Development proceeded so favorably that the next month the Air Force set aside funds for the purchase of 124 of the aircraft, designated the F–86D. [42]

For the long term, the board of senior officers, dissatisfied with interceptor aircraft prospects, agreed that the Air Force needed a design competition among aircraft companies to provide a modern, all-weather interceptor. The board decided on 1954 as the probable operational date for the new interceptor, referred to as the "1954 interceptor." [43]

Unhappy with the results of previous efforts to design a reliable interceptor, Fairchild and Saville supported a different approach in developing the 1954 model, an aircraft projected to meet high performance challenges presented by future Soviet intercontinental jet bombers. In May 1949 Fairchild asked leaders in the aircraft and electronics industries to come to Washington so he could explain the method to be used in developing the new interceptor. The Vice Chief reminded the industry leaders that in the past the Air Force had written rigid specifications for designing aircraft. In his opinion, this method did not best utilize the scientific and engineering talent available. Fairchild, therefore, proposed an experiment. He would have Saville brief industry leaders on the air de-

F–102 Delta Dagger. The 1954 "interim" interceptor, this plane became America's first operational delta-wing aircraft.

fense situation and outline general requirements for an advanced interceptor. Next, the designers and engineers would carefully consider the problem and submit their evaluations to Fairchild. [44]

Unfortunately, Fairchild received few of the thoughtful replies he anticipated. Instead, he was deluged with letters from various aircraft and electronics firms, intent on establishing themselves as prime contractors in air defense, submitting performance estimates that exceeded realistic expectations. While industry response disappointed, the 1954 interceptor marked an important milestone in aircraft development. Fairchild decided to build the interceptor to conform to the hitherto untested weapons systems approach to aircraft development. This method recognized that the increasing sophistication of weapons demanded that their parts not be manufactured as completely isolated components. The weapons system concept ensured that each aircraft would be designed "as a whole from the beginning so that all the characteristics of each component were compatible with the others." [45] Ultimately, the 1954 interceptor, in its first stage, became the Convair F–102, a delta wing, all-weather interceptor, but it was not operational until 1956.

Further Organizational Changes

In April 1949 further changes occurred in the continental air defense command and organization structure. General Stratemeyer became Commanding General of the Far East Air Forces (FEAF) while General Whitehead assumed command of CONAC. An outstanding air commander in the Pacific during World War II, Whitehead had operated directly under General George C. Kenney. Tagged "the Butcher of Moresby" by the Japanese, Whitehead was an aggressive combat commander. He remained in the Pacific after the war as head of FEAF. When world tensions were their greatest in 1948, he turned to air defense, making the Fifth Air Force's aircraft warning service in Japan fully operational and prepared for action. Upon appointment to lead CONAC the following year, Whitehead made it clear that he would not be content to play second fiddle to Saville. The fiery general, determined to take complete control of continental air defense, would not accept the air defense organizational arrangements he inherited from Stratemeyer.[46]

Fairchild wanted Whitehead in CONAC for his organizational abilities as much as for his tactical and air defense operations expertise. When Stratemeyer had transferred responsibility for operational air defense to Saville in March 1948, radar and fighter units in the field received administrative, personnel, and logistical support from the individual continental air forces. Under actual deployment, Saville would command the units; however, Whitehead thought this arrangement lacked sufficient decentralized control. He decided to create two regional air defense operational forces, the Eastern Air Defense Force and the Western Air Defense Force, and to invest their commanders with suitable powers for dealing with unforeseen conditions. Whitehead's staff now controlled air defense planning, and Saville had no prime role in air defense.[47]

Although Saville remained the obvious Air Force authority on air defense, Fairchild probably never considered placing him at the head of CONAC when Stratemeyer moved to FEAF. One reason was Saville's relatively junior status among Air Force general officers. More important, perhaps, Fairchild recognized that Whitehead's breadth of experience in all phases of tactical operations as well as his administrative skills made him the choice for the major job at CONAC. Fairchild apparently hoped to merge Whitehead's and Saville's talents. Unfortunately, these two tough, volatile personalities had clashed during the war when Saville, preferring to fight in Europe, spurned Whitehead's offer of a staff position in the Pacific theater. Bruised egos persisted between them, and it was doubtful whether they could reconcile their differences and work together harmoniously.[48]

Just before Whitehead's reorganization was to become effective, Col. Jacob E. Smart, an Assistant Deputy for Operations on the Air Staff involved in air defense planning, prepared a summary of important air defense accomplishments since the end of World War II. In his analyses, Smart determined that Saville was primarily responsible for whatever progress had been made in air defense and advised Whitehead to extend his tenure in ADC. Smart conceded that Saville's methods were often unorthodox, as when he used his connection with Fairchild to bypass the chain of command. This, along with a brusque manner, made Saville a "thorn in the side to many people. Nevertheless," continued

Smart, "*he has produced the only tangible results toward building an air defense system that has* [sic] *been produced since the end of the war.*" Smart emphasized Saville's role in obtaining congressional authorization for the interim program. He concluded:

> His [Saville's] actions, however unorthodox they may appear, have been taken with the tacit consent of General Vandenberg and General Fairchild. He has undoubtedly had to "play by ear" in many instances and has irked many important and would-be important people, but he has got away with it all and has *got things done.*[49]

Smart need not have feared that Saville would be left out in the cold. Although Whitehead and Saville would not work together, Fairchild was still bound to put his air defense expert's talent to good use. On September 1, 1949, Saville became Director of Military Requirements, a position Fairchild had held during the early months of World War II. In re-creating the position for Saville on the peacetime Air Staff, Fairchild urged his protege to approach Air Force combat force requirements in the same hard-driving, innovative spirit he displayed as head of ADC. In fact, given his interest and capabilities, Saville's assignment to Headquarters USAF would not restrict his role in air defense developments.[50]

An internal debate resulted from the Air Force approach to postwar air defense. In a period of defense budget cutbacks, President Truman and the Congress were not inclined to spend the vast sums needed to develop, equip, and staff advanced air defense systems, especially since most military and civilian intelligence sources estimated that the Soviet Union, the most probable future threat, would not acquire an atomic capability before 1952 at the earliest. (Air Force intelligence predicted an earlier date.) Even if the Soviets possessed "the bomb," their first bomber capable of one-way attacks against the continental United States, the Tu–4 Bull, appearing in public for the first time in a 1948 air show flyover, posed only a limited threat. The Soviets had 300 Tu–4s in production by 1949, but the plane's range was insufficient to allow it to attack the continental United States and return home, and the Soviets had yet to demonstrate the capability to refuel the aircraft in flight. Little sense of urgency existed regarding air defense among members of Congress, government officials, and the public.

The Air Force was somewhat less complacent. Contrary to predictions made by the other civilian and military intelligence agencies, Air Force analysts believed a serious Soviet intercontinental threat would develop rapidly and thought the best way to counter it would be with SAC. Recognizing the service's responsibility for providing a minimum air defense, in 1946 ADC staff officers began drawing up various short- and long-range plans for U.S. air defense. These plans, generally too ambitious given the congressional and public mood at the time, seemed unlikely to be funded. General Fairchild, disturbed at the lack of progress when he became Air Force Vice Chief of Staff, called upon the service's most knowledgeable air defense authority, General Saville, to develop a cheap air defense plan. With a more realistic chance of being approved by Congress, this plan would lay the foundation for future modernization and expansion. While these steps seemed sufficient, events in the latter half of 1949 motivated the public to question whether the Air Force was doing all it could to provide air defense for the United States.

Chapter 5

Broadening Dimensions: Air Defense as a Public Issue

That public complacency about the nation's air defense status had started to diminish became evident in August 1949. The Boeing Company announced plans to shift production of its B–47 jet bomber from Seattle, Washington, to a facility in Wichita, Kansas. Air Force leaders apparently encouraged Boeing to make this move because Wichita seemed less vulnerable to air attack than Seattle. Boeing employees and Seattle businessmen, not surprisingly, were less than enthusiastic about the planned move. They complained to their congressional representatives who, in turn, brought the case to Secretary of the Air Force Stuart Symington.[1]

To explain the Air Force position, Symington agreed to attend a meeting in Seattle arranged by the city's Chamber of Commerce. In preparation he asked Chief of Staff Vandenberg why he sponsored the move in the first place. Symington wanted to know, in particular, if the Air Staff planned eventually to transfer all west coast production inland. Vandenberg replied that no such plans were being developed. He claimed, however, the case of B–47 production in Seattle was unique. The B–47, with the Convair B–36, was one of the two advanced strategic weapons the Air Force planned to deploy in the near future. The Soviets might consider a heavy sacrifice in men and aircraft worthwhile if they could slow or halt B–47 production in Seattle by launching one-way attacks.[2]

Ernest Gruening, Governor of Alaska, also attended the Chamber of Commerce meeting. He believed he had a stake in the controversy because Soviet bombers on route to Seattle would probably travel over Alaska and could attack targets there. Gruening became outraged after listening to the Air Force's reasons for wanting to make the shift. He told Symington:

> I am shocked that it is the Air Force, supposedly the striking arm of the military establishment, that is initiating this "turn tail and run" behind the Rockies policy. I am amazed that the flying branch of our armed forces, instead of emu-

General Hoyt S. Vandenberg becomes Chief of Staff, U.S. Air Force. Administering the oath is Chief Justice Fred Vinson. Others in the photograph are, *left* **to** *right,* **Secretary of National Defense, James V. Forrestal, Air Force Chief of Staff General Carl Spaatz, and Secretary of the Air Force W. Stuart Symington.**

lating the eagle, the American symbol of air power, should
follow the example of lesser birds and pursue a policy that
is both ostrich-headed and chicken-hearted.

Gruening went on to suggest that the Air Force pay more attention to air defense and construct a radar screen along the northern and western coasts of Alaska to warn of approaching bombers. In addition, to employ large numbers of fighter-interceptors would assure "the Russians would never be able to fly across Alaska heading this way. Their planes would be shot down. They would have to fly . . . around the Aleutians . . . and Puget Sound would be as far away as Wichita." The governor charged, mistakenly, that his suggestion to construct a northern radar screen was a completely new idea to Air Force planners. Although his accusations belied Air Force air defense efforts, Gruening's views apparently contributed to a compromise whereby the Air Force agreed to build B–47s in both Wichita and Seattle.[3]

The Revolt of the Admirals

In addition to the Boeing controversy, the Revolt of the Admirals in the summer of 1949 tested Air Force willingness to perform its air defense responsibilities. Naval officers objected to Air Force procurement of the B–36 strategic bomber in light of Secretary of Defense Louis A. Johnson's decision to cancel the aircraft carrier *United States*. The B–36 controversy brought to the forefront the failure of the services to cooperate on missions, including air defense.

Navy leaders feared the Air Force would attempt to consolidate all air power into one branch of the military. Although some airmen doubtlessly harbored such a wish, the Air Force concerned itself more with its establishment as the primary strategic force than with the unlikely possibility of stripping the Navy of all its air resources. [4]

The Air Force believed the 65,000-ton *United States* was designed to carry aircraft capable of delivering atomic bombs, making the carrier a threat to its monopoly of strategic aviation. Although the Navy denied it, there was at least some truth in this view as the Navy had shown interest in the development of carrier-based nuclear arms delivery since 1945, although the Key West roles and missions conference had delegated primary responsibility for strategic aerial operations to the Air Force. Both services believed they had ample cause to distrust the other when Johnson announced the cancellation of the *United States*. Many high-ranking Navy officers interpreted this move as the first step by the Defense Department to eliminate the naval air arm. [5]

Denied their aircraft carrier because of scarce funding and defense officials who considered the B–36 a more important weapon, naval officers lashed out at Air Force mission prerogatives. One thrust of the Navy's criticism stated that the Air Force neglected tactical air requirements and concentrated almost exclusively on the strategic mission. This overlapped into an indictment of the Air Force approach to air defense. Admiral Arthur W. Radford, for instance, believed that Air Force dedication to the strategy of the "atomic blitz" had resulted in an absence of suitable fighter aircraft that "may have grave consequences for future security of our bases and our homeland." Symington reported to President Truman that the Navy charged that the Air Force "in the interest of pushing the B–36 . . . had canceled fighters and other aircraft to the detriment of the air defense of the United States and the air support of the Army." [6]

In testimony before the House Armed Services Committee, Symington and Vandenberg attempted to answer the Navy. Admitting the bulk of Air Force resources was assigned to strategic forces, they nevertheless convinced the congressmen that the Air Force was doing all it could within budget limitations to provide air defense and support of ground forces. The Air Force leadership favorably impressed Congress by providing a well-planned, informative, coordinated presentation. Navy officers, on the other hand, often spoke without the complete support of their civilian chiefs. [7]

In the course of the hearings, the Navy criticized the performance of the B–36, claiming its most advanced fighter, the McDonnell F2H Banshee, could easily intercept and destroy the bomber. The Navy also boasted that the Banshee was superior to contemporary Air Force interceptors. None of this meant that the Navy had an interest in assuming primary responsibility for U.S. air defense from the Air Force—it wanted to enhance its strategic role in national defense—but it did spotlight the question of Air Force–Navy coordination in air defense matters. [8]

As part of the Key West agreements, the Navy had agreed to cooperate with the Air Force by providing sea-based air defenses to help protect the coastlines against enemy bombers. But the Chief of Naval Operations soon stated that "a routine and continuing peacetime commitment of naval forces to continental air defense is not intended." The Air Force considered this attitude unhelpful, at the least, because of the increasing realization that Navy radar picket ships and airborne early-warning radars could make an important contribution to air defense. Carrier-borne early-warning planes had a curious history. They were designed by the Navy in response to Japanese suicide attacks in World War II. Since the Navy had a head start in this field, the Air Force decided to suspend research in 1948 to save funds and avoid duplication of effort. Unfortunately, the Air Force failed to coordinate its actions adequately with the Navy which also had other priorities—early warning for air defense not being among them. For the moment, little if anything was done to advance what appeared to be a promising concept. [9]

Meanwhile, the final judgment of the House Armed Services Committee on the B–36 affair promised to salvage something from this unpleasant episode by calling for greater teamwork between the services. For air defense, this implied joint Air Force–Navy training exercises and the establishment of procedures whereby naval forces, particulary fighters, would be used in an emergency. The new Chief of Naval Operations, Admiral Sherman, expressed special concern that the Navy do its share in providing for the air defense of the United States. Joint maneuvers were held, and the Navy supplied more aircraft and picket ships for air defense duty. Still, it remained clear that the Navy wished to win for itself a more pronounced strategic role. Assisting the Air Force in its continental defense mission hardly ranked among its priorities. Major responsibility for air defense rested foursquare with the Air Force and, from all appearances, the Navy wished to keep it that way. [10]

Impact of the Soviet Atomic Bomb

Public and congressional concern about air defense had surfaced for the first time since the end of World War II during the Boeing controversy and the B–36 hearings. However, the Soviet Union's atomic test generated far more concern. On September 3, 1949, an Air Force B–29 reported unusually high radioactivity measurements over the North Pacific near the Soviet Union's Kamchatka Peninsula. Soon after, the Air Force collected enough evidence for the Atomic Energy Commission to conclude that the Soviets had tested an atomic device. On September 19, American and British scientists met with AEC and Pentagon officials to assess the event more precisely. They agreed that the fission products the Air Force bomber filtered from the air over the North Pacific had come from an atomic bomb exploded on August 29.[11]

President Truman announced the event to the American people on September 23, calling it an "atomic explosion." He claimed not to be particularly surprised the Soviets had accomplished the feat so soon, stating that such a "probability has always been taken into account by us." Public statements of military leaders reinforced the President's view. General Omar N. Bradley, Chairman of the JCS, acknowledged that while the "explosion" was doubtlessly that of an atomic bomb, the occasion did not call for hysteria. He said the fact that an industrially backward nation could make an atomic bomb did not imply necessarily that the same nation could produce bombs in quantity and launch nuclear attacks.[12]

Truman and his military leaders tended to play down the effect of the Soviet atomic capability, but a number of people inside and outside the government and defense establishments were disturbed. For the first time since Pearl Harbor, civilians became especially anxious for improved air defenses. According to the commander of the 25th Air Division in the west, strong civilian pressure built to have air defenses in place and functioning along the west coast. Senator Warren Magnuson of Washington told Symington of his concern about the protection of his state, home of the Hanford atomic energy plant. Magnuson vowed to do everything in his power to assure that the west coast and Alaska were defended adequately.[13]

It would be largely up to General Fairchild to initiate and direct studies of Air Force air defense requirements under the new circumstances. The new emergency could hardly have come at a worse moment for the Vice Chief. Long plagued by heart and other health problems, Fairchild, worn down, seriously considered retirement. Vandenberg, fortunately, prevailed upon him to remain at his post during this tense period.[14]

On September 30, 1949, Fairchild called an Air Staff conference to discuss the impact on Air Force plans of the Soviet development of the atomic bomb. Interestingly, even though many American airmen had touted an atomic offensive as unstoppable when the United States had possessed the only nuclear weapons, no high-ranking Air Staff member present at the meeting suggested that the Soviet atomic capability rendered air defense irrelevant. In fact, representatives from the Deputy Chief of Staff for Operations suggested that the time had arrived for the Air Force to promote air defense to the same priority as the strategic retaliatory forces. That idea, however, got quickly shot down. Saville made what most of the officers attending the meeting considered the more practical suggestion of urging Congress to appropriate funds for the completion of the radar screen. Fairchild and even Saville did not dispute the status of SAC as the prime Air Force weapon and deterrent. [15]

Thus, in forming its response to the enhanced Soviet threat, the Air Force knew it would have to tread warily. Within the context of U.S. overall strategy, no one questioned the requirement for air defenses. The question that arose, as it would for the next ten years, was how much could be devoted to the mission in light of what were, in the opinion of the Air Force, more pressing requirements, especially those of SAC. The Air Staff believed it had to ensure its views were not misinterpreted as advocating air defense at the expense of the strategic forces. Following this line of thought, Symington told Secretary of Defense Johnson in November 1949 that the Soviets would only be deterred from attacking the United States by the fear of a devastating retaliatory attack. But if they did attack, he said the Air Force would have to be prepared with the best air defenses affordable. [16]

Fairchild followed Symington's lead in budget hearings held in early 1950 stating, "The period which we all realized must some day come where intercontinental air warfare is possible is now at hand." He reiterated Symington's belief that the Air Force now had to maintain both its strategic and air defense forces in a state of immediate readiness. The Air Force believed the strategic forces to be of primary importance in the sense they provided the United States with its most formidable deterrent to war. At the same time, said Fairchild, the responsibility of the Air Force lay in providing "the greatest degree of air defense attainable within the means available." The air defense forces had to be trained and on alert continuously to meet a sudden enemy air attack. [17]

The problem was funding. The Air Force could not escape the Truman administration's decision to allow it only forty-eight groups. Symington told congressmen who advocated stronger air defenses that an increase to seventy groups would solve many difficulties. For the moment, the best way the Air Force could strengthen its air defenses under the constraints of the budget lay in reducing greatly tactical forces assigned to ground support operations.[18] That decision did not please the Army, but the Air Force had to assign priorities under the changed circumstances.

Fairchild and his top Air Staff officers had decided that air defense would remain less important than bombardment, even though the Soviet Union had detonated an atomic bomb. Although the American atomic striking force would, as Fairchild told Symington and Vandenberg, retain its primacy, Soviet possession of the bomb would, in the opinion of the Air Staff, force acceleration of air defense plans and projects by from one to three years. Vandenberg and Symington agreed with this analysis.[19]

Fairchild accordingly directed the Air Staff to review the Air Force position within the framework of a seventy-group program; he thought that, under the changed circumstances, the administration could conceivably allow the Air Force to expand to seventy groups if pressed. Thus far the Air Force had only Saville's permanent radar program to show for its long-range planning effort, and that continued to await final authorization from Congress. Fairchild wanted the Air Staff to examine means for completing the program. In addition, he asked for suggestions on how to increase the effectiveness of Air National Guard units assigned to air defense duties. Finally, he called for more and better cooperation with the Army and Navy in deploying picket vessels and antiaircraft artillery units.[20]

Fairchild directed General Anderson, Director of Plans and Operations, to spearhead the review. Anderson and his staff worked tirelessly for three months and then formed an air defense team under Col. T. J. Dayharsh to refine their findings. On December 29, the JCS asked Vandenberg to present proposals for using air defense means and for increasing those already available. Vandenberg and Fairchild asked Dayharsh and his air defense team to present their ideas at a JCS meeting held on March 2, 1950, and at the second USAF Commanders' Conference held the following month on Ramey Air Force Base, Puerto Rico.[21]

The meeting with the JCS focused on establishing goals for a minimum air defense by 1952. At Ramey, planners familiarized commanders with the thinking behind the plan as well as with its contents. Referred to as the Blue Book plan, it stipulated that a minimum air defense could be in place and operating by mid-1952. Brig. Gen. Charles P. Cabell, the Air Staff Intelligence Director, noted that the Air Force expected the Soviets to have between 45 and 90 atom bombs by that time, and from 70 to 135 by mid-1953. Cabell said the Soviets already possessed sufficient Tu–4 bombers, trained aircrews, and bases of operation to deliver their complete stockpile of bombs.[22] Anderson estimated July 1, 1952, as the critical date when the Soviets would pose a dangerous threat. Anderson also explained that the same date marked the earliest time by which the Air Force could set up, in an orderly manner, an operational air defense system.[23]

By the time the Blue Book plan was completed, funds had been found to start construction on the 85 radar stations and 10 air division control centers authorized for the United States and Canada under the permanent radar program. Congress had permitted Department of Defense and Bureau of the Budget officials to reprogram $50 million of the overall Department of the Air Force appropriation, at their discretion, to initiate construction of the permanent program. Symington, disturbed about "robbing" other projects in order to begin radar construction, nevertheless approved the action, as did Secretary of Defense Johnson and the Bureau of the Budget. The Air Force accordingly transferred $33 million from its maintenance and operations appropriation and $17 million from the aircraft purchase appropriation. Soon after, General Joseph T. McNarney, with Johnson's permission, reprogrammed $4 million from family housing.[24]

Despite the difficulties the Air Force had in funding the permanent radar stations, Blue Book planners felt it necessary to add twenty-four additional stations in the United States. As Anderson explained at Ramey, the permanent program

> was planned to meet a forecasted Russian capability in 1953 of sporadic, dispersed attacks against our resources. It did not include a coverage of areas in which certain units of our retaliatory forces are located and was intended only as the basic framework for an ultimate aircraft control and warn-ing system.

Now, said Anderson, the probability that the Soviets would control a stockpile of forty-five to ninety bombs made it necessary for the Air Force to provide protection for exposed SAC bases. The Air Staff had considered two possibilities in meeting this problem. The first would involve moving the bases inside the permanent radar system. The second would extend the warning system to include the bases. Since it was expected to cost approximately $100 million to move the bases, the Blue Book recommended adding additional radar stations. The plan suggested sixteen stations, eleven in the immediate vicinity of the bases and five on the southeastern coast of the United States, to "add needed warning for inland targets and combat units." The eight remaining stations would be located in Canada, three built by the United States and staffed by Whitehead's CONAC units, with the Canadian government's agreement.[25]

In the area of weapon strength, the Blue Book specified a need for the Air Force to have sixty-seven all-weather squadrons operating by 1952. The planners agreed with Saville's recommendation that each squadron possess at least twenty-five all-weather aircraft with an average of two-and-a-half crews per aircraft. Thus could the squadrons stand twenty-four-hour alert, train adequately, and have aircraft ready for duty during emergencies. As for deployment, Blue Book planners called for the squadrons to defend, in order of priority, the atomic weapons storage sites of SAC; the Hanford, Washington, atomic energy facility; and major American cities, with Washington and New York heading the list.[26]

The Air Force asked the JCS to approve and act upon the Blue Book plan without delay. Specifically, the Air Force asked that a joint committee be formed to determine how much each service could contribute to the system. The JCS turned the Blue Book over to the Joint Strategic Plans Committee for further study. The committee members agreed that current air defenses were inadequate and that July 1952 was when an operational air defense system should be in place. They also recommended that the Air Force provide the numbers of radar stations and interceptor squadrons proposed in the Blue Book plan. Furthermore, the committee suggested that the Navy furnish twenty-five radar picket ships to man ten stations, and that the Army provide fifty-one battalions of guns (each battalion to consist of three to twelve batteries), fifteen more than the Air Force proposal. In conclusion, the committee believed the plan "to be a sound approach, in principle, to the *optimum* (as opposed to the Air Force definition of the minimum) air defense system required." [27] Two formidable difficulties remained. First, the Air Force had to persuade Congress to approve the funds needed to implement the plan. Second, the Air Force had to persuade the Army and Navy to donate their resources to air defense.

Roles and Missions Dilemmas

Blue Book planners had decided a minimum air defense system for 1952 required a seaward extension of radar warning. They recommended the Navy establish ten picket ship stations to meet this need, six operating off the east coast and four off the west. The planners expected the picket ships to assist in identifying inbound overwater flights while providing additional warning for air defenses in the coastal areas.[28]

The Air Force needed Army and Navy cooperation. During World War II and through the first two years of Air Force independence, airmen had hoped to amalgamate into the Air Force air defense components controlled by other services. Because the Army and Navy resisted, the Air Force could only make agreements with the land and sea forces to train together and make emergency air defense plans. Because the mission was primarily an Air Force one, air leaders worked to obtain centralized control. But the Army and Navy both proved jealous of their prerogatives in allowing their forces to become Air Force controlled, even in an emergency.

The Blue Book plan considered the possibility that shore-based Navy and Marine fighter squadrons would compose part of, or supplement, squadrons assigned to defend the continental United States. As noted, the Navy opposed this idea, stating it had "other use" for its aircraft. As for the Army, the Air Force sought but did not receive an Army estimate of antiaircraft artillery, so the Air Force proceeded to make antiaircraft artillery estimates unilaterally. As the Air Staff perceived the situation, Army guns would be most needed on SAC bases, atomic installations, population centers, and industrial centers.[29]

Before the Soviet atomic explosion, almost no Army antiaircraft artillery units were on air defense duty in the United States and Alaska. The Army had worldwide antiaircraft responsibilities and believed its guns could be better used if its units were abroad than if they were on domestic alert against an improbable Soviet bomber attack. Airmen, who took the Soviet intercontinental threat more seriously, became angered, and quickly pointed out that the Army had fiercely resisted all Air Force attempts to absorb artillery units but had done little if anything to prepare its antiaircraft artillery units to assist in continental defense. The irony in the Air Force protests was that many airmen had disparaged the worth of antiaircraft artillery before World War II (as some ground officers had ridiculed the fighter). However, events in the war had removed any doubts that antiaircraft artillery played an integral part of air defense, and the Air Force now wanted the Army's guns on alert.

Immediately after President Truman announced the Soviet atomic bomb, the Army finally received the motivation and funds to act, establishing gun defenses for the atomic energy plants. It soon created an Antiaircraft Artillery Command. One of the purposes of the new command was better coordination with the Air Force, but disagreements between the services on how antiaircraft artillery fit into the overall air defense organization remained unresolved.[30]

One reason for Army unwillingness to give the Air Force control of antiaircraft artillery was that, before World War II ended, the Army had started to develop a surface-to-air missile, later called Nike. The missile showed enough promise to make ground forces commanders question the wartime concept of assigning air defenses to the area control of an Air Force commander. Unlike most artillery, surface-to-air missiles are long-range weapons and thus lessen the threat to friendly aircraft during joint air defense operations. Army planners, believing little danger existed to the interceptors, reasoned the missiles should be free to fire without the consent of an Air Force director. Further, the Army view was that two separate defense systems, one run by the Air Force and one by the

Army, should exist. In September 1946, however, the War Department had upheld the Air Force belief that antiaircraft artillery units should be controlled by the air commander.[31]

The Army could not reconcile itself to that concept, and from the end of the war until the establishment of the Antiaircraft Artillery Command, it claimed to be too hard pressed for resources to respond to Air Force requests for antiaircraft artillery in continental air defense. During these years another problem arose when the Air Force began to develop an unmanned interception missile. The Air Force had been interested in this concept since nearly the end of World War II when Germany demonstrated the feasibility of the V–2, a liquid-fueled missile flying at an altitude of about 60 to 70 miles and having a range of approximately 300 miles. After the war, the Air Force supported a number of surface-to-air missile projects, finally settling on the so-called BOMARC (Boeing–Michigan Aeronautical Research Center) unmanned interception missile. When the Army forged ahead in developing Nike, the Air Force cited duplication of effort as the reason for its attempt to assume control of all guided missile development. The JCS decided in November 1949 to assign missiles to the services according to function, with the Army retaining Nike as a successor to antiaircraft artillery and the Air Force continuing development of BOMARC as an unmanned interceptor. The Army considered the decision a guarantee of a continuing air defense role and a factor in forming a separate antiaircraft artillery command.[32]

After losing its battles to integrate antiaircraft artillery units into the Air Force and to control all surface-to-air missile development, the Air Force took solace in the fact that antiaircraft artillery units were now deployed at the Hanford and Oak Ridge atomic energy plants, and its leaders were optimistic that the units would shortly be stationed on SAC bases as well. But if fighter and antiaircraft artillery components were assigned to defend the same location, the controversy over rules of engagement would almost certainly recur.

In this area the two services remained poles apart. The Air Force continued to believe that the area air defense commander, usually an Air Force officer, should decide when antiaircraft artillery units would open fire. The Army maintained that "inner artillery zones" should be established over critical targets like Hanford and Oak Ridge, where the antiaircraft artillery commander could override hold-fire orders placed by the Air Force director. The Air Force countered that to permit this would be to forego the concept that "air defense was an operation of integrated components in which each . . . contributed to the total operation . . . and each was employed in conjunction with the others."[33] For the moment the controversy remained unresolved, leaving the Air Force and Army unable to work together effectively in air defense operations.

117

Although Air Force hopes for amalgamating Army and Navy units for air defense had vanished by fall 1949, airmen still wanted guarantees of unambiguous control of *all* components in an emergency. The Air Force would have had a better case had it worked out the mechanics of such a situation. When still in ADC, Saville and his staff had attempted to prepare for the JCS a detailed doctrinal statement on how and when the Air Force would control Army and Navy forces in an emergency. But Saville left ADC before the work was finished, and the services remained far from agreement on the matter at the time of the Soviet atomic test.[34]

In November 1949, Vandenberg vigorously reminded his JCS counterparts of their air defense responsibilities. He told the Chiefs that the Air Force thought the Soviet Union might already possess a stockpile of atomic bombs. In the face of this possibility, Vandenberg believed that air defense had become "so urgent and vital to the security of the nation" that drastic action was called for. As a first measure, he suggested the Chiefs act at once to pool the resources of the defense establishment to provide for air defense. Secondly, he thought the situation demanded an urgency and priority similar to the Manhattan District Project, responsible for developing the American atomic bomb in World War II. Vandenberg said he realized that this would be expensive, but the current situation cried for determined actions.[35]

Vandenberg's case was buoyed by the State and Defense department's joint study, "United States Objectives and Programs for National Security," completed in spring 1950. This National Security Council (NSC) policy paper, NSC 68, designed, in part, to outline the needs for increased spending on defense, called present military plans and programs "dangerously inadequate in time and scope. . . ." This new consensus required the JCS to examine all military programs in terms of cost and requirements. In regard to air defense specifically, NSC 68 estimated the Soviets could seriously damage U.S. vital centers in a surprise attack in 1954 if opposed by America's programmed air defenses for that period. The Army's Chief of Staff and the Chief of Naval Operations, apparently influenced by NSC 68, agreed to keep their minds open on the crash program suggested by Vandenberg. However, they decided to postpone direct action on the crash program until new studies of overall military requirements were completed. The JCS began immediately to look for funds that could be taken from lesser priorities to improve current air defenses. In this regard, the Chiefs obtained Johnson's support of Air Force efforts to expedite installation of the permanent radar stations.[36]

In attempting to persuade the Army and Navy to contribute more willingly and substantially to home air defense, Vandenberg had a dilemma. The other services believed they had enough to do supporting their major responsibilities, without contributing more than was absolutely necessary to a mission recognized to be primarily an Air Force concern. This problem was not unique to the Air Force. Both the Army and Navy were often frustrated when, for example, they asked for closer co-operation from the Air Force in close air support and antishipping roles. Nevertheless, Vandenberg recognized that after the Soviets gained an atomic capability the time was right to pressure the other services into increasing their home air defense outlays. After four years of sporadic deliberations, the Army decided to establish an antiaircraft artillery command, and the Chief of Naval Operations directed fleet commanders in February 1950 to cooperate with the Air Force for emergency deployment of Navy forces in air defense operations. Neither action guaranteed Air Force control of the other services' forces in an emergency, but the changes indicated that the Army and Navy took their air defense responsibilities more seriously. Negotiations by the Air Force involved more than those by the Army or the Navy, for the air defense concept had wide implications. Canada also participated extensively and would become even more important as time went on and the systems expanded. For the present, the JCS supported preliminary talks between the U.S. and the Royal Canadian air forces for installing air defenses in Canada. In addition, the pace of negotiations quickened within the Permanent Joint Board on Defense for setting up an American unified command to provide air defense protection on leased bases in Newfoundland and Labrador.[37]

Pressure on the Air Force to increase the effectiveness of the air defenses increased steadily from late 1949 through the first half of 1950. The Chairman of the JCS, General Bradley, urged faster actions on the radar stations. Without this, he warned, "an atomic attack on the industrial heart of the nation is entirely possible." *Time* magazine reported that the Air Force needed to speed work on the radar systems and needed more and better interceptors. Representative Thor C. Tollefson of Washington, commenting on the B–47 production controversy in Seattle, claimed that the people of the northwest were unhappy with the Air Force's apparent inability to protect them from air attack. Dr. Vannevar Bush, writing to Bradley, was "appalled" by the condition of U.S. air defenses and wondered if the Air Force was doing all it could to provide sufficient defense without overburdening the nation's economy and taking funds from the strategic forces. By March 1950, private citizens wrote also to Symington and Vandenberg to express their concern. The letter writers, usually well informed, worried that the air defenses would be inadequate in an emergency.[38]

Public concern about air defense increased because the Soviets developed an atomic capability far sooner than most intelligence experts had predicted. Although President Truman claimed not to be surprised, the administration had failed to warn the American people that their atomic monopoly might be short-lived. As the department with the primary responsibility for air defense of the United States, the Air Force had, at least since Fairchild and Saville intervened, tempered its emphasis on the defense issue only by the overriding necessity of readying SAC. At best the Air Force could only appeal to Congress and map various plans, of which they had no dearth. The most detailed and farsighted plans, however, would be worthless without funding.

Now that an air attack appeared possible, funding appeared more likely because the public and Congress now showed some interest in air defense. The most interested and influential supporters included Representative Carl Vinson of Georgia. Vinson told Symington he meant to do all he could to see that the Air Force received what it required in men, radars, and interceptors to assure adequate continental air defense. Encouraged by Vinson's support, Headquarters USAF advanced the completion date from July 1, 1951, to December 31, 1950, for the most essential radar stations. [39]

In April 1950, the Air Force pledged to complete the entire permanent radar system by mid-1952. Even when completed, it would not detect and track low-altitude air attacks any better than the Lashup systems currently in operation. As exercises held in early June 1950 in the 25th Air Division indicated, insufficient low-altitude coverage could, and probably would, result in disaster during an actual attack. Saville, aware of this problem when he devised the permanent system, had advised the use of civilian ground observers until low-altitude coverage could be provided by small, unmanned radars relaying data to the permanent stations. The Air Staff agreed that until such equipment was developed, installed, and operating, air defenses would have to rely on the eyes and ears of ground observers for low-altitude sightings. [40]

The Air Staff accordingly began organizing an Air Force–sponsored GOC. General Whitehead formulated a plan and in February 1950 submitted his ideas for the use of observers in the northeast and west coast defense areas. Whitehead called for a total of 160,000 civilian volunteers to operate some 8,000 posts. They would report to 26 filter centers staffed by air reservists and civilians under the guidance of small cadres of Air Force enlisted personnel. Headquarters USAF and the Office of the Secretary of Defense approved the plan, and by June 1950 CONAC prepared to enforce it as soon as funds became available. [41]

Meanwhile, talks between the U.S. Air Force and the Royal Canadian Air Force took on a new sense of importance as a result of the Soviet atom bomb. If the Soviets attacked, they would doubtlessly do so over the shorter northern routes, and radar stations were needed in Canada to provide early warning for both nations. [42] In June 1950, the U.S. and Royal Canadian air forces agreed on the proposed Radar Extension Program, including construction of thirty-one radar stations in Canada. The U.S. Air Force would pay the cost of constructing and equipping at least eighteen of these stations. Whitehead's forces would operate eight of them, extending U.S. radar coverage north of the border. Further, emulating the CONAC Lashup program, the Canadian Air Force assigned additional forces to air defense and established a temporary air defense system while awaiting final approval of the Radar Extension Program. The Canadians soon had three temporary radar stations operating and had assigned a second fighter squadron to air defense duty. Assisted by the Bell Telephone Company of Canada, the Canadian Air Force also initiated preparations for a Canadian GOC. The Canadians were encouraged to take this step when Whitehead's staff officers acquainted them with CONAC's plans to form an observer corps. U.S.-Canadian negotiations for joint air defense procedures were generally smooth and cordial. [43]

Vandenberg and Fairchild wanted to make optimum use of civilian expertise in planning air defense systems. Like Spaatz and Arnold previously, they called upon the skills of Dr. Theodore von Karman, Chairman of the Air Force Scientific Advisory Board. Von Karman established a committee to devise an appropriate Air Force position on air defense for the immediate future. The members of this group would "try to determine from the combined viewpoints of physical sciences, economic and social aspects and the capabilities of the Air Force just how far the nation could go toward an ideal perfect air defense, in view of other unavoidable requirements of National Security." Another group of board members and other scientists would work closely with Whitehead's units located in the northeast. They would try to develop techniques and equipment that could "produce maximum effective air defense for a minimum dollar investment." [44] The Air Force hoped to build a technologically advanced air defense at low cost, but the task would prove impossible.

Meanwhile, in January 1950, the Air Force established the Air Research and Development Command (ARDC) and, on the Air Staff, the new office of Deputy Chief of Staff for Development. These changes were encouraged by a report submitted by a special Scientific Advisory Board committee on research and development headed by Dr. Louis N. Ridenour. Since the end of World War II, the research and development function in the Air Force had been divided among different staff and command agencies, often with overlapping responsibilities. The Air Staff, by establishing ARDC and the staff position for development, was intent on building a more cohesive, better organized, and clearly directed technology structure. [45]

These events had to have a profound effect on the course of continental air defense. It was becoming exceedingly clear to Air Force planners that, in the future, the Air Force would have to depend on technology instead of on overwhelming resources to supply the advantage over the Soviet Union. That technology would be applied to developing air defense systems seemed almost certain, especially with the appointment of General Saville to the new post of Deputy Chief of Staff for Development. In this assignment Saville directed the leading edge of Air Force efforts to optimally utilize current scientific research. On arriving at the Pentagon, Saville began soliciting the opinions of prominent scientists on how advanced technology could be used to improve air defense operations. As in his advocacy of the interceptor of the future, Saville intuitively believed that technology still on the drawing board or in the laboratory could eventually be developed and incorporated in a modern air defense system. Ivan A. Getting, one of the major scientists who worked closely with him at this time, considered Saville "a very remarkable man. He thoroughly believed in the application of modern science and technology to the problems of the Air Force and strongly felt the need of bringing about much more positive thinking in combining military problems with advancing science and technology." [46] Saville consulted the eminent scientist Dr. George E. Valley of MIT, who told him that the technology might soon be available to support the production of more effective radar and accurate data handling. The ability, Valley said, lay with computer technology, still an elementary science. Valley believed the Air Force could support development of this technology without endangering the buildup and modernization of SAC. [47] With that assurance, Saville advocated in the Pentagon that the Air Force support computer-related research for air defense purposes.

Air Defense Forces in the Field

Whether or not the Air Force decided that computers were the wave of the future in air defense, General Whitehead, as head of CONAC, confronted problems concerning the present. As the officer directly in charge of most of the nation's forces for air defense, Whitehead believed he could not afford to rest with intelligence estimates that the Soviets would not be ready to launch an air attack against the United States until 1952. For the CONAC commander, no time could be lost in making his forces combat ready. According to his deputy, Brig. Gen. Herbert B. Thatcher, Whitehead "was always seeing war around the corner, always looking for it." [48]

Interestingly, although Whitehead and Saville could not work together, they shared similar personal and professional qualities, both putting everything into their work, tackling assignments relentlessly. As one

Lt. Gen. Ennis C. Whitehead

of his subordinates later recalled, "General Whitehead, once he told you something . . . you had better do it. There were no half-way measures with him. He wanted a hundred percent, and if he could get a hundred and two out of you, that's what he wanted." [49]

General Fairchild had told Whitehead to consider air defense his command's most important mission. Whitehead, because of his enthusiasm for the job, interpreted this to his commanders as signifying that the Air Staff had come to regard air defense as "the most important mission assigned to the USAF." Whitehead might have also reached this mistaken conclusion because Fairchild ordered the Air Staff to accord CONAC air defense units, temporarily, the same priority for resources reserved since late 1948 for SAC. [50]

As one of its first actions under this provision, the Air Staff authorized an increase in the number of Lashup stations. This action permitted Whitehead to install a temporary radar warning and control system in the Los Angeles and San Francisco areas; provide radar coverage for the atomic energy installation in Oak Ridge, Tennessee; expand radar coverage over the Hanford, Washington, atomic energy plant; and increase radar coverage over the southern and western approaches to the Seattle-Hanford region. In addition, Whitehead received the additional officers and enlisted men needed to initiate an air defense command structure in the expanded Lashup system. The Air Staff also assisted him in his efforts to maintain fighter-interceptors on air defense alert and to institute

F–86D Sabre. This interceptor version of the Sabre did not become fully operational until 1953.

air weapons control (ground control intercept) procedures.[51]

Whitehead, pressing to achieve around-the-clock operations with the forces at his disposal, put tremendous strain on the people in air defense units, but the CONAC chief was not deterred. His commanders acknowledged that he was "hardboiled," "tough," and "would brutally test you." His methods, nevertheless, seemed to achieve positive results. By June 1950 most of the additional Lashup stations and heavy radar equipment authorized in fall 1949 were either operational or about to become so. Fifteen additional stations were soon added, making the total forty-three.[52]

To use the expanded and improved radar coverage fully, Whitehead sought permission to disperse his twenty-three fighter-interceptor squadrons from the eight bases they occupied to twenty bases. The Air Staff approved the idea, but it could not implement the plan immediately because of insufficient funds. In another development, the stateside squadrons began to receive F–86 Sabre jets. While the Sabre proved an outstanding aircraft in wartime air superiority, it had not been designed specifically for air defense (squadrons did not start to receive the F–86D modified for air defense until 1953). In the meantime, F–94As, the first jet interceptors modified specially for air defense, became available and were stationed on bases in the Pacific northwest.[53]

As Lashup systems proliferated and the performance of pilots and planes improved, Whitehead attempted to extend their periods of oper-

F–94 Starfire, the United States' first jet-powered, all-weather fighter. This plane was the first to shoot down, with only a radar image, a target drone.

ation. After a ten-day exercise in the northwest early in 1949 proved the competence of weapons controllers and air crews to perform successful intercepts, Whitehead authorized his area commanders to begin active air defense to the limit of the capabilities of their forces. This was possible because Saville had previously initiated arrangements with the Civil Aeronautics Administration and Military Flight Service to provide flight plan data to the 25th Air Division in the northwest and the 26th on the east coast. The respective control centers received prompt information when bomber-type aircraft penetrated the divisions' active defense zones. Now, under Whitehead's orders, the 25th and 26th air divisions attempted to intercept tracks that could not be identified positively by flight plan correlation. The aircrews received orders to shoot down violators of airspace over the atomic plants in Hanford, in Oak Ridge, and in Los Alamos, New Mexico, if those violators committed a blatantly hostile act such as dropping bombs or paratroopers, or firing on interceptors and ground targets.[54]

Headquarters USAF, however, concerned about possible errors, such as the shooting down of civilian aircraft, decided that Whitehead had moved too fast. On January 17, 1950, he received orders to cease all interception operations. Arming the fighters and investing them with authority to shoot down aircraft was, as the Air Staff expressed it, "a new step in our concept of the air defense of the United States." [55]

In discussions following the Air Force decision, Whitehead's staff

125

proposed that all civil and military pilots be required to file flight plans when their routes took them through sensitive, defended areas. As expected, much opposition to this suggestion arose because it promised to complicate operations in flight control centers. Also, civilian airlines feared passengers would be uneasy knowing their flights were subject to interception. Despite their uncertainties, affected civilian and military agencies agreed to file voluntary flight plans when traveling over defended areas. In April 1950, Headquarters USAF authorized CONAC to resume interceptions with armed fighters against aircraft off their flight plans. Operations were at first limited to areas over the atomic energy installations. In time, CONAC's authority to make interceptions increased to include aircraft approaching the east coast of the United States. Further, Canada agreed to provide flight plan data on aircraft approaching the United States from across the northern border.[56]

By June 1950, the 25th Air Division in the northwest was the most advanced Lashup sector. In February it had experimented by implementing twenty-four-hour-a-day operations, apparently attaining Whitehead's goal in at least one sector. But the 25th soon returned to an eight-hour-a-day, five-day-a-week work schedule because of personnel shortages. In subsequent months, the 25th received increasing numbers of enlisted graduates of Air Training Command electronics schools. Still, its radar and control stations remained desperately understaffed in several skills, especially radar repair.[57]

Despite its problems, the 25th Air Division conducted an air defense exercise from June 18 to 24, 1950. SAC bombers launched sixty strikes in that period aimed either on Seattle or the Hanford atomic plant. As part of the defensive forces, Air National Guard fighter units and a Coast Guard cutter assisted the 25th. According to Col. Clinton D. Vincent, 25th Air Division Commander, the radar-equipped cutter proved a valuable asset in extending early warning. Vincent reiterated the Blue Book planners' recommendation that Navy picket vessels be an integral part of the air defenses.[58] Notwithstanding Coast Guard and Air National Guard assistance, the division's overall effectiveness was judged unsatisfactory. If subjected to high-level attack (17,000 to 25,000 feet), Seattle would have received sufficient warning for its population to take cover, although the defenses would probably have been unable to prevent the city from being bombed. Had the attack been staged from low altitude, Seattle citizens would probably not have had time to seek shelter. As for Hanford, the facility would have had an even chance of being forewarned of a high-altitude attack, but the odds were much less for a low-level assault.[59]

In the wake of the exercise, Col. George S. Brown, one of Whitehead's most knowledgeable staff officers who would later become Air

Force Chief of Staff and Chairman of the JCS, evaluated the nation's air defenses:

> . . . we have a training establishment which, incidentally, has some actual operational capability. We are, therefore, not fulfilling our primary mission since, in effect, we are still preparing to provide for the air defense of the continental United States and are not yet capable of providing a minimum acceptable defense.[60]

Although Brown's observations were accurate, the Boeing controversy, the B–36 hearings, and, especially, the Soviet atomic explosion all worked to raise public, and military, consciousness of air defense. Now, in mid-1950, the Air Force remained, as Brown noted, a long way from providing adequate air defense. Fairchild and Saville led a drive to identify immediate and long-range goals and to construct a framework conducive to further expansion. Increases in the number of radars and fighters deployed, personnel assigned to air defense duties, and stepped-up scientific research showed advancement; yet, more progress was needed. Such was provided, but in a most unexpected fashion, on the other side of the world—on June 25 North Korean forces crossed the 38th parallel into the Republic of Korea.

Chapter 6

Continental Air Defense in the Korean War Period

As soon as word reached Headquarters USAF of the North Korean invasion of South Korea, General Vandenberg acted. Placing air defense forces in the continental United States and Alaska on around-the-clock alert, he directed his commanders to intercept and destroy all unknown aircraft penetrating the identification zones around atomic energy installations or heading inland from the sea or from the north toward defended areas.[1] These precautions seemed necessary because Vandenberg and the JCS thought that the Communist attack on Korea could be the prelude to a Soviet-inspired general war. For the next several months, Air Force air defense forces were on special alert against a Soviet air attack.[2]

If the Soviets attacked, the Air Force knew little about what tactics they might use. As a RAND analyst summarized the predicament:

> They [Soviet bombers] might come in at a high altitude or low altitude. They might come in many different ways as far as whether they exploit saturation tactics, or try to sneak through the defenses or so on. And since we don't know anything really about their doctrine of strategic air, we have a tremendous gamut of possibilities to worry about . . . we always have to look at the worst possibility.[3]

As the RAND analysis made clear, a paucity of reliable intelligence information caused the Air Force endless worry in preparing to meet a Soviet strategic air offensive. Addressing the Air War College a few weeks before the start of the Korean War, General Saville assessed the optimally conceived air defense as able to destroy sixty percent of attacking enemy bombers. A more likely success rate would be thirty percent. In any case, said Saville, the percentages would not mean much until the nature of the enemy threat could be determined more accurately. Saville emphasized the need for more accurate intelligence data to gauge Soviet capabilities and Soviet plans for launching an intercontinental attack.[4]

To gather information on Soviet intercontinental capability and bomber tactics, the Air Force used information from German and Japanese ex–prisoners of war who had been forced to work in Soviet industrial facilities from 1945 to 1949, information supplied by Soviet defectors, current and wartime attaché reports, and German intelligence materials captured at the end of World War II that included aerial photography of the Soviet aircraft industry.[5] The Air Force and other military and civilian intelligence agencies also used secret agents, decryption devices, electronic eavesdropping, and balloon and aircraft reconnaissance operations. But the nature of Soviet society and its obsession with secrecy precluded first-rate U.S. intelligence until very high-altitude surveillance aircraft appeared later in the 1950s.[6]

Largely ignorant of Soviet intentions, the Air Force believed it had to prepare to face the worst. Stalin had proved since the beginning of the Cold War that he was not intimidated by American or European military power. In fact, Soviet provocations in eastern Europe and divided Berlin seemed evidence that "the threat posed to America's European allies by the Red Army was probably greater than the threat America's atomic monopoly posed to the Soviet Union's survival."[7] The communist aggression in Korea—if it was, as strongly suspected in the United States, orchestrated or approved by the Soviet Union—was consistent with Soviet aggressiveness since the end of World War II and was more dangerous because the American atomic monopoly had been broken.

Although the Soviets were attempting to make inroads in Europe and probably in Asia, the question remained whether they would launch an air attack against the United States if they could. The Air Force adhered to the administration position outlined in NSC 68. The authors of this important policy paper argued, in part, that the Soviet Union was determined to achieve world domination and would use any means at its disposal to obtain its goal: "There is no justification in Soviet theory or practice for predicting that, should the Kremlin become convinced that it would cause our downfall by one conclusive blow, it would not seek that solution."[8]

If the Soviets attacked, their long-range delivery vehicle would almost certainly be the Tu–4 Bull, patterned after the Air Force B–29. Not a true intercontinental bomber (neither was the B–29 nor its successor, the B–50), a Bull could reach every important government and industrial site in the United States on a one-way mission, and American planners believed the Soviets would sacrifice airplanes and crews to attack selected targets in the United States. Although intelligence sources had identifed only 30 Bull bombers in operational units in early 1950, 415 were expected to be available by mid-year and 1,200 by mid-1952. The mid-1952 date was when the Air Force expected the Soviet Union to be ready to stage a decisive attack against the United States. By then,

American bomber crews would be better trained and navigation and radar equipment would be improved. Moreover, the Soviets were trying to increase the Bull's range, develop an aerial refueling capability (the United States had this capability in 1949), and produce and operate a long-range bomber by mid-1952. The Air Force, incidentally, marked 1952 as the earliest date for completion of an operational air defense system in the United States.[9]

The threat of a Soviet intercontinental air strike seemed a real danger. The probability that the United States would not strike first in a future atomic war only further reinforced this perception. SAC officers had identified as targets important industrial and military facilities in the Soviet Union, but these would most likely be struck in retaliation. Some officers in SAC and in the Air Staff advocated a preemptive offensive if reliable intelligence indicated an imminent Soviet attack. Less likely, a "preventive" war could start if the Soviets were preparing for a future first strike, and the United States would have the moral right to intercept it, thereby gaining the initiative. The general agreement in SAC and Headquarters USAF was that neither preemptive nor preventive attacks were realistic options for war plans. In the United States, the military complied with government policy, and notwithstanding his tough rhetoric, President Truman believed "starting an atomic war is totally unthinkable for rational men."[10]

The Air Force had to accept the probability that in a future war it would have to meet the first strike before it could retaliate. If the Soviets were to attack, they would have to use their entire stockpile of atomic bombs, estimated at between ten and twenty. They would doubtlessly strike at night, when the propeller-driven Tu–4 would have little if anything to fear from the few American interceptors then on alert. SAC preparations for retaliation could take days while sufficient bombers deployed to forward bases and became armed with atomic weapons. Meanwhile, if the Soviet war plan was well conceived, it might include provisions for evacuating people and industry to outlying areas. A Soviet first strike could not be considered any more improbable or irrational than Japan's attack on Pearl Harbor, so the enhancement of air defense since the outbreak of fighting in Korea seemed logical.[11]

General Vandenberg was especially concerned with the air defense of Alaska—an important military staging area in light of the polar concept, and a possible target for enemy bombers approaching the U.S. mainland. Air Force fighter forces in Alaska, undermanned and equipped largely with obsolete F–82s, were plagued with frequent mechanical breakdowns. Before hostilities began in Korea, the Air Force had decided to phase out the Twin Mustang. The aircraft performed so inefficiently that it had not been marked for transfer to Air National Guard units, as was the jet F–80; it was marked for disposal. In the meantime, no F–

131

82 parts were being manufactured, nor were they normally interchangeable.[12]

Worsening matters in Alaska, ground-based radar equipment remained extremely scarce. General Frank A. Armstrong, head of Alaskan Air Command, implored Vandenberg to send additional equipment, saying "any kind that will make a blip will do." In response, the Air Staff supplied Armstrong with enough equipment and personnel for five additional radar stations.[13] Equally important, one squadron received F-94 all-weather interceptor jets as replacements for the F-82. Like the Twin Mustang, the F-94 was to serve temporarily until the Air Force could substitute the F-89. The F-94A, received by the squadron in Alaska, was lightly armed with four .50-caliber machineguns. This gun sufficed when combined with the Hughes APG-32 radar, the first American postwar intercept radar to become operational. A backseat radar operator acquired the target on his scope and directed the aircraft until the pilot could take aim with a radar image in his optical sight. In late 1949, an F-94A pilot shot down (for the first time) a target drone without having actually seen it.[14]

In November 1950, Armstrong and Lt. Gen. William Kepner, now head of the Alaskan unified command, conducted a two-day test of the air defenses. Although the F-94s and additional radar equipment were judged improvements, Kepner and Armstrong found numerous problems. The radar coverage continued to show gaps, identification of aircraft remained too slow, and communications were inadequate. Fighter base facilities were poor, and the Army did not provide nearly enough antiaircraft artillery units, primarily because of requirements in Korea. The final report concluded that had the exercise strike force consisted of Tu-4 bombers, the raiders probably would have completed their missions successfully.[15]

Meanwhile, in CONAC, Whitehead directed his commanders to try once again to institute twenty-four-hour-a-day, seven-day-a-week operations. The recall of Air Reserve controllers, radio technicians, and other air control and warning specialists promised to make this possible. Unfortunately, the Air Force lack of tactical air resources soon resulted in the transfer of many of Whitehead's personnel to radar units in Korea. In short, Whitehead found it as impractical as Kepner and Armstrong had to begin around-the-clock operations in Alaska. Whitehead consequently ordered the continental radar systems to operate at the peak efficiency of individual units.[16]

Fighter-interceptor units adopted similar procedures. During daylight hours each squadron kept from two to eight aircraft on fifteen-minute alert, depending on the number of aircraft available. In addition, each squadron kept a third of its complement of operational aircraft on three-hour alert. Operational aircraft crews excused from alert duty performed routine training.[17]

These schedules meant that trained personnel in the Eastern and Western air defense forces worked under intense pressure. The few skilled people available had to put in seventy- to eighty-hour weeks and had to be on call at all times. Leaves and passes were necessarily restricted. Such conditions could easily have undermined morale because the direct threat posed to the United States as a result of the Korean War appeared oblique at best. Air defense commanders, therefore, made special efforts to explain the necessity of extended operations to their subordinates. Members of the 26th Air Division in the east, for example, learned that the Soviets possessed enough long-range aircraft to deliver their entire stock of atom bombs in one strike, and they might do so! Because it seemed unlikely the United States would receive advance intelligence of such an attack, the first indication would probably be radar detection of a large wave of unidentified aircraft. The 26th Air Division was reminded that its mission was to be ready to oppose and defeat such a threat.[18]

In the fighter-interceptor units, combat ready became a familiar term after the start of the Korean War. The 52d Fighter Wing, based on McGuire Air Force Base, New Jersey, provided a good example of what this implied. One of the few wings able to assume full-time operations, the 52d's combat crews rotated through 24-hour alert duty. Reflecting the tenseness of the period, each crewmember carried a .45-caliber pistol when on alert and on all air defense missions. Moreover, fearing sabotage, the wing's F–82s remained under continuous armed guard in lighted areas. Recognizing the severe limitations of their aircraft, crewmembers devised last-ditch ramming tactics whereby radar observers would bail out and pilots would use the vacant starboard side of the fighter for ramming enemy bombers. All in all, the crews were "brought to a keen edge . . . ready for fighting when the order came." [19]

The state of communications between Washington, the major commands, and air defense divisions became a major concern of the Air Force and all air defense components. The day the war began, the U.S. Air Force Operations Staff set up an emergency command post on the fourth floor of the Pentagon to serve as a reception point for radio messages between Vandenberg and his FEAF commanders during Air Staff after-duty hours. In mid-July 1950, the installation of direct telephone lines between Whitehead's headquarters and the 26th Air Division's headquarters marked the beginning of the Air Force air raid warning system. It became a rudimentary national warning network in August when President Truman had a direct telephone line installed between the Air Force Pentagon post and the White House.[20]

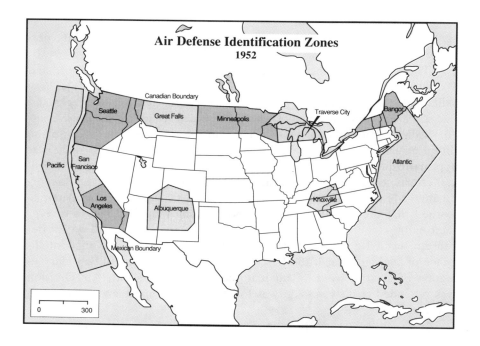

Air Defense Identification Zones
1952

The emergence of an air defense command and control structure allowed General Whitehead to expedite arrangements initiated as early as 1948 for alerting all military installations and state and national civil defense authorities of an approaching air attack. By fall 1950, communications and procedures existed for this purpose. As in World War II, degrees of alert were designated by color codes. "Yellow," when transmitted by air division centers to civilian and military key points, meant the possibility of attack. "Red" signified an imminent air attack. "White" meant all clear. The air defenses subsequently adopted the term "Air Defense Readiness" to use for alerting air defense and other specified military forces when commanders suspected danger but were not convinced of the necessity to alert the entire nation.[21]

Other significant improvements in air defense procedures developed during the first months after the start of the war, as in July when the JCS agreed on the mandatory filing of flight plans for military pilots flying through defended areas. The Air Force, with cooperation from the Civil Aeronautics Administration, pressed for similar control of civilian air traffic. In September, Congress empowered Truman to impose such control whenever the safety of the nation seemed threatened. Meanwhile, the Air Force defined more precisely the areas in which mandatory filing would be required. The restricted areas, since 1948 variously named "active defense areas" or "defense zones," now became "air defense identification zones." [22]

To enhance air defense principles further, on August 24, 1950, President Truman concurred with a proposal initiated by Vandenberg for clarifying conditions under which fighter-interceptors could open fire. At the start of the Korean War, fighters could fire only after intruders had committed a clearly hostile act. The new ruling permitted firing when the intruder was "manifestly hostile in intent, or . . . bore the military insignia of the U.S.S.R., unless properly cleared or obviously in distress." (The ruling required not just radar contact, but that the intruder be visually sighted, before firing could commence.) [23]

Another significant event in air defense was the August 1, 1950, agreement on antiaircraft artillery procedures reached by Vandenberg and Army Chief of Staff General J. Lawton Collins. Largely the product of negotiations in April between Major Generals Frank F. Everest of the Air Staff and Charles L. Bolte of the Army General Staff, this Collins-Vandenberg agreement allowed air division commanders to exercise operational control of all antiaircraft artillery units assigned to their sectors. Division heads were expected to establish flexible conditions under which the units would go into action. Everest and Bolte proposed that while sector commanders would be authorized to issue hold fire orders to antiaircraft artillery commanders, these orders would be imposed for as short a period as practicable. Everest and Bolte agreed that the commanders had to be free to fire at aircraft that *they* determined hostile, unless otherwise directed. [24]

The Collins-Vandenberg agreement formalized the rules of engagement described by Bolte and Everest in April. Just as important, it authorized Whitehead and Brig. Gen. Willard W. Irvine, named to head the new Antiaircraft Artillery Command, to establish an antiaircraft artillery component at each echelon of the air defense forces. The officers in charge of the artillery units were expected to serve as the principal advisers to their respective air defense chiefs. Antiaircraft artillery commanders in the field, therefore, would be assured that the orders they received had been confirmed by or, at the very least, coordinated through their own services. This agreement was expected to alleviate interservice conflicts. [25]

General Irvine began to put into effect the organizational provisions of the Collins-Vandenberg agreement in late August. He established the Eastern Antiaircraft Artillery Command on Stewart Air Force Base, New York, and the Western Antiaircraft Artillery Command on Hamilton Air Force Base, California. He also moved his headquarters from the Pentagon to Mitchel Air Force Base, a better location from which to coordinate air defense matters with Whitehead. From all appearances the Korean conflict served as the impetus that at long last moved the Army and Air Force to seek compromises, put aside interservice jealousies, and reach sensible agreements on the position of antiaircraft artillery in air defense.[26] Unfortunately, time brought more problems.

The outbreak of the Korean War—following so closely on various incidents of Cold War tension in Eastern Europe and Berlin, the Soviet atomic explosion, and the defeat of the Chinese Nationalist government by the Chinese Communists—obliterated the limit on military expenditures imposed shortly after the end of World War II. The Air Force believed more money would be available not only for all its critical programs, especially those involving SAC, but also for air defense. Congressman Carl Vinson reinforced this belief early in August 1950 when he told Vandenberg that the House Armed Services Committee wanted to help the Air Force achieve its goals. Still, said Vinson, the committee was unhappy with the progress of certain Air Force programs, including the permanent radar system. Vinson decided to establish a special radar subcommittee to evaluate periodic Air Force progress reports on the system.[27]

The call for rapid improvements in air defense also appeared in the media. Retired General Carl Spaatz, now a military analyst, offered his opinion in *Newsweek*. Spaatz wrote that time was running out and the United States could ill afford to postpone safeguarding the nation from nuclear attack. He recommended immediately strengthening all components of the air defenses.[28]

New men now assumed the job of creating new air defense systems and forces and of reassessing future needs. General Fairchild, who, although seriously ill for some time, had remained at his post at Vandenberg's request, died three months before the start of the Korean War. His death cost the Air Force the services of an outstanding planner and theorist. It also adversely affected the fortunes of his protege, Gordon Saville. "When Santy died," Saville said later, "my heart went flat, I was through." He felt that, as long as Fairchild was Vice Chief of Staff, "I could survive, I was willing to fight. But when there wasn't any Santy . . . there wasn't any place [to] go." Soon after Fairchild's death, Saville planned his own retirement, in part because he feared the prospects for improved air defense were diminished without Fairchild's backing. Saville thought no one was left on the Air Staff to deny the continuous demand for resources made by SAC's strong-willed commander, General Curtis E. LeMay. Of course, Saville realized his personal prospects had also dimmed drastically by Fairchild's death. He had accumulated by flaunting his connection with the Vice Chief, by his unconventional style, and by his abrupt manners numerous enemies on the Air Staff in the course of starting the air defense buildup. Although he remained at his post as Deputy Chief of Staff for Development until June 1951 while he completed ongoing projects and his successor was chosen, Fairchild's death weakened Saville's influence in Air Staff councils.[29]

Gordon Saville's contributions to the development of air defense in the United States cannot be denied. He was an adept student, theorist, practitioner, seer, and salesman of and for the concept. Blunt and outspoken, a small, compact bundle of nervous energy and continually flowing ideas, he never hesitated to present his views regardless of how unpopular they were to his superiors. In the process he gained a staunch admirer and backer in Fairchild, and many powerful adversaries able to counter Fairchild's support. Perhaps a larger degree of tact and diplomacy would have permitted Saville to receive the accolades due him as the progenitor of the sophisticated air defense networks that would emerge in a few years after his retirement.

In selecting Fairchild's successor, Vandenberg had no dearth of talent from which to choose. General Lauris Norstad filled the position temporarily but deferred shortly to General Nathan F. Twining. Having served with distinction in both the Pacific and European theaters in World War II, recently Twining had briefly been Deputy Chief of Staff for Personnel in the Air Staff and, before that, head of the Alaskan unified command. His dealings with the Army and Navy in Alaska proved useful when he became involved with inevitable interservice disputes, some involving air defense, as USAF Vice Chief of Staff and later as Chief of Staff and Chairman of the JCS.[30]

Another crucial change in the Air Force command occurred when Secretary of the Air Force Stuart Symington left office in April 1950. Although Symington resigned quietly, he was profoundly disturbed by Secretary of Defense Johnson's belief that a forty-eight-group Air Force was adequate in the face of the Soviet atomic threat. Thomas K. Finletter, Symington's successor, had served as head of President Truman's Air Policy Commission in 1947 and, like his predecessor, was determined to provide the Air Force with the best air defense capability possible—as long as the offensive forces lost no funds in the process. Finletter chose John A. McCone as his undersecretary and made him principally responsible for expediting completion of the radar system.[31]

The Korean War galvanized Congress into increasing defense expenditures, benefiting air defense programs. Johnson permitted Finletter to increase the priority of the radar programs, and Congress responded in September 1950 with a supplemental appropriation of nearly $40 million. The Air Force thus could now build the stations and purchase new search and height-finder equipment more quickly. Now, apparently, the Air Force had no excuses for not implementing rapidly the permanent system as Representative Vinson expected.[32]

On October 2, however, Deputy Chief of Staff (Comptroller) Lt. Gen. Edwin W. Rawlings, advised Assistant Secretary of the Air Force

Eugene M. Zuckert of scheduling problems. Shortages of building materials had caused construction delays, and a strike at the General Electric plant in Syracuse, New York, in September (where the AN/CPS–6B long-range radar was being manufactured) had impeded equipment deliveries.[33] Zuckert passed the news on to McCone who, on October 30, carried it to the House Armed Services Committee. At the same time, McCone promised Vinson that the Air Force expected to have the first twenty-four radar stations in operation no later than March 1, 1951, and the remainder completed by the end of June 1952. For the moment, Vinson was satisfied.[34]

Soon after fighting began in Korea, the Air Force examined its worldwide radar control and warning requirements. Twining, agreeing that the permanent system was inadequate in the United States, authorized the mobile radar program. Whitehead was to receive twenty-four radar stations, increased from an original sixteen, to protect SAC bases. The new program also included twenty mobile radar stations to fill what were perceived as gaps in the permanent system. To minimize costs, the Air Force planned to select sites requiring "minimum access roads, grading, clearing, and construction of hardstands on which the mobile equipment could be placed." The Air Force intended to operate the new radar stations with tactical air control groups, units that could be housed on air bases and moved to the stations for training, during alerts, and in actual emergency, should one arise. Twining decided to support the program with funds targeted for the tactical forces because units trained to operate the mobile radar stations could perform the same job in Korea, if necessary.[35]

As with the radar station programs, the Korean War also proved an impetus to the buildup and improvement of the civilian Ground Observer Corps (GOC). In July, Whitehead directed his commanders to make every effort to improve all phases of the GOC program and to bring it to maximum capability because low-altitude attacks still posed a danger. He was anxious for the U.S. program to at least keep up with that of the Canadians. By October 1950, the Royal Canadian Air Force had instituted a ground observer system, the Long Range Air Raid Warning System, capable of twenty-four-hour-a-day, seven-day-a-week operations. Using radio communications, volunteer observers reported sightings to the nearest Canadian Air Force radar of any aircraft they could recognize with four or more engines.[36]

By November the Air Force considered the American GOC system to have a limited capability. Of the 26 filter centers planned, 19 were being installed in the east and 7 in the west. Each filter center personnel authorization included 1 officer, 3 airmen, and approximately 500 civilian volunteers. Observation posts, which reported to filter centers, required at least 25 volunteers to operate continuously.[37]

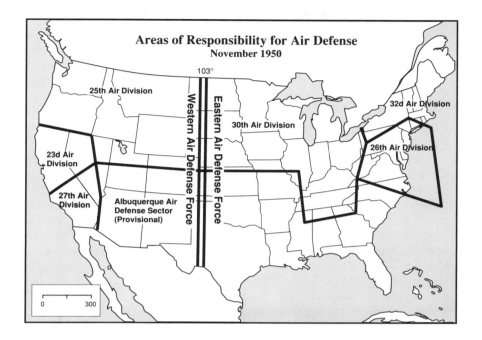

In early November the Air Force conducted a ground observer test in the east designed primarily "to revive interest of current members . . . tired from lack of activity." The final report indicated that, while enthusiasm was generally high, the GOC, with its present manning and training, could provide continuous tracks to the radar system only in a few areas. The exercise confirmed that recruitment and training remained the most urgent immediate tasks. Station personnel frequently mishandled ground observer information, failing to correlate it properly with information from radars. The report recommended that radar station commanders encourage teamwork among Air Force members and civilian volunteers. [38]

Reorganization and the Impact of the Chinese Intervention

A mid-1950 reorganization assigned the tactical forces from CONAC's numbered air forces to regional air defense and tactical air organizations, but almost immediately planning started for another, far more extensive change. Before the Korean War, Vinson and the House

Armed Services Committee expressed displeasure with progress in air defense. The Committee also questioned whether the Air Force was making its best effort to provide sufficient air support for the Army. In May 1950, Vinson told Maj. Gen. Thomas D. White, Air Force congressional liaison officer, that the Air Force had to increase the resources and efficiency of its tactical forces or risk losing its mission to the Marine Corps.[39] Although joking, Vinson made an important point that the Air Force heeded.

The Air Staff began planning to reorganize CONAC in response to Congress's and its own concerns about the strength of the tactical and air defense forces. Staff members consulted Whitehead, who suggested establishing a separate air defense command so that air defense activities could receive undivided attention and supervision. Reiterating a suggestion Stratemeyer had made two years earlier, Whitehead asked that the new headquarters be moved inland to make it less vulnerable, proposing Ent Air Force Base, Colorado, as a location. He also asked that a third regional command be formed, a Central Air Defense Force. He reasoned that when the Eastern and Western air defense forces became fully staffed, logistical and administrative difficulties would arise.[40]

On November 10, 1950, Vandenberg and Twining notified Whitehead that the Air Force had approved activation of a separate Air Defense Command with headquarters on Ent. Whithead's other recommendation that a third air defense region be formed remained undecided.[41]

In addition to making air defense the sole mission of a major command, the Air Force reestablished TAC as a major command. As Vandenberg explained to General John K. Cannon, then serving as head of U.S. Air Forces in Europe:

> Reduction of strength and the [postwar] economy program necessitated consolidation of Air Defense Command and Tactical Air Command into CONAC. Our increased strength now indicates the reestablishedment of these commands under these headquarters. I feel that this must be done at once. I propose to assign Whitehead as Air Defense commander and you to command the TAC with your headquarters at Langley. Your backing . . . in the tactical field and your standing with the Army . . . uniquely qualifies [sic] you for this command.

The reorganization provided for an increase to three major Air Force commands—a new Air Defense Command under Whitehead, a reestablished Tactical Air Command under Cannon, and a restructured Continental Air Command—with jurisdiction over the air defense and tactical forces, when before there had been just one. The primary task of CONAC would be to administer and supervise the Air Reserve forces. Headquarters USAF set December 1, 1950, as the effective date for the reorganization. Whitehead began selecting who on his staff would accompany him to Ent and who would remain on Mitchel as a cadre for the new CONAC to be established there.[42]

Whitehead and the staff officers who accompanied him to Colorado Springs were handicapped by the uncertainty of Air Force programs that changed several times in the weeks immediately before and after fighting started in Korea. When the war began, the Air Force expected by mid-1954 to have 69 wings (the Air Force described a wing as 2 or more squadrons and support elements). In August 1950 Vandenberg told the JCS that the Air Force required 130 wings to meet its commitments in Korea while maintaining combat-ready forces in Europe and the continental United States. The Chiefs decided on a 95-wing program, and in September President Truman agreed.[43]

Neither the JCS nor the President clarified just when the Air Force would actually attain 95 wings. From August until November 1950 budgetary pressures and the satisfactory progress of the war in Korea postponed a decision on just when the Air Force would expand to meet its new goals. This situation changed abruptly when the Chinese Communists launched a massive counterattack against United Nations forces on November 26. On December 15 in a radio and television report to the American people, Truman declared a national emergency. The true significance of the Chinese attack, he said, proved that the Communist leaders were "willing to push the world to the brink of general war to get what they want." Secretary of State Dean Acheson told Congress that "the Russians [were] behind all these movements" and the United States had "to face the possibility now that anything can happen anywhere at any time."[44] In ordering his Air Force commanders to take whatever actions they deemed necessary to increase readiness and effectiveness in their forces, Vandenberg noted that the JCS believed the Chinese attack increased the chances for a general war.[45] The Chiefs recommended that forces and equipment scheduled for 1954 be ready by 1952 or sooner, and Acheson's successor as Secretary of Defense, George C. Marshall, and President Truman approved their proposals.[46]

Congress approved Truman's requests for supplemental funds to meet the new goals set for 1952.[47] For the Air Force this included a special appropriation for the mobile radar program and increases in radar and aircraft procurement. Congress also supported the President's imposition of mandatory control over civilian air traffic in an emergency. As of December 27, 1950, civilian and military aircraft operating within the air defense identification zones had to file flight plans for air defense identification purposes.[48] Truman and Marshall also increased the call to active duty of Reservists and National Guardsmen to meet manpower requirements engendered by the decision to move military programs ahead two years, and the President decided the states would be primarily responsible for implementing civil defense measures, with the newly created federal Civil Defense Administration providing coordination and guidance.[49]

The Air Force intended to supply Whitehead with forty-five fighter-interceptor squadrons (constituting approximately fifteen of the ninety-five wings allocated) under the new 1952 program.[50] As head of ADC, Whitehead hoped to upgrade his command's capabilities immediately. Finletter assisted by ordering the federalization of fifteen Air National Guard fighter squadrons in February 1951 (he was delegated to do so) and of another six squadrons in March, and by assigning them to ADC.[51] Twining also earmarked an additional fifteen National Guard fighter squadrons for the air defense mission and obtained Truman's permission to authorize Whitehead to federalize them in an emergency. As Twining told Maj. Gen. Milton A. Reckord, Chief of the National Guard Bureau, Whitehead could now use all Air Guard forces in an imminent or actual enemy air attack.[52]

With the additional funds contained in the 1952 budget, the Air Force increased orders for all-weather interceptors (F–94s, F–89s, and F–86Ds), and Air Training Command prepared to expand radar observer and all-weather interceptor schools for pilots. If aircraft deliveries and aircrew training progressed as anticipated, all forty-five of ADC's fighter-interceptor squadrons would be ready for all-weather operations by mid-1953.[53]

A potentially embarrassing situation developed when the Air Staff informed Vandenberg that the permanent radar system could not be completed according to the deadline Under Secretary McCone had given to the House Armed Services Committee. McCone had told Vinson that the first twenty-four stations would be operating by March 1, 1951, and the rest by the following July. Although construction had proceeded smoothly, equipment deliveries had fallen behind schedule, and installation of the new radars proved more difficult than expected.[54]

The Air Force had initially planned to use older equipment of the type deployed in the Lashup system on many of the permanent stations. The basic Lashup radar, the long-range AN/CPS-5, could not provide low-altitude coverage. Although funds became available to purchase new equipment for all permanent stations after the start of the Korean War, some on the Air Staff favored moving equipment from Lashup stations onto permanent stations as soon as construction ended. Whitehead objected, and Lt. Gen. Idwal H. Edwards, Deputy Chief of Staff for Operations in the Air Staff, supported him. Discussions, during a conference in Edwards's office on December 6, 1950, assured Whitehead that Lashup equipment would not be moved to the permanent sites or decommissioned until the new sites could receive the new radars.[55] However, the older World War II–type radar, the CPS-5, at only 165 miles outranged the first new radar deployed, the CPS–6B. Like its World War II predecessors, the CPS–6B could not provide low-altitude coverage. Its new moving-target indicator, expected to improve tracking coverage of aircraft, also failed to live up to expectations.[56]

Whitehead did not fully appreciate all this when he opposed moving Lashup equipment onto permanent sites. The decision meant the Air Force could not meet the deadline for completing the first-priority radar stations nor the July 1951 deadline for completing the permanent system. McCone reluctantly wrote Vinson that completion dates were based on the plan to use older radars, operational on interim sites, in new sites until improved radars could be produced and installed. Now, however, because of the entry of the Chinese Communists into the Korean War, the Air Force again believed the possibility of a general war existed. Under the circumstances, the Air Force did not want to risk transferring older radars to new sites and losing radar coverage temporarily. Completion of the permanent system would be delayed until at least November 1951, and McCone asked the House Armed Services Committee for patience and understanding. Worker strikes had interfered with equipment delivery, and shortages of building materials had slowed construction and installation. Still, said McCone, the Air Force intended to overcome these difficulties and provide the nation with the best possible aircraft control and warning service as soon as practicable.[57]

Although McCone's explanation appeared to satisfy the Armed Services Committee, not everyone in Congress thought the air defense programs moved as fast as they should. Senator Henry Cabot Lodge's belief that "domestic air defenses are so feeble as almost to invite attack" led him to propose expanding the Air Force to 150 groups and, apparently, allocating far greater resources to air defense.[58]

While Lodge's suggestion to expand the Air Force was greeted enthusiastically by Air Force leaders, they expressed concern that it might precipitate an immediate overinvestment in air defense to the detriment of the strategic forces. Their concern reflected the theme that prevailed through the history of continental air defense. From the mid-1930s, the Air Force had advocated air defenses capable of exacting an extreme price from any attacker of the American homeland, but few if any Air Force leaders believed even the most potent air defense could, by itself, ensure a favorable outcome in an intercontinental war. For that purpose, strategic forces needed to be primed and ready for offensive action. As air defense assumed more public significance, the Air Force became increasingly disturbed when emphasis on air defense came at the expense of SAC.

In early 1951 Vandenberg told the House Committee on Appropriations that the Air Force believed "the most tenable means to prevent large numbers of atomic bombs from dropping on this country is to retaliate by destroying these weapons and the means for their delivery at their source." Strangely, the congressmen did not challenge this statement. They might have questioned how, if the United States chose to forgo the option of a first strike attack, the Air Force planned to "retaliate" by destroying bombers and bombs "at their source." The Air Force had claimed repeatedly that the Soviet atomic threat was credible only if the Soviets used their complete supply of bombers and weapons in attacking the United States.[59]

Vandenberg believed an adequate air defense system contributed to deterrence.* But, in what became an oft-quoted statement, he announced publicly in February 1951 that the most the American people could expect from the air defense system was for it to destroy thirty percent of attacking bombers before they reached their targets. He realized many Americans would be shocked to find the nation so vulnerable to air attack. Putting most of the Air Force budget into building static defenses, however, was not the answer. "Even if we had many more interceptor planes and AA [antiaircraft] guns and a radar screen that blanketed all approaches to our boundaries," he said, "a predictable 70 percent of the enemy's planes would penetrate our defenses." Regardless, as Chief of Staff he promised that the Air Force would do everything within its power to make U.S. air defenses the best in the world. But he wanted Americans to accept the fact that "the offensive always has a crushing advantage in aerial warfare, and there is no prospect that the balance will change in the foreseeable future." [60]

Vandenberg based his estimate of maximum effectiveness of an air defense system on the findings of a committee led by Dr. Valley. In March 1950 the Valley Committee estimated that the system proposed in the Blue Book plan would destroy about ten percent of enemy bombers. The committee members' subsequent investigations led them to believe the Air Force could raise this to thirty percent by bringing present equipment and forces to peak efficiency. In the meantime, while the Air Force attempted to reach this goal, Valley recommended that MIT establish an air defense laboratory. The laboratory would research and develop new equipment, including computers, for automating data handling and transmission which might eventually enable the defense systems to destroy far more than thirty percent of an enemy bomber fleet attacking the United States.[61]

---

*Deterrence, which became a commonly used term in the Cold War period, had been practiced in relations between contending parties throughout history. A good definition is supplied by military analyst John M. Collins [*Grand Strategy: Principles and Practices* (Annapolis, Md.: Naval Institute Press, 1973), pp 34-35]:

> Deterrence aims at obviating war. It is a compound of threats, the *capability* to carry them out, and the *will* to execute, if necessary. Successful combinations preclude unwanted aggression by imposing on deterees the prospect of exorbitant costs in relation to anticipated gains. The product is stability.

Using the skills of civilian scientists in projects of military significance was not new to the Air Force, but the use of scientists for matters of air defense soon became unprecedented. Some of the nation's outstanding scientists devoted themselves to developing advanced air defense systems; their efforts were crucial to the system that emerged in the second half of the 1950s. However, when some scientists proposed to the Air Force what seemed an optimal defense system, disagreements developed between the scientists and the airmen.

After the Chinese moved their forces into Korea in November 1950 and world tensions increased, the Air Force began to analyze the effectiveness of various weapons systems suggested by Valley, as well as of those suggested by the Weapons Systems Evaluation Group (WSEG) organized by the Secretary of Defense and comprised of military officers and civilians. The WSEG had been making an independent study of air defense since early 1950. It had concluded that the existing system was dangerously inadequate and that the one scheduled for operation in 1952 would be little improved. [62]

On the basis of Valley's and the WSEG's evaluations and recommendations, the Air Force moved to have leading scientists at MIT, over the objections of some faculty members who objected to the university's continued involvement in military research and development, work on the air defense problem. MIT President James R. Killian, Jr., became convinced that, if the university could improve the nation's defenses, it should do so. [63] He insisted that a new study group be formed to confirm the need for an air defense laboratory and to select the projects it should investigate. Killian also insisted that, if the laboratory was established, its resources and findings be made available to the Army and the Navy. Thus could MIT research requirements for fleet defense operations and defense of overseas military bases as well as those for continental air defense. [64] The Air Force agreed with Killian's conditions, and a new study group called Project CHARLES, led by Dr. F. Wheeler Loomis of the University of Illinois, began to examine the feasibility of an air defense laboratory. [65]

Vandenberg wrote Killian about the major deficiencies in the air defense system that the Air Force hoped the laboratory (if established) would solve. Paramount among them, according to the Chief of Staff, was that verbal and manual methods of communicating and displaying aircraft position plots obtained by radar were too slow, used telephone lines inefficiently, and could not deal with a high level of air traffic. Vandenberg believed the Air Force needed "improved means for the rapid collection, transmission, processing, and display of information on the air situation. All these things should, as far as possible, be done automatically and without human intervention." He was also disturbed by the Air Force's inability to track low-flying aircraft on radar. He outlined

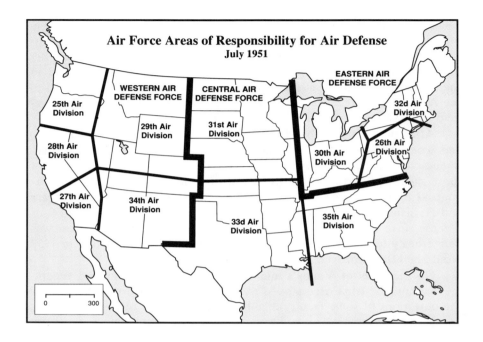

Air Force Areas of Responsibility for Air Defense
July 1951

EASTERN AIR DEFENSE FORCE

WESTERN AIR DEFENSE FORCE

CENTRAL AIR DEFENSE FORCE

25th Air Division

29th Air Division

31st Air Division

32d Air Division

28th Air Division

30th Air Division

26th Air Division

27th Air Division

34th Air Division

33d Air Division

35th Air Division

0   300

related needs as including airborne radar equipment that would afford true all-weather capability and a method to detect aircraft approaching the United States by overwater routes. This latter need presented a special problem because of the curvature of the earth and the line-of-sight radar beam. Radar could detect hostile aircraft flying at high altitudes only about an hour before they reached the American coastlines. Low-flying planes could be detected only a few minutes *after* they crossed the coastlines. Radar picket ships and patrol aircraft could alleviate these problems somewhat but, in the number needed for adequate coverage, would be very expensive to operate. In summary, Vandenberg told Killian:

> The foregoing problems by no means exhaust the list of technical difficulties faced by the Air Force in connection with its responsibility for air defense. Among others I might mention the problem of bringing all-weather fighters safely back to base under instrument conditions; the problem of coordinating fighter interceptors, antiaircraft artillery, ground-countermeasures; the problem of controlling friendly air traffic in such a way that a minimum interference with normal operations is produced, while the identification of friendly aircraft is facilitated and so on.[66]

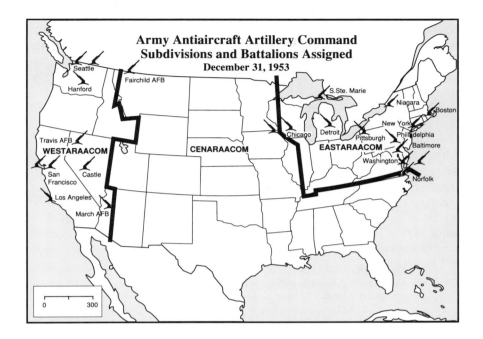

The need for an air defense laboratory to investigate the myriad problems seemed obvious to Vandenberg. Clearly, the Air Force was determined at this stage to forge ahead with its laboratory approach to air defense. From all indications, the Air Force had the utmost faith in the scientists.

Content in the knowledge that some of the nation's best scientific talent would soon be delving into the air defense problem, Whitehead proceeded to organize his new command. Notwithstanding minimal facilities at Ent and scarce housing at Colorado Springs, Whitehead and his staff remained optimistic. They were especially relieved, as was Twining, that ADC Headquarters at last operated inland, a less appealing target for enemy raiders. They were also pleased that the command was far from the distractions offered by New York City, in contrast to the situation at Mitchel Air Force Base.[67]

General Irvine's Army Antiaircraft Artillery Command Headquarters also left Mitchel to join ADC in Colorado Springs. Because of crowding on Ent, Irvine and his staff worked in a hotel in downtown Colorado Springs. There they prepared to take command on April 10, 1951, of forces consisting of 23 battalions—6 of automatic weapons, 9 of 90-mm guns, and 8 of 120-mm guns.[68]

No sooner had ADC been activated than Whitehead reopened his case for a third regional command to supplement the Eastern and Western air defense forces. In late January 1951 Twining agreed; Central Air Defense Force activated on March 1, 1951, with headquarters on Grandview Air Force Base (redesignated Richards-Gebaur AFB in 1957), south of Kansas City.[69]

For the next six months Whitehead concentrated on organizing and readying his forces for any eventuality. Then, having done his best to bring ADC to peak efficiency, he decided to retire because of ill health. Although Headquarters USAF disappointed him with less support than he believed his job required, he left gracefully. "Having had the privilege," as he expressed it, "of guiding ADC through its first half-year of separate existence," he told Vandenberg that it had been "a trying time for all of us as we worked to organize this command during a period of unparalleled peacetime expansion." Essentially, he said, it had been a case of improvisation in many areas:

> Our supply of skilled and experienced personnel has been meager. We had to utilize our materiel sources to the limit. In many cases, fighter squadrons which have just been called to active duty remain on barely adequate bases because permanent ones . . . could not be made available economically in a short time. All work done on the temporary bases was limited to the rudiments of necessity. In most cases the original squadron equipment was retained and shepherded carefully. A similar program was followed for the AC&W program . . . . Sites originally designed for smaller numbers of personnel, are necessarily accommodating many.[70]

General Benjamin W. Chidlaw, a graduate of West Point, replaced Whitehead. Although he had commanded tactical air forces in World War II, he earned his reputation in technical and engineering assignments; he had directed the first Air Force jet engine and aircraft development programs. As head of the Air Materiel Command, he had been closely associated with air defense matters, especially those dealing with acquisition and installation of equipment in radar stations.[71] Because air defense appeared destined to become a concept imbued in sophisticated technology, Chidlaw seemed the perfect officer to lead ADC.

Chidlaw examined closely the assets and capabilities of ADC against the demands of the mission. He had been led by Vandenberg's public statements to believe that under the ninety-five-wing buildup ADC would be capable of stopping two or three of every ten attacking bombers. After looking more closely at the matter, he believed Vandenberg had been too optimistic. That, exclaimed Chidlaw in an Air Force major commanders' meeting, "scared the hell out of me but plenty!" He told the conferees in November 1951:

General Benjamin W. Chidlaw

I said to myself . . . how do you know you're right—how do you know that your people have come up or even close to being right? Well, the answer was call in the greybeards, the scientists, the mathematicians . . . and let's see if the odds are of such . . . an order. This I did. First, I called RAND. They have been studying this problem for many, many months. Their figures coincided with mine almost on the button. Now I got more scared than ever, so I thought I had better check again. Get a checker to check the checker. So, we did that. We talked with personnel of the Weapons Systems Evaluation Group . . . . We got hold of Dr. Valley and his crew . . . at Cambridge . . . . All agreed that this figure of ten percent could, even under certain conditions generally adverse to the defense, be overly optimistic. [72]

In October 1951, RAND, which had been performing air defense studies since early 1947, submitted a major study of requirements for 1952 to 1953. Concluding that the Soviets would possess from 100 to 500 Tu–4 bombers armed with 100 atomic bombs by the end of 1953, RAND analysts warned that the air defenses would not be able to cope with such a threat. They recommended that ADC's data handling, aircraft identification, and ability to guard against low-level attack be improved rapidly. The WSEG concluded similarly. It emphasized low-level defense, warning that new intelligence revealed that Soviet long-range forces were developing such tactics. [73]

Evaluations made by RAND and WSEG supported the recommendations and conclusions of the final Project CHARLES report. The report surmised that technology existed for solving air defense problems and suggested that MIT proceed to organize an air defense laboratory as proposed by Valley and seconded by Vandenberg. Killian and MIT agreed, and when the Air Force accepted the major cost of the venture, the Army and Navy assented. By December 1951, MIT had instituted the so-called LINCOLN Project, predecessor of the Lincoln Laboratory. [74]

Loomis, leader of Project CHARLES, agreed to serve as Lincoln's first director. He continued work started by the Valley Committee to find a "quick fix" for current air defense equipment and operational problems, but the major LINCOLN Project program was to develop a centralized digital air defense system, as begun by the Valley Committee. This decision marked a watershed in continental air defense. [75]

Valley and his associates decided that, in the long run, the permanent system then being deployed could best be characterized as "an animal . . . lame, purblind, and idiot-like . . . , [and] of the comparatives, idiotic is the strongest." Valley thought that it made "little sense for us to strengthen the muscles [weapons], sinew [communications], or the eyes [radar], if there is no brain [a data-processing center]." [76]

As Valley saw the problem, even after the permanent system was fully established, air defense would remain a local operation, without central control. Telephone and teletype communications remained far too slow to permit an overall air defense commander rapid decisionmaking as the air battle whirled around him. Even if the central commander received all the timely information from the various radar stations, he could not assimilate the voluminous incoming data quickly enough. At the local level, targets identified on radar were recorded on plexiglass with grease pencils. Moreover, radio communication between weapons controllers and interceptor pilots lacked speed and precision. According to the Valley Committee the entire air defense apparatus was woefully sluggish. [77]

Although these problems might have seemed insurmountable, Valley believed he recognized an answer in automation—specifically the computer. After World War II, industrial applications of automation had just begun and military applications were only dimly perceived. This situation, however, would soon change.

In 1946 the first all-electronic digital calculator was tested and operated. The next year at MIT, Dr. Jay W. Forrester designed a computer called WHIRLWIND. Its program, funded by the Office of Naval Research, originally sought to analyze aircraft stability. Forrester envisioned his machine as being equipped to accept radar pulses that "could

150

Plexiglass plotting board at the Combat Operations Center, Ent Air Force Base

trigger the machine to calculate airplane speeds, directions, and distances, all within microseconds." Some Air Force officers in research and development, Saville prominent among them, believed the computer could eventually be used for air traffic control and air defense. In air traffic control, the computer would be tasked with keeping planes apart; in air defense, it could provide information allowing aircraft to come together, as with fighters intercepting enemy bombers. Largely through the persuasive efforts of Saville, then Deputy Chief of Staff for Development, the Air Force decided to share the costs of WHIRLWIND development with the Navy.[78]

By mid-1952 the Lincoln Laboratory led the way in development of the computerized air defense system. As Secretary of the Air Force Finletter pointed out, the Air Force now had some of the most eminent scientists of World War II and postwar years at work on the problem. He was confident that "no other source . . . either in education or industry possessed an air defense development potential to [equal] that of MIT." [79]

Confronting Realities

Despite all of the Air Force's hopes for the computerized network of the future, present air defense problems still needed solutions. Regardless of the best Air Force efforts to expedite completion of the permanent radar system, it became operational at approximately the time scheduled. When Chidlaw took over ADC, only one station functioned: the 25th Air Division's station on McChord Air Force Base, Washington, equipped with new CPS–6B combination search and height-finding radars. Fourteen more permanent stations came into operation by the end of 1951, two equipped with the first AN/FPS–3 search radars, and the others with CPS–6Bs.[80]

Fortunately for the Air Force, pressure from the House Armed Services Committee regarding progress on radar stations lessened as the situation in Korea stabilized. Twining and his top Air Staff officers had momentarily considered slowing work on other projects to speed completion of the radar stations, but reduced tensions influenced them not to do so. The program therefore moved ahead, with the permanent system nearly completed by late 1952.[81]

To obtain the skilled personnel required for staffing radar stations, the Air Staff agreed to let ADC hire civilian experts. By summer 1951, about 300 electronic engineers from the Philco Corporation worked for ADC. The program also included communications specialists from the Radio Corporation of America. These technical representatives worked closely with ADC personnel for many years.[82]

With the establishment of Lincoln Laboratory, changes occurred in the permanent system. By early 1953, Chidlaw commanded eleven divisions whose sectors encompassed the whole nation. Chidlaw also commanded three regional centers and his own Combat Operations Center on Ent, none of which had even been contemplated in the original program. Now, the Air Force looked forward to the centralized system as the best way to facilitate the changeover from manual to automated systems. The Combat Operations Center on Ent also reflected the pivotal role Colorado Springs began to assume in all facets of air defense.[83]

ADC had planned to add forty-four mobile radar stations to the emerging permanent system: twenty-four to provide protection for six SAC bases and twenty to serve as low-altitude "gap fillers."[84] On January 18, when the final site surveys for the forty-four stations were complete and contracts for their construction were arranged, Chidlaw suspended all activity on the mobile programs. His staff, along with RAND and WSEG analysts, had decided that, for maximum efficiency, ADC defenses had to be deployed in a double perimeter in the northeast, the

Early computers. Patch panel of an early IBM computer (*above*) and component parts of a UNIVAC (*below*).

northwest, and California. These deployments would be supplemented by island defenses around the SAC and Atomic Energy Commission installations located beyond the perimeter-protected areas.[85] As described by Maj. Gen. Frederic H. Smith, ADC Vice Commander, the goal would be to encircle these "complexes of vital targets . . . [with] two lines of radar, with the inner perimeter located approximately 70 miles from the edge of the target area, and the outer line extended 120 miles." ADC planned to base its interceptor forces within the perimeter lines to detect and destroy enemy bombers before they reached their targets.[86]

153

General Frederic H. Smith

Although the term "double perimeter" sounded innovative, the concept merely reiterated the principle of selected, in-depth deployment Saville and his staff had called for in 1948. By reopening the case for the concept, Chidlaw said, in effect, that the permanent radar system served as the nucleus for in-depth air defenses around selected areas. As a first step, Chidlaw asked Vandenberg to allow ADC to replan the location of the forty-four mobile stations. Vandenberg, in turn, directed Twining to have the Air Force Council* study the matter, assuring that it would be considered within the context of overall Air Force requirements. A major question asked whether SAC bases would receive adequate protection under the double perimeter system. The council answered yes, and on February 13, 1952, Vandenberg recommended that the Air Force proceed with the double perimeter plan. Vandenberg pledged Chidlaw complete Air Staff support, but he warned the plan's implementation was subject to available funds.[87]

In October 1952 Chidlaw called for a second-phase mobile radar program, and in mid-1953 he proposed a third phase. The resulting 104 stations were all to be operational by 1956. The Air Force approved

---

* The Air Force Council was established by Vandenberg on April 26, 1951, to speed the policy and decisionmaking process in the Air Staff. Chaired by Twining, the council consisted by July 1951 of the five Deputy Chiefs of Staff and the Inspector General [Futrell, *Ideas, Concepts, Doctrine*, p. 154]. An earlier Air Council had been formed in June 1941 with the establishment of the AAF.

Chidlaw's recommendations, again pending the availability of funds.[88] Smith told the Air Staff that the addition of 104 stations would provide ADC solid coverage at medium and high altitudes over the double perimeter zones. These radars would not, however, solve ADC's continuing dilemma in detecting aircraft flying below 5,000 feet. Smith suggested that small automatic radars be developed to supply low-altitude data. The Air Staff approved the requirement, contingent, as always, on funding.[89] Electronic detection of aircraft flying at low altitudes continued to elude the Air Force, despite its best efforts to solve the problem, in the years ahead.

The Air Force stepped up attempts to extend the outer fringes of the double perimeter areas seaward. Every major air defense study since 1947 had urged that picket ships and early-warning and control aircraft be developed and acquired. Unfortunately, progress had been thwarted by lack of money and the inability of the Air Force and Navy to agree on how and where the overwater detection forces would operate and, most importantly, who would command them.

Shortly after the Korean War started, Whitehead requested that Headquarters USAF ask the Navy to assign enough picket destroyers for ten stations on the east and west coasts.[90] Vandenberg promptly passed the request to Admiral Sherman, Chief of Naval Operations, who died before he could act on the issue. His successor, Admiral William M. Fechteler, promised to make the ships available, but probably not before 1954. Vandenberg asked the Navy to provide the ships sooner, to no avail. The Navy, believing that destroyer-type picket ships should be developed for both fleet and continental air defense, had begun to reequip former destroyer escorts for air defense duty and had stationed one off the east coast to work with ADC in determining radar, communication, and procedural needs. The Air Force approved these developments, but thought the sea service did not move fast enough in providing picket ships for home air defense and in assigning them to stations on the coasts.[91]

Navy reluctance to commit to an expensive picket vessel program to support the Air Force continental defense mission figured prominently in the Air Force decision to procure early-warning and control aircraft. The Navy had pioneered the use of early-warning aircraft in World War II and had begun to modify its Lockheed Constellation for fleet defense in 1950.[92] The ADC and Air Proving Ground kept abreast of the projects, and by spring 1951 were impressed sufficiently to suggest that the Air Force purchase forty of the aircraft. By mid-1951, the Air Staff had developed a program for Lockheed to deliver ten EC–121s (the Air Force designation for early-warning versions of the plane) by spring 1953 and thirty-eight over the succeeding two years. The program grew subsequently to include fifty-six planes.[93]

155

With approval of the double perimeter concept in early 1952, Childlaw decided to locate the airborne early-warning force on two bases, one on each coast. The forces were expected to extend the radar coverage and to detect an approaching enemy aircraft in time for interceptors to scramble and engage bombers as far seaward as possible. By mid-1953, ADC radar operators and technicians trained at Navy airborne early-warning schools in San Diego, California, and Patuxent, Maryland. Because of labor difficulties, however, Lockheed delayed the delivery date for the EC–121s to February 1954.[94] The Air Force could only prepare its personnel to accept the aircraft, and wait.

Without reliable low-altitude radar, the Air Force relied on the civilian GOC. As ADC commander, Whitehead had done his best to institute around-the-clock operations for the GOC, but he never reached this goal. His determined recruiting effort paid off, for in the period after the start of the Korean War, large numbers of patriotic citizens volunteered their services in providing for the nation's defense.[95]

In June 1951 ADC employed 8,000 observation posts and 26 filter centers staffed by 210,000 volunteers in the first nationwide exercise of the GOC. The two-day test was not impressive. The average time for data to pass from observation posts through filter centers to radar stations that directed interceptor operations exceeded eight minutes. By then, many bombers would have completed their missions.[96]

Soon after the tests, the Air Force realized it would have to make the GOC more effective; it had no alternative for supplying adequate low-altitude coverage.[97] During Childlaw's first ADC commanders' conference, held in Colorado Springs in October 1951, Vice Commander Smith proposed that the GOC operate continuously along the Atlantic and Pacific coasts and along the Canadian-American border. At a minimum, said Smith, the GOC should operate around the clock in those areas from May through October, when long daylight periods prevailed over most of the Soviet Union. American intelligence sources assumed that, if the Soviets attacked, they would do so in daylight to give their air defenses an advantage against SAC retaliatory assaults.[98]

Smith increased his efforts to improve the GOC after the commanders' conference. A year after the Korean War began, the American people perceived less of a threat of general war and their patriotic urge to support observation posts subsided. To overcome this apathy, Smith believed the Air Force had to demonstrate why the GOC was vital.[99]

Accordingly, Smith put the GOC on twenty-four-hour-a-day operations and increased its training. A test on October 24, 1951, of Eastern Air Defense Force's ability to assume its posts in an emergency intensified his commitment to continuous operations. An hour into the test, only twenty-nine percent of the observation post personnel had reported in; after three hours, only seventy-five percent of the posts were staffed and operating. These results supported Smith's contention that the GOC served little purpose unless it could respond rapidly to an actual attack.[100]

Chidlaw agreed completely with Smith. He asked Maj. Gen. Roger M. Ramey, Air Staff Director of Operations, to grant the GOC higher priority for funds, materiel, and personnel support. Chidlaw hoped to have at least a portion of the GOC on twenty-four-hour-a-day duty by spring 1952. The ADC chief told Ramey he knew that continuous operations of the GOC could raise concerns about an imminent enemy air attack; still he believed that he had to train and use all the forces available to him. Ramey soon afterward told Chidlaw that the Air Staff agreed to increase its support of the GOC.[101]

The news prompted Chidlaw's staff to plan to put 32 filter centers and 8,483 observation posts on 24-hour duty in 27 of the 36 states where the GOC would operate.[102] Subsequent exchanges between the Pentagon and Colorado Springs determined that the plan would become effective on May 17, 1952, and be called Operation SKYWATCH.[103] Vandenberg, announcing its beginning on April 23, said, "we are fulfilling the requirement for low altitude surveillance throughout a vital part of the nation. In so doing we are strengthening many of the weaknesses in the radar network since visual observers are effective in many cases where radar is of little or no aid."[104]

To the astonishment of the Air Force, the Association of Civil Defense Directors criticized SKYWATCH because of a letter issued by the Central Air Defense Force stating that SKYWATCH was not an emergency measure, only the next step in the orderly establishment of an air defense system. Civil defense leaders, however, thought that if conditions were so perilous as to demand placing the GOC on continuous operations, "this should be announced in unmistakable terms by appropriate authority."[105]

To help clarify the matter, the Air Force arranged a meeting in the Pentagon among Defense Department personnel, state civil defense officials, and representatives from the Civil Defense Administration. Here, Millard Caldwell, head of the Civil Defense Administration, supported the view held by the state civil defense spokesmen. He said that the Air Force had to be honest with the American people if it asked them to make the sacrifices required by SKYWATCH. "The people on Main Street," said Caldwell, "believe that the Air Force can keep the attacking planes, or a very high percentage of them, from getting through. . . ." Now, however, they heard they needed civil defense *and* a GOC.[106] Caldwell and the state civil defense officials apparently wanted the Air Force to emphasize the air defense threat, thereby calling attention to the concurrent need for more and better civil defense programs.

157

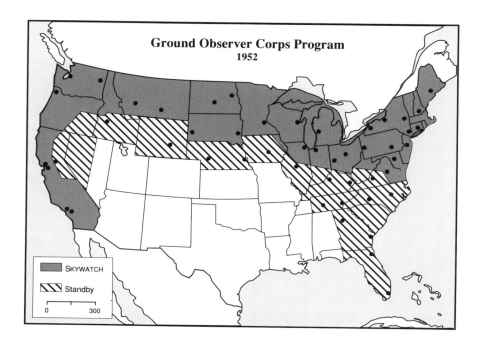

Air Force Secretary Finletter and Generals Twining, Chidlaw, and Smith, the principal Air Force representatives at the meeting, agreed the Air Force had failed to show the public the urgent need for the GOC. According to Finletter, while the JCS thought the year "1954 will be the most *dangerous* for the security of the United States," he referred to General Bradley's view that "this does not mean Soviet Russia will not precipitate World War III tomorrow." Therefore, stressed Finletter, the twenty-four-hour watch was needed to guard against the present, not a future, Soviet threat. Twining added that SKYWATCH would remain a vital element in the air defense network until effective low-altitude radars were developed and installed. [107]

The Air Force argument persuaded state and federal civil defense directors to support starting SKYWATCH in July 1952. The Air Force proceeded to launch a massive publicity campaign for the GOC, assisted by the Advertising Council Incorporated, a nonprofit organization sponsored by America's advertising agencies. President Truman pitched in by making a personal appeal for SKYWATCH. In addition, the Air Force public relations department composed pointed radio spot announcements, for example, "Who will strike the first blow in the next war, if and when it comes? America? Not very likely. No, the enemy will strike first. And they can do it too—right now the Kremlin has about a thousand planes within striking distance of your home." Another spot announcement heard was, "It may not be a very cheerful thought but the Reds right now have about a thousand bombers that are quite capable of destroying at least 89 American cities in one raid. . . . Won't you help protect your country, your town, your children? Call your local Civil Defense Office and join the Ground Observer Corps today." [108]

On July 14th SKYWATCH began. Contrary to the original plan calling for twenty-four-hour-a-day operation only from May through October, the Air Force decided to operate SKYWATCH year round. [109] The favorable response its publicity campaign elicited (by mid-1953 the GOC had about 305,000 volunteers) doubtlessly contributed to the Air Force decision. Although the GOC required many procedural, equipment, and facility improvements before it could be considered truly effective, the citizenry now seemed convinced of the necessity for SKYWATCH.

As the Air Force planned SKYWATCH, airborne control and warning, and the double-perimeter radar programs, its leaders knew their efforts would be worth little without Canadian assistance and cooperation. The history of Canadian and American cooperation for North American defense predated World War II, but like the Americans, the Canadians had improved their air defenses little after the war. It took the Soviet atomic explosion and the outbreak of the Korean War to galvanize them. Although Canada had a separate air defense organization since December 1948, as late as December 1950 it had only three operating radar stations. The problem this represented for Canada, and for the United States, was underscored by Whitehead's remark that "our highly industrialized, highly populated border, which just so happens to be that border facing the threat to our national security, is wide open and will continue to be so until we extend our presently programmed radar net northward." [110]

The U.S. Air Force and Royal Canadian Air Force had agreed on a jointly financed Radar Extension Program in mid-1950. In October 1950 the JCS established the U.S. Northeast Command as a unified command designed to defend the United States through the area defined by Labrador, Newfoundland, northeastern Canada, and Greenland, where the United States had obtained or leased bases during World War II. [111]

By November 1950 the United States and Canada agreed that the Radar Extension Program would consist of thirty-three radar stations. The United States would build and equip twenty-two and supply personnel for eighteen. The plan was submitted to the Permanent Joint Board on Defense on February 6, 1951, and soon after, the JCS and Canadian Combined Chiefs of Staff approved it. Secretary of Defense Marshall wrote to Secretary of State Acheson urging expedition of a formal agreement between the two countries so that U.S. and Canadian air forces could complete the program as soon as possible. [112] Expecting early action, the Canadians established an Air Defence Command on June 1, 1951. They also increased their fighter-interceptor force to six squadrons (the Canadian Air Force expanded to a total of nine interceptor squadrons during the Korean War) and expanded their temporary radar control and warning system to five stations.[113]

The urge to build up the air defenses, which was prevalent at the start of the Korean War and which had resurfaced when the Chinese entered the war, was beginning to fade. By April 1951 the United States still had not contributed to the Radar Extension Program, and the Commander of the Royal Canadian Air Force, Air Marshal Wilfred A. Curtis, was perturbed. Through the next decade, no group would advocate as forcefully for closer Canadian-American relations in air defense than the officers of the Canadian Air Force. Curtis wrote to Undersecretary McCone, asking that funds be provided as quickly as possible so that the Canadians could begin work on the stations. Quick action was necessary because of the limited period available for construction at many northern stations. McCone brought the matter to Finletter who got the issue moving. President Truman approved, and on June 13, 1951, the U.S. government released $20 million for construction of the radar stations. Hume Wrong, Canadian Ambassador to the United States, and Acheson formally concluded the agreement on August 1 in an exchange of notes. Agreeing with Wrong's request, official announcements avoided depicting the program as American military aid to Canada. They stated that the accord provided for establishing radar systems in Canada as part of the defense of North America.[114]

By June 1952 the joint Canadian-American committee on the Radar Extension Program was replaced with a greatly expanded agency that included personnel from the Canadian Air Defence Command, the American Air Defense Command, the Northeast Air Command, Headquarters USAF, and the Royal Canadian Air Force. The agency, designated "Project Pinetree Office," located in Ottawa, Ontario.* Stations constructed under its aegis would later become the Pinetree Line.[115]

Status of the Fighter-Interceptor Forces

In May 1951 Headquarters USAF redesignated all fighter squadrons assigned to air defense duty "fighter-interceptor" squadrons. This im-

---

* In related developments, the United States negotiated rights to base military personnel and to establish air defense forces in Greenland and Iceland. In both cases, precedents had been set during World War II. As they had done with Canada, Denmark (which exercised sovereignty over Greenland) and Iceland cooperated willingly with the United States.

plied, in part, that the squadrons were to be equipped and trained to fly intercept missions in all weather. While a few squadrons possessed this capability by mid-1953, most continued to be restricted to fair-weather operations. In ADC five squadrons still operated with F–51s, and fifteen operated with F–80, F–84, and F–86 day jets. Six ADC squadrons and all those assigned to the Alaskan Air Command and Northeast Air Command now had Lockheed F–94As and F–94Bs, welcome replacements for the completely inadequate F–82s. The Starfire was not really an all-weather interceptor; it lacked the deicing equipment needed to operate in winter skies.[116] Lt. Gen. Arthur C. Agan, destined to command ADC in the late 1960s, was a wing and air division commander when the F–94 was introduced. He described the Hughes radar as "fairly simple and fairly effective against the kind of targets that we had then. If [we] had a non-jamming target within the performance envelope that an F–94 could deal with—the F–94 could do the job." [117]

The F–94C model, an aircraft that included deicing equipment, was scheduled to be the Air Force's first all-weather interceptor. It was not flight tested until late June 1951 and not delivered to ADC until March 1953.[118] The Northrop F–89 Scorpion thus became the Air Force's first operational all-weather fighter. Design and engine problems prevented delivery to ADC of the first models, designated the F–89B, until June 1951. An improved "C" model debuted in January 1952, but shortly after, three disintegrated in the air, killing the crews. Because structural weaknesses in the aircraft apparently caused the accidents, Air Materiel Command restricted the operational speed of the aircraft to 350 knots pending correction of the problems. In the meantime, the Air Force issued a hold order on the purchase of additional Scorpions while Northrop worked to solve the problem.[119]

In summer 1952, eight airmen died when four more F–89Cs fell apart in the sky. Subsequently, the Air Force grounded all Scorpions until their airframes could be strengthened. To compensate for this action, the Air Staff temporarily transferred F–94As and F–94Bs from the Air Training Command to ADC. By mid-1953, the modified Scorpions went back into service, but hopes that the plane was finally reliable were dashed by more accidents. Another year passed before Northrop produced what was considered a trustworthy model, the F–89D, and the Air Force could begin to purchase and use these aircraft in greater numbers.[120]

In April 1953, ADC received the first North American F–86Ds. The Air Force had been somewhat skeptical about the worth of the one-man, all-weather version of the famed Sabre jet when General Saville first recommended it in 1949. However, by this time the Air Force had decided most ADC squadrons would be equipped with the "Dog," as some pilots affectionately called it. The F–86D had a limited range be-

Fighter-Interceptor Squadrons Assigned
December 1946 - June 1954

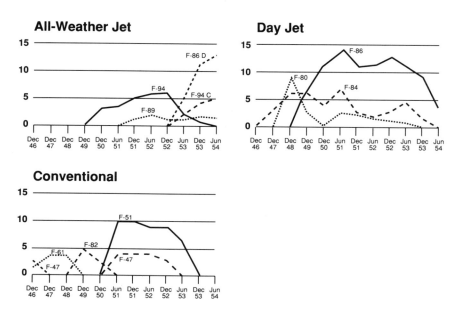

cause pilots had to use its fuel-consuming afterburners to reach altitude. The plane, bigger and heavier than the day Sabres, was less maneuverable. Still, problems with the F–86D did not approach the severity of those the Air Force suffered with the F–94 and especially with the F–89. By June 1953 fifteen ADC squadrons were changing to the F–86D, and others were preparing to receive it.[121]

All of the Air Force's interceptors in the 1950s were equipped with more sophisticated and lethal weapons. Many aircraft carried up to 104 so-called folding-fin air-to-air rockets, more powerful as interceptor weapons than machineguns or cannons. The rockets were conventional weapons, although the Air Force explored the possibility of using nuclear-tipped tactical rockets in future air defense.[122]

During this period the Hughes Aircraft Company worked closely with the Air Force to develop a revolutionary airborne radar. Beginning with Saville's experiments in the Florida air exercises of 1935, the Air Force had relied heavily on a GCI system to vector its aircraft onto the trail of approaching enemies. The evolution of radar allowed the weapons director on the ground to position an interceptor to conform with the blip the controller viewed on a radarscope. After receiving positioning directions from the controller, the pilot would turn on his nose radar

Fighter-Interceptor Aircraft on Hand
December 1950 - June 1954

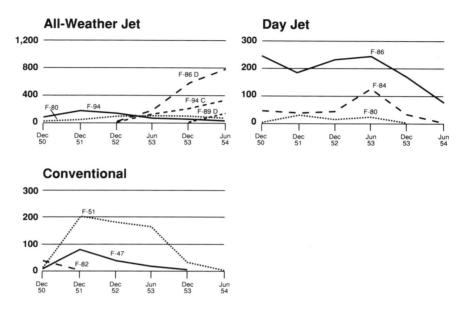

and seek the target. If the pilot found the "bandit" (an unidentified intruder would be referred to as a "bogey"), he would usually attempt to destroy him by attacking from behind, the so-called tail-on maneuver.

In the late 1940s, the Air Force and Hughes began developing another technique, the lead collision course. This technique would require a powerful fighter radar so that targets could be seen from much greater distances than previously possible. Since interception of an enemy from the side instead of from behind would enable an interceptor pilot to aim at a larger target, an improved radar would allow detection of an enemy from a greater distance, and the pilot could fire rockets at the side of the opposing aircraft without having to maneuver for a dangerous close-in tail attack. For this method to work, black box equipment had to be used to determine when to fire the rockets at a target's future position, calculated on the basis of its speed.[123]

The technology for the lead collision-course interceptor first appeared in the F–89D in 1953. With an enlarged Hughes E–6 radar, the system included an analog/digital computer interacting with an autopilot. Complementing these components were the Scorpion's 104 folding-fin air-to-air Mighty Mouse 2.75-inch rockets. Developed by Army Ordnance and first installed on the F–89B, the rockets could fire simulta-

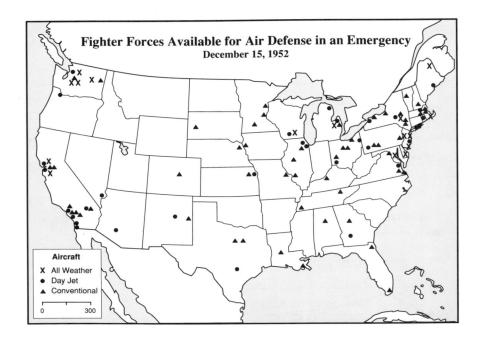

neously from wing pods to blanket "an area of sky bigger than a football field." [124] Further improvements in the electronics of the lead collision-course system were incorporated in the F–89H model and in the F–102, which became the premier Air Force interceptor in 1956.

The development of new electronic technology leading to more effective tactics for air interception resulted largely from Fairchild's and Saville's advocacy for the weapons systems approach—the development of an airframe around its various weapons systems—in procurement. Although synchronization in development and production was not all it might have been, black box units (that could be mounted or removed from aircraft in a single package) and other electronic components installed in aircraft were now recognized to be as important as the quality of the airframe itself in the development of a potent military aircraft.

While the burgeoning sophisticated technology in the Korean War period made continental air defense glamorous and exciting, crews and maintenance personnel left to guard the homeland often suffered considerable hardship. By December 1951 ADC regulations stipulated that four aircraft be kept on alert on each stateside airbase during daylight hours—two for takeoff in five minutes and two in fifteen minutes. The remaining aircraft in each squadron had to be ready to operate within three hours. When the all-weather F–94Cs began to arrive, night alert requirements

ADC Day Conventional Fighters (Jet)
Interceptors Possessed
1951 - 1954

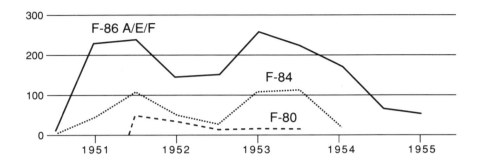

increased. Alert aircraft parked at the end of a runway; their crews lived alongside in trailers or a similar type of "ready shack." In 1952 alert hangars for the aircraft and aircrews began to be provided. As Chidlaw described life on the alert line:

> Pilots . . . in order to maintain the proper alert status spend as much as 100–101 hours a week on the base. Add to this the sleeping time and driving back-and-forth time required, and you get a picture of just how little time they have left for recreation or to spend with their families. This is an acute morale problem, but one which we see no ready solution. . . .[125]

Although the subsequent assignment of additional crewmembers and the gradual improvement of alert facilities ameliorated the situation, on flight lines and in radar stations long duty hours remained the norm in ADC.

The introduction of new, all-weather night fighters eliminated some of the boredom of training and alert duty. After flying the new aircraft, however, some pilots realized boredom had its advantages. General Daniel "Chappie" James, ADC commander in the late 1970s, recalled:

> From 1951 to 1956 I was intimately involved in the air defense mission. I use the word intimately advisedly. I submit there can be no greater intimacy between man and machine than for the man to be strapped to a flaming hulk of hardware over the ocean searching for an unknown on a stormy New England night. In the six years that I drove all-weather fighters there were many such occasions. I experienced my fair share of those heralded moments of stark terror.[126]

TABLE 1. ADC Day Fighters (Jet) Possessed

Aircraft	Jan 1, 1951	Jun 30, 1951	Dec 31, 1951	Jun 30, 1952	Dec 31, 1952	Jun 30, 1953	Dec 31, 1953	Jun 30, 1954	Dec 31, 1954
F–80A/C		47	35	18	17	15			
F–82F	26								
F–84C/D/G	43	109	46	21	110	115	21		
F–86A/E/F	236	241	145	154	263	229	177	64	53
Total	305	397	226	193	390	359	198	64	53

TABLE 2. Interceptor Squadrons Assigned ADC, by Type

Aircraft	Jan 1, 1951	Jun 30, 1951	Dec 31, 1951	Jun 30, 1952	Dec 31, 1952	Jun 30, 1953	Dec 31, 1953
F–47D		3	3	3	1	1	
F–47N		1	1	1	1		
F–51D		9	9	8	7	7	
F–51H		1	1	1			
F–80A		1	1				
F–80C		1	1	1	2	1	
F–82F	3						
F–84C		4	1	1	1		
F–84D	3	3	1				
F–84G					4	5	1
F–86A	15	11	10	8	6	6	4
F–86D					1	11	30
F–86E		3	1	2		1	1
F–86F				1	8	5	4
F–89B			2	2	1		
F–89C				1	2	3	3
F–94A		5	5	3	3	2	2
F–94B		2	5	7	6	6	1
F–94C						4	8
Total	21	44	41	39	43	52	54
Squadrons not equipped with aircraft	1	0	0	1	3	4	3
Squadrons possessing aircraft	20	44	41	38	40	48	51

In the first half of the 1950s, ADC commanders believed that Headquarters USAF did not appreciate fully the work, sacrifice, and difficulty air defense personnel experienced. Chidlaw noted almost all ADC officers received efficiency reports below comparable grades at other major commands. He believed this was due to ADC's higher standards and suggested that excellence be gauged throughout the Air Force as it was in his command.[127]

Chidlaw's successor, General Earle E. Partridge, demanded equal terms of recognition and promotion for ADC personnel. Low retention rates for all-weather interceptor crews and weapons controllers particularly distressed him. He blamed this on the fact that ADC was not permitted to award promotions for excellence in bombing and navigation competition, as SAC could. As he remonstrated to Twining:

> There is something wrong with a system that permits one command to promote its outstanding team members without allowing other commands to do the same. Surely the air crew who can consistently place their interceptor in a position to deliver a knockout blow against a high speed, high altitude enemy bomber or the controller who can consistently guide the air crew to a successful interception in adverse weather conditions deserve [sic] as much recognition as their SAC counterparts. I believe the defense of Pittsburgh, Cleveland, and Detroit, not to mention the SAC bases themselves, is as important to our interests as is the timely destruction of key targets within the Soviet Union.[128]

Spot promotions for ADC personnel, despite well-reasoned arguments presented by Partridge and his predecessors, did not come. The Air Force showed unequivocally where its priorities lay—in SAC.

Thus the Korean War had provided an impetus to air defense preparedness. The threat of general war produced stepped-up programs to improve all Air Force components for continental defense. Although facts were few concerning Soviet intentions, intelligence sources indicated the Soviets continued to update the Tu–4, to plan for a true intercontinental bomber, and to increase their atomic stockpile. In response, increased funding for U.S. air defense (and all other programs) allowed the Air Force to upgrade current components and investigate new technology for future systems. Yet, important questions remained. Air defense was necessary, but at what cost? Terms such as "no free ride," "minimum" air defense, "optimum" air defense, and "damage limitation" were bandied about in Air Force councils and among government officials and scientists studying the concept. Before a decision was reached on the size and scope of future air defense systems, these terms would have to be defined more precisely, as would the nature of the threat posed by Soviet bombers.

Chapter 7

An Integrated, Efficient, Highly Potent Air Defense System

In 1954 the administration of President Dwight D. Eisenhower supported the development of a large and sophisticated continental air defense buildup. Air defense would undergo a technological transformation to match in importance the development of radar in the late 1930s. However, the automated systems that would eventually revolutionize air defense operations were still being perfected in research laboratories in the early 1950s. For the forces on alert in the field, computerized systems remained years away. Field forces had to make the best use of equipment at hand, regardless how inadequate, and hope to meet the test if called upon. An incident during the spring of 1952 highlighted the problems of the defenses.

Next to the Real Thing

On April 16, 1952, Col. Woodbury M. Burgess, General Chidlaw's intelligence chief, received a "troublesome piece" of information from Headquarters USAF. The information, categorized as an "indication," implied that it came from a clandestine source and concerned Soviet military movements. Burgess and his intelligence staff remained in the ADC Combat Operations Center. By late in the evening they had received no further information to confirm the warning, so Burgess decided they could go home. Meanwhile, he informed Maj. Gen. Kenneth P. Bergquist, ADC operations deputy, of the special intelligence, and Burgess and Bergquist decided there was no reason at that time to inform either General Frederic H. Smith, ADC Vice Commander, or Chidlaw of the incident.

Shortly after midnight, the Western Air Defense Force operations center on Hamilton Air Force Base, California, notified Colorado Springs of four vapor trails sighted one hour and twenty-seven minutes earlier over Nunivak Island in the Bering Sea, heading east by southeast. The information originated at the Elmendorf, Alaska, center and was transmitted through McChord Air Force Base, Washington, which provided the only communications links between the two systems. A captain on duty in the intelligence section on Ent received the news and promptly phoned Colonel Burgess, who hurriedly returned to the Combat Operations Center. Once there, he directed that the Royal Canadian Air Force be informed of the sighting; he also notified General Bergquist who rushed back to the center.

By 0220 Bergquist had alerted his counterparts in the Eastern, Central, and Western air defense forces, and the various direction centers had been instructed to direct northern and coastal radar stations to be especially vigilant. Bergquist also attempted to confirm the sighting with the Alaskan center, but before the call could be completed, the line between McChord and Elmendorf went dead, leaving all involved "simply exasperated." Bergquist now phoned General Smith, saying "We have something hot—I think you better come over."

When Smith arrived in the Operations Center, he and Bergquist considered calling an Air Defense Readiness alert. This procedure, formulated and instituted by Whitehead, allowed ADC to bring individual sectors or the whole command onto full combat readiness. Smith and Bergquist had a difficult decision, because calling an alert would mean awakening hundreds of ADC and other Air Force personnel and ordering them to duty stations with no time for explanations. The result of such an order was uncertain since the procedure had never been tested.

No sooner had Bergquist and Smith begun considering what to do than the decision was, in effect, made for them. At 0310 the intelligence duty officer came running to Smith with word that "Eastern [Air Defense Force] has just called in and reported five 'unknowns' coming in over Presque Island [Maine]." One minute later Smith ordered ADC on full Air Defense Readiness alert. At the same time, notification went out to the air defense region commanders, to General LeMay of SAC, and to the USAF Command Post in the Pentagon over hot lines, specially installed for such emergency situations. At this time Smith also notified Chidlaw who, like air defense personnel all over the country, quickly reported for duty. Meanwhile, commanders of TAC, Air Research and Development Command, Air Proving Ground, and Air Training Command, all pledged to commit radar and fighter units in an emergency, were contacted by commercial toll calls. The Army Antiaircraft Artillery Command did not receive the alert until 0341. Then, General Irvine's staff ordered "all units on site to man their guns, and other units to prepare to move."

Within fifteen minutes from the time the alert was called, Ent, region, and division air defense centers began operating with full teams.

Also within fifteen minutes, telephone and teletype lines throughout the aircraft control and warning network were operating, an accomplishment Chidlaw called "A miracle of dead-of-night efficiency." On fighter bases, the number of aircraft in immediate readiness increased from 88 to 240 within the first hour.

Chidlaw canceled the operation at 0550. Communications had not been reestablished with Elmendorf, nor had the mysterious contrails over Nunivak been identified. In the east, sightings were narrowed to three "unknowns," which interceptors identified as friendly. These were French, British, and Pan American airliners that had drifted from their scheduled courses on flight plans other than those reported to the Presque Isle site. No one blamed the pilots; they had reported their changes in flight to Canadian flight-monitor stations. Communications between the stations and ADC's Presque Isle radar site had failed, and the course changes were not identified in the Eastern Air Defense Force's identification logs.

No sooner had Chidlaw canceled the alert than the Pentagon called the Operations Center. Air Staff officers believed that ADC had panicked and taken more drastic measures than the situation required. Chidlaw, however, refused the call and told Bergquist, "Tell 'em if the situation occurs again, I'll do the same thing," and he went off to bed.[1]

Later, when the incident could be seen in greater perspective, the Air Staff acknowledged the "general misinterpretation of its meaning" regarding the original intelligence of Soviet military movements. Even more important, the Air Staff admitted that the alert pointed up many weaknesses in operating procedures. Improvements needed to address a broadened role for the USAF Command Post in future alerts, and the installation of hot lines among all commands committed to furnishing augmented forces for air defense in an emergency became urgent. The thirteen to thirty-nine minutes it had taken ADC to alert cooperating commands over commercial toll lines was unacceptable; SAC had been alerted by hot line in eight seconds.

Chidlaw told Vandenberg that the alert had made "more of our top Air Force people . . . aware of the very thin margin of evidence on which we too frequently must base our decisions."[2] If that thin margin was to be overcome, the nation would have to make a substantial investment in sophisticated technology applicable to air defense systems. The debate over how much to invest in air defense, meanwhile, went on during the Korean War period not only in Air Force councils but also in specially formed, civilian-led committees and among influential scientists and journalists. Their assessments would be crucial in deciding the future of continental air defense.

East River

The Air Force assumed a seemingly paradoxical approach toward air defense. In late 1952, Generals Chidlaw and Smith of ADC joined with Generals Vandenberg and Twining and the JCS in opposing a recommendation pending before the National Security Council for an extensive air defense network.

Events leading to this paradox began in the summer of 1951 with a study called East River, cosponsored by the Air Force and the National Security Resources Board (established to advise the President on the coordination of mobilization problems involving the military, industry, and civilians). In the East River project, many of the nation's most distinguished scientists gathered to consider air defense from a civil defense perspective.* After months of study, the project director, retired Army Maj. Gen. Otto L. Nelson, Jr., submitted an interim report to Secretary of Defense Robert A. Lovett on April 7, 1952. The study group concluded that civil defense could not be effective without a capable air defense system. The project members assumed that "an adequate air defense . . . must and will be provided." Specifically, they said, the air defenses needed to provide warning to the civilian population and to operate so effectively that civil defense would only need to deal with limited leakage through the defensive net.[3] Not surprisingly, Lovett told Nelson that civil defense planning based on such a belief was naive. He said that while "it would be highly desirable if we could have such protection . . . in the foreseeable future it is unrealistic to expect such a high percentage of kills." Lovett suggested the East River members resume their study with the assumption that, while an enemy could not launch a saturation attack against all important targets, "crippling" attacks on some would be likely.[4]

After receiving Lovett's advice, East River's final report dealt more with air defense deficiencies than with civil defense needs. The report claimed that civil defense officials had to have at least an hour of early warning of an impending air attack to take appropriate action. It also devoted, as one Chidlaw staff officer commented, excess time to proposing ways for alleviating weaknesses that were already "well known to all responsible for providing the air defenses of the United States." [5] Although the report did not discernibly affect the state of either the civil or air defenses, the project proved important because its members concluded that more could and should be done to improve air defenses, and they

---

* The Army, not the Air Force, was the military service invested with the greatest civil defense responsibilities [B. Franklin Cooling, *The Army Support of Civil Defense, 1945–1966: Plans and Policy,* 2 vols (Washington, D.C., The Office of the Chief of Military History, 1967)].

with many of those who supported their views were influential enough to carry their arguments to the highest levels of government.

Views presented in the East River report soon became public knowledge through newspaper and magazine articles. For Americans who relied on the press for information about the condition of their country's air defenses, the messages could be confused or contradictory. For example, in February 1952, at the same time the Air Force campaigned to increase participation in the GOC with radio spot announcements and billboard and newspaper advertisements, an article appeared in the widely read *Saturday Evening Post* that threatened to negate Air Force efforts. The article, "Night Fighters Over New York," exaggerated the prospects for air defense weapons and computerized command and control systems of the future. According to the article, "Thousands of these new supersonic terrors [jet interceptors] will soon be beating up the airwaves in the country's incredible new air defense network." This was hardly an accurate appraisal for short-term air defense prospects in the early 1950s. Moreover, ADC feared it could foster undue complacency and hurt recruiting for the GOC.[6]

Unhappy as it was with the *Saturday Evening Post* article that overstated prospects for air defense in the immediate future, the Air Force was even more disturbed by the tone of articles written by the newspaper columnists Joseph and Stewart Alsop. Starting in 1952 and for the next three years, the Alsop brothers published several pieces accusing the Air Force of being the major foe of air defense preparedness.

Joseph Alsop had served as an aide to Maj. Gen. Claire L. Chennault in China during World War II, where he directly observed an effective early-warning and control network in operation. He also learned the irascible general's view that U.S. airmen overemphasized strategic bombing.[7] Although it is pure speculation how much, if at all, Joseph Alsop's World War II experiences influenced his and his brother's subsequent reports on Air Force air defense programs, their articles could not cover the complete story of the Air Force's plans, programs, and aspirations for air defense since 1948. The ensuing exchanges between the columnists and Air Force defenders frequently presented complicated technological and economic problems as a simple conflict between the Air Force leadership and the scientific community. The scientists, some with close connections to the Alsops, offered brighter prospects for air defense than Air Force leaders believed practicable. Indeed, the Air Force came to suspect that the scientists were giving the Alsops much of the information for their articles.

The Alsops began their campaign by reiterating Vandenberg's estimate that the existing air defense system could destroy only ten percent of an enemy's attacking aircraft, at best. They pointed out that, in reality, the "terrifyingly feeble" air defense system could not be expected to achieve even this kill ratio, except perhaps in daylight and good weather. (Chidlaw agreed with this assessment.) Their dismal assessment could be rectified with "new weapons . . . new techniques . . . heavy investment and by great national effort." The columnists believed that in three or four years the United States could have an essentially leakproof air defense network. "This is a defense so strong," they said, "that even suicide air missions to the most vital American targets will look like a waste of men, machines, and atomic raw stuff." [8]

The Alsops concluded the nation could not afford to lose time in constructing such a "near-total air defense." As for cost, they proposed that the defense budget be increased by approximately $4 billion a year for several years for air defense alone. And, in a warning apparently directed at the Air Force, the Alsops wrote, "If this great issue is not faced, those who have refused to face it will carry an unbearable burden of blame, when the time of danger is suddenly upon us and we find that we are not defended in the air." [9]

Unfortunately, the Alsops offered few specific proposals regarding what the nation could do to achieve an airtight defense. While they mentioned the Army's Nike missiles and referred to other components, such as radar equipment and all-weather fighter-interceptors, the article seemed to suggest it was only necessary to produce and use these systems in quantity to accomplish the task. It soon became clear, however, that some distinguished scientists who were investigating the air defense situation, and whom the Air Force suspected of being the Alsops' sources, had much more in mind than just increasing the quantity and quality of current and programmed forces.

The Summer Study Group

The Summer Study Group, which James Killian of MIT described as "an ad hoc undertaking of the [Lincoln] Laboratory," met from June through August 1952 in MIT's Sloan Building in Cambridge. Dr. Jerrold R. Zacharias, also of MIT, a highly esteemed physicist and a participant in the Lincoln Laboratory and East River projects, organized and led the group. The group consisted of about twenty full-time scientists and engineers plus as many part-time consultants, all with some knowledge of air defense. Although later misidentified as consisting primarily of Lincoln members, only six of the many hundreds of scientists and engineers assigned to or in some manner associated with Lincoln participated in the summer study. Among the former East River members on the study group were Zacharias and Doctors Albert Hill, Lloyd Berkner, Isidor I. Rabi, and J. Robert Oppenheimer. Hill headed the Lincoln project,

Berkner was chief of Associated Universities and guided the completion of the final East River report, and Rabi and Oppenheimer were major contributors in the Manhattan District Project, which developed the first atomic bomb. [10]

The original purpose of the group seemed to differ among its members. Killian said the project originated because of doubts as to whether Lincoln's air defense study was exhaustive enough. Lt. Gen. Laurence C. Craigie, Saville's successor as Air Force Deputy Chief of Staff for Development, thought the group's purpose was to define the nature of the probable threat to North America from air attack between 1958 and 1964. This objective involved addressing various criteria, among which were determining the feasibility of remote early-warning systems and deciding when intercontinental ballistic missiles (ICBMs) would pose a danger to the United States. Craigie also wanted the scientists to explore the question of whether defense against such missiles was possible. [11]

Hill, in informing the Air Staff why Lincoln was sponsoring the project, laid out the group's priorities. First, the scientists would concentrate on the possibility of devising an early-warning network capable of providing three to six hours' warning against the approach of aircraft. Second, said Hill, they would focus on the establishment of an interceptor force to take best advantage of early warning. Finally, the scientists would examine defenses against ICBMs. [12]

As Hill promised, the group's final report emphasized the early-warning problem. Accepting East River's conclusion that three to four hours of early warning were essential to alert and disperse the interceptor and bomber forces, Hill and his associates set out to specify how this could be accomplished. Clearly, detection of approaching aircraft had to be made in the far north as Stratemeyer's planners had pointed out as early as 1947. The questions the Summer Study Group attempted to answer were, Where should an early-warning network be installed? and How could it be equipped, manned, and operated most economically?

The group knew that Canada had begun considering an early-warning plan of its own. Two Canadian agencies, the National Defence Council and the Defence Research Board, were assessing the possibility of using inexpensive radar equipment developed in the McGill University electronics laboratory for this purpose. Through new communications devices, aircraft sightings made at unmanned radar stations in the north could be relayed to small, manned area stations. These would pass information to the main stations in the southern part of the country. The Canadians also considered installing a low-cost unmanned radar chain in mid-Canada along approximately the 55th parallel (corresponding to the Hudson Bay area in the east). [13]

Summer Study Group members journeyed to Canada to observe the McGill device in operation. They also attended briefings and demonstrations of radar and communications equipment that American manufacturers were developing and that promised to perform in warning-line operations as well as and as inexpensively as the Canadian equipment.[14]

The scientists ended their work in late August 1952, and Hill and Zacharias convened a formal briefing to convey the group's conclusions and recommendations. The full membership along with some hundred persons from the Defense Department and from industry attended the briefing. The thrust of the briefing was, as later expressed in the group's written report, that not only was a distant early-warning line feasible, but its installation would enhance significantly the status of continental air defense.[15]

As the scientists envisioned it, a distant early-warning network would function as a 200- to 400-mile-wide zone stretching from Alaska to Greenland just under the Arctic Circle. The zone would extend seaward from Alaska to Hawaii and from Greenland to Scotland. Estimated costs totaled approximately $370 million to install the zone and $106 million per year to operate it.[16]

The scientists moved that the Defense Department implement the project immediately. From available intelligence estimates, the Summer Group had concluded that, by the end of 1954, the Soviet Union would possess enough atom bombs to seriously threaten North America. Accordingly, they suggested that the Defense Department complete the northernmost portion of the warning line by that time. This could be done if survey parties began work in early 1953 and construction started that summer. In the meantime, plans and preparations for full development of the warning line could go forward.[17]

In the final, most provocative section of its report, the Summer Study Group addressed the possible objection that its proposal for an increased emphasis on air defense grew from a Maginot Line philosophy. On this point, the scientists doubtlessly knew that since the end of World War II the Air Force had repeatedly pointed to the historical example of France's Maginot Line in making a case for powerful strategic forces. The Air Force objected to relying primarily on a defensive strategy, a virtual "Fortress America," as unwise. It believed grave dangers would result for the United States. Although defenses could raise the threshold of uncertainty for an attacker, limit damage to critical areas, and exact a heavy price for an attacker, defenses could not in themselves deter or win wars; winning wars was clearly the province of SAC, which had to be given the men, planes, and equipment it needed to fulfill its mission.

Such were the Air Force arguments against a Maginot Line philosophy. The scientists, however, had another definition of what this strategy constituted:

> The Maginot Line psychology is the psychology of a nation
> that puts "all its eggs in one basket" in a military sense. The

French put their entire effort in a single rigid defensive concept, the Maginot Line, and failed to maintain the balance of forces needed to meet any situation that the enemy might pose. The antithesis of the Maginot Line is the balanced military force. . . . The history of warfare is replete with examples of failure because of "Maginot Line" psychology, i.e., excessive reliance on a single weapon or weapons system. The great emphasis placed in recent years on the development of an effective "retaliatory force" in the belief that this constitutes an adequate defense is another manifestation of this psychology. Again, we put "all our eggs in one basket. . . ." We conclude, therefore, that continued dependence on a retaliatory force as our sole defense represents the development of a dangerous Maginot Line psychology. [18]

The Summer Study Group's final report greatly disturbed the Air Force. Since the end of World War II, the Air Force had been, for all practical purposes, alone in calling for air defense improvements. Involving scientists in postwar air defense was originally an Air Force attempt to modernize future systems. Now, airmen felt, in effect, accused of having concern only for offensive retaliation.

Even before the Summer Group had started its investigations, the Air Force apparently had misgivings regarding the scientists' intentions. Finletter told Killian and Provost Julian Stratton of MIT that the Air Force feared the project would "get out of hand." Killian, however, assured Air Force leaders that the study would be "kept in bounds." He believed the scientists' work would enhance the research in air defense occurring in the Lincoln Laboratory and, by doing so, would benefit both Lincoln and the Air Force. The final report seemed to confirm Air Force apprehensions. The scientists misinterpreted the Air Force don't-put-all-your-eggs-in-one-basket position because of the Air Force's orderly, less costly approach to creating air defenses. Although the Air Force did not oppose the *eventual* construction of a warning line in the far north, its first priority lay in strengthening the double perimeter system and improving the forces and weapons that comprised it. [19]

The Air Force believed the Summer Group recommendations contradicted Killian's assurances that the study would not get out of hand. Subsequent events validated the major Air Force concern (although not stated specifically in the Summer Group's final report) that accelerating the progress of air defense programs would have to occur only at the expense of SAC. This fear increased when, after receiving the report, President Truman directed Lovett on September 24, 1952, to determine the cost and feasibility of building an early-warning line. [20]

The Summer report received the President's attention, in part, because Secretary of State Acheson, influenced by Paul Nitze, head of the State Department Policy Planning Staff, supported it. Nitze was closely associated with the Summer Group and had sat in on many of its meetings.[21] The eminent reputations of many members of the group, notably of Robert Oppenheimer, also made Truman carefully consider the report. According to Zacharias, Oppenheimer served as only one of many part-time consultants to the group. Zacharias had expected, and was proved correct, that Oppenheimer's name would influence other prominent scientists to participate in the study project.[22] The Air Force, however, laid more blame on Oppenheimer than he probably deserved for the report's recommendations. The Air Force leadership considered Oppenheimer its most renowned opponent to orderly air defense.

Events leading to this view preceded the Summer Study Group. The Air Force's first impression of Oppenheimer appears to have come from Project VISTA. Conducted against the background of the Korean War, when developments indicated Communist aggression could assume dangerous forms other than a large-scale nuclear attack, VISTA examined, in part, how atomic weapons could be used in conventional warfare. Oppenheimer contributed to the report, compiled by scientists in the California Institute of Technology at the request of the three services, by reviewing and revising a chapter dealing specifically with use of smaller nuclear weapons on the tactical battlefield.[23]

Oppenheimer addressed the question of allocation of fissionable materials for making atomic weapons. He suggested that these materials (in short supply in the fall of 1951) be more equitably given to the tactical and defensive air forces for nuclear tipped missiles. This notion had some acceptance in the Air Force. General Lauris Norstad, commander of the air forces in Europe, the main geographical focus of VISTA, approved Oppenheimer's ideas; hovever, the Air Force leadership in the Pentagon took another view. In recommending more tactical nuclear weapons, Oppenheimer seemed to suggest taking scarce material for the manufacture of atom bombs from SAC. The Air Staff also took exception to his campaign against establishing a second weapons laboratory to expedite development of a fusion (hydrogen) bomb, a crucial Air Force priority. During the Atomic Energy Commission's 1954 hearings held to investigate whether Oppenheimer posed a security risk (more for his left-wing connections than for his views on military matters) David T. Griggs, the Air Force Chief Scientist from December 1952 to June 1953, testified:

> It became apparent to us [Griggs, Vandenberg, and Finletter] . . . that there was a pattern of activities all of which involved Dr. Oppenheimer. Of these one was the VISTA project. . . . We were told in the late fall, I believe of 1951, Oppenheimer and two other colleagues formed an informal committee of three to work for world peace or some such purpose as they saw it. We were told that in this effort they considered that many things were more important than the

development of the thermonuclear weapon, specifically the air defense of the United States.[24]

Maj. Gen. Roscoe Charles Wilson, who described himself as "first of all a big-bomb man," was the only other Air Force representative to testify at the Oppenheimer hearings. Wilson, Army Air Forces liaison with the Manhattan District Project and, in postwar years, a member of an atomic research committee, also claimed to be disturbed by a "pattern of action on Oppenheimer's part beginning with his VISTA activities."[25] Like Griggs, Wilson reported few specific facts, but Oppenheimer lost his security clearance.

Joseph Alsop, a friend of Oppenheimer's, suspected Air Force complicity in Oppenheimer's losing his security clearance. Shortly after the hearings concluded, Alsop coauthored with his brother Stewart an article for *Harper's Magazine* entitled "We Accuse." Their article, like Emile Zola's work of the same name, an attack on the accusers of French Capt. Emile Dreyfus in the 1890s, pulled no punches.

The Alsops argued that the unpopularity of the VISTA findings within the Air Force derived from the project participants' proposal to divide the atomic stockpile: part to a reserve; part for tactical use, including air defense; and part to SAC. According to the Alsops:

> The Air Generals, no great believers in atomic plenty, have been fighting tooth and claw for five years to keep the entire atomic stockpile as the Strategic Air Command's monopoly asset. Compared to SAC, the Air Force Generals cared very little about tactical air which was one of the reasons for all the difficulty in Korea.

Oppenheimer's suggestion that there be a new distribution of atomic weapons, said the Alsops, "reduced most of the leaders of the Air Staff to a condition of apoplectic fury. . . . The Air Generals, who cared even less about air defense than tactical air, had pooh-poohed the whole idea." Moreover, the Alsops believed that the Air Force interpreted the Summer Study Group's report "as nothing less than a sinister, insidious, direct attack on strategic air power." [26]

This vituperative article reflected the charges made by Air Force critics over the past two years. Because the Alsops' columns and articles received wide readership, the Air Force had early described in public terms how its approach to air defense and tactical air power complemented its other missions. As the former commander of the air defense forces, retired General Ennis Whitehead, stated to newly appointed Vice Chief of Staff Lt. Gen. Thomas D. White, unless the Air Force could prove that it was committed to depth and flexibility and to the needs of SAC, a grave danger existed that "the Maginot Line boys from MIT" would be able to persuade Congress and the public to support a "Great Wall of China concept." [27]

In fact, Vandenberg had personally reiterated the points described by Whitehead soon after the Summer Study Group's report appeared. Appearing on the nationally televised "See It Now" broadcast, Vandenberg claimed the Air Force was doing everything it could to provide the nation with formidable air defenses. Still, he cautioned, it was important to distinguish between defense in land warfare and air defense. On the battlefield, defense principally required the ability to shoot back and hit the sources of an enemy's fire. In air warfare, however, sources of enemy fire were usually enemy air bases, and destroying them required powerful offensive air action.[28]

Early in 1953, Vandenberg presented his ideas to the Board of Directors of the Advertising Council of America. "Developments," he said, have "given rise to a certain amount of wishful thinking. The hope has appeared in some quarters that the vastness of the atmosphere can in some miraculous way be sealed off with an automatic defense based upon the wizardry of electronics." While the Air Force fully attempted to provide the most up-to-date air defenses, said the Chief, it was important to remember that even the most advanced technical systems could not substitute for fighter aircraft, crews, and antiaircraft artillery. The Air Force believed these forces needed to be fully manned and operating at peak efficiency before a computerized air defense system and an early-warning network were established. On the topic of air defense in general, Vandenberg expressed these thoughts:

> I have often wished that all preparations for war could be safely confined to the making of a shield which could somehow ward off all blows and leave an enemy exhausted. But in all the long history of warfare this has never been possible. The shield is neither the strongest deterrent to aggression nor the surest guarantee against defeat. It is not the defense that the aggressor fears most; it is the realization that he may receive a harder blow in return. . . . Certainly it is not the state of our defenses that has restrained our potential enemy in the recent past, and is continuing to restrain him—instead he fears the risk of a retaliatory attack.[29]

In his desire to restrain what he saw as an overemphasis on air defense, the Chief of Staff was joined by no less an authority than retired General Gordon Saville. Many years later, Saville recalled bitterly that there had been a period "after I got out of the business when the air defense of the United States was basically determined by MIT." It disturbed him that the scientists could have suggested, as he believed they had, that an impenetrable air defense could be constructed. As an outspoken advocate for air defense, Saville had nevertheless maintained that leakproof defense nets were impracticable.[30] In the March 1953 issue of *Air Force Magazine* he suggested that in air defense both those who would call for a perfect defense and those who would be content with the most minimal system were equally mistaken:

> In this endeavor as in all others, the extremists are wrong and their councils are deadly. We must select the most suitable instruments of air defense and fit them together into a weapons system which will economically and successfully defend people, cities, factories and SAC bases. [31]

Saville made an especially important point in mentioning the protection of SAC bases. Although interceptor units were on alert at SAC bases and the Army contributed antiaircraft artillery components, widespread destruction of bombers sitting on the ground would probably still occur if the Soviets launched a surprise attack and prompt early warning was not provided. The specter of Pearl Harbor still haunted military commanders for, as Whitehead reminded Vice Chief of Staff General White, the United States could not be expected to take the first "bite" in a future conflict, and "we might be flattened by the first attack." [32]

In this period, the Air Force began to worry seriously about the vulnerability of its strategic forces. Intelligence sources predicted improvements in the quality and quantity of Soviet bombers. Stalin had ordered a new design bureau under V. M. Myasischev to develop a bomber capable of a range of 9,940 miles, to reach the United States and return home. But by 1953 only one prototype Mya–4 Bison had been produced, though the Soviets were known to be working feverishly to build more. Stalin had not invested all his hopes in Myasischev; he had Tupolev working on a similar long-range bomber. Tupolev, like Myasischev, had problems developing and outfitting suitably powerful engines. He soon decided that a pure jet would not achieve enough range, so he decided to concentrate on building a turboprop aircraft, eventually the Tu–20 (Tu–95) Bear. As with the Bison, one prototype Bear was in production by the end of 1953. [33]

Near the end of 1953 the only threat the Soviets could muster with even pretensions of intercontinental range remained the obsolete Tu–4 Bull, of which approximately 1,800 had been produced by the end of 1953 (about 1,000 were in service at the time, matched with 50 atom bombs). The Air Force expected this situation to change within a few years as work progressed on the Bear and Bison programs as well as on a medium-range jet bomber, the Tu–16 Badger. While the Soviets improved their bombers and produced more bombs, the Air Force worried about the vulnerability of its SAC bases. Like the Soviets, but, as events developed, with far more success, the Air Force was upgrading its intercontinental bomber force. Concurrently, the number of bomber bases in the continental United States increased. Because of greater bomber range, bomber bases in England could be recalled to the United States, resulting in the continental United States having 30 SAC bases in 1954

Russian planes. Tu–95 Bear (*above*) and Tu–16 Badger (*below*).

compared to the 17 it had 6 years earlier. Vandenberg understood that while it was, for the moment, safer to have B–36, B–47, and B–50 bombers stationed in the continental United States rather than in Britain, for example, this situation would not necessarily continue if Soviet long-range bomber programs progressed smoothly. He admitted that if the enemy attacked, even using the Tu–4, he would aim some if not most of his bombs at SAC bases, hoping to gain an immediate, stunning victory, or at least cause confusion and lessen the ferocity of retaliation.

> Hence this long-range striking force must be protected against surprise. Viewed in this light the whole air defense

> program takes on new significance. It becomes more than a
> means of merely reducing disaster and making an attack
> more costly to the enemy. It is an additional safeguard for
> the preservation of that force which has been the deterrent
> to aggression and which remains the principal guarantee of
> our survival as a nation.[34]

Vandenberg's analysis marked a watershed in the Air Force approach to
air defense. "Merely reducing disaster and making an attack more costly
to the enemy," the task of active air defense forces, would remain an Air
Force responsibility. But by indissolubly linking early warning with SAC
integrity, Vandenberg assigned the warning aspect of the air defense mission preeminence over active defense measures, a situation that continued
in coming years.

None of this implied, however, that the Air Force immediately embraced the concept of distant early warning. A RAND report issued in
November 1952 strongly influenced Air Force views. RAND analysts
agreed that a distant early-warning line "may possess desirable features"
but that the best solution for protecting SAC bombers would be to
devise alternate basing modes, build bomb shelters, and maintain more
aircraft on alert. The analysts also considered the Air Force desire to
delay implementation of a warning system until an extensive test period
could be conducted in the far north.[35]

Meanwhile, the Air Force continued to question the motives of the
most outspoken advocates of a highly developed air defense system, the
scientists of the Summer Study Group. In fact, within the corridors of
the Pentagon the rumor circulated that the scientists believed a leakproof
defense could be built that would obviate the need for a strategic striking
force. This idea, incredulously received by Air Force officers, became
public in May 1953 in a *Fortune* article by Charles J. V. Murphy, an Air
Force Reserve officer with close ties in the Air Staff. Murphy, who did
not sign the article, attributed the notion to an informal group that had
preceded the Summer Study team in the spring of 1952. The group, said
Murphy, called itself ZORC for the first letters of the names of its members—Zacharias, Oppenheimer, Rabi, and Charles (Charles Lauritsen).[36]

During the Oppenhemier hearings the following year, David Griggs
testified that Finletter and Vandenberg had heard that ZORC wanted to
eliminate SAC to ensure that the military budget could support an air
defense buildup.[37] Furthermore, in the July 1953 issue of *Foreign Affairs,*
Oppenheimer called for a greater emphasis on air defense and implied
that the Air Force had not met its responsibilities in this matter. He re-
counted that a "high officer in the Air Defense Command" had told him
it was not "really our policy" to provide air defense for Americans
against atomic attack. The unnamed officer's rationale for this statement
was the task "is so big a job that it would interfere with our retaliatory
capabilities." [38]

In truth, although Oppenheimer and the other scientists favored an increased emphasis on air defense, no facts support the idea that they conspired to disestablish SAC. The existence of ZORC, derived from hearsay, cannot be taken seriously. It now appears that both the Air Force and the scientists either misunderstood or distorted each other's position. The scientists seem to have been motivated by an intense desire to improve the status of continental air defense. They were, perhaps, overoptimistic about how new technology could produce a perfect or near-perfect system. Yet no tenable evidence exists that Oppenheimer and his associates suggested building the optimal air defense by abolishing SAC. That idea grew from Air Force fears and suspicions.

On the other hand, some of the scientists—and their supporters in the media—erred in assuming the Air Force was only concerned with the buildup of its strategic forces. Certainly the needs of SAC would continue to demand priority, but other missions could hardly be neglected, especially in the wake of the Korean War, which reinforced the requirement for effective air power in many guises. Regarding continental air defense, the Air Force supported an approach whereby the forces and warning networks composing the inner defenses would be developed and perfected before the far northern warning line was implemented. Statements by Air Force leaders indicated they knew the warning line could serve not only for air defense purposes but also as a trip wire, alerting bombers to disperse and prepare for retaliatory actions. The Air Force, other than ADC, was dubious that a bolt from the blue would occur without having a crisis develop and SAC bombers put on upgraded alert. The distant warning line was thus considered useful but not a pressing need to be funded at the expense of more important programs.[39]

While requirements for air defense were debated acrimoniously in public view, the issue was also thrashed out less conspicuously in the inner councils of government. On September 18, 1952, Jack Gorrie, Chairman of the National Security Resources Board, received a briefing from retired Maj. Gen. Otto L. Nelson, Jr., and Dr. Lloyd Berkner on problems involved in building a distant early-warning line. Gorrie left the briefing convinced a warning line was needed and could be constructed, for purposes of civil defense. On September 24 he brought his case before President Truman and the National Security Council. He persuaded the President to request a Defense Department estimate on the feasibility and cost of an early-warning line that could be activated early enough to permit civil defense measures.[40]

Truman forwarded Gorrie's request to Secretary of Defense Lovett, who asked the Air Force to investigate the matter. This action might have been considered incongruous since the Air Force position was well known. Nevertheless, Lovett considered the Air Force the agency best qualified to lead the preliminary investigation. The Air Force therefore assembled a working group of representatives of ADC, the Air Staff, the Lincoln Laboratory, and RAND under Maj. Gen. James E. Briggs, Assistant Deputy Chief of Staff for Development. Briggs worked quickly and, by October 14, presented his conclusions to members of the National Security Council, the JCS, and other high government officials. Not surprisingly, Briggs's ideas reflected the Air Force reaction to the Summer Study Group's conclusions, namely, that a distant warning line was

> unwarranted at this time since it would involve corresponding decreases in the same amount expended for our offensive capability. Moreover, many of the equipments forming the basis for such an Air Defense system [were] in the embryonic stages of development, and without adequate testing millions could be spent with little additional security. [41]

In effect, Briggs did not reject outright the concept of distant early warning (whether for civil defense, air defense, or bomber dispersal), but he called for more analysis and research and development.

Truman approved Briggs's recommendations, and Lovett promptly executed them. In mid-November 1952, a reallocation of 1953 Department of Defense funds provided $20 million required for research and development of new electronic communications equipment and for establishing experimental stations. [42] In addition, Lovett opened negotiations to have Western Electric Company conduct the experimental project. He convinced Mervin J. Kelly, President of Bell Telephone Laboratories, to head an air defense study group consisting of military representatives, industrial leaders, scientists, and engineers. Kelly was charged with reviewing the need for a distant early-warning system as measured against other air defense priorities. At the conclusion of his investigation, Kelly was to recommend policies and programs to make continental air defense more effective. [43]

Earlier, RAND and ADC had given their support to the Air Force's go-slow approach in regard to the warning line. According to RAND analysts, a pressing need existed to concentrate funds on more important air defense improvements in the near future. These included low-altitude overland radar; implementation of airborne early-warning and picket ship coverage; and more and better local-defense weapons such as the Nike missile, to be deployed around coastal cities and SAC bases. [44]

Speaking for ADC, General Chidlaw warned of

> the possibility that someone in high office, alarmed or excited by the enthusiasm or the genuine apprehension of the scientific group [the Summer Study Group], might push the panic button, thus causing a hysterical approach and an out-of-balance approach to the air defense question.

185

The ADC staff and unit commanders, said Chidlaw, were more concerned than anyone in acquiring the means to accomplish their mission. They also believed there had to "be a definite spot, a peak, in our air defense preparations . . . beyond which the returns do not justify the means, a point of diminishing returns." [45] This view agreed with the ideas of Air Force leaders in the Pentagon. As Brig. Gen. John K. Gerhart, Deputy Director of Operations in the Air Staff (and future commander of NORAD), warned, the Air Force might be forced "by NSC decision to program billions on defense gadgetry at the expense of our deterrent strike and air superiority forces." [46]

The JCS agreed with the Air Force's cautious approach to air defense, a tactic also favored by the Department of Defense, even by ADC. President Truman decided, nonetheless, to take immediate steps to build the distant early-warning line. The arguments of his civilian advisers, especially those of Acheson and Nitze, undoubtedly swayed him. When informed of the President's decision, the JCS asked him not to make a public announcement until Kelly's air defense study group completed its investigations. The Chiefs feared that the American people would believe the military intended to focus undue attention on defense rather than on offense. Truman honored the Chiefs' request; his decision appeared in a classified document, NSC 139, issued on December 31, 1952. In this document, the President moved the "period of maximum danger," set by the JCS in 1950 as 1954, back one year to 1955. By that time, he said, it was crucial that an effective air defense system be in operation. Although he did not define what an effective air defense might be, or what one would cost, Truman identified early warning as a key element. He believed the early-warning network should be operational by December 31, 1954, and completed by the end of 1955. [47]

Soon afterward, Lovett directed the JCS to plan for the establishment and operation of the distant-warning system. He also made the Air Force responsible for conducting in the last days of the Truman administration the early warning-line experimental project. Before leaving office, Lovett cleared the appointment of the Kelly Committee with Charles E. Wilson, the new Secretary of Defense under President Dwight D. Eisenhower. Consequently, the work of the committee proceeded uninterrupted despite the change of administrations. [48]

Wilson, the former President of General Motors, apparently agreed to adhere to NSC 139. The Chiefs reinforced the urgency of air defense planning when they briefed the new Secretary in early February 1953 on the state of the air defenses. They told him that the threat to the United States would become serious by 1954 or 1955 and that 65 to 85 percent of the atom bombs launched by the Soviets (in 1953 they possessed approximately 200 bombs) could be delivered on targets in the United States. [49]

With Wilson's approval, General Bradley, Chairman of the JCS, instructed the service chiefs on March 11, 1953, to submit individual plans and project forces available as of December 31, 1955, for the land, sea, and air defense of the United States. Essentially, each service was to prepare an estimate of the forces it could allocate from anticipated force levels to defense and still meet the requirements of other missions. These plans would eventually be submitted to the JCS as a plan for achieving an effective continental air defense.[50]

Contrary to the Alsop reportage, the Air Force took this increased emphasis on air defense seriously. Although Air Force leaders used every opportunity to make their case for not reinforcing the defense forces at the expense of SAC—NSC 139 contained some assurances to that effect—the Air Force hastened to meet the directives of the national command authorities.

General Twining, successor to Vandenberg on June 30, 1953, as Chief of Staff, and General White, new Vice Chief of Staff, personally guided Air Staff work on the new defense plans. White cautioned the Air Staff that "perhaps the Air Force would find that it had to reduce or eliminate some of its lesser responsibilities" to meet its air defense commitments.[51] Twining even said that the absolute primacy of SAC's mission might have to be reconsidered. He foresaw "the distinct possibility that the future activities of the Air Force may well be primarily grouped into two equally important functions, air defense and strategic air operations."[52]

Twining wanted the Air Force to obtain ostensibly exclusive jurisdiction over all aspects of air defense planning. The Air Force would submit a completely new plan for air defense against which the JCS could measure proposed allocations received from the other services.[53] The USAF War Plans Division of the Directorate of Plans prepared the proposal with the assistance of other Air Staff agencies and members of Chidlaw's Colorado Springs staff.[54]

In brief, the plan proposed to add 29 mobile and 135 low-altitude stations to ADC's radar system. The plan noted the requirement for the computerized system being developed in the Lincoln Laboratory, but it did not attempt to predict when the system would be ready for installation. Four squadrons (40 aircraft) of control and warning planes would be deployed under the plan, and the Navy would furnish 20 radar picket ships. These, along with 5 Texas Towers, to be built off the Atlantic coast, could extend radar coverage seaward. Texas Towers, which resembled oil drilling platforms used in the Gulf of Mexico, were huge, manned platforms to serve as radar sites. The Air Force hoped the towers and other air defense improvements could be functioning by the end of 1955.[55]

The Air Force favored constructing a far northern warning line, once its feasibility had been proved in tests. Many questions remained, however, as to how personnel and equipment functioned in arctic environments. In the meantime, the Air Force advocated U.S. support for a Canadian project, the Mid-Canada Line. This line, if fully completed, would extend from Newfoundland across Canada along approximately the 54th parallel and would then run north along the Alaska highway before connecting with the Alaska radar system. Further, the seaward barriers would extend from Alaska to Hawaii and from Newfoundland to the Azores. ADC would operationally control ninety Air Force airborne early-warning aircraft and thirty Navy picket ships.[56]

As for the weapons force, the Air Force hoped to have seventy-five fighter-interceptor squadrons functioning by the end of 1955. Unfortunately, development of the 1954 interceptor (initially the F–102A), Fairchild and Saville's experiment in a weapons systems approach to aircraft development, had lagged. The Air Force thus had to rely on the F–89 and F–86D for its frontline interceptors at least through 1955. Meanwhile, a project was under way to adapt an air-to-air guided missile, the Falcon, designed for the 1954 interceptor, for use on the F–89. As with so much else connected with home air defense, Saville influenced the early development of the guided air-to-air missile. During his tour as Deputy Chief of Staff for Development, he stimulated the Hughes Aircraft Company to develop the prospectively potent weapon.[57] While Hughes, under Saville's not so gentle prodding, made immense strides, the missile would not be ready before the end of 1955. The Air Force's only hope of achieving a substantial increase in the destructive power of its interceptors before then lay in equipping them with rockets carrying atomic warheads. This issue proved too sensitive and controversial to be approved quickly.[58]

The Air Force's BOMARC and the Army's Nike remained the only surface-to-air missiles scheduled for use in the air defense network. BOMARC was not expected to be ready for deployment until the end of 1955. As for Nike, the Air Force suggested that the Army Antiaircraft Artillery Command be increased from 66 to 110 battalions and that 47 be equipped with Nikes. In addition, the Air Force also considered using a new air defense missile—the Talos. Developed for fleet defense by the Navy, Talos could be converted to a ground-to-air point-defense role in which it might be as good as or even better than the Nike. The Air Force hoped to equip 20 squadrons with the Talos missile, permitting it to participate actively in the ground-to-air defense mission. Airmen trained to maintain and use Talos could then be employed later as cadres for BOMARC.[59]

Not surprisingly, the Army and the Navy did not share the Air Force's views on how many and what kind of forces they should provide for air defense. The Army, for example, preferred sixty-one Nike battalions by the end of 1955, not the forty-seven suggested by the Air Force.[60] The Army did not see the Talos as a superior weapon to Nike, nor did it intend to let the Air Force usurp its ground-to-air continental defense role.

For its part, the Navy reiterated its long-held belief that it should be solely responsible for and equipped to handle overwater surveillance and warning. At one time, of course, the Air Force had been prepared to concede the mission to the Navy, but when the Navy did not move as quickly as the Air Force wanted, the Air Force ordered early-warning aircraft and planned to deploy them on the east and west coasts. Now, however, after the Air Force had prepared its own seaward warning forces, the Navy appeared ready to act on the issue. According to the new Navy concept, the commander in chief of the Atlantic Fleet and his counterpart in the Pacific would provide both continental air defense warning and antisubmarine capabilities. To accomplish both missions, the Navy wanted 3 wings (133 aircraft) of early-warning planes and 36 destroyer-escort ships converted for use in picket vessel operations. With these, the Navy claimed, it could place in the Atlantic and Pacific by the end of 1955 barriers able to detect 95 percent of any enemy aircraft flying from 500 to 30,000 feet and approaching the American coasts. Although the Navy's estimate of early-warning aircraft requirements coincided approximately with the Air Force's, each service believed it should own and operate the aircraft. The respective estimates on the required number of picket vessels also differed significantly: the Navy believed it could do the job with 36; the Air Force believed the Navy should provide 50.[61]

The JCS could do little to resolve the differences between the Navy and the Air Force. Although most of the service chiefs preferred to solve roles and missions questions through individual negotiations, a centralized air defense organization with authority to make decisions was needed.[62]

While the services struggled with their respective air defense responsibilities, the Kelly Committee completed its work and submitted to Wilson a report, which included little specific guidance. Ambiguities became apparent when the Alsops concluded that the report "fully confirmed" the findings of the Summer Study Group,[63] whereas Charles Murphy, the Air Force Reserve officer-journalist, labeled it an "impressive rebuttal of the Summer Study Group." [64]

In most respects, the report merely confirmed the ideas and projects instituted or under consideration for air defense. Discounting the possibility of building a near-perfect defense, the report emphasized that American military planning had to concentrate on offensive capabilities. The committee supported construction of the Mid-Canada Line, pointing to the need for a far northern warning line if the new experimental program to develop equipment and facilities succeeded. The committee also approved the automated ground control system being developed in the Lincoln Laboratory and, in a related matter, advocated a vigorous civil defense program.[65]

After five months of study and investigation, the Kelly Committee approved the projects under way or close to implementation. One committee recommendation, prompted by interservice disputes on air defense allocations and missions requirements, appeared to influence later developments: Kelly suggested to centralize "responsibility for air defense . . . under a single agency with broad authority." [66]

Thorough as the report appeared, Wilson decided a more comprehensive study was needed. Another committee composed of, as Wilson put it, our own people (the previous Democratic administration had appointed Kelly) therefore joined the plethora of past and present air defense study groups. Retired Army Lt. Gen. Harold R. Bull, one of President Eisenhower's most valued staff officers in World War II, chaired the new committee,* and General Smith, the ADC vice commander, joined as the Defense Department's representative. Members of the Office of Defense Mobilization, the federal Civil Defense Administration, and the Interdepartmental Committee on Intelligence and Security served to ensure the study would be conducted with a broad view. Bull was asked to review Kelly's findings, study the present and future threat of air attack, and examine air defense measures under way and programmed. He would then recommend physical and organizational improvements necessary in the immediate future and estimate the cost.[67]

Soon after the Bull Committee convened, President Eisenhower's new National Security Council issued its first major policy statement. Initially, the Eisenhower administration discounted Truman's warning of a Soviet threat to the United States by the end of 1955. Eisenhower's long-range policy called for a steady, continuing analysis of the nation's military needs and a calm, fiscally sound buildup. Consistent with this approach, Eisenhower reduced Truman's proposed 1954 defense budget, assuming it contained expenditures not mandatory for strengthening the military. The new President believed the Soviet threat could be met within a balanced budget by eliminating waste and unessential programs. This strategy was to establish and maintain strategic offensive forces capable of damaging the Soviet Union sufficiently so that making war with the United States, on any conceivable scale, presented an unacceptable risk. A complementary goal was to institute a continental air defense

---

* Bull had previously been chosen by Eisenhower to lead a civil defense survey committee (the Bull Board) in December 1946 [Cooling, *Army Support of Civil Defense,* Vol II, pp 17–23].

strong enough to prevent disaster "and to make secure the mobilization base necessary to achieve . . . victory in the event of a general war." [68]

The Decision to Proceed

Soon after he assumed office, Eisenhower made clear he intended to rely heavily on the JCS, particularly on the chairman, to attain his military objectives. In his mid-1953 reorganization of the Defense Department, the President selected Admiral Radford as Chairman of the JCS and increased his authority. [69] Radford had been one of the Air Force's most outspoken opponents in the late 1940s during the interservice disputes culminating in the B–36 controversy. He was, however, completely loyal to the President and could be expected to uphold Eisenhower's views in JCS councils. In addition to Radford, Eisenhower appointed Admiral Robert B. Carney as Chief of Naval Operations, and General Twining replaced the ailing General Vandenberg as Air Force Chief of Staff. General Matthew B. Ridgway, a hero in Korea as head of the Eighth Army and Douglas MacArthur's successor in Japan, became Army Chief of Staff. Ridgway, odd man out on the new JCS, believed that Eisenhower's policies overemphasized long-range nuclear capabilities and that the ground soldier remained a decisive factor in warfare. The President instructed the chiefs to spend a month, beginning in mid-July, reappraising the nation's military programs. [70] They were then to confer with Secretary Wilson on ways to identify and reduce sources of waste, inefficiency, duplication, and excessive cost in the Defense Department budget. [71]

On July 22, in the midst of these arrangements, General Bull submitted his report, which the National Security Council circulated as NSC 159. Limited strictly to defense needs, Bull's report stated unequivocally that the inadequacy of the current defenses constituted an "unacceptable risk to our nation's survival." Bull recommended the United States continue to develop air defense measures as rapidly as possible even though the Soviet threat could take years to materialize fully. [72]

In many ways the Bull report agreed with Air Force plans for air defense. Like the Air Force, Bull assigned top priority to completing the Mid-Canada Line and its seaward extensions and to setting up contiguous surveillance and warning systems off the coasts. The committee proposed that the following be completed on a second-priority basis: the Lincoln automated system, the gap-filler radar program, a fighter-interceptor force of 75 squadrons (as the Air Force had proposed), an improved aircraft identification system, and a far northern warning line if experimental tests proved it workable. Bull estimated a cost of $34 billion to com-

General Nathan F. Twining accepting a second tour as Chief of Staff, United States Air Force. Administering the oath on June 30, 1955, is Secretary of the Air Force Harold D. Talbott.

plete these projects. Since the 1954 budget contained $4.3 billion for air defense improvements, the buildup would require more than 8 years for completion if expenditures for air defense remained unchanged. [73]

On August 4 the outgoing Chiefs of Staff told Secretary Wilson (and two days later told the National Security Council) that they favored a stronger air defense. They urged, however, that improvements not be undertaken at the expense of more important requirements. The chiefs also questioned the priorities outlined the Bull report. Consequently, the National Security Council postponed making a recommendation on the Bull proposals until September 1, 1953, when the new service chiefs were scheduled to meet with the council to present their ideas. [74]

On August 12, 1953, Americans learned that the Soviets had exploded a thermonuclear device, less than a year after the United States had demonstrated the feasibility of the fusion bomb. Not a superbomb—it had a different configuration and lower yield—the Soviet weapon could be carried in an aircraft, whereas the American one could not. Just as four years earlier when the Soviet Union first exploded an atomic device, a public cry immediately arose for better continental air defenses.

The Eisenhower administration minimized the event, much as President Truman had done in response to the Soviet's atomic test in 1949. On August 26 Admiral Radford told reporters the Soviet thermonuclear experiment had been foreseen and would not severely alter America's basic military plans. He acknowledged a need for the United States to strengthen its air defenses.[75]

While the JCS considered new defense goals in light of the enhanced Soviet threat, the National Security Council developed a more definitive statement on defense policy. In terms of air defense, the National Security Council recommended implementing the programs suggested in the Bull report to the extent they did not detract from a balanced budget. Eisenhower accepted this advice and directed Wilson to solicit more concrete ideas from the JCS on various air defense matters.[76]

National Security Council policy paper NSC 159/4, an amended version of the Bull report, became a key document in the history of continental air defense. It was the first postwar air defense directive approved at every level of military command—at the presidential, at the Office of the Secretary of Defense, and at the JCS levels. The Air Force could at last proceed to build a modern air defense system knowing it had the complete backing of *all* elements in the national command structure.

Events moved fairly rapidly. Using NSC 159/4 as justification, the Air Force Council on October 28, 1953, asked the Air Staff Budget Advisory Committee to include funds in the 1955 budget to construct the facilities required by ADC to convert to the Lincoln automated system.[77] On December 2, the council recommended approval of the ADC 323-station low-altitude gap-filler radar program.[78] On the same date, the council agreed to the ADC request for 29 additional stations under the "third phase mobile radar program." Many of these stations would provide coverage along the U.S.-Mexican border and the Gulf of Mexico.[79] On January 11, 1954, the council recommended funds be added to the 1955 budget to construct five Texas Towers to complement the picket ships and early-warning aircraft system that the Air Force, with Navy support, hoped to establish off the east coast.[80]

NSC 159/4 also facilitated closer cooperation between the United States and Canada in air defense matters. The two nations formed a Military Study Group and, under its direction, a Scientific Advisory Team. American and Canadian scientists studied prospects for the Mid-Canada and far northern warning lines. Concentrating first on the Canadian-inspired (and eventually built) Mid-Canada Line, the scientists agreed it could and should be constructed. Erected generally along the 55th parallel, it could detect penetration by hostile aircraft and could discriminate between incoming and outgoing air traffic.[81] The Permanent Joint Board agreed the U.S. and Royal Canadian air forces should plan the line; on December 8, 1953, the JCS authorized General Twining to contact his Canadian counterpart to discuss the project.[82]

Another, even more provocative, National Security Council paper, NSC 162/2, followed NSC 159/4. Better known as New Look, NSC 162/2 warned of the determination of the United States to use its nuclear striking force if attacked. The New Look, as one JCS summary stated, was intended

> to minimize the threat of Soviet aggression by maintaining a strong security position with emphasis upon offensive retaliatory strength and defensive strength—this to be based upon a massive retaliatory capability . . . an effective continental defense system, and by combat forces of the United States and its allies suitably deployed to deter or counter aggression and to discharge initial tasks in the event of a general war.[83]

The New Look program has often been interpreted as synonymous with "massive retaliation," espoused publicly in January 1954 by Eisenhower's Secretary of State, John Foster Dulles. Described as "a revival of the spirit of the offence in military strategy," [84] the New Look emphasized strategic air power. The United States would not compete with the Soviet Union in a conventional arms buildup, and local wars, like the war in Korea, would be fought primarily by allies with American help. Perhaps the essential New Look strategy was to deter the Soviets from engaging in or supporting large- or small-scale conflicts, understanding the United States reserved the right to retaliate.

President Eisenhower and his chief civilian and military advisers emphasized home air defense. Throughout his term in office, Eisenhower addressed the United States' inability to launch a preventive or preemptive attack on the Soviet Union. Such an attack was contrary to American democratic and moral ideals. Even if a month of advanced warning allowed preparation, Eisenhower foresaw difficulties in obtaining secret congressional approval and explaining his actions to the American people. Despite all the advantages, the President finally concluded that "it would appear impossible that any such thing would occur." [85] Under the circumstances, Eisenhower realized the nation had to be capable of sustaining the first blow in a future nuclear war, "a blow that would almost certainly be a surprise attack and one that would make Pearl Harbor, by comparison, look like a skirmish." [86]

The President thus set as the military's first objective "the capability to deter an enemy from attack and to blunt that attack if it comes—by a combination of effective retaliatory power and a continental defense system of steadily increasing effectiveness." [87] The objective, said Eisenhower, demanded priority in all defense planning. The National Security Council, in reviewing its air defense decisions of late 1953 and early

1954, agreed completely with Eisenhower, although the council now believed the Soviet Union would not have a significant capability for launching strategic nuclear attacks until July 1957.[88] Meanwhile, Admiral Radford emphasized quality continental air defenses and offensive retaliatory power.[89] The Air Staff concluded from such statements that the two most important Air Force missions in order of importance were to develop and maintain a massive nuclear retaliatory capability and to develop and maintain an integrated and effective continental defense system.[90]

The new national emphasis on air defense enabled General Chidlaw, his staff, and ADC commanders to speak forthrightly on air defense needs. Since 1948 the ADC commander had been directed to develop and operate a minimum air defense system. Chidlaw's statement in late 1952 that there was a limit, a point of no return, to an air defense buildup exemplified the pressure this policy put on ADC. This view supported the contention, consistently voiced by the Air Force as its primary mission, that it had to maintain a strategic air force capable of deterring or winning a nuclear war with the Soviet Union. Now, under Eisenhower's New Look, the JCS charged the air defense chief with establishing an effective system even though the Eisenhower cuts in the military budget hit the Air Force hard. Forces to achieve an effective air defense system were not to be acquired at the expense of SAC, which would fulfill the primary objective.

Chidlaw's deputy, General Smith, had commanded pursuit squadrons before World War II and, after performing impressive combat service in the Pacific during the war, headed the Eastern Air Defense Force in 1950. Smith (who later became Air Force Vice Chief of Staff), stimulated by the intricacies of air defense, approached the subject cerebrally, much as Saville had. In March 1954, Smith indicated how ADC planned to develop and use the "integrated, efficient, and highly potent air defense system" the Eisenhower administration planned to install. According to Smith, a basic premise of New Look strategy was that in a future war the United States would be attacked by "masses of thermonuclear weapons." To meet this threat, he said, ADC required the most advanced weapons and warning systems. Moreover, highly trained and motivated personnel would be needed to work in the sophisticated air defense command and control environment, made possible by computers. In broad tactical terms, the purpose of active defenses would be to engage and destroy an enemy as far away from his target as early warning and rapid reaction would permit. Smith described his scenario of a future air battle after the defenses had been alerted to an approaching attack:

> Bombers will be met by extremely fast interceptors armed
> with rockets and missiles, some with atomic warheads, fol-
> lowed by unmanned supersonic interceptors homing to the

targets by their own radar, and finally by short range missiles. All of this complex network . . . will be knit together by high speed computing machines capable of carrying scores of tracks and controlling an equal number of interceptors by the automatic transmission of intercept data to our fighter aircraft.[91]

Most of the technology Smith described had been researched and was being tested. Events in the next few years would determine whether the new administration's decision to strive for an effective defense would produce the sophisticated system he envisioned.

Chapter 8

Defensive Systems Become Operational

When the Eisenhower administration decided to build an effective continental air defense, the Air Force planned to have its components in place and functioning as soon as possible. The wide-ranging postwar debate over the role and purpose of strategic air defense thus culminated in an extensive buildup of radars, aircraft, missiles, and command and control networks designed to defend the United States against attack from manned bombers. By the end of the 1950s, most of the complicated and expensive apparatus was in place and functioning, although a potentially more lethal weapon than the bomber had emerged—the intercontinental ballistic missile (ICBM).

SAGE: A Command and Control Network for Air Defense

In Kingston, New York, on August 7, 1958, an engineer pushed a button activating one of the largest and most highly developed computers of the time. Moments later, a BOMARC surface-to-air missile rose from Cape Canaveral, Florida, to intercept a simulated enemy bomber over the Atlantic Ocean.[1] This marked the first time the SAGE (semi-automatic ground environment) air defense system had, by remote control, guided the firing of a missile. SAGE, the heart of a network designed to coordinate all air defense components in existence and the world's first major command and control system, established a new technology with far-ranging military and nonmilitary applications.[2]

The origin of SAGE can be traced to Air Force actions after the Soviets exploded their atomic device in August 1949. In one of its most important actions, the Air Force established an air defense study group led by Dr. Valley in December 1949. Formally known as the Air Defense Systems Engineering Committee, its emergence coincided with the

197

A SAGE component, a 64 × 64 magnetic core memory

appointment of General Saville as Deputy Chief of Staff for Development. The committee worked closely with Saville but reported to Chief of Staff General Vandenberg through the Scientific Advisory Board.[3]

Valley Committee members visited numerous air defense sites and became discouraged by what they saw. The most striking problem involved the use of primitive equipment and methods in ground-controlled interception (GCI). Members were astounded and distressed by "the completely inadequate and antiquated means provided for the control of . . . interceptors."[4] Valley believed a solution to the problem might lie in the use of new technology, especially that of computers. It was imperative to devise a system that could gather data from radar stations and relay and process the information as quickly as possible so that defensive weapons could be unleashed in time to repulse a rapidly approaching invader. Current manual systems, relying heavily on voice communications, could not be expected to assume this function fast enough in a high-speed battle between jet bombers and fighters. According to Valley, however, the WHIRLWIND computer, developed in the late 1940s by Jay W. Forrester, might eventually provide a breakthrough in air defense.[5]

Because of Valley's suggestions, the Air Force became the leading supporter of MIT's Lincoln Laboratory, established in 1951 to study air defense in depth. Yet, as late as fall 1952, the Air Force was studying prospects for another air defense automation project, based on the British Royal Navy's Comprehensive Display System (CDS). A centralized surveillance scheme, the CDS used storage and retrieval of data from telephone and teletype components. As CONAC commander, General Whitehead had encouraged Headquarters USAF to adapt the system for American air defense. Members of the Air Staff who traveled to Europe to observe CDS agreed the system might be applied to American air defense. Radars could be assigned to geographic areas, each under a central combat center. With several radars feeding information to such a post, perhaps a hundred planes could be tracked, ten times more than at an individual site. Even after six years of development, CDS was not nettable (it could not exchange data automatically among different combat centers as the more advanced systems being developed by Lincoln promised to do).[6] Despite this drawback, the Air Force still had hopes for it. On the basis of tests conducted by the U.S. Navy (interested in CDS for fleet defense) and evaluated by Air Proving Ground technicians, Maj. Gen. Morris R. Nelson, Air Force Director of Requirements, decided in June 1952 that CDS was the only affordable system capable of improving existing air defenses.[7]

CDS prospects in American air defense brightened considerably when the University of Michigan Willow Run Research Center proposed to correct deficiencies in CDS and to modify it for use in the Air Defense Integrated System (ADIS). ADIS would Americanize CDS by making it possible to transfer data electronically between combat centers. The Michigan proposal faced vigorous opposition by Lincoln Laboratory members who feared ADIS would drain financial support and interest from their laboratory.[8]

Responding to the Michigan challenge, Lincoln officials, with the concurrence of Maj. Gen. Earle Partridge, now head of Air Research and Development Command, formulated a substitute program for ADIS. They proposed to develop the Lincoln Transition System built around a central digital computer receiving data from radar sites. Lincoln representatives believed this operation could begin by 1955, one year earlier than Michigan's estimates for ADIS. Conceivably, advanced radars and Boeing's BOMARC interceptor missile could enable the Lincoln system to defend against ballistic missiles.[9]

General Chidlaw and his staff in ADC feared the Lincoln plans might be too far-fetched. He favored assigning priority to the less complicated Michigan system. Chidlaw told Vandenberg that ADIS appeared to ADC

> to be well thought out using known techniques and provides a high degree of flexibility with optimum application of human judgment in concert with maximum automaticity.

> It also appears to be compatible with other service systems now being developed and can readily integrate missile weapons.

The Lincoln system, on the other hand, seemed "rather nebulous." Chidlaw recommended that it "be directed towards future threats such as the intercontinental missile and not towards the present manned aircraft threat." [10]

General Twining told Chidlaw the Air Staff shared his belief that the Michigan system showed the most immediate promise. However, said Twining,

> your view that the Lincoln system effort should be re-aligned toward an intercontinental ballistic missile threat is not shared by my staff. It is felt that the enemy threat from manned bombers and air-breathing missiles to ballistic or glide missiles will not be a sudden one, and that it will not have been completed by 1960. Our air development program should be accordingly shaped to meet the widely differing requirements of these threats through the period of their probable co-existence. At each potential target, point defense systems . . . appear to be required for defense against the ballistic missile; a decentralized surveillance system with centralized control of our area air weapons is the goal for air-breathing missiles. [11]

RAND analysts monitored the progress of the two systems. Although they considered the Lincoln air defense system the most promising for the 1960s, they agreed with Chidlaw that the Michigan system seemed more likely to meet short-term needs. RAND therefore recommended the Air Force implement CDS in its original form, then improve it after it was operating. [12]

In the course of its investigation, RAND discovered "a basic attitude of distrust of Lincoln in the Air Force and that relations between Lincoln and the working level USAF people have frequently been unpleasant." RAND also determined that the Air Force often failed to understand what the Lincoln scientists were attempting and recommending, though the Air Force was clear in its wish to ensure that the laboratory's efforts not be "sporadic and erratic" by offering specific guidance. [13]

Dr. James Killian, MIT President, pressed Lincoln's case against the Michigan project. In January 1953 he asked Secretary of the Air Force Finletter if Air Force sponsorship of both Lincoln and Michigan did not, in effect, indicate a lack of faith in Lincoln. Killian proposed that the Defense Department perform a "technical evaluation" of Lincoln, paying "particular attention to the relationship of its program to air defense systems based upon centralized digital computation." If the evaluation showed that an agency other than MIT was better qualified to lead the way in air defense research, Killian said,

we stand to withdraw. Since the project involves real hazards for the Institute, particularly financial hazards, and
since it is not the kind of project that the Institute as an
educational institution would normally wish to undertake,
we feel it is important that there be no question in regard to
our serving as contractor. [14]

Killian's views disturbed the Air Force. Despite all the problems Air
Force leaders had and continued to experience with the scientists, they
acknowledged the MIT expertise and wanted to continue an affiliation
with the university. Two years earlier, Killian had to be induced even to
consider establishing Lincoln. He had just refused as being contrary to a
university's activities a request by the Navy to do classified work on
antisubmarine warfare. But General Saville, along with scientists Louis
Ridenour and I. A. Getting, had persuaded Killian that "the dangers to
the nation from attack by airplanes carrying A bombs was a different
order of magnitude than the dangers of the need of protecting ship-
ping." [15]

Now, Finletter hastened to assure Killian that the Air Force valued
Lincoln's work and that a "technical evaluation" was not called for. The
Air Force, he said, continued to regard Lincoln as its best hope for developing a suitable ground environment for electronic defense. At the
same time, Finletter, defending Air Force support of the Michigan
project, said Michigan offered hope of suggesting improvements in air
defense to be "realized in the Air Defense Command after a few years,
perhaps before the revolutionary LINCOLN program materializes in its
entirety." It was, therefore, Air Force duty to support and capitalize on
Michigan's efforts. Finletter promised Killian this in no way lessened Air
Force support for Lincoln. [16]

General Partridge also solicited Killian's approval of dual development. He pointed out it would be impractical for the Air Force to accept
one system and completely exclude another "because of the limited available facts concerning the operational and technical capabilities, state of
development and cost of either system." He asked MIT and Michigan to
cooperate in resolving the problems involved in creating an automated
air defense system. [17] Partridge also asked Chidlaw and his staff to give
equal support to MIT and Michigan. [18]

Only two months after Partridge pleaded for cooperation, the Air
Force decided to discard its dual-development approach to building the
air defense ground environment. On April 10, 1953, at a conference held
in Partridge's headquarters between his staff and members of the Air
Staff, the Air Research and Development Chief heard that Headquarters
USAF had decided to cancel its support of the Michigan system and that
the Air Research and Development Command planned to finalize a production contract for the Lincoln Transition System [19] (the Lincoln Transition System was redesignated the SAGE System in 1954).

The Air Force decided to take this important step for a number of reasons. Most important, Finletter's and Partridge's reassurances had failed to mollify Killian. To allow MIT to withdraw from the air defense program would mean a huge financial loss for the Air Force which had already invested substantial sums in Lincoln. Another factor in the Air Force decision to support Lincoln alone was the views of the new Secretary of the Air Force in the Eisenhower administration, Harold E. Talbott, and his Assistant for Research, Trevor Gardner. On March 28, 1953, Talbott and Gardner visited Dr. Albert G. Hill, Lincoln Director. Hill told them the laboratory had serious financial problems and found it difficult to attract topflight scientists.[20]

Lincoln's power play proved successful when Talbott and Gardner decided it was time for the Air Force to drop its dual-development policy and to invest all its resources in one agency. Thus, a policy that had earlier been called dual development was now denounced as a duplication of effort. Partridge and his Vice Commander, Maj. Gen. Donald L. Putt, accordingly arranged a meeting with the University of Michigan's President Dr. Harlan Hatcher to break the bad news. Hatcher conceded that some of Michigan's objectives and many of its components were similar to Lincoln's and agreed to withdraw from the project.[21] The Air Force investment with Lincoln was safe.

This action proved unpopular with the ADC staff in Colorado Springs. ADC officers, responsible for the day-to-day air defense of the United States, believed Michigan's plans were less ambitious than Lincoln's and offered better prospects for the near term. Vice Commander Smith sent Headquarters USAF a list of air defense requirements needed before the Lincoln system could be deployed, which most optimistically was estimated to be 1955. The requirements included filling gaps in radar coverage below 5,000 feet and identifying friend from foe more quickly and reliably.[22] The Air Staff knew of these and other deficiencies in the air defenses described by Smith. That Smith chose to reiterate them may have been his way of warning that to await the outcome of the Lincoln venture before investing in present air defense improvements might prove tragic. Since 1946, officers directly responsible for air defense worried about the present threat, while Headquarters USAF concerned itself more with future needs.

Once Lincoln had been invested with the sole responsibility it had so eagerly sought, the Air Force expected positive results. As Partridge told Killian,

> [N]ow that the Air Force is placing its entire dependence
> and emphasis on the Transition system to the exclusion of
> all other efforts in this field, the discharge of the associated
> responsibility becomes . . . vital to the nation. . . . Full co-
> operation and assistance on the part of the Lincoln Labora-
> tory and MIT . . . [is anticipated] for a period of years

through successful production, installation and operation of the system.[23]

Cooperation necessitated that the Air Force support the MIT scientists wholeheartedly. Problems could still occur because Air Force relations with scientists working in air defense had been quarrelsome at best, and often bitter. The Air Force position was that scientists should initiate ideas and devise new technologies to make air defense more effective. The general feeling was that Summer Study Group members had gone beyond their mandate in advocating extensive air defense improvements which, the Air Force feared, could overemphasize defense at the expense of SAC. Eisenhower's decision to forge ahead in air defense and to build up SAC would have seemed to end the argument. As the RAND analysts reported, however, animosity between the Air Force and the scientists continued, and Air Force reluctance to make MIT solely responsible for development of the air defense ground environment seemed to support their view. The Lincoln threat to withdraw completely from the program could not have been expected to relieve tensions. The Air Force decision to yield to MIT demands emphasized how the service was placed in a distinctly uncomfortable position. Mistrustful of the scientists, Air Force leaders still had to execute Eisenhower's dictum to build an effective air defense. The Air Staff knew that MIT talent could, eventually, meet that goal most effectively.

A change in attitude was required, and the Air Force set out to instill a mutually respectful relationship with the scientists, engineers, and other technicians involved in SAGE. Lincoln received extremely wide latitude in designing and developing the system, befitting the need for creativity and productivity. The commanders of ADC, Air Research and Development Command, and Air Materiel Command asked for and received periodic briefings from Lincoln and the assigned project officers. Generally, Lincoln and the other agencies involved in SAGE had complete freedom to establish their own management structures and modes of operation. Many years later, a participant in SAGE remembered that

> those of us who were designing SAGE believed in it, and I don't know how we could have done the job if we didn't. But as the buyer of the thing you [the Air Force] had every right to be terrified. I was amazed at the time and I'm still amazed at the unflagging support of the Air Force. Truly remarkable.[24]

Indeed, the Air Force had every reason to be concerned, because computer technology remained an unexplored discipline. The initial work on the computer that eventually became SAGE began in the late 1940s in the MIT Digital Computer Laboratory. From Forrester's initial work in designing the WHIRLWIND computer for the Navy, the Air Force became aware that a similar machine could be applied in air de-

203

fense operations. Forrester and Lincoln later designed WHIRLWIND II specifically for air defense use. The production version of WHIRLWIND II—in Air Force nomenclature, the AN/FSQ-7—resulted from a joint effort among Lincoln Laboratory, Air Force Cambridge Research Laboratory, and International Business Machines Corporation (IBM) personnel.

The AN/FSQ-7 proved decidedly better than the manual system in performing GCI functions. In the early 1950s, GCI methods resembled those used in World War II, although in some systems improved radars had been installed. Each site consisted of a search radar, a height-finding radar, and devices for communicating with interceptor pilots. Radar operators analyzed their scopes in darkened control centers where aircraft appeared as blips on the scopes and target information was supplied by telephone from adjacent GCI sites. In major control centers, large plexiglass boards depicted the local geography, and airmen used grease pencils to mark the boards to show aircraft in the vicinity.[25] All in all, this method would not suit the direction of a high-speed air battle fought in ever changing positions.

The centralized command and control data-processing system, SAGE, would improve this situation. Analog computer–equipped direction centers with interconnecting communications would process radar signals and coordinate weapons used in an air battle. Radars and computers would combine to present a clear picture of the speed, location, and direction of all planes within radar range. A single radar, the basic air defense element, would be replaced by SAGE, now controlling several radars in a single operations center by linking them to a computer through telephone lines or ultrahigh frequency (UHF) radio waves. In addition to receiving information from radars, SAGE computers would be supplied with additional data from such sources as Texas Towers, picket ships, early-warning aircraft, and the GOC. The SAGE computer would create a composite picture of the air situation as it developed. Generated radarscope displays would provide information so that controllers could decide how to deploy the various weapons to destroy an invader. The semiautomatic system required human judgment; it was designed to combine "the talents of man with the best aptitudes of machines."[26]

The key to automating air defense procedures lay in the WHIRLWIND computer. First tested in 1951 on Cape Cod, Massachusetts, the automated network consisted of a control center in Cambridge where the computer was housed, a long-range radar at South Truro, also in Massachusetts, and numerous short-range gap-filler radars. By 1954 more radars had been added, and the whole operation had become steadily more realistic. The Air Force integrated an F-86D squadron in the Cape Cod system and diverted SAC training flights into the area so intercep-

AN/FSQ-7 radar. Shown here is part of the maintenance control console of the central computer.

tors could train against B–47 jet bombers. By the time the Cape Cod system evolved into an experimental SAGE sector in 1954, more than 5,000 sorties testing various components had been flown against it. Still developmental, the computer generally performed well. Cape Cod did much to validate the Lincoln efforts.[27]

While Lincoln and IBM continued to build and refine the computer to be used in SAGE, equally critical attention focused on computer programming. Like the computers, computer programs were elementary in the early 1950s. Progress in programming would prove crucial in determining success or failure for the automated environment. Changes in radars, tactics, and weapons implied an enormous, continuing programming effort.[28]

Lincoln agreed to prepare the master programs, assisted by RAND which employed a sizable number of programmers, considering how young the discipline was. So many software designers became involved in SAGE that RAND created a special entity for them, the Systems Development Corporation (SDC). Although technically a Lincoln unit, SDC did much of its work at RAND Headquarters in Santa Monica, California. RAND designers developed the Model I software that allowed realistic training for technicians scheduled to operate the first direction center, expected to debut on McGuire Air Force Base, New Jersey.[29]

RAND's and Lincoln's programming tasks included synchronizing the SAGE data link with such diverse weapons as supersonic fighters, antiaircraft artillery, and surface-to-air missiles. Planning for the control of Army Nike missiles and antiaircraft guns within SAGE presented a major challenge for the Air Force. Not only technical considerations but also sensitive roles and missions questions were involved. After seven years of discussion, the JCS in 1954 had finally authorized creation of the joint-service command for continental air defense (CONAD). Commanding CONAD would be an Air Force officer, while the Army and Navy would perform designated missions (the primary Army contribution would be antiaircraft artillery and missiles). The new organization did little to change old perspectives; the Air Force continued to advocate centralized control of all air defense weapons, and the Army continued to believe it needed extensive freedom to operate its guns and missiles effectively. The Army Antiaircraft Artillery Command resisted subordinating itself to what it believed would be restrictive control in SAGE. From the Air Force perspective, weapons systems functions could overlap under attack. Army defense forces were designed basically for point, or short-range, operations; in contrast to the longer range of Air Force interceptors, considered area defense weapons. Interceptors in pursuit of invading bombers could, during confusion of battle, enter the airspace defended by Army guns and missiles. Aircrews feared finding themselves in such a situation that could be more dangerous than facing the enemy. They believed Army gunners prone to shoot at aircraft indiscriminately, "sorting them out on the ground later." [30]

Reflecting a desire for at least partial autonomy in air defense operations, the Army proceeded to develop its Missile Master control system, a semiautomatic fire-direction system intended to improve coordination of missile-firing units. Previously, an Army air defense command post controlled units that manually plotted targets on a map. Missile Master was expected to provide a "rapid, automatic, electronic system for transmitting data and coordinating the target information and defensive effort." [31]

The Air Force considered Missile Master a blatant duplication of effort; it wanted Army missiles and guns exclusively controlled by SAGE. General Partridge, who replaced Chidlaw as CONAD commander in 1954, argued "we cannot afford to waste any weapons once the air battle starts, nor can we afford to waste any dollars through unnecessary duplication of equipment and tasks in building our air defense system." [32]

No resolution of this dispute satisfied both the Air Force and the Army. The services were as reluctant as ever to compromise in the seemingly endless quarrel over control of antiaircraft guns and missiles for air defense. After countless Air Force and Army proposals and separate JCS studies on the fate of Missile Master, Secretary of Defense Charles E. Wilson decided the matter in June 1956. He ruled that SAGE control all weapons for air defense and the Army deploy Missile Master. SAGE commands would be relayed to antiaircraft artillery batteries and missiles through Missile Master. Although Wilson's decision did not address Missile Master redundancy, it satisfied the Air Force by keeping intact the principle of centralized control of air defense forces under an Air Force commander.[33]

The Air Force knew engineering and communications networks would prove instrumental in determining SAGE efficiency. Early in the program, Western Electric and Bell Telephone Laboratories, selected as engineering consultants, formed a group called Air Defense Engineering Service (ADES). Burroughs Corporation Research Center also began to develop special equipment for automatic processing and transmission of radar data to computers. Like almost everything connected with air defense, the work performed by ADES and Burroughs proved difficult and expensive. Congress, it appeared, conforming with the post–World War II pattern, would lose enthusiasm after the danger subsided and the invoices appeared for programs hastily authorized in periods of seemingly dire peril. This proved true with SAGE, which in 1953 had been approved during the Korean War when world tension was high, but in 1956 the Air Force estimate of an annual communications expense of $200 million produced congressional shock waves. (The Air Force successfully solicited the American Telephone and Telegraph Company to reduce its rates, but the Federal Communications Commission–approved savings of about $14 million yearly were hardly noticeable.[34]) By 1956 the very large investment in SAGE prohibited the withdrawal of government support.

Under SAGE the Air Force planned to divide the continental United States into eight air defense regions with eight combat operations centers, and into thirty-two air defense sectors with thirty-two SAGE direction centers. Because of its strategic significance, the northeast would receive the first SAGE installations, which, housed in concrete, shock-resistant, aboveground buildings, would rely on air conditioners to prevent the primitive computers inside from overheating and melting.

The SAGE system became nominally ready on June 26, 1958, when the New York sector became operational. The ambitious Air Force plans for SAGE deployment, however, were never realized. This failure was due in large measure to the perception of many in Congress and in the Eisenhower administration that by the late 1950s the Soviets had decided to concentrate overwhelmingly on ICBMs (SAGE was solely an antiaircraft system). Cuts in antibomber defense programs in the 1960s resulted.

The first intensive use of computers in air defense was not without difficulties. Indeed, many problems arose, although some of the more serious involved not the equipment but the adjustment process for people working within the system. In the manual air defense network, personnel

SAGE direction center. This installation is located at Stewart Air Force Base in New York state.

in control centers exercised substantial authority over their environment, visually identifying blips on radarscopes, making calculations, and telephoning sightings to other control centers. The information flowed slowly enough to allow unhurried responses, though this method would almost certainly fail under actual attack. As a RAND analyst judged the situation, "the scene in an Air Defense Direction Center during a SAC System test or major exercise was that of hurried conferences with many people putting their heads together to make decisions." [35]

In SAGE, information flowed into control centers at an unprecedented rate. Commanders and weapons directors had to assimilate information and make quick decisions to vector interceptor pilots accurately to their targets. Unfortunately, many people assigned to work in the first SAGE installations were initially uncomfortable with the new system. A RAND analysis found that

> the first thing that can be said about the SAGE system going newly into the field, and into operational use, is that the experienced Air Defense crews attempted very quickly to circumvent the central computer. This was not done in

malice; rather, it was the response of Manual Air Defense System operators to an extremely confusing, very different way of operating. They had habits, ways of working, and ways of thinking about Air Defense that no longer fit in the SAGE environment. Therefore, they almost unconsciously attempted to make the SAGE environment as much as possible like the Manual Air Defense system with which they were somewhat experienced. . . . Men who are confronted with a new system will almost always distrust it—complain about the hardware—try to use the old ways.

As the analysis made clear, the air defense personnel were not modern-day Luddites; they were merely confused by rapid changes confronting them in their work place. RAND suggested they be taught more about computer-based systems, the functions of a computer program, and the importance of people to the system.[36]

Despite its problems, SAGE proved an outstanding achievement. Coordinating its efforts with multiple civilian and military agencies, and working in a new and relatively untested technology, the Air Force produced the first prototype, large-scale command and control system for air defense. Moreover, SAGE served as a major sponsor and testing ground for the fledgling American computer industry. It played a seminal role in the rapid advance of computer sciences in the years following its implementation. It also substantiated the Air Force belief that computers deployed over a wide area could exchange large amounts of military data rapidly and effectively. SAGE enabled the Air Force to acquire a unique understanding and competence in the design, development, and operation of computer systems that would eventually benefit such diverse operations as SAC target selection planning and personnel records management. In fact, all components of the military, not only the Air Force, gained in later years from Air Force experiences with computers for air defense. Never tested during war, the Air Force air defense endeavor left its clearest legacy on the development and manufacture of sophisticated technology.

Warning Lines

SAGE was designed to control and fight the air defense battle. To do so effectively required prompt and accurate information of enemy movements, not only flowing from sectors to combat operations centers but also needed as soon as possible after the enemy left his bases. To obtain such information, the United States and Canada constructed three early-warning lines—the Pinetree Line, the Mid-Canada (McGill) Line,

Pinetree Line. The domes of a Pinetree Line radar outpost dominate a winter scene in Quebec, Canada.

and the Distant Early Warning (DEW) Line—built consecutively to extend the warning network as far north as possible.

The first line completed, the Pinetree, performed warning and GCI activities. Functioning in 1954, it extended on both sides of the Canadian-American border and consisted of over thirty stations. The United States absorbed two-thirds of its cost and provided most of its staff. Meanwhile, Canada alone designed, constructed, paid for, and operated the Mid-Canada Line. The Mid-Canada Line, not really a radar warning line, was an unmanned microwave "fence" that signaled when something flew by (even flocks of geese—it suffered from many false alarms). Although it could not accurately gauge the altitude, number, speed, or direction of an attacker, it served Canada's purpose by providing a rudimentary first warning (or second warning if the DEW Line was built), a benefit the Pinetree Line provided for the United States. Moreover, as many Canadians viewed the situation, building and assuming responsibility for the line absolved Canada from any financial obligation to support the far more expensive DEW Line.[37]

The far northern warning line had been the subject of bitter controversy between the Air Force and its civilian proponents. When members of the Summer Study Group investigated early work on the Mid-Canada Line (then referred to as the McGill Device) in the summer of 1952, they returned home convinced that if a warning fence was feasible under the fierce weather conditions that prevailed along the 55th parallel in mid-Canada, then another, potentially even more valuable, warning line

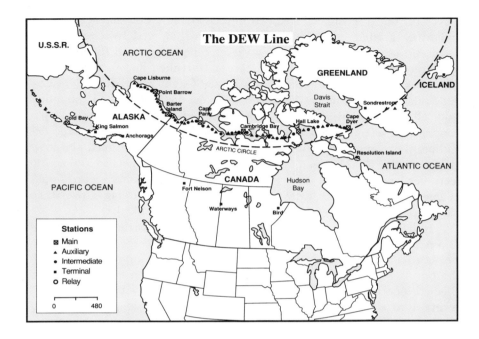

might be built in the frozen arctic wastes. The Air Force, meanwhile, had been reluctant to support the project, suspecting it was part of a scheme by the scientists to build an impenetrable air defense that would drain funds from SAC. Also, though the DEW Line could offer early warning for SAC bombers based in the United States, the Air Force believed the widely dispersed bases and bomb shelters provided no better solution, an attitude endorsed by RAND. Despite Canadian experiments in mid-Canada, the Air Force thought that building a vast and complicated warning network in the frozen tundra might prove unworkable.

Notwithstanding its objections, the Air Force played a major role in determining the feasibility of building the DEW Line. The first important step occurred when the Lincoln Laboratory established an experimental outpost on Barter Island, on the northeast coast of Alaska. To decide what equipment was necessary under arctic conditions, Western Electric Company personnel traveled to Barter in February 1953. The Air Force furnished supplies and provided advisers.[38]

Once the men and equipment had assembled on Barter, work proceeded rapidly. Lincoln scientists developed automated alarm circuits that sounded an audio alert when the radars picked up a target. Operations center controllers were thus freed from constantly monitoring their radarscopes. "Scatter" radio communications, which bounced radio

211

waves off the troposphere, avoided unpredictable arctic magnetic forces and other ground interference. Scientists also adapted two new radars for arctic use. Powered by nearby diesel generators, both functioned in temperatures as low as minus 65 degrees fahrenheit and in winds up to 150 miles per hour. One conventional line-of-sight radar, the AN/FPS–19, could detect aircraft as high as 65,000 feet and outward to 160 miles. Like all line-of-sight radars, this one suffered from low-altitude short-comings; an enemy flying lower than 5,000 feet could easily escape detection. To compensate for this deficiency, scientists designed the low-altitude AN/FPS–23 which could detect low-flying targets as low as 200 feet over land or 50 feet over water. So that neither would record flocks of migratory birds, both were set to disregard objects flying slower than 125 miles per hour—a feature the Mid-Canada Line lacked.[39]

Installation of an eighteen-site test line across northern Alaska and into northwestern Canada began in July 1953 with a huge sealift of materiel northward from Seattle and Portland in Washington state, through the Bering Strait, to Point Barrow and Barter Island in Alaska. Western Electric operated from a former World War II Navy base at Barrow, where it designed and tested the twenty-eight-foot-long, sixteen-foot-wide, ten-foot-high boxlike modules needed to house men and equipment required to construct the DEW Line. The Air Force airlifted into Barrow modules fabricated in the continental United States and then disassembled into panels. The civilian contractor employed to construct the sites reassembled the modules and, using tractors, towed them over the tundra to sites on trails marked by air-dropped flags. By early 1954, the experimental line was operating with a few preproduction AN/FPS–19 search radars and short-range AN/FPS–23 gap-filler radars. The line consisted of two main stations (one on Barter Island and the other on Point Barrow) and of seven auxiliary and nine intermediate stations. The main and auxiliary stations, equipped for full surveillance and warning, possessed both search and gap-filler radars. All information funneled over scatter communications into sector control in main stations, where controllers identified sightings as friendly or unknown. Data on unknowns then passed to Canadian and American air defenses to the south.[40]

By spring 1954 Air Staff concerns about the feasibility of building the DEW Line had been largely resolved. One Air Staff report noted that some problems remained with false alarms in the short-range radars, which Lincoln scientists had confidence they could correct. Regardless, the Air Force judged the overall experiment successful; the long-range radars were ready for full production, and communications equipment had performed satisfactorily. Most important, supplies could reach workers and technicians performing difficult tasks in an inhospitable climate.[41]

DEW Line. A module (*above*), airlifted in component parts from the United States and now reconstructed and ready for installation on the DEW Line, is towed from an assembly tent before its trip to its final destination in the far north. Men from a construction crew (*below*) head for "home" after a day's work erecting a DEW Line site.

The United States still had to obtain Canada's permission and cooperation to build the DEW Line. The Air Staff predicted few problems after Canada decided to construct, man, and operate the Mid-Canada Line without financial or other U.S. aid. The Air Staff interpreted this as a sign that Canada not only would agree to construction of the DEW Line but also would press for its installation as soon as possible.[42] Indeed, on September 2, 1954, Canada approved the DEW Line in principle in a formal diplomatic note. This enabled the Royal Canadian and U.S. air forces to begin site surveys and to assemble construction materials on Canadian soil. Canada accrued two important benefits from construction of the DEW Line.

DEW Line. Workmen (*left*) prepare concrete foundations which have their footings in natural rock as they begin construction at a DEW Line post. Inspectors (*right*) view construction progress at a main station, where a tower to house electronic equipment will be built.

> Firstly, Canada secured what the United States had up to that time assiduously endeavored to avoid, namely, an explicit recognition of Canadian claims to the exercise of sovereignty in the far north. Secondly, it diminished the threat of hostile encroachments into the Canadian Arctic by making it clear that the region constituted a part of a security zone of North America and NATO.[43]

Canada, in fact, benefited in other ways from the DEW Line. All costs for building the line were to be paid by the United States—a situation Canadians could justify since Canada bore the total cost of the Mid-Canada Line—and Canadian materiel and labor would be used for DEW Line construction, a situation that would garner Canada significant economic benefits.[44]

To coordinate DEW Line matters more efficiently, the two air forces formed the Military Characteristics Committee. The committee and Western Electric both completed preliminary site surveys. Members of the Location Study Group, representing the navies and the air forces of both nations, made some independent surveys to determine the required length and route of the line and on November 12, 1954, submitted their recommendations. They proposed a route from a spot between the Arctic Circle and latitude 70 degrees north on the west coast of Greenland across Canada to join with the two sectors already operating from Barter Island to Cape Lisburne, Alaska.[45] This generally conformed to the final shape of the DEW Line, although modifications and extensions occurred.

DEW Line. A tower (*left*) for temporary communications goes up at one of the DEW Line locations. A U.S. Air Force inspector (*right*) watches as frozen ground is blasted in preparation for the erection of a radar antenna.

In December 1954, Secretary of Defense Wilson's office contracted with General Electric to design, engineer, procure, construct, and install the DEW Line.[46] By this time, according to Assistant Secretary of the Air Force (Financial Management) Lyle S. Garlock, the DEW Line had "the highest priority within the Air Force," and the service pushed for the line to become fully operational as soon as possible.[47] This view resulted less from the DEW Line being instrumental in allowing interceptors to shoot down enemy bombers far from their targets, although that was a consideration, than from the DEW Line implications for warning and defending SAC. General Partridge succinctly expressed the Air Force perception of its air defense mission:

> As a matter of doctrine, we believe that the best defense is a good offense, and we believe that our primary mission in the Air Defense Command is to defend the bases from which the Strategic Air Command is going to operate. We believe also that we have to provide a reasonable, an equitable protection for the key facilities, the population centers and our industry.[48]

In January 1955 the JCS approved installation of an initial, or basic, segment of the DEW Line, to stretch from Cape Dyer on Baffin Island, Canada, to Cape Lisburne, Alaska, and to consist of fifty-seven substations centering on six main stations.[49] Canada and the United States signed a formal agreement to that effect in May 1955. Soon afterward, Western Electric began construction with the goal of completing work

DEW Line site to supply to the Strategic Air Command and the air defense net early warning in response to the manned bomber threat

on the fifty-seven stations and having them ready for operational testing by mid-1957.[50]

DEW Line construction, which started in spring 1955 and ended in early 1957, has been described as

> the most costly construction task ever accomplished in so short a time. Meeting the engineering, construction, and logistical problems involved in maintaining the system every minute or every hour of every day, week, and month, throughout extraordinary achievement. Never before had there been such a mammoth intrusion into the Canadian Arctic.[51]

Because extensive work could be accomplished only in brief periods of the year in the far north and because most construction sites were isolated, supply and transport became paramount. Whereas sea and land routes moved supplies partway, many final sites could only be reached by air transport. Advance construction parties, usually traveling by ski-planes or snow tractors, built airfields by clearing a patch of earth large enough to accommodate C–46 or C–47 transports carrying D–4 tractors. The tractors then carved out landing strips at least 6,000 feet long for use by relatively large C–124 Globemasters.[52]

In 1956 land, water, and air transports (Air Force and commercial) carried 167,183 short tons of supplies to DEW Line sites, at a cost of 25 military and civilian aircraft-related fatalities. Extraordinary efforts had produced a nearly complete DEW Line by the end of 1957. Before giving the Air Force responsibility for the line, Western Electric performed more than one million tests of electrical and communications equipment. The date of July 31, 1957, when responsibility passed to the Air Force, marked the better part of a decade that had been spent planning the line. During the remaining decade, operation and testing of stations, sorting of procedures and defining of tasks, and extension of the line's boundaries east and west occurred.[53]

Other Warning Systems

As the DEW, Mid-Canada, and Pinetree lines were being planned and implemented, the Air Force began establishing other control and warning systems. These systems not only supplemented the northern early-warning lines, they also patrolled areas beyond the range of northern radars. Navy picket ships performed that function aided to some extent by airborne early-warning and control aircraft. In addition, Texas Tower radar platforms, fastened to the ocean floor, extended east coast radar coverage 300 to 500 miles seaward. The expected gain was at least thirty critical minutes to prepare the air defenses for the anticipated Soviet bomber threat.

The 5 planned Texas Towers, deployed about 100 miles off the northeast Atlantic seaboard, could furnish advance warning for key northeastern industrial sites, likely targets of Soviet bombers. In fact, the towers could be placed only on this location because only on the continental shelf off the northeast coast was the water shallow enough to build them. Here, the affixed towers could be equipped with large, long-range radars resembling those used inland, a major advantage over much smaller shipboard and airborne radar. The littoral towers were not restricted by space and weight, as were ships and aircraft. Because of the tower's supposedly fixed and stable locations, the data they provided could be deciphered immediately and precisely. Towers were thus better suited to perform weapons control functions than were radars located on ships or planes. Coastal towers had the same capabilities as inland installations; early-warning aircraft and picket ships did not.[54]

The Air Force originally intended to deploy five Texas Towers, but the plan eventually called for three. Partly because Headquarters USAF wanted to economize, it persuaded ADC that airborne control and warning aircraft could protect the areas where Texas Towers 1 and 5 were to be installed. The three remaining towers did not meet Air Force expectations and, in one instance, caused a major tragedy.

When preparing to activate the towers, the Air Force estimated that twenty-two men could maintain continuous operations. This number

Texas Tower. One of four radar platforms placed on the continental coast of the northeastern United States, this facility was part of a control and warning system developed to defend the United States from overwater attacks.

proved grossly inadequate; by 1957 usually six officers and forty-eight airmen staffed each tower. Required were not only radar operators and technicians but also personnel for plumbing, refrigeration, medical, and cooking chores. Also unique specialists such as marine enginemen dealt with maritime matters pertaining to tower operations. Totally unprepared to fill these positions with qualified people, ADC, in frustration, proposed transferring the whole operation to the Navy and Marine Corps. Headquarters USAF, unwilling to turn the entire operation into such a joint enterprise, turned down the ADC recommendation.[55]

Personnel assigned to Texas Towers usually worked in shifts of one month aboard a tower and one month ashore, their service time counting as an overseas isolated tour. They spent much duty time trying to operate the radar and communications equipment used in this peculiar environment, a difficult job at best. The Air Force occupied TT–2, 110 miles east of Cape Cod, in December 1955. Tower and crew alike suffered the effects of constant vibration from the rotation of the radar dish and the operation of diesel generators and other equipment. Only when the AN/FPS–20A broke down or needed service, all too frequent occurrences, was there relative relief from the incessant and resonating buzz. The surrounding water and the footings driven into the ocean floor even trans-

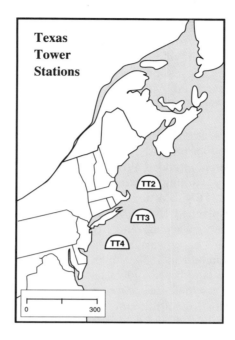

mitted distant sounds up the steel legs to be amplified through the whole structure. The tower stood

> like a three-pronged tuning fork . . . . Matters were not im-
> proved when, every half-minute or so during the frequent
> fog days, the dismal sounding foghorn croaked out its for-
> lorn message.[56]

Their instability in the face of Atlantic storms eventually negated whatever real advantage the towers had over ships and aircraft as early-warning radar platforms. The worst example was TT-4, 84 miles southeast of New York Harbor. Operational in early summer 1957, its design and faulty construction made it an engineering nightmare. Anchored in over 30 fathoms of water, a depth twice that beneath TT-2 and three times the water under TT-3, TT-4 rocked ominously in even moderate seas. Navy underwater survey teams identified and corrected some of the problems with the supports, but nothing could offset the continual damage below the surface. The crew abandoned the structure on September 10, 1960, in the face of Hurricane Donna. Two days later the storm battered the tower with 132-mile-an-hour winds and waves in excess of 50 feet, doing enough damage to force the Air Force and its construction contractor to specify February 1, 1961, as the date to begin

completely renovating TT–4. A caretaker crew of 14 contractor maintenance workers and 14 Air Force personnel stayed behind. On January
15, 1961, a fierce winter gale bore in on the hapless station and ripped
off all 3 of its legs in succession. Its 28 occupants sank with the platform
into the sea; none survived.[57] The Air Force decommissioned the last of
the towers, TT–3, on March 25, 1963, ending a less than glorious venture.

Airborne early-warning and control aircraft, another project meant
to extend advance warning seaward, proved more worthwhile than
Texas Towers. The Navy ended World War II as the only service developing airborne early-warning systems, and it continued tests by adapting
radars to Grumman TBM–3W torpedo bombers and PB–1Ws (converted
B–17s). The Navy planned to use these planes in antisubmarine warfare
and in offshore early-warning and tracking roles. Interested in the
Navy's progress with early-warning aircraft, the Air Force participated
in various tests beginning in 1950, which involved Navy PB–1Ws working with Air Force land-based radars and interceptors. These tests convinced Air Force air defense commanders that early-warning planes
could compensate for low-altitude deficiencies in its line-of-sight ground
radars, then reasonably effective at ranges of about 150 miles against
medium and high-altitude targets and only half this distance against low-
altitude aircraft.[58]

The Navy primarily promoted early warning not for continental defense but for fleet defense and other missions applicable to naval operations. Accordingly, ADC urged Headquarters USAF to use naval hardware and tactics and to take the lead in early-warning aircraft for home
defense. By November 1950, the Air Force carefully watched tests conducted by the Navy on its PB–1W, equipped with an AN/APS–20B
search radar set and an AN/APS–45 height finder. In mid-1951, the Air
Force chose a larger version of this aircraft, the Lockheed Super Constellation, and equipped it with the same radars for airborne early warning. In November 1951, ten of these planes had been ordered from Lockheed, but first deliveries were delayed until 1953, largely because of industry strikes.[59]

When the EC–121 Warning Star arrived in the Air Force, its hump-
back and its crescent-shaped dish and antenna on top earned it the nick-
name "Pregnant Goose." Intended for early-warning and weapons control activities, the Warning Star had a combat radius of about 1,000 nautical miles, could cruise at approximately 200 knots, and had a service
ceiling of less than 24,000 feet. More important, it possessed on-station
capabilities supplied by 4 radars.[60]

The Air Force eventually based the EC–121s on two permanent
sites, one at Otis Air Force Base, Massachusetts, and the other at
McClellan Air Force Base, California. On the east coast, the planes origi-

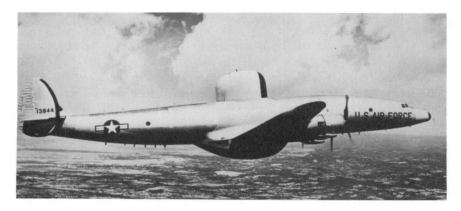

RC–121C. Bulging with electronic detection devices, the highly specialized search and communications equipment within this airplane was designed to give the defense maximum warning against the approach of unidentified air and surface ships.

nally patrolled an area between Texas Towers and Navy picket vessels, stationed beyond the radius of the Warning Stars. Off the west coast, only picket vessels supplemented the planes. Unfortunately, throughout much of the 1950s troubles plagued the early-warning aircraft. Problems with radar and communications equipment continued. Frequent malfunctions in electronic systems often grounded planes over long periods for repairs. Aircraft able to patrol usually missed crew members with key specialties, especially weapons controllers. [61]

Tests and exercises conducted by ADC in the late 1950s indicated that Warning Stars did not perform their missions successfully, mainly because of difficulties with the electronic equipment. Progress in ADC's persistent attempts to fix quirks in the system seemed excrutiatingly slow, and by 1959 ADC reacted similarly as it had after its experience with the Texas Towers: it wanted to transfer the whole airborne early-warning mission, planes included, to the Navy. Calmer heads prevailed at Headquarters USAF, and the transfer did not occur. [62]

Time proved the Air Force decision to continue improving, refining, and developing its airborne early-warning program to be correct. Positive results came slowly. In the latter 1960s, the EC–121's electronic and radar systems improved substantially, its range increased, and it carried automatic data links to the SAGE network. Airborne early warning became especially compelling in the 1970s when Boeing produced the Airborne Early Warning and Control System (AWACS) aircraft. Specifically designated the Boeing E–3A, it incorporated detection, tracking, and electronic countermeasure capabilities and interceptor-controller functions, and its performance far exceeded that of the first Warning Stars.

The GOC remained the last warning against enemy bombers until 1959. When the Air Force began Operation SKYWATCH in 1952, ADC and especially its deputy commander, General Smith, believed the GOC indispensable to air defense. At the time, no better method existed for detecting low-flying aircraft approaching or traveling over American territory.

By 1957 the situation seemed to have changed. The medium-range and distant-warning lines were functioning or soon would be. The same was true for Texas Towers and airborne early warning. All were expected to provide low-altitude support. The Air Force expected these systems would lessen or obviate the need for the GOC. Regardless that Texas Towers appeared a most inglorious failure and the EC–121 program was experiencing prolonged growing pains, the Air Force decided to deactivate the GOC.

Some officers in ADC argued that the GOC was needed until low-altitude gap-filler radars and other surveillance systems became truly dependable, but Headquarters USAF decided in the late 1950s that the increased speed of modern jet bombers made the GOC obsolete. The GOC had never performed efficiently and had become just another expense on an already strained budget. In early 1958, the views of Maj. Gen. Hugh Parker, head of Western Air Defense Force, reflected the disenchantment of commanders in the field with the GOC. Parker told Lt. Gen. Joseph H. Atkinson, head of ADC, that "surveillance information submitted by the GOC has not been timely, nor has it been accurate enough to be acted upon by the air defense system. It is logical to assume that this situation would not change during an actual war. . . ." [63]

Parker's analysis prevailed in the Air Staff, and Headquarters USAF abolished the GOC, even though difficult. Over the years many volunteers had come and gone, but a corps of experienced civilians remained who consistently staffed GOC posts and frequently served in remote locations under considerable personal hardship. The Air Force would find it difficult to tell these dedicated individuals that their services, once thought essential, were no longer wanted.

The Air Force nevertheless proceeded to phase out the GOC, ending twenty-four-hour-a-day operations in many observer posts on January 1, 1958. In July the GOC celebrated the sixth anniversary of SKYWATCH. The Air Force had publicized previous anniversaries, but in 1958 military personnel in the GOC minimized the occasion. Soon, civilian observers joined the Ready Reserve, and many military personnel moved to other assignments. The GOC deactivated on January 31, 1959, ending a noble experiment that, if nothing else, allowed concerned citizens to become informed about, and actively participate in, home air defense operations.[64]

Deciding the fate of the GOC was one of many problems the Air Force had to confront in its surveillance and warning programs. Reflecting the historic pattern of fluctuating allocations for U.S. defense, by 1956–1957 the money promised for air defense during the Korean War now proved difficult to obtain. At the end of 1957, ADC operated 182 radar stations, which reported surveillance data to 17 control centers. Of this number, 32 had been added during the last half of the year as low-altitude, unmanned gap-filler radars. The total consisted of 47 gap-filler stations, 75 Permanent System radars, 39 semimobile radars, 19 Pinetree stations, and 1 Lashup station. The single Texas Tower in operation also counted as a functioning continental radar station.[65]

The Air Force instituted plans to obtain radars with greater height-finding and range capabilities. A 1955 interservice study, Project LAMP-LIGHT, had predicted that the existing and programmed search radars were vulnerable to electronic countermeasures (ECMs) that might make them useless in combat. As a possible solution, the LAMPLIGHT group recommended the development of radars that could quickly be tuned to different frequencies when they encountered jamming. Although frequency agility could not eliminate the ECM threat, it was expected to combat it as effectively as any other means available. ADC grew anxious to have new radars available during the 1959–1962 period, but Headquarters USAF warned that new technology generally meant delays in equipment production. Moreover, it was expected to be difficult to obtain funds for radars designed to counter the manned bomber after the Soviets launched Sputnik in October 1957, an indication of the potential for ICBM attacks against the United States.[66]

As anticipated, problems arose in funding and developing the new technology. The Air Force decided to equip its operating search radars with antijamming modifications, known as fixes. Exercises held between ADC and SAC in October 1956 and January 1957 highlighted the need for these modifications. In both exercises, SAC bombers, using the most up-to-date ECM equipment, virtually blinded the defensive radars. General Partridge of CONAD and General Atkinson of ADC pleaded with Headquarters USAF to expedite the antijamming fixes.[67]

The promise of a new ICBM threat meant a series of financial disasters for continental ground radar programs. Funds for frequency-agility radars decreased by $29 million for fiscal year 1960, and the Air Force projected a delay in the program until 1965. This decrease, combined with an austere new design for SAGE station deployment (especially in the south and southwest), indicated Congress's reluctance to allocate vast sums for bomber defense in the 1960s as the threat of Soviet bomber attack appeared to decrease with the concomitant growth of the Soviet Union's missile force.[68]

The Air Defense Weapons Force

Scientists and other proponents of air defense in the early 1950s advocated a system whose primary function would be to save the lives of North American citizens. The Air Force view was that the DEW Line and other warning components offered a degree of insurance that the American retaliatory capability would not be destroyed in a Soviet first strike. Air Force spokesmen consistently stated it was a chimera to believe that a one hundred percent defense could ever be built. If an enemy aimed his attacks on America's great cities, most bombers would get through the defenses and cause widespread nuclear destruction.[69]

Despite this gloomy prognosis, the Air Force believed it was responsible for doing everything it could to limit damage to American soil if not to overseas installations while destroying as many enemy bombers as possible. The Air Staff and the ADC remained convinced that the Soviets could not believe they would be allowed to attack uncontestedly American cities, important defense facilities, or, most important, SAC bases. Notwithstanding its emphasis on retaliatory capabilities, the Air Force in the 1950s took seriously the mission of direct defense against bombardment.

Nowhere was the capability to destroy enemy bombers given more consideration than in ADC. Chidlaw and his successors carefully noted Soviet progress in bomber development; ADC's interest began to peak in 1954 with the onset of the bomber gap. The bomber gap first appeared in the Soviets' 1954 May Day air show when one Bison jet bomber flew by the reviewing stand. The following year, many more Bisons appeared during the May Day parade. As events later indicated, the Soviets probably used multiple flyovers of the same aircraft to give observers the impression they possessed more planes than they did. They successfully impressed western military attachés and other spectators with the strength of their military aircraft programs. In the wake of the apparently thriving Bison program and with the development of the Tu–95 Bear and the 1953 thermonuclear explosion, a 1955 CIA national intelligence estimate (NIE) claimed that "the USSR is devoting a major aircraft production effort to the development of massive intercontinental air attack capability." The NIE predicted that if the current trend persisted, by 1959 the Soviet long-range air force would be more powerful than SAC forces.[70]

General LeMay, SAC Commander, agreed with the NIE during 1956 Senate Airpower Hearings:

Combat-Ready Aircraft and Aircrews

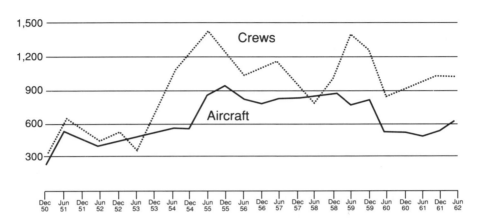

> The Soviets will enjoy a numerical advantage in long-range bombers in the period 1958–1960. We would be fool-hardy to assume they would not also provide the weapons, bases, refueling capability, maintenance capacity, training, and professional personnel to support this numerical superiority in aircraft. . . . I can only conclude that they will have greater striking power than we will have in the time period under our present plans and programs.[71]

The bomber gap implications were far more decisive for strategic offensive programs than for air defense. LeMay's prescription to counteract the Soviet bomber threat was to expand the Air Force fleet of B–52 bombers, which became operational in 1955. Congress agreed. Shortly after LeMay's ominous predictions of Soviet bomber strength, the gap began to recede. Critical intelligence information gathered by CIA-controlled U–2 surveillance planes dispelled the bomber gap myth (although the Air Force, partly for parochial reasons, continued to insist that a bomber gap existed even after the CIA and the other military intelligence agencies had deduced otherwise).

In ADC, Chidlaw and his staff officers reacted to the bomber gap scare with stepped-up measures to improve the air defense combat force, the leading edge of which were fighter-interceptors. Since 1948 the Air Force had tried unsuccessfully to develop a true all-weather jet interceptor. The F–80, F–84, and F–86 day fighters had served as expedients, as had the all-weather F–94Cs and F–86Ds. The F–94C was merely a night-fighter version of the F–80, one of the Air Force's earliest jet aircraft. As for the F–86D, it was largely the result of General Saville's pressuring the Air Force to convert the F–86, the best Air Force fighter

225

in the early 1950s, into a single-seat interceptor, which proved only an interim solution because the Dog required frequent modifications. Furthermore, many pilots thought that the equipment in all-weather interceptors demanded a two-seat aircraft. The F–86D was described by one air defense commander as "a fine airplane for a two-headed fellow with four arms." There remained, of course, the F–89, but the Scorpion, although a two-seater, experienced endless structural and mechanical problems, making it the target of even more criticism from pilots than the F–86D.[72]

To perform the air defense mission adequately, the Air Force had invested much of its hopes in the 1954 interceptor. Convair won the contract for the aircraft in July 1951, but later that year the Air Force realized the plane's specifications were too advanced for Convair to fulfill the contract by 1954. Basically, ADC wanted a long-range, extremely fast aircraft capable of operating at high altitudes. As Chidlaw viewed the situation in August 1954, a few months after the lone Bison appeared in the Moscow air day parade:

> The picture as we see it now is grim. Intelligence experts state that we could expect a Soviet capability by December of 1955 of attacking our major industrial targets and key SAC facilities with 200 heavy bombers at altitudes approaching 55,000 feet and at speeds of .8 Mach to .9 Mach with the capability of delivering 1 to 5 megaton yield bombs. If this is true, then frankly, the interceptors currently considered for contract are of marginal value to us. In the case of the F–102A, for example, we are fighting to attain a maneuverable ceiling of 50,000 feet.[73]

The F–102A Delta Dagger referred to by Chidlaw became the interim model of the 1954 interceptor the Air Force encouraged Convair to build while it continued its development of the ultimate interceptor, the F–102B, which became the F–106 Delta Dart. In effect, the Air Force approved a two-step production scheme for Convair: limited production of the F–102A with the J–57 engine to precede mass production of the F–102B with its more powerful J–67 engine and state-of-the-art Hughes fire control (electronics and radar) system. Meanwhile, the fire control system installed in the interim F–102A would include advanced features such as an automatic flight control system, a semiautomatic armament selection device, and a data link with SAGE. Hughes had difficulty delivering this sophisticated package, and when ADC began accepting the aircraft in 1956, the system remained incomplete and some components were virtually untested. In 1958, when Hughes had more time to perfect the system, it spent three to four months making modifications. More modifications occurred beginning in 1960 when the Air Force decided most of its Delta Daggers would have to be equipped to meet the elec-

Table 3. Air Defense Aircraft

Aircraft	Dec 1950	Jun 1951	Dec 1951	Jun 1952	Dec 1952	Jun 1953	Dec 1953	Jun 1954	Dec 1954	Jun 1955	Dec 1955	Jun 1956	Dec 1956	Jun 1957	Dec 1957	Jun 1958	Dec 1958	Jun 1959	Dec 1959
F-82	26	19	4																
F-94A&B	60	82	144	117	93	20	45	14											
F-89B&C		4	25	51	60	31	62	40											
F-80		41	37	17	15	15													
F-84	43	103	38	16	41	115	21												
F-86 (day)	236	255	174	192	215	229	180	82	37										
F-47		96	70	72	43	17													
F-51		213	195	149	172	160	31												
F-86D						123	601	798	783	1,026	1,041	1,014	710	345	36				
F-94C						103	187	265	201	196	199	172	164	116	52	20	16		
F-89D								76	118	183	250	222	106	104	34	12			
F-86L													56	393	576	419	327	188	133
F-89H												72	112	107	78	40	49	21	
F-89J													15	124	242	286	264	260	207
F-102A												5	97	301	428	517	627	611	482
F-104A																51	100	86	90
F-101B																		73	188
F-106A																		18	97
Total	365	813	687	614	639	813	1,127	1,275	1,139	1,405	1,490	1,485	1,260	1,490	1,446	1,345	1,383	1,257	1,197

F–106A Delta Dart. The "ultimate" interceptor, this airplane became the last model to be devoted solely to air defense.

tronic countermeasure threat. New devices allowed the fire control system to be "tuned automatically, change frequencies at random, rapidly reestablish a broken 'lock' on a target and otherwise combat electronic jamming." [74]

Equally important as the Delta Dagger's fire control system was its configuration. The delta wing, which had influenced the Air Force to select Convair's design, was not a new idea. Its inception was in the wind tunnels of Nazi Germany, and the British considered the wing best for high-speed performance. The first successful delta wing aircraft, the experimental XF–92A, had been developed by Convair and successfully test-flew in September 1948. This experimental model later gave rise to the Delta Dagger and the subsequent Delta Dart. Convair's first tests of the delta wing F–102 showed the aircraft incapable of supersonic flight, considered by ADC commanders absolutely necessary to catch Soviet bombers. This inadequacy arose from a design problem of aerodynamic drag on the wing. In the early 1950s, inadequate equipment and facilities hampered supersonic wind tunnel tests. Test aircraft, often miniature models, failed to correspond dimensionally to the actual product. Only in December 1951 when Richard Whitcomb of the National Advisory Committee for Aeronautics (NACA) developed a new supersonic aircraft design sharply reducing the fuselage cross section over the delta wing and subsequently lessening aerodynamic drag were these problems overcome. Known as the area rule, Whitcomb's concept soon became a standard feature of all high-performance aircraft; it gave their fuselages the familiar Coke-bottle shape characteristic of future fighters. Amplifying and expanding the area rule, Convair engineers installed a sharper nose on the F–102A, added fairings to both sides of the plane's body, and installed a more powerful engine. With these changes, the Delta Dagger achieved supersonic speed, and 875 interim F–102As were eventually built. [75]

An F–102A phase-out began in 1959 with the introduction of the long-awaited F–106. Development of the F–106 had suffered unforeseen delays with the J–75 engine and final cockpit design. By 1957, Headquarters USAF seriously considered canceling it altogether, but ADC persisted and this time won the debate. Problems with development of the aircraft's intricate fire control system and powerful propulsion system pushed its operational date forward to 1959. With these problems solved, the plane received an electronic system that included a digital computer, tying it into the SAGE network. Data links enabled pilots to receive information faster and to fire their weapons more accurately. The addition of the Pratt and Whitney J–75—P–17 afterburner-equipped engine gave the F–106 a fifty percent increase in power over the F–102's engine. In fact, the Delta Dart's top speed (Mach 2+) made it about twice as fast as the Delta Dagger. The Dart remained durable enough to appear in modified versions in Air National Guard units in the 1980s. Eventually, 340 F–106s were built. [76]

Although satisfied with the eventual performance of the F–102 and F–106 interceptors, the Air Force was dissatisfied with the many years it took to develop and produce either one. During this period, ADC had pressed for other century series aircraft for the defense forces, supplementing its fighter units even if it had to accept aircraft not specifically designed for air defense. Such was the case with the Lockheed F–104 Starfighter, best suited for tactical air superiority. ADC staff officers thought the Starfighter could have limited use as a day fighter, even though too small to be equipped with data link equipment and thus disqualified from operating in the SAGE system. Despite the Air Research and Development Command's recommendation that the "limited capability interceptor" should not be assigned to defense units, Headquarters USAF acquiesced in ADC's requests for the F–104 to help fill the gap between the F–102A and F–106. Accordingly, ADC received six F–104 squadrons in April 1956. The small fighters remained in test status through 1957 and became operational the following year. At the end of 1958, ADC had one hundred F–104s but already planned their retirement with the expected deployment of the Delta Dart. ADC's Starfighters

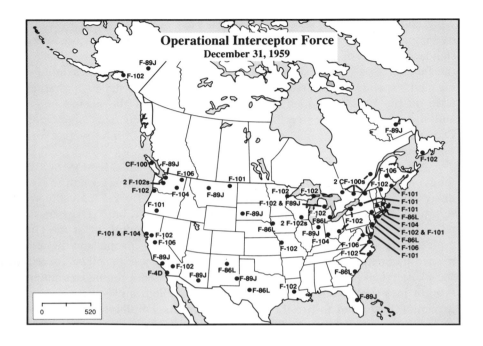

Operational Interceptor Force
December 31, 1959

therefore transferred to Air National Guard units in 1960, only to return
to ADC in 1963 in the aftermath of the Cuban Missile Crisis of the pre-
ceding year. The last F–104 air defense squadron did not deactivate until
1969.[77]

A far better century series aircraft, produced to fill the gap in anticipation of the 1954 interceptor, was the McDonnell F–101B Voodoo. In
its early development as the XF–88, the aircraft was intended to perform
long-range penetration missions. But in the early 1950s, ADC realized
the plane could meet the standards for an interceptor. At the time, ADC
considered for service as stop-gap all-weather fighters the F–101, an advanced version of the F–89, and an interceptor model of the North
American F–100. The F–101 appeared the most promising of the three,
and Headquarters USAF agreed with the ADC choice in February 1955.
On the basis of its experiences with the 1954 interceptor, Headquarters
USAF insisted that all the "kinks be ironed out" before it accepted delivery of the plane. So, when the first Voodoos became operational in 1959,
the Air Force received a thoroughly tested machine, linkable with
SAGE. Surprisingly, the F–101B did not rate far behind the touted F–
106 in terms of performance, although its fire control system was markedly inferior. With the Delta Dart, the Voodoo became the heart of the
fighter-interceptor force in the 1960s and remained, modified and im-

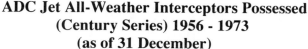

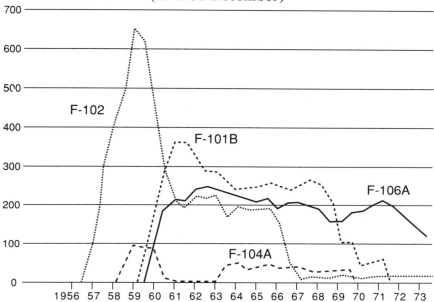

ADC Jet All-Weather Interceptors Possessed
(Century Series) 1956 - 1973
(as of 31 December)

proved, in service with Air National Guard and Canadian units in the 1980s.[78]

Air Force leadership of the 1960s would have been shocked by the thought that the Delta Dart and Voodoo would remain first-line interceptors for more than 25 years. As early as April 1953, ADC asked the Air Staff to consider the need for a long-range interceptor with a 1,000-mile radius, a combat altitude of 60,000 feet, and a speed between Mach 1.5 and Mach 2. Staff officers in Colorado Springs thought such an aircraft would be needed to exploit the improved surveillance coverage that programmed early-warning systems would provide. An ideal interceptor would destroy enemy raiders as far as possible from their targets in North America. The F–106 and F–101B could not meet ADC standards for long-range performance.[79]

Headquarters USAF agreed with ADC that a long-range interceptor was needed, but budget and specification problems delayed awarding the contract until June 1957, when North American was chosen. Designated the F–108, the aircraft would be a Mach 3, two-seat, twin-engine, stainless steel interceptor. Its range would permit it to reach the DEW Line, but when there, its range would have exceeded that of ground control.

F–101B Voodoo. Designed as a strategic penetration fighter, this model of the Voodoo served as an all-weather fighter and, with the Delta Dart, became the heart of the fighter-interceptor force in the 1960s.

This potentially fatal handicap could be overcome if an advanced airborne intercept radar would allow the plane to operate in tandem with other F–108s. All these plans came to nought, however, in the 1959 budget crunch. Forced to choose between a projected Mach 3 bomber—the B–70, also being built by North American—and the F–108, Air Force Chief of Staff Thomas White decided to scrap the fighter and keep the bomber in development. White readily conceded the requirement for an interceptor with the proposed characteristics of the F–108, but he reasoned that the Air Force's greater need was for a weapon that would constitute the most potent threat to the Soviets, and "hands down, the B–70 wins that argument." [80]

The effect of the looming ICBM threat eventually consigned the B–70 to the F–108's fate. White's rationale for choosing the bomber over the fighter reflected long-established Air Force doctrine favoring strategic offensive forces in any consideration of weapons systems. White explained:

> Of course, our philosophy is based on the fact that offense is the best defense. . . . I am perfectly certain that . . . air defense could absorb the national budget, and . . . still could not guarantee 100-percent defense. So, in the final analysis, it is a matter of judgment at what level you balance out between offense and a minimum adequate defense. [81]

GAR–1 Falcon. This infrared-seeking guided aircraft rocket is shown fitted in its launching position under an aircraft's wing.

When the Korean War started in 1950, Air Force interceptors carried machineguns as primary armament; by the end of 1954, F–86Ds, F–94Cs, and F–89Ds carried 2.75-inch folding-fin air-to-air rockets (FFARs). Because development on the radar-guided air-to-air Falcon missile had lagged, this weapon did not enter the air defense inventory until 1955. The first to arrive, the Guided Air Rocket-1 (GAR–1), came in March 1956, two years later than expected (F–89H interceptors carried the rockets). The GAR–2 radar-guided missile, relying on infrared guidance, appeared soon after. In the next few years, Hughes improved the missiles' accuracy as it developed more sophisticated models in both radar and infrared categories. [82]

As ADC viewed the situation, the Falcon, in its various guises, did not provide a sufficiently lethal force because it required a direct hit on its quarry or had to come extremely close to its quarry to be effective. Compounding the problem were intelligence reports that indicated Soviet bombers carried jamming devices capable of disrupting radar-guided rockets. Part of the ADC solution to defeating such ploys lay in the development of nuclear air-to-air missiles packing so much destructive power that their detonation in the vicinity of an enemy would ensure his annihilation. [83]

ADC first submitted a formal requirement for atomic weapons in 1952. Although sympathetic, Headquarters USAF could not do much at the time. Atomic materials were just becoming plentiful, and those available went to SAC, uncontestedly. Besides, the development of small atomic warheads to fit inside an interceptor's air-to-air rockets was expected to be difficult. Protection of military and civilian personnel in contact with the weapons would be a major task in itself. ADC, confident difficulties could be overcome, continued to argue for atomic capability.[84] In 1954 the JCS finally approved the ADC request. Douglas Aircraft received a contract for development of an atomic rocket, and the Atomic Energy Commission started to develop a suitable warhead. The rocket, temporarily called Ding Dong and subsequently designated the MB-1 Genie, flew on an F-89J, the aircraft judged most adaptable in the shortest time. The JCS set January 1, 1957, as the target date for air defense forces to become operational with nuclear weapons. To expedite initial development, the first rockets had no guidance systems; this was later corrected.[85]

The target date for delivery of the MB-1 was technically met on January 1, 1957. Inventories at Wurtsmith Air Force Base, Michigan, and Hamilton Air Force Base, California, included rockets and F-89J aircraft. Not until July 1957 did the rocket and its warhead actually fire in an atomic test in Nevada. Although the test involved no target, the warhead detonated as required. To prove the weapon safe for air defense over populated areas, several volunteers stood directly below the detonation in the Nevada desert, marking the last firing of a nuclear air defense weapon until 1962. In 1958 the Soviets announced a moratorium on atmospheric nuclear weapons testing, and the United States followed suit.[86] Ultimately, ADC hoped to equip its advanced century series interceptors with nuclear armed guided rockets, but nuclear weapons proved to have less impact on air defense forces than ADC had envisioned in the early 1950s. First, safety considerations severely restricted realistic training, and second, reliability and sophistication of conventional weapons improved substantially in the next two decades.

Concurrently, the Air Force better understood what its new weapons and electronics systems implied for air defense fighter tactics. Before the early 1950s, Air Force interceptors, armed with fixed guns, had to train their weapons on a bomber for an appreciable time in order to score a kill. To obtain the necessary lead angle for the guns, a fighter had to fly slightly ahead of the target and turn with it. If all went as planned, a curved course brought the interceptor closer on the bomber's rear as the attack progressed. Because interceptors had to attack from relatively short range and bombers were usually well armed in the rear, the chance for a successful interception remained relatively low. The development of rockets changed fighter tactics: a single shot could destroy a bomber. Interceptors now had to be in firing position for just an instant, eliminating the need to follow the bomber on a curved course and allowing an attack from any direction. Increased rocket range also obviated the dangerously close range required by fighters to achieve kills.[87] Yet in the late 1950s rear attack tactics resurfaced with the use of infrared guidance systems that homed in on the heat emanating from a target's tail section. Thus rear attack methods, predominant in World War II, remained in use.

No matter how the interceptor pilot approached his prey, he depended on ground instructions, especially with establishment of the SAGE network.

> Gone were the days of the "heads-up" fighter pilot with his few instruments to follow and the seat of his pants to fall back on when something went wrong. The jet all-weather pilot flew by the radar scope and the beam given him by his co-partner, the radar director on the ground. An error on the part of either member of the team and the enemy would slip away unharmed into the night or fog. Perhaps never before in the history of combat aviation was the success of a mission so dependent on ground-air teamwork as it was in air defense operations.[88]

The controller, the team member on the ground, often became extremely dissatisfied with his job. Under the best of circumstances, air defense alert duties could prove trying; the general routine consisted of waiting and boredom. Air defense stations, often located in remote, isolated areas, also fostered low morale. Judging by the high annual turnover rate in their ranks, weapons controllers more than likely either left the Air Force at the end of their tours or switched to other specialties. ADC estimated in 1954 that, of the 988 officers assigned to weapons controller duties, only about half were fully qualified. This statistic was attributed largely to poorly selected personnel attending the controllers school at Tyndall Air Force Base, Florida. In May 1954, ADC suggested that the Air Force attempt to select better qualified, more highly motivated officers, offer them more effective training, and make a career in weapons control more attractive. Although the Air Force increased staffing rates significantly and many controllers enjoyed and took pride in their work, morale problems continued.[89]

BOMARC

In the 1950s, the Air Force strove to create a composite air defense force. The philosophy of not relying on a single weapons system, such as manned aircraft, could be stated: "Analysis of any one weapon system will reveal weaknesses which could be exploited; however, it is extremely difficult to find any one specific weakness which is common to a composite weapon system."[90] This conviction partly explains the Air Force attempts over a ten-year period to develop an unmanned interceptor to complement and supplement its other defensive weapons.

As early as 1945 the Army Air Forces (AAF) had asked Boeing to study prospects for developing a ground-to-air pilotless aircraft (GAPA). AAF interest in this concept began during World War II when Germany launched V–2 surface-to-surface liquid-fueled missiles against Britain. The V–2, with a range of only 300 miles, was not particularly accurate. It could, however, attain supersonic speeds, inviting prospects for similar, though more deadly, weapons in the postwar world.[91]

Boeing's GAPA experiments envisioned a missile effective up to 35 miles. Although one test missile fired successfully and the Army and Navy were testing various other short-range surface-to-air missiles, the JCS decided to halt GAPA studies in 1949. The Air Force did not contest their decision; its concept of air defense called for striking an enemy bomber as far from its target as possible. Accordingly, Air Materiel Command asked Boeing to join with researchers at the University of Michigan's Air Research Center in January 1950 to examine the feasibility of building an accurate, long-range, supersonic missile for air defense. By June 1950 experts at Boeing and Michigan agreed that a missile could be developed to fly at speeds from Mach .09 to Mach 3 at a ceiling of 80,000 feet and with a range of 200 miles. The missile, to be called BOMARC ("BO" for Boeing and "MARC" for Michigan Air Research Center), was expected to become operational by 1956.[92]

Many Air Force technical specialists doubted that the 1956 operational date for BOMARC could be met. Time proved them correct. The scientists' estimates proved too optimistic, and by the end of 1954 BOMARC's operational date had slipped to 1959. Strictly speaking, the Air Force achieved operational readiness in December 1959 when one missile was ready to be deployed at McGuire Air Force Base, New Jersey. This accomplishment came after seven years of testing and attempts to mate BOMARC with a nuclear warhead and integrate it into SAGE.[93]

Overall, BOMARC proved a major disappointment for the Air Force. In the early 1950s, air defense commanders foresaw 4,800 missiles deployed at 40 sites in the continental United States. In actuality, fewer than 500 missiles deployed on 8 sites in the northeastern United States and on 2 sites in Canada. Testing did not end with the activation of the McGuire missile site; it continued until August 1963 when 215 missiles had been expended in tests that usually failed to meet standards. By the end of 1964, the inactivated BOMARC A was converted into a drone.

An IM–99 BOMARC missile being launched at the Air Force Missile Test Center, Patrick Air Force Base, Florida, on April 15, 1960

The improved BOMARC B finally achieved a measure of reliability. It could be equipped with a nuclear warhead and synchronized with SAGE. This was an air-breathing, rocket-boosted missile with a range

237

exceeding 400 miles in its advanced versions and with a speed of Mach 2.5. Powered by a ramjet engine, BOMARC B was guided to its quarry by the SAGE system; it then homed in on the target by radar. It remained in the air defense inventory until 1972.[94]

When BOMARC developed into an efficient system, the Soviet manned bomber threat was no longer a major public concern. As early as 1959, funds for testing and deployment were declining. Congressional enthusiasm for funding a weapon designed to defeat the bomber waned as the ICBM appeared to be the more dangerous threat. By the early 1960s, air defense had been assigned a low priority in Congress. Requirements became far more compelling for antimissile defense and, to a greater extent, for the burgeoning Atlas, Titan, and Minuteman offensive ICBM programs. After the Air Force achieved its goal in attempting to improve BOMARC, it did not want to deactivate the missile. It made a case that the bomber threat had not disappeared completely, and Congress allowed a relatively small deployment in the eastern United States and Canada until the early 1970s.

It was in March 1954 that the Eisenhower administration decided to install an "integrated, efficient, and highly potent air defense system." As the decade ended, most components of this system were in place and functioning. The far northern DEW Line constituted the earliest array of warning radars. Approximately 1,000 miles south of the DEW Line lay another radar screen, the Mid-Canada Line, built along the 55th parallel and extending from coast to coast. The third radar chain, the Pinetree Line, a joint enterprise of the United States and Canada, existed along the border. Extending the radar screens were sea patrols consisting of Navy picket ships, Texas Tower radar platforms, and earlywarning surveillance aircraft. In addition, until 1959, the GOC supplied a last-resort warning service. The system had the ingredient most important to defense—depth. Because of the likelihood that one of the warning devices would fail to function properly, suitable backup systems should also have been available.

Theoretically, the DEW Line would detect unidentified planes approaching from the north during an actual attack. High-wave scatter broadcasts would relay this news to the Combat Operations Center in Colorado Springs. SAC bombers would be alerted while forward-based interceptors obtained positive identification. If enemy aircraft were positively identified, friendly fighters would seek and destroy them while other friendly fighters scrambled to assist. Immediate warning from the far north would provide four to six hours for preparation, allowing the air battle to be directed from Colorado Springs. If a far less likely (given the range of Soviet bombers) flank attack from the sea routes occurred, the preparation time would be less and the battle would probably be more decentralized, with sector commanders making more decisions at the local level. Enemy aircraft evading defensive fighters, when practically upon their targets, would come under fire from Army antiaircraft artillery and missiles and from additional interceptors directed by the sector Air Force officer in charge. SAGE, on the basis of radar information and with the use of digital computers to direct interceptors, missiles, and antiaircraft artillery, would actually deploy the weapons. Thus the whole air defense network responded to orders from Colorado Springs, but the direction of individual battles depended largely on automatic systems and the judgment of commanders in the air defense sectors.

How this complex command and control system would have functioned during the confusion of battle is difficult to determine in retrospect. Exercises between ADC and SAC predicted advantages for the offensive forces; for example, defenses were easily deactivated electronically. Still, SAC was the preeminent force of its kind in the world, and during the 1950s and early 1960s the inferior Soviet long-range bomber force could not hope to match its power and capabilities. The primary ADC objective remained to allow SAC sufficient warning for dispersing its bombers and launching retaliatory raids, not to shoot down enemy bombers. Countless communications tests among the warning lines; the Colorado Springs Command Post; the SAC Command Post in Omaha, Nebraska; and the Pentagon indicated the feasibility of such an approach.

Chapter 9

Organizing to Meet the Threat

In the second half of the 1950s, concurrent with Air Force efforts to bring defense systems to operational status, restructuring of the air defense organization occurred. Thorny debate among the three services on roles and missions, as well as delicate negotiations between government and military officials in Washington and Ottawa, produced a more cohesive and sensibly organized command and control and planning network for North American air defense.

Continental Air Defense Command: A Joint Command for Air Defense

Since the 1948 Key West conference, disagreements among the services over air defense roles and missions had prevailed. One decision made at Key West was to invest the Air Force with primary responsibility for continental air defense. The Army's contribution was to be anti-aircraft guns and missiles, and the Navy's, picket early-warning vessels and limited numbers of ship- and land-based fighter squadrons.

In the first years after Key West, the Defense Department attempted to achieve a measure of coordinated joint planning for air defense. This was part of an overall Defense Department effort "to provide formal machinery for effecting essential interservice coordination in certain fields of joint interest." In 1951 the JCS directed the services to revise the *Joint Action Army-Navy* publication that had served as the basic authority for interservice coordination in the pre–World War II years and to reissue it as the *Joint Action Armed Forces*. In the course of the project, the Army proposed the establishment of joint training centers to oversee training for air defense, air support of ground troops, and airborne and amphibious operations. The training centers would report to the JCS through service executive agents. Under the terms of the proposal, the Army would oversee tactical air support and airborne centers; the Air Force, the air defense center; and the Navy, the amphibious center. To

the Air Force, however, the proposed arrangement seemed an encroach-
ment by the Army on Air Force missions, and the joint training centers
were never created. A revised plan, approved by the JCS in April 1951,
preserved Air Force control over tactical aviation as well as over air defense and airborne operations. In addition, the JCS decided to implement
another Army recommendation that six joint boards be established. A
board chairman would report to the service chief with primary responsibility in the respective mission and would be appointed by that service.
The Air Force would head three boards—air defense, tactical air, and air
transport; the Army would manage the airborne troop board; the Navy,
the amphibious board; and the Marine Corps, the landing force board.[1]

The idea did not appeal to the Air Staff, which thought too many
boards and committees already existed for solving interservice problems.
General Vandenberg, Air Force Chief of Staff, preferred making personal accommodations with the other service chiefs, but the JCS decision
forced him to support the boards. In notifying General Chidlaw, head of
ADC, of the pending formation of the Air Defense Board, Vandenberg
acknowledged the need to compromise with the Army. Vandenberg told
Chidlaw that the Air Force would at least head the Air Defense Board
and would retain "full responsibility for its functions in this critical
area."[2]

Vandenberg appointed Maj. Gen. Grandison Gardner to chair the
joint Air Defense Board, activated on July 7, 1951. Although he had no
special expertise in air defense, Gardner came to his post with a varied
background. He held a master of science degree from MIT, had headed
the Air Proving Ground, had been the first AAF Comptroller General,
and had served as deputy to the Chairman of the U.S. Strategic Bombing
Survey. His first tasks were to develop doctrine and procedures for air
defense and "to evaluate tactics and techniques . . . the adequacy of
equipment . . . [and] joint training, and make appropriate recommendations thereon."[3]

Gardner could not have been pleased to know how Headquarters
USAF felt about the boards. In early February 1953, when Secretary of
Defense Wilson ordered the services to eliminate nonessential functions,
the Air Force suggested abolishing all joint boards. The Air Staff continued to advocate deciding most interservice roles and missions questions
by consultations with the service chiefs. Despite Air Force opposition,
the JCS, Army, and Navy elected to keep the boards functioning. The
Air Force took consolation in the fact it headed three of the boards, so
its views were likely to predominate.[4]

In a related matter, the Air Force also opposed creation of a unified
command for air defense, not a completely new idea but one that received increased attention as air defense became an important issue in
late 1953.[5] When General Twining succeeded Vandenberg as Air Force

Chief of Staff in July 1953, he accepted the Air Staff's recommendation against a unified command for air defense. Twining reiterated to Admiral Radford, JCS Chairman, the Air Force preference for personal agreements, such as those made between Vandenberg and Army Chief of Staff General Collins on the employment of antiaircraft artillery, rather than for boards or joint commands to solve air defense problems.[6] In practice, personal agreements were usually cumbersome and subject to frequent reexamination. The Collins-Vandenberg agreement, for example, did little to end Army–Air Force disputes on coordination of antiaircraft artillery and interceptors in the air defense battle. Perhaps Twining, like Vandenberg, opposed an air defense unified command because he feared increased multiservice authority in a mission dominated hitherto by Air Force concepts and doctrine.

Admiral Radford, however, had his own ideas on the subject. Strong willed, he received President Eisenhower's complete support. On January 15, 1954, he informed the service chiefs that "in an era when enemy capabilities to inflict massive damage on the continental United States by surprise attack are rapidly increasing, I consider that there is no doubt whatsoever as to the duty of the Joint Chiefs to establish a suitable 'joint command' [for air defense]." [7]

Though he did not heed Air Force arguments, Radford nevertheless conceded to it the preeminent place in a future unified command. He asked Twining to devise whatever organization was necessary, whether it "fit the presently agreed definition of a unified command or not." Radford only requested that the command be composed of forces from all the services and be able to coordinate air defense responsibilities. He wanted the command led by an Air Force general officer, invested with adequate control over forces assigned to the Air Force Air Defense Command, the Army Antiaircraft Artillery Command, and the Navy offshore surveillance and warning systems. Navy commanders in chief in the Pacific and Atlantic would command the early-warning and picket vessels used in the sea barriers. Meanwhile, Air Force commanders in the unified Northeast Canada and Alaska air commands would operate with the same degree of autonomy as before. Radford concluded that all unified commands were to respond, as much as possible, to the needs of the unified air defense command.[8]

After Radford and Twining had discussed the matter further, Twining instructed General Partridge, his Deputy Chief of Staff for Operations, "to reverse our previous position." In discharging this order, Partridge told the Air Staff that, because the creation of a unified command for air defense was now inevitable, the Air Force should establish a dominant position by preparing to write the command's charter and directives. As events unfolded, Radford and the JCS elected to assign preliminary work to the Joint Strategic Plans Committee, although this did not mean the Air Force was eliminated. By early March 1954, the committee had drawn up "terms of reference" based on Radford's proposals, and it submitted them to the JCS and Headquarters USAF, which forwarded them to Chidlaw and his staff in Colorado Springs for comment.[9]

Two months later, Chidlaw returned a complete plan for what he called the United States Air Defense Command. The plan established at each echelon an Air Force Air Defense Command headquarters and a joint service air defense headquarters. It also established a naval command in Colorado Springs to have charge of picket ships and, possibly, blimps in the offshore warning systems. When necessary, Navy representatives would be assigned to lower echelon air defense forces, and similar arrangements would be made with Army antiaircraft artillery units. Chidlaw considered this plan the simplest and most effective method devisable. He believed that relocating the three component commands in Colorado Springs promised "intimate staff relations, mutual trust, respect, and understanding, at the same time making possible the maximum joint staff representation.[10]

Under Chidlaw's plan, the Air Force retained the same operational control over antiaircraft artillery units as specified in the 1950 Collins-Vandenberg agreement. Similarly, it gave ADC control over Navy forces in offshore warning systems. Chidlaw believed that, when the joint command was established, the need for Gardner's Joint Air Defense Board would be obviated. Chidlaw suggested that the JCS work for an agreement with Canada for a combined North American air defense command, reasoning the air defense of the United States involved Canada too, "basically because it is impossible to defend vital Northern U.S. targets without the fullest cooperation of the Canadians."[11] Although the Canadians and Americans had been cooperating in air defense since World War II, the two nations would soon seriously consider establishing the dual command Chidlaw suggested.

Chidlaw asked the JCS to review his ideas quickly so he could continue with more comprehensive plans for a joint command.[12] Before the Chiefs could reply, the Army protested what it perceived as a high-handed attempt by the Air Force to consolidate absolute control over the air defense mission through the new command. Lt. Gen. John T. Lewis, who led the Antiaircraft Artillery Command, believed the commander of the new unified organization, designated by Radford to be an Air Force officer, would be "placed in an intolerable position . . . finding it almost impossible to command impartially and without prejudice."[13]

To Lewis's dismay, the JCS adopted Chidlaw's proposal and most of its provisions. Ignoring serious reservations on the part of the Army, Secretary Wilson approved formation of the new command on July 30, 1954, and the JCS directed it be established on August 2. Designated

Continental Air Defense Command (CONAD), the organization official-ly came into being on September 1, 1954, commanded by Chidlaw and headquartered in Colorado Springs.[14] General Lewis became deputy for antiaircraft artillery matters, and Rear Adm. Albert K. Morehouse became deputy for Navy forces in air defense.* Also on September 1, responsibility for air defense of the United States passed from the Air Force Air Defense Command to CONAD, and from the Air Force to the JCS (although the Air Force served as executive agent of the new command).[15] When he succeeded Chidlaw the following year, General Partridge gave Congress a succinct description of CONAD. It was, he said, the only "joint command." All other commands that came directly under JCS jurisdiction consisted of forces from each of the services and

> it is customary for the overall commander to operate his forces through the component commanders by issuing his orders to them and having them, in turn, pass the instruc-tions to their subordinate units. The air defense procedures are so vitally concerned with the time of reaction that in Continental Air Defense operations, the units of the Army, Navy, and Air Force are operated directly by me and my subordinate commanders. In other words, the Army, Navy, and Air Force provide the units for air defense purposes, but the actual control of these units in the air battle is a re-sponsibility which I must carry out as Commander-in-Chief of the Continental Air Defense Command.[16]

The CONAD Commander thus received enormous authority not only over the Air Force but also over the Army and Navy forces desig-nated for air defense. This situation disturbed the Army, which made an especially important (some Army officers would say the most important) contribution to the mission in the form of antiaircraft artillery and sur-face-to-air missiles, which were increasing in range and accuracy. For the moment, though, Army protests to the JCS went unheeded; Radford maintained that the Air Force should be prominent in the command. Meanwhile, the Air Staff pressed to abolish the Joint Air Defense Board because it duplicated work being done in Headquarters CONAD. In De-cember 1954, the JCS agreed and moved to eliminate it.[17]

Although the Air Force had at first feared losing control of air de-fense under terms of a joint command, CONAD's establishment seemed, if anything, to strengthen the Air Force position. CONAD included the Air Force Air Defense Command and Army and Navy forces as joint command components, but all parts were not equal. ADC Headquarters served as CONAD Headquarters, and Air Force officers occupied prac-

---

* Morehouse took command of the new Naval Forces for CONAD (NAVFOR-CONAD) when that headquarters was established in Colorado Springs later in the year. The Navy, with less of an investment than the Army in continental defense, usually did not dispute the dominant position of the Air Force in the new command.

THE EMERGING SHIELD

tically all important positions throughout the command. Partridge justi-
fied this inequality by claiming only Air Force officers were qualified to
fill critical posts. He believed that competence as a staff officer in air defense operations required "an intimate knowledge of offensive and defensive aerial warfare"; Army and Navy officers, according to Partridge,
did not possess such knowledge.[18]

The Army vigorously opposed the dual arrangement involving
ADC and CONAD. Lt. Gen. Stanley R. Mickelsen, Lewis's successor in
the Antiaircraft Artillery Command, strove to have more Army officers
at headquarters level, "in view of the major contribution that ARAA-
COM [Army Antiaircraft Artillery Command] is making in the CONUS
air defense effort." Mickelsen charged that "if USAF officers occupy all
or nearly all key positions . . . it becomes obvious that the CONAD is
'joint' in name only . . . ."[19]

The Army repeatedly took its case to the JCS and finally received a
positive response in June 1956. By then, Partridge had agreed to make
changes ensuring greater Army and Navy representation at headquarters
level. But the time for in-house reform had passed, and the Secretary of
Defense approved a JCS recommendation to separate the Headquarters
ADC staff from the Headquarters CONAD staff. This distinction meant
ADC would concentrate on Air Force combat-related activities while
CONAD had administrative responsibilities and joint-service planning.
The change allowed Army and Navy officers to fill numerous positions
in Headquarters CONAD. The replacement of Partridge as Commander
of ADC by Lt. Gen. Joseph H. Atkinson made Partridge's position in
CONAD more nonpartisan.[20]

Tranquillity among the services remained elusive where air defense
was concerned. The Army, for example, continued to argue for greater
freedom in antiaircraft operational procedures from those offered in the
Collins-Vandenberg agreement. Partridge complained he had too little
authority to allocate Army and Navy forces effectively. While the three
services debated and feuded in CONAD, Canada joined the air defense
equation.

North American Air Defense Command

As domestic air defense organization changed, the Air Force and
JCS considered the need for a combined air defense command with
Canada. The notion was by no means novel. According to General
Charles Foulkes, Chairman of the Canadian Chiefs of Staff Committee
(the Canadian equivalent of the U.S. JCS), Canadian military officers had
identified the need as early as 1946.[21] Since 1951, when Royal Canadian

246

Air Force liaison officers began serving in Colorado Springs, the U.S. and Canadian air forces had developed closer relations. Operationally, agreements had evolved for allowing the JCS and Canadian Chiefs of Staff Committee to order joint air defense procedures in an emergency. Air commanders in Canada and the United States had extensive authority to order interceptors to enter the other's air space in pursuit of identified hostile intruders. Deployment of the respective early-warning lines, of course, made it imperative that both air staffs coordinate plans for close tactical cooperation. American and Canadian airmen shared other common goals and concerns; both air forces constantly battled to obtain the greater share of their nations' military budgets. For the Royal Canadian Air Force (RCAF), with no equivalent to SAC, air defense became as important and compelling a mission as U.S. Air Force strategic bombing.[22]

As early as 1948, the RCAF formed an autonomous air defense fighter group equipped with De Havilland Vampire jets. In January 1950, flight tests had begun on the Canadian-made and -developed A. V. Roe (Avro) CF–100, which became the mainstay of Canadian fighter units in the 1950s. Canada's air defense squadrons also possessed the Canadian-manufactured Canadair F–86 Sabre, greatly improved by replacement of the original engine with the 16,000-pound-thrust Orenda engine, made by Avro for use in its CF–100.[23]

Sadly, the Avro CF–105 Arrow all-weather fighter, the aircraft with the potential to become Canada's most important contribution to North American air defense, never became operational. Before the combined U.S.-Canadian command received serious consideration, the Canadian Air Staff had assessed the need for a replacement for the CF–100. It received permission from the government to permit the superb Avro engineering and design team to develop an advanced interceptor that would operate in the harsh northern environment.

When the aircraft first flew in 1958 (after the establishment of the combined command), the most knowledgeable observers, including Air Force officers in both countries, judged it outstanding on the basis of its rate of climb, speed, and weapons systems. In fact, the Arrow seemed superior to all other interceptors, Canadian or American. But soon after the plane debuted, a new Conservative-led government decided that since the ICBM had become the most dangerous threat, Arrow-type aircraft were unnecessary. The Arrow's escalating costs, largely resulting from the Canadian Air Staff's decision to go "first class" and to invest in expensive state-of-the-art fire control and air-to-air missile systems, reinforced this judgment.[24]

Another factor led to the Arrow's early demise: the United States would not, as the Canadians had hoped, purchase substantial numbers of the aircraft. Although U.S. Air Force officers had encouraged Canadian

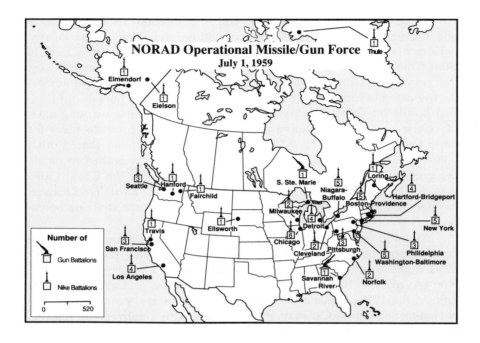

NORAD Operational Missile/Gun Force
July 1, 1959

production of the plane and had closely watched its progress, no Americans committed themselves to buy Arrows. Former Liberal Prime Minister Lester Pearson offered a partial explanation in 1957, recalling his travails in trying to sell the CF–100 to the U.S. Air Force:

> I know also from my own experience in the past that when we tried to get the United States interested in the CF–100, some years ago, at a time when the CF–100 was admitted in Washington to be certainly the best all-weather fighter on the continent, we made no progress at all. The aircraft industry down there was not going to allow any interference with its own right to produce its own aircraft for its own government. I believe the minister [Conservative Prime Minister John F. Diefenbaker] will be having the same trouble with the CF–105.[25]

Pearson correctly believed that U.S. officials preferred to avoid creating a brouhaha in the American aircraft industry. The Air Force would have been forced to challenge existing restrictions on importing foreign aircraft (rescinded for Canada after the fate of the Arrow had been decided) had they tried to purchase either the CF–100 or the CF–105. Furthermore, when the interceptor reached production, the U.S. Air Force was reconsidering its antibomber programs in light of the new Soviet ICBM threat. It had canceled its own advanced interceptor,

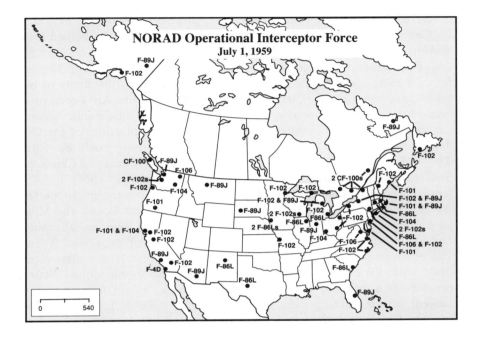

the F–108, and had dropped planned F–106 updates. No U.S. market existed at the time for an expensive, foreign-manufactured interceptor, regardless of its capabilities. Thus, in the end, those Arrows that were built were cut for scrap.

Canada opted to deploy the BOMARC surface-to-air interceptor missile, a weapon slow to mature. Two BOMARC–B squadrons, at first unarmed but equipped after the Cuban Missile Crisis with nuclear warheads, were installed in northeast Canada. In 1961, after their interceptor force had become practically obsolete, the Canadians accepted delivery of sixty-six F–101B Voodoos equipped with Falcon air-to-air missiles from the United States.[26]

The rise and fall of the Arrow highlighted the tentative Canadian approach to air defense and overall defense relations with the United States in this period. On the one hand, Canada possessed a long and proud military history. In the twentieth century, its soldiers, sailors, and airmen had compiled distinguished records in both world wars and in Korea. It had taken the lead in creating the North Atlantic Treaty Organization (NATO), signaling its intention to continue to play a military role in world affairs. Its air force, a small, highly professional organization, enthusiastically worked to increase air defense ties with the United States, and its aircraft engineers and designers were outstanding. On the other hand, Canadians valued their independence and sovereignty, and no Canadian government could survive that appeared to be bullied into making defense agreements with the United States.

The question of a joint Canadian-American command for air defense, a minor political issue in the United States, was the focus of intense debate in Canada. Consequently, the JCS and the Air Force proceeded slowly in approaching Canada for making an agreement. American military authorities realized the gap between the priorities of the Canadian Air Force and those of the Canadian government could be wide. The JCS told Secretary Wilson that they and the Canadian Chiefs of Staff Committee considered North America a "strategic entity for defense purposes." They realized the Canadian government might prefer the existing arrangement whereby the Permanent Joint Board, the Military Cooperation Committee, and the Canada-U.S. Regional Planning Group coordinated and negotiated defense plans and programs. These and other committees, established during World War II and afterward, dealt with various U.S.-Canadian defense needs. If the United States pressed for a different system, the JCS feared it "might jeopardize the current working arrangement . . . ." This JCS belief followed the position the Chiefs took a year earlier when they told Wilson that Canadian military planners were "unable to arrive at negotiated positions without agreement on a governmental level. A combined U.S.-Canadian command would in all probability be equally restricted." The JCS did not believe a joint command would be "sufficiently effective to warrant the expense in money and personnel involved." The Chiefs maintained that U.S. members of the Permanent Joint Board and the Military Cooperation Committee* should remain alert to "any significant change in the Canadian attitude" and inform American authorities immediately.[27]

The JCS correctly perceived that Canada's political leadership would consider the issue of a joint command to be a hot potato. Canada's politicians were uneasy about close bilateral defense ties with the United States, conceivably so strong it could dictate terms to Canada. More appealing to Canada was linking North American defense with NATO. For a great many reasons, the most important being a profound determination to keep exclusive control over SAC, the United States opposed this step. In the words of the noted historian of North American air defense, Joseph T. Jockel, "Letting the Europeans get closer, via NATO, to North American defence, would bring them that much closer

---

* The Permanent Joint Board on Defense was established in 1940 to consider in the broad sense the defense of the north half of the western hemisphere. Two civilians from each nation and military personnel represented the board. Representatives from the foreign offices of the United States and Canada, as well as military officers, made up the Military Cooperation Committee, established in 1946.

to SAC's retaliatory power." [28] At the time, Europeans expressed little interest in the defense of North America.

SAC itself was a touchy subject for Canadian politicians. Most Canadian authorities, military and political, believed that, like it or not, the defense of North America would require Canadian participation. Soviet bombers attacking the industrial northeastern United States would leave radioactive fallout over major Canadian cities located close-by. Also compelling was a moral imperative: without Canadian cooperation, air defense of the United States was futile, just as air defense of Canada was impossible without U.S. resources. Canadian geography offered critical advantages of early warning and defense in depth. By the mid-1950s, it was clear that the major purpose of air defense was not to shoot down enemy bombers—it was to allow SAC sufficient warning to retaliate— and Canadian leaders realized this. In 1956, a House of Commons member assessed the real purpose of the warning lines as not to ready forces to destroy bombers but rather

> to give the [SAC] bombers a chance to get into the air so that they will not be destroyed on the ground and in order that they can launch a countermeasure of massive retaliation . . . . Well, if that is the hope it does not hold out much comfort for the rest of us because we are going to be burnt to a crisp anyway. [29]

Although racked by uncertainty, the Canadian Liberal government, continuously in power for thirty-two years, allowed military and diplomatic discussions on a joint command to proceed in 1956 and 1957. Talks continued between the U.S. and Canadian air forces; in addition, the Joint Canadian-U.S. Military Group, a subgroup of the Military Cooperation Committee, examined the issue. At the end of 1956, the Military Group recommended an integrated American-Canadian command for air defense. The JCS approved the recommendation in February 1957, as did the Secretary of Defense the next month. The Canadian Staff Committee also supported the plan and advised the new government under John G. Diefenbaker, elected June 10, to do likewise. On August 1, 1957, a joint communique released in both national capitals announced the approval of an integrated command for air defense. [30]

The establishment of command headquarters occurred September 12, 1957, at Ent Air Force Base, Colorado Springs. At that time no diplomatic agreement existed between the United States and Canada. The new Conservative government under Diefenbaker, which had won a shocking upset victory over the Liberals in June, was, according to General Foulkes, "stampeded" by the General Staff Committee into accepting the integrated command. [31] Diefenbaker apparently believed the creation of the command, as negotiated by the former Liberal government, a foregone conclusion. He quickly discovered his error when Parliament asked why it had not been formally consulted in the matter. Diefenbaker, backing away from a potential political scandal, tried unsuccessfully to tie the new command to NATO, which only damaged his credibility more at home and provoked a diplomatic row with Washington, where the JCS remained adamantly opposed to any link between the new integrated command and NATO.[32]

Meanwhile, diplomatic notes were not exchanged until May 1958, when the command had been operating for eight months. Terms of the agreement, as signed by Canadian Ambassador Norman Robertson and U.S. Assistant Secretary of State Christian A. Herter, gave the North American Air Defense Command (NORAD) the mission of defending the continental United States, Alaska, and Canada against air attack. NORAD would include as component forces the U.S. Army Air Defense Command (formerly the Antiaircraft Artillery Command), U.S. Naval Forces CONAD, the Air Force Air Defense Command, and the Air Defence Command of Canada. The NORAD commander in chief had assigned operational control over all component commands, air defense forces in Alaska, and all other Canadian and U.S. air defense units made available to him. CONAD, meanwhile, would address U.S. responsibilities outside NORAD's jurisdiction, including American air defense weapons employing atomic warheads.[33]

General Partridge became the first NORAD commander, and Air Marshal C. R. Slemon, a staunch advocate of American-Canadian cooperation in air defense, his deputy. The two nations agreed that an American would always command NORAD with a Canadian as his deputy.

RCAF officers in NORAD considered the air defense of North America a single problem and agreed the command's primary purpose would be to provide early warning and defense for SAC's retaliatory forces. However, the Diefenbaker government came under pressure because of Parliament's apprehension that Canadian views would carry little weight against the might of the American military machine. Air Marshal Slemon received instructions from his government "to fight to the last ditch to safeguard Canadian sovereignty . . . ." Much to his relief and gratification, Slemon found that

> although we were a little partner making a relatively small contribution to the operational capability of the joint effort, our views were considered in exactly the same light as our partners, the Americans. I guess this is the most outstanding reaction I had apart from the great friendliness that engulfed we strange Northerners when we appeared on the scene.[34]

General Partridge, probably having learned some lessons from dealing with the U.S. Army and Navy in CONAD, wasted no time in designating the Canadians as equal rather than as "little" partners. He proved this immediately by appointing a Canadian officer Deputy Chief of Staff for Operations in NORAD, the position Slemon considered "the guts of our joint effort." Canadian political authorities monitored closely the progress of the new command, and Partridge's attitude served to lessen Canadian apprehensions and ensure NORAD's harmonious beginning.[35]

Through the years, NORAD developed successfully. Although the Canadians generally contributed only between eight and twelve percent of the funds for the command, the United States used Canadian territory for airbases and early-warning stations. Late in 1958, Canadian and U.S. air force officers embarked on a program called Continental Air Defense Integration, North (CADIN), to integrate the two nation's defenses in the SAGE system. In the active defense forces, Canadian pilots and controllers proved their expertise and professionalism in exercises with their American counterparts. At the planning level, Canadians held critical staff positions and participated in defining air defense concepts and doctrine for North America.

It would be wrong to assume that operations always ran smoothly in NORAD. Besides questions of general policy, conflicts could arise on the day-to-day operational level. For example, an American commander might be absent from Colorado Springs and a U.S. President would have to give orders to the Canadian deputy. Conceivably, the deputy might not have time to consult with his government before executing orders involving both U.S. and Canadian forces. Many authorities in both nations believed that "there would be a coincidence of national interests in such an emergency." As one Canadian historian pointed out, "The United States has always been careful never to place any restrictions on the authority of the Canadian deputy on the assumption, presumably, that there could never be a conflict in authority." [36] Had the United States, in truth, ever needed to take unilateral action, it could have done so through CONAD, its specified command for air defense.

A unilateral response, in fact, occurred in the Cuban Missile Crisis of October 1962. On October 22, as world tensions heightened, the United States demanded removal of Soviet intermediate-range ballistic missiles in Cuba. American components in NORAD were put on a high level of alert. Canadians, meanwhile, disagreed over the seriousness of the situation. The Canadian government, annoyed at not being consulted in advance (the United States had determined as early as October 16 that missile sites were being constructed in Cuba, but it informed only Britain among its allies), resolved that it would not be dictated to by the United States. Accordingly, Canada kept its forces temporarily on normal status. This created friction, not only between the two governments but also wherever Canadian and American air force officers worked side by side in NORAD. The situation grew especially stressful in the northern 30th NORAD region, partly in Canadian territory, where Canadian officers served as Vice Commander, Director of the Combat Center, and Director of Exercises and Systems Evaluation. When the Combat Center went on advanced alert, its Canadian Director technically remained on normal air defense status for two days longer. Full Canadian diplomatic support did not come until October 25, when Canadian forces in NORAD joined those of the United States at the highest readiness state.[37]

The delayed response in the crisis led to harsh criticism in Canada and the United States. It caused a review of Canadian defense policies in Parliament and contributed at least partly to the fall of Diefenbaker's Conservative government shortly thereafter. The new Liberal government subsequently agreed to arm Canadian BOMARC and CF–101B squadrons with nuclear warheads (Canada had previously hesitated to take this step) in confirmation of the nation's total commitment to North American air defense.[38] The missile crisis inadvertently set the stage for closer U.S.-Canadian defense relations that have since prevailed. It proved to Canada that during an emergency, the United States would respect its sovereignty. The crisis also showed that nations like the United States and Canada with convergent interests would not always agree in an emergency.

For the national leadership of the two countries, the establishment of NORAD came not a moment too soon. Within weeks after the combined command began functioning, the Soviets launched Sputnik, the first orbiting Earth satellite, a feat that signaled Russian capabilities with long-range rockets. Nothing could have made clearer the need for a missile defense. It is doubtful whether the United States or Canada would have seen value even in an antibomber defense had not the Soviet ICBM threat emerged as unequivocally as it did. Instead of having to justify its existence, NORAD now turned to adapting its missions and functions to a new and more dangerous threat, patent to all.

Chapter 10

Epilogue: Impact of a New Threat

On October 4, 1957, the Soviet Union launched into orbit an artificial satellite called Sputnik. With a diameter of twenty-three inches and weight of eighty-four pounds, Sputnik had a resounding effect on, among other things, the course of future U.S. military priorities. American observers considered especially significant the capability of the ballistic missile that launched the satellite to carry a nuclear warhead. Nevertheless, the Eisenhower administration took the news calmly. Supplied with information from U–2 reconnaissance overflights and radar surveillance of Soviet missile tests, the President claimed Soviet possession of an ICBM before the Americans would not be catastrophic; the Soviet Union did not yet maintain the forces or operational capability to launch an ICBM attack against the United States. Eisenhower's nonalarmist views, however, were not shared by many prominent officials, scientists, journalists, and other informed citizens. Resulting controversies about the U.S. technological decline and the possibility of a missile gap were to have profound implications for the scope and composition of U.S. Air Force bomber defense programs.[1]

Sputnik did not catch the Air Force completely by surprise. Although its post–World War II air defense programs logically concentrated against the manned bomber, the Air Force recognized a future need to defend against ballistic missiles. As early as January 1946, the AAF had explored defense concepts to be used against threats like the German V–2, a liquid-fueled ballistic missile. The AAF foresaw a missile defense system that included electronic jammers, automatic weapons control, and computer devices for guiding surface-to-air countermissiles. The defensive missiles were predicted to have to destroy ICBMs traveling as fast as 5,000 miles per hour and at altitudes ranging from sea level to 100 miles above the earth.[2]

The AAF Guided Missiles Division, established immediately after World War II, examined the problem in broad perspective. It decided:

> The advent of atomic explosives and energy made all previous defense planning obsolete. It is now considered technically feasible, as a result of extensive research, to send long

range missiles carrying atomic warheads, at supersonic speeds to any point of the earth's surface. As all nations must be considered as being able to construct and use such missiles, it becomes imperative that a defense system be established to cover all approaches to the U.S. . . . . No nation can survive if the enemy's first blow is successful in atomic warfare.[3]

The Air Materiel Command's Engineering Division proceeded to make some preliminary investigations into the characteristics of a missile defense system. Their research showed little promise, and the Guided Missiles Division admitted in December 1946 that "there is absolutely *no* materiel available today capable of detecting, identifying, intercepting, and destroying such missiles [ICBMs] once they are launched." [4]

Realizing the problem deserved a more exhaustive examination than it could provide, the AAF late in 1946 turned to the University of Michigan's Willow Run Research Center. Scientists there decided the likelihood was nil that developments in technology might provide defense against hostile missiles in the near future.[5]

By April 1947, the AAF concluded that "scientists as a whole have thrown up their hands at the problem of devising a defense against ground missiles of the V–2 variety." [6] Although neither the Air Force nor the scientists it employed gave up completely on the concept of ICBM defense, little progress took place in the next few years. Strategic defense became a secondary concern compared to the more immediate need—for antibomber defense.

The Air Force took important action only in July 1953 when intelligence sources indicated Soviet missile programs were progressing more rapidly than anticipated. The Air Research and Development Command asked the Lincoln Laboratory to study the ICBM defense problem. On the basis of the Lincoln recommendations, the Air Force entered into three study contracts with aircraft-electronics companies to develop methods for detecting, identifying, and destroying ICBMs. Called collectively WIZARD 3, the study reports confirmed Michigan's view that existing technology would not solve the ICBM interception problem. WIZARD 3's suggestions led to production of a high-powered line-of-sight radar with a 3,000-mile range. In combination with computers, this radar calculated a missile's trajectory. Highly accurate, a WIZARD 3 radar located on a hill near Cambridge, Massachussetts, could detect missiles fired from Patrick Air Force Base, Florida.[7]

Meanwhile, the Air Force and the Army competed for control of the ICBM defense mission, their rivalry predating Air Force independence. Army Ground Forces had contracted with the General Electric Company in 1945 on Project THUMPER, designed like similar AAF projects to study defense prospects against V–2–type missiles. Also in 1945 the Army started research and development on its Project Nike family of missiles, envisioned as potential antimissile weapons. Despite these actions, the AAF believed that since it had major Army air defense responsibilities, it would have the missile defense mission once its independence was assured. After establishment of the Air Force, defense officials procrastinated in defining responsibility for the antimissile function. Thus the Army and Air Force continued separate research projects in ICBM defense.[8]

Air Force and Army research and development efforts came slowly. In the early 1950s it was difficult to judge when the missile threat would emerge in earnest. A RAND report issued in December 1953, on the eve of development of the huge air defense system, urged continued efforts not only to defend against the bomber but also to prepare more determinedly to develop missile defenses. RAND predicted that Soviet ICBMs would eventually "make obsolete nearly the entire air defense system except for the lingering bomber capability." Hence, RAND proposed a more intense study of missile defense concepts, continual reassessment of intelligence information, and, later, a shift from the air defense system toward an ICBM defense network. RAND guessed that the missile threat would be real by 1960, although the bomber would continue to pose a threat in the foreseeable future. RAND therefore did not oppose the air defense buildup just beginning; it urged starting no new major weapon system solely for defense against the manned bomber. RAND analysts presumed, mistakenly, that some primary components of the air defense system, like SAGE, could also perform missile defense functions.[9]

The Defense Department did not adopt immediately the RAND recommendation for a gradual shift in emphasis to missile defense because too little was known of Soviet ICBM plans. In the second half of the 1950s, however, improved electronic intelligence and high-altitude surveillance overflights confirmed the Soviets' advancing offensive missile programs. The United States was not prepared to meet this impending danger, as Headquarters CONAD reminded the JCS in 1956:

> Russian development of intercontinental and intermediate range ballistic missiles, as well as earth orbiting satellites, poses a threat which cannot be countered by the existing air defense system. The weapons or ground environment now or soon to be available to counter the air breathing threat [is] of limited value against ballistic missiles or satellites operating at very high speeds and altitudes. We therefore face a requirement for developing, in an extremely short time, a vast improvement in the detection and destruction capabilities of the air defense system.[10]

CONAD did not wait for a JCS response to its caveat before initiating action. It assigned ADC, as a natural extension of ADC's bomber defense mission, responsibility for providing and operating an ICBM defense system.[11]

Responsibility for ICBM defense was not decided as easily. The Army, adamantly opposed to the mission going to ADC, believed it was the only service currently developing weapons (Nike and its variants) that stood any reasonable chance of defeating ICBMs. In mid-1956, Lt. Gen. Stanley R. Mickelsen, head of Army Air Defense Command, claimed that "NIKE is capable of killing any known guided missile and will be effective against the intercontinental missile when it materializes." Adding substance to Mickelsen's claim, in November 1956 the Army began development of the Nike Zeus, designed specifically as a high-altitude antimissile missile.[12]

On November 26 Secretary Wilson ruled that principal responsibility for antimissile defense, unlike that for air defense, would not be assigned to just one service. The Army would assume responsibility for point-defense missiles, "leaving to the Air Force missile defense developments other than the point defense portions specifically assigned to the Army."[13]

Wilson's directive was vague, but it appeared the Air Force would concentrate on developing long-range (area) missile defenses. Further clarification did not come until January 16, 1958 (after Sputnik), when Wilson's successor, Neil McElroy, told the Air Force to continue "as a matter of urgency" its WIZARD program research in early-warning radars, tracking and acquisition radars, communication links between early-warning radars and the active defense system, and a SAGE data link in a missile defense network. McElroy said these elements would all be needed in a Nike-Zeus defense system. "The Air Force program," McElroy concluded, "will be limited at this time to work in [these] areas."[14]

McElroy's directive that the Air Force concentrate on ICBM surveillance presaged the course of its missile defense activities for years to come. Whereas the Air Force had made various attempts to work toward an active missile defense system since the end of World War II, its investigations indicated such systems infeasible. In 1959 Air Force Assistant Secretary for Research and Development Richard E. Horner told a House Appropriations Committee that no active missile defense, including Nike, was judged by the Air Force likely to work. Instead, said Horner, the Air Force thought funds would be better spent on offensive ICBMs.[15]

In succeeding years, the Air Force did not neglect active ICBM defense altogether, for the Defense Department charged it to examine ways of destroying missiles during the boost and midcourse phases of flight. It achieved no significant progress, however. Its most promising venture, probably the dual-role Minuteman, envisioned the offensive ICBM used as an interceptor missile, but the venture showed little progress. The Army's Nike-Zeus and Nike-X Sentinel/Safeguard systems, originally intended for point defense but developed into an area-defense network by the late 1960s, overshadowed it.[16]

Whereas Air Force active missile defense efforts were limited, Air Force efforts to implement ICBM early-warning systems were not. As early as June 10, 1955, U.S. Air Force General Operational Requirement (GOR) 96, "A Ballistic Missile Detection Support System," called for three northern radar sites to detect and track Soviet ICBMs launched over the polar routes toward North America. Because a Soviet ICBM would need thirty-three to forty-six minutes to fly to the United States and fighter-interceptors and SAC bombers would need at least fifteen minutes of tactical warning to become airborne, the three radar sites would allow interceptors to meet an anticipated second-wave bomber attack aimed at key forces and installations that the more destructive but as yet less accurate missiles might be expected to miss. Most important, early warning of ICBM attack would allow time to prepare U.S. strategic bombers and, perhaps, ICBMs, for retaliatory strikes.[17]

When issued in 1955, GOR 96 aroused little interest in the Defense Department. Not surprisingly, the Air Force received a far more positive response when in the weeks after Sputnik it submitted GOR 156, "Ballistic Missile Defense System," closely resembling the earlier plan. GOR 156 called for a ballistic missile early-warning system (BMEWS) capable of providing radar coverage over crucial northern points. This system would have to be completely reliable, operate continuously in all weather, incorporate electronic countermeasure devices, discriminate between real and false alarms, and ensure overlapping radar coverage between Canadian and Soviet portions of the Arctic perimeter for 2,600 miles. The Air Force recommended that radar sites be placed in Great Britain, Greenland, and Alaska to assure coverage above the Soviet land mass. Radar sites would be equipped with communications to relay information to the ADC/NORAD Combat Operations Center and the SAC Command Post at least fifteen minutes before Soviet ICBMs reached their targets.[18]

The decision to construct BMEWS was arrived at without the bitter debate that preceded authorization of the DEW Line. The Air Force by this time had embraced early warning as the major tenet of air—or missile—defense. Upon submission, the Defense Department and Congress quickly endorsed GOR 156. Construction on the radars started in summer 1958, and December 31, 1960, marked the initial operation of the first radar in Thule, Greenland. Site II at Clear, Alaska, began operating in June 1961; the last BMEWS site at Fylingdales Moor, Yorkshire, England, attained initial operational capability on September 15, 1963. The Thule and Clear sites were oriented to cover the possible transpolar missile trajectories and bomber routes out of the Soviet Union, whereas the radars in England could provide data both on ICBMs fired over the pole at the United States and on intermediate-range ballistic missiles (IRBM) launched against Britain from the western Soviet Union or Eastern Europe. Tests proved all three radar sites could transmit enemy ICBM data to the NORAD Combat Operations Center. NORAD would then simultaneously transfer information to display facilities in SAC Headquarters and to the three display facilities in the Pentagon: the Joint War Room of the JCS, the Defense Intelligence Agency, and the Air Force Command Post. The Air Force believed the most reliable ICBM detectors would ultimately be early-warning satellites. The Air Force finally deployed the world's first active military satellites, called SAMOS (Satellite and Missile Observation System) and MIDAS (an infrared Missile Defense Alarm System), in late 1960.[19]

Effects of the ICBM Threat on the Air Defenses

As the Air Force prepared to meet the Soviet missile challenge in the late 1950s, Air Staff planners did not believe the danger of bomber attack had disappeared. The Air Force thought the Soviet Union would retain "a large and effective manned bomber force" until ICBM systems could become more accurate and sophisticated and could be deployed in force. As President Eisenhower had pointed out in the midst of the public furor caused by Sputnik, Soviet missiles would not immediately pose a deadly threat. Bombers would supplement a Soviet ICBM attack upon North America until at least 1962 and maybe longer.[20]

With the ICBM heralding a new age in warfare, some observers in Congress and the Defense Department began to fear that funds spent on bomber defense were funds wasted. Skepticism grew on the worth of the still-expanding air defenses, and it motivated the Defense Department to issue, on June 19, 1959, the Master Air Defense Plan. Key features of the plan included a reduction in BOMARC squadrons, cancellation of plans to upgrade the interceptor force, and a new austere SAGE program. In addition, funds were deleted for gap-filler and frequency-agility radars.[21]

In January 1960, during House Appropriations Committee hearings, Representative George H. Mahon noted $30 billion had been spent on air defense in the 1950s, and invoices were still coming in. General Nathan Twining, Chairman of the JCS, told Mahon that, while air defenses had to be continuously reappraised, he believed no wholesale reductions were immediately indicated. He said that NORAD Commander in Chief General Laurence S. Kuter (who had succeeded Partridge on August 1, 1959) "feels very strongly that we are not devoting enough of our time and effort to air defense." [22] As the officer with primary responsibility for North American air defense, Kuter fought hard for additional air defense hardware and personnel. He believed that the Soviets could

> place a force of about 200 bombers over North America until at least 1970. All or part of these could be directed against hardened ICBM sites [the first American offensive ICBM squadrons became operational in 1960]. The method of attack will probably be in conjunction with, but following a USSR missile attack. [23]

In the early 1960s, the Air Force accepted the supposition that the Soviets would follow an ICBM attack with waves of strategic bombers. Therefore, the need seemed apparent to ensure survival of interceptors through dispersal procedures and hardening of air defense command and control facilities. Survival of these facilities became even more compelling with the realization that the facilities might eventually be configured to function as anti-ICBM warning and direction centers, both at the headquarters and operational levels. Combat Operations Center (COC) in Colorado Springs had direction of the air defense battle. When ADC had moved to Ent Air Force Base in January 1951, COC facilities were located in an office building and comprised of a latrine with the plumbing removed and part of a hallway. A much improved 15,000-square-foot concrete block COC became operational on Ent in May 1954. CONAD commander General Partridge remained unsatisfied. In December 1956 he requested that the Air Staff consider an underground location for the COC from which its personnel could, by using computers, oversee the decentralized air defense battle and assume control of ICBM defense when the threat developed (which he estimated would occur by 1960). He envisioned the new COC would require a near one hundred percent probability of surviving an attack from multimegaton weapons, large duplexed computers to provide simultaneous two-way data transmission for both bomber and missile defense operations, communication and display facilities, self-sufficiency in a 5-day battle for about 195 people, and an independent water and power supply. [24]

Although the Air Staff supported Partridge's requests, the JCS and Defense Department considered them less than urgent and took no action. In July 1958 Partridge reminded the JCS that the present command post was susceptible to dangers far less than a nuclear attack, but which could render incalculable damage:

> It has been recognized for several years that the facilities at Ent are quite inadequate both from a point of view of availability of floor space as well as security. The Combat Operations Center is a concrete block building of extremely light construction and is exposed to the traffic on the adjacent street so that a man with a bazooka passing in a car could put the establishment out of commission. [25]

NORAD, Cheyenne Mountain. General L. L. Lemnitzer, Army Chief of Staff; Admiral Arleigh Burke, Chief of Naval Operations; Mr. Neil McElroy, Secretary of Defense; General Earle E. Partridge, NORAD Commander in Chief; and General Thomas White, Air Force Chief of Staff, take a telescopic look at the site of the new underground North American Air Defense (NORAD) Command Operations Center (COC) (*above*). The COC, under Cheyenne Mountain's protective shield of granite (*below*), housed the defense of the North American continent.

On February 11, 1959, the JCS approved, in principle, the building of a new COC and assigned its development and production management to the Air Force. After much investigation, the Air Force accepted a recommendation made by RAND that the new COC be placed outside Colorado Springs, in Cheyenne Mountain. Before beginning to tunnel out the granite mountain, the Air Force had to update and amplify its concept of the COC to include an integrated air and space early-warning mission. In August 1960, an Air Research and Development Command study described the future COC as "a hardened center from which CINCNORAD would supervise and direct operations against space attack as well as air attack." The COC's function would thus evolve

NORAD Command Operations Center. ADC and NORAD personnel dine within the completely self-sufficient NORAD Command Communications Center located underground in the Cheyenne Mountain Complex in Colorado.

from air defense to missile defense and control of space surveillance and tracking systems.[26]

Excavations for the hardened COC in 9,565-foot-high Cheyenne Mountain ended on May 1, 1964, and its underground structures were completed in December 1965. Built under 1,500 feet of rock, the center could withstand effects of nuclear attack from weapons of up to 30 megatons where overpressure on the surface would be 600 pounds per square inch. Eleven buildings, mounted on steel springs to protect electronic equipment, were built in a series of interconnecting chambers. In an emergency, a sealed COC could operate for 30 days with only filtered air recirculated inside the mountain. The COC had its own power plant, heating and air conditioning systems, dining areas, sleeping facilities, storage areas, and a dispensary. Southeast of the buildings, underground reservoirs contained diesel fuel, drinking water, and water for industrial uses.[27]

The integrity of the control center, housed in the Cheyenne Mountain complex, was critical. Also important to safeguard was the widespread SAGE apparatus. Under ICBM attack, even if Air Force fighter-interceptors managed through timely warning and dispersal procedures to escape missiles, if SAGE blockhouses were destroyed, fighter-interceptors would have no regional command and control facilities to fight the expected second-wave Soviet bomber attack.

The first SAGE regional battle post began operating in Syracuse, New York, in early 1959. Called a combat center, an aboveground, windowless, cement block structure housed it. SAGE regional commanders, usually major generals, supervised the air battle in subordinate sectors. Use of the AN/FSQ–8 computer permitted these commanders to receive nearly instantaneous pictures of operations in their sectors. Brigadier generals usually commanded the sectors themselves, where the layout of direction centers resembled that of regional combat centers. A major difference: direction centers used a different computer, the AN/FSQ–7, designed especially for weapons control activities. The continental United States had twenty-one direction centers and three regional combat centers. Most direction centers lay along the nation's perimeter, and the combat centers were sited in Syracuse, New York; Madison, Wisconsin; and Tacoma, Washington. By the end of 1961, when the number of centers had increased, the NORAD commander controlled eight regional centers, including manually operated ones (those without computers), located in Alaska and northeast Canada. [28]

Thus in the early 1960s an air defense command and control system existed in which air surveillance data flowed through battle centers with speed and accuracy. The massive, confidence-inspiring concrete blockhouses, with their wondrous computers and consoles, quickly became the pride of local communities and favorite inspection stops for dignitaries. A disquieting concern, however, persisted. Because blockhouses were hardened to withstand overpressures of only 5 pounds per square inch, the Air Force feared that Soviet ICBMs could destroy all or part of SAGE before the first enemy bombers had penetrated the DEW Line. [29]

Protecting SAGE was not a new problem for the Air Force. The original system planners abandoned their ideas of protecting underground centers and communications as too costly. They sought survival through dispersal and redundancy. First conceived as a large system, if one SAGE direction or combat center was destroyed, another would assume its defense area. Unfortunately, cutbacks in air defense, starting in the late 1950s, adversely affected these plans. Although the Master Air Defense Plan of 1959 was not complete, the SAGE design came to resemble more a perimeter defense system in contrast to offering defense in depth. Complicating matters, eight direction centers existed on or near SAC bomber bases and ICBM sites; another three shared bases with SAGE combat centers. More than likely, these facilities would be destroyed in first-strike ICBM attacks on SAC bases. Poor planning in the pre-ICBM period and fiscal concerns had conspired against the safety-in-numbers theory. [30]

Under the circumstances, the Air Force decided to resurrect the concept of underground regional combat centers, called Super Combat Centers. As the Air Force considered means to safeguard the blockhouses, IBM announced development of a transistorized, or solid-state, computer in spring 1958. The computer would be able to process 5 to 7 times more data than the vacuum tube computers used in SAGE. Just as

Semiautomatic ground environment. The first SAGE post to become operational, this combined direction center–combat center was located at Syracuse, New York.

important, the improved computer would not only do more, it would occupy less space. Impressed by IBM claims, the Air Force wanted to install new computers in the 300- to 500-foot deep Super Combat Centers, thus attaining an estimated hardness of 100 to 200 pounds per square inch. Communications systems would be dispersed 14 or more miles from the centers to provide an additional level of protection. Super Combat Centers would replace present unhardened combat centers and, in critical locations, direction centers as well. In February 1960, these Air Force designs became moot. A presidential committee decided that, while it might be possible to harden the centers sufficiently, their communications systems would still be highly susceptible to blast damage, especially to electromagnetic pulse, the emission and propagation of potentially damaging electromagnetic radiation caused by nuclear weapons.[31]

The Air Force finally adopted an alternative proposal designated Backup Interceptor Control (BUIC). BUIC was devised by ADC and Air Force Systems Command (previously Air Research and Development Command) in response to limited funding for survivable control centers. An aboveground, decentralized system, it relied on second-generation solid-state computer technology. It was conceived as a backup to SAGE, which it closely resembled. BUIC centers, colocated with radar stations, differed from SAGE regional combat and direction centers, which were separated from their data sources. Even if communication links failed or were destroyed, BUIC would continue functioning because its radars supplied its information.[32]

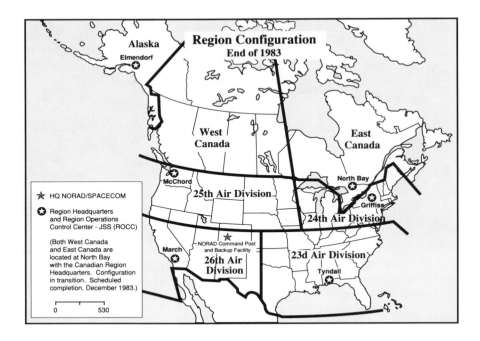

Exposed BUIC centers were not the best solution. As Soviet strategic forces became more powerful and reliable, the Air Force believed the only survivable command and control system would be an airborne radar that was effective over land. As early as 1962 the Air Force began exploring possibilities for an Airborne Warning and Control System (AWACS). The EC–121's airborne radars suffered from ground clutter—radar impulses emanating from the terrain that masked reflections of aircraft. Perfecting engineering solutions for early-warning devices over land was expected to be a formidable undertaking in a period of retrenchment for air defense programs.[33]

Aftermath: Deterioration of the Air Defenses

In 1957 Soviet Premier Nikita S. Khrushchev called the manned bomber obsolete, believing its functions could be performed more efficiently and lethally by missiles. In fact the powerful Soviet military establishment did not share Khrushchev's complete faith in ballistic missiles as the *sine qua non* of modern weapons. (This controversy probably contributed to the Soviet leader's downfall in 1964.) By the time of the

Cuban Missile Crisis in 1962, developmental problems with the missile program left the approximately 200-plane bomber force the largest intercontinental component in the Soviet arsenal.[34]

Reviewing Soviet defense spending patterns, a RAND analysis indicated that from 1951 to 1961 Soviets spent more overall on medium-range weapons, such as the Tu–16 Badger bomber, than on intercontinental weapons of any kind. The Badger, although possessing a combat radius of less than 2,000 miles, could reach NATO targets and SAC bases in Europe. During the first half of the 1950s, the Soviets spent less than 2 percent of their total military budget on strategic weapons, including Bear, Bison, and ICBM development programs. During this period, even though the Soviets attained atomic capability, they adhered to Stalin's primary post–World War II objective: consolidating their gains in Europe.[35]

In the second half of the 1950s, Soviet expenditures for intercontinental weapons increased. RAND estimated that by 1961 the Soviet Union had invested twelve to thirteen percent of its defense budget for long-range forces, in contrast to eight to nine percent for strategic requirements in Europe. This trend, part of the so-called nuclear revolution in Soviet military affairs, centered on ballistic missile research and development, not on strategic bombers.[36]

In the competition for funds, the long-range bomber force lost out not only to the Red Army, to medium-range bomber and medium-range ballistic missile (MRBM) forces, and to ICBMs, but also to air defense. Because of their experiences in two world wars as well as their current objectives, the Soviets chose to balance their offense and defense more closely than the United States did.[37] Air defense ranked on Stalin's list of postwar military objectives just behind consolidation of Soviet power in Europe and ahead of gaining an intercontinental and atomic capability. In the immediate years after World War II, the Soviet Union spent 3 to 4 times as much on air defense as on *all* its strategic aerospace programs. By 1956 the Soviets committed about 550,000 military personnel to air defense; the United States dedicated approximately 130,000 people from all services to air defense operations. The pattern only started to change markedly in the early 1960s with the growth of the Strategic Rocket Force, awarded independent status in 1960. Yet even at that time, spending favored strategic defensive forces. In the United States, offensive spending had dominated since the end of World War II; in the early 1960s, spending for strategic offensive forces exceeded by about 4 times that for air defense.[38]

Despite these comparisons, the U.S. investment in air defense had not been paltry. Only by a comparison with strategic offensive forces do air defense budgets in the 1950s appear small. Conventional forces suffered the biggest losses in the Eisenhower administration. By 1960, as a result of the investment of billions of dollars in research, development, and hardware, the nation reaped its reward: the most sophisticated air defense system ever built. In December 1961, NORAD controlled more than 100 squadrons of F–101B, F–102, and F–106 fighter-interceptors in addition to BOMARC and Nike surface-to-air missiles. SAGE was tied into 78 radar sites of the DEW Line, 98 radars were installed in the Mid-Canada Line, and 256 were in the Pinetree Line. Navy picket ships and dirigibles, Texas Tower radar platforms, and EC–121 early-warning aircraft represented the eyes of the vast system.[39]

Twenty years later, 5 U.S. Air Force and 10 Air National Guard squadrons, assigned to air defense duties, still had 1950-era F–106 and F–101B interceptors. Only 66 long-range radars remained in the United States and Canada; DEW Line radars had declined from 68 to 31; and Texas Towers, the GOC, radar picket ships, Nike antiaircraft missiles, and EC–121 early-warning aircraft had all been eliminated. Yet the Soviet bomber threat had not changed significantly. Twenty years later, the Soviet bomber force remained constant at about 200 aircraft.

The U.S. perception of the threat, however, changed drastically. Although the Air Force envisioned a future Soviet intercontinental attack featuring ICBMs and strategic bombers, it received only limited support to counter this dual threat. After Sputnik, Congress and the public focused on the missile. Most defense officials in the 1960s agreed that, since the nation was vulnerable to ICBMs, vulnerability to bombers had little relevance. Secretary of Defense Robert S. McNamara held that air defense could not be separated from missile defense. Despairing of ever seeing a truly effective ICBM defense, he reasoned that Soviet missiles could eliminate air defense systems in a first strike, rendering them useless should subsequent bomber waves appear in North American skies.[40]

Although McNamara and his assistants in the Defense Department searched for more appealing strategies, the policy that emerged embraced the most extreme option: massive retaliation, popularly referred to now as mutual assured destruction (MAD). This policy had fateful consequences for air defense. The notion that both superpowers would be deterred from starting a general war by the realization that any nuclear missile or bomber attack would invite a devastating counterattack actually rested on the belief that no really effective defense remained possible. McNamara and his staff believed that attempts by either side to deploy expensive and risky strategic defense systems would be countered easily by modest additions to the offensive holdings of the other side. By accepting that the offense in war had achieved an irreversible dominance with atomic weapons, the United States and the Soviet Union could avoid a never-ending arms race and save their defense outlays at the same time.[41] According to one commentator, MAD became so decisive

TABLE 4. Comparison of Defense Department, Air Force, and ADC Budgets

Budget	1961	1962	1963	1964	1965	1966	1967	1968	1969	1970	1971
Defense Dept	$46,029	$50,441	$51,208	$50,979	$50,866	$66,150	$73,436	$75,219	$79,432	$77,035	$72,941
Air Force	$19,887	$19,573	$20,430	$20,002	$19,402	$23,480	$24,708	$25,053	$26,126	$24,274	$22,729
ADC*	$2,719	$2,154	$1,775	$1,685	$1,496	$1,441	$1,394	$1,383	$1,353	$1,293	$1,291
Air Force, as a percent of Defense Dept	0.4298	0.3880	0.3989	0.3923	0.3814	0.3549	0.3364	0.3330	0.3289	0.3151	0.3116
ADC, as a percent of Defense Dept	0.0617	0.0427	0.0346	0.0330	0.0294	0.0217	0.0189	0.0183	0.0170	0.0167	0.0176
ADC, as a percent of Air Force	0.1367	0.1100	0.0868	0.0842	0.0771	0.0613	0.0564	0.0552	0.0517	0.0532	0.0567

* This figure includes all monies allocated for the command or by other Air Force major commands for ADC programs.

Source: Figures for fiscal years 1961 and 1962 were obtained from hearings before the Subcommittee on Department of Defense of the Committee on Appropriations and before the Committee on Armed Services, Senate, 89th Cong., 1st Sess., on H.R. 9221, 1965, Pt 1, p 206, and from HQ ADC DCS Comptroller, Directorate of Budget. Figures for fiscal years 1963 through 1969 were obtained from the Air Force's Force and Financial Program, May 1970. Figures for fiscal years 1970 and 1971 were provided by HQ ADC DCS/Comptroller, Directorate of Budget.

Table 5. Air Defense Matrix

Year—Event	DEW radars	AWACS	EC-121	Ground Observer Corps	SAGE/BUIC, Canada	BUIC Centers, USA	SAGE Centers, USA	Picket ships	Texas Towers	Gap-filler radars, USA	Long-range radars, Canada	Long-range radars, USA (CONUS)	Hawk	Hercules	Nike Ajax	BOMARC squadrons, Canada	BOMARC squadrons, USA	Intrcptr squadrons, Air National Guard	Intrcptr squadrons, Canadian	Intrcptr squadrons equipped (reg)	Intrcptr squadrons assigned (reg)
1946—ADC established																		30		4	4
1947—Independent Air Force established												2						50		7	7
1948—CONAC established; first RCAF interceptor squadron				2								5						38		11	11
1949—NATO established; U.S.S.R. A-bomb				2				1				18						38		20	20
1950—Korean War								2				18						38		20	21
1951—ADC reestablished				5				2				58						16		41	41
1952—Lincoln Laboratory Summer Study Group			1	27				2				81						16		40	43
1953—U.S.S.R. H-bomb			1	34				2			8	85						52		51	54
1954—CONAD established			11	32				2			25	86			83			70		55	57
1955			30	38				6	1		28	90			161			69		58	61
1956—New New Look			80	56				10	2		35	106			218			69		65	69
1957—Sputnik; NORAD established	58		70	26				10	3	44	35	115			242			55		64	71
1958—First SAGE center	58		90	9			1	11	3	75	32	135			232			41	3	58	60
1959—Master Air Defense Plan	64		90				5	11	3	114	32	157		80	172		2	42	3	56	56
1960—Kennedy-McNamara Administration; Khrushchev cancels bombers	64		90				13	10	3	90	34	153		99	162		5	40	3	41	41
1961—Tushino Airshow; Triangular/CADIN Agreements	68		91				19	10	2	95	31	147		128	82		8	29	3	41	41

Year – Event																		
1962 – Cuban missile crisis	68	91			20	11	2	95	31	152	8	132	48	10	26	5	42	42
1963 – Continental air defense study	40	71			16	11		86	34	144	8	132	23	10	26	5	40	40
1964 – Canadian White Paper	40	72			15	11		92	35	147	8	133	2	8	21	3	39	39
1965 – Bombing of North Vietnam begins	40	83			15			89	35	142	8	129	2	8	21	3	37	37
1966 – AWACS/OTH-B/F-12 plan presented	40	76			13			86	35	137	8	111	2	8	21	3	31	31
1967 – F-12 Program ended	40	54		12	13			68	33	137	8	111	2	8	21	3	28	28
1968 – Tet offensive; Czech invasion	40	67		12	11			17	30	125	8	94	2	8	21	3	19	19
1969 – Nixon term begins	33	65		12	10			16	30	93	8	81	2	7	19	3	14	14
1970 – Planned AWACS buy reduced to 42	33	37	2	12	6			30		79	8	75	2	7	19	3	14	14
1971 – Cuban plane at New Orleans	31	33	2	12	6			28		71	8	52	2	7	19	3	11	11
1972 – SALT (ABM) Treaty	31	27	2	12	6			28		71	8	52	2		19	3	9	9
1973 – Watergate; ADC mission change	31	28	2	12	6			25		75	8	52			19	3	7	7
1974 – AWACS buy reduced to 37	31	15	2	1	6			25		80	8	4			18	3	6	6
1975 – IBM Study	31	8	2	1	6			24		72	8	4			13	3	6	6
1976 – OTH-B cancelled, then restored	31	4	2	1	6			24		72	8	4			10	3	6	6
1977 – ADC reorganization planned	31		2	1	6			24		56	8	7			10	3	6	6
1978 – Danson-Brown letters lead to JUSCADS	31		2	1	6			24		55	8	7			10	3	6	6
1979 – ADCOM reorganized; AWACS reduced to 28	31	4	2	1	6			24		46	8	7			10	3	6	6
1980 – PMD change making JSS primary war C^2	31	7	2	1	6			24		42					10	3	6	6
1981 – Air Defense Master Plan published	31	7	2	1	6			24		42					10	3	5	5

"as to make those who support[ed] a capable air defense posture almost shrug their shoulders and give up with the futility of it all." [42]

MAD, in its implications for air defense, was not accepted by the Soviet Union. Unlike the United States, the Soviet Union did not consider air and missile defense two sides of the same issue.

While the Soviets agreed to an antiballistic missile (ABM) treaty in 1972, they never stopped developing and refining their bomber defenses. McNamara called the continued buildup of Soviet air defenses "fanaticism," best explained by "their strong emotional reaction to the need to defend Mother Russia." [43] The Secretary of Defense did not believe that the building of bomber defenses by one side while the other was dismantling its contributed to destablization, a process he fervently wished to avoid.

The pattern established in the 1960s continued into the succeeding decade. The Air Force failed to evaluate U.S. air defense and ICBM defense independently, although it generally accepted the idea that bomber defense without ABM defense was worthless. Secretary of Defense James Schlesinger expressed this view during testimony to the Senate in 1974:

> Without an effective antimissile defense, precluded to both the U.S. and U.S.S.R. by the ABM treaty of 1972, a defense against Soviet bombers is of little practical value. [44]

Air defense, one of the least emphasized defense priorities in the period of U.S. involvement in the war in Southeast Asia, rarely became the public issue it had in the past. Occasional incidents occurred to reveal inadequacies of the air defense and warning systems. On October 5, 1969, a defector from the Cuban Air Force piloted an armed MiG–17 undetected from Havana to Homestead Air Force Base, Florida. [45] In October 1971 an unidentified plane carrying Cuban officials to a sugar cane conference passed completely unseen until the pilot requested landing instructions from the New Orleans airport. This second occurrence prompted a congressional investigation which revealed that deterioration of the warning systems and active defenses had made the 1,500-mile southern border between Florida and California practically defenseless. The Chairman of the House Armed Services Committee, F. Edward Hebert, demanded the situation be corrected. In May 1972 Secretary of Defense Melvin R. Laird established the Southern Air Defense Network consisting of ten radar sites and interceptors on alert at four bases along the previously unprotected areas. [46] Although welcomed by ADC, these additional radar sites fell well short of filling the gaps that had developed in other approaches to North America.

Throughout the period that air defenses were reduced, the Air Force protested the cutbacks, pointing out that the Soviet strategic bomber force, while not increasing as had been foreseen in the 1950s, had remained stable and still posed a threat. *Air Force Magazine*, a publication that could be relied upon to represent the Air Force view, continuously called for air defense improvements. In a July 1970 editorial describing air defense as "The Forgotten Front" it reported that

> it is outstanding that some members of Congress and so many reporters and commentators have apparently written off the Soviet bomber threat. Ten years ago, it was regarded seriously. Yet since then, the Soviets haven't reduced their bomber force much, if at all, while at the same time the USAF Aerospace Defense Command has been cut to the bone. It's hard to escape the conclusion that the United States is *more* vulnerable to air attack today than it was a decade ago, when we did worry about it. [47]

Despite its concern, the Air Force was reluctant to make air defense a cause célèbre. As much as it wanted an improved defense, the Air Force believed improvements should come from additions to its funding. Following a historic pattern, the Air Force showed no willingness to relinquish anything in favor of air defense. The Air Staff did not weaken offensive deterrent forces in the service of air defense; neither did it consider reductions in other missions during the Vietnam conflict.

As the war in Southeast Asia declined, the Air Force reflected on its approach to air defense in the wake of fifteen years of force reductions. In 1974 Air Force Chief of Staff General George S. Brown admitted that the continental air defense forces had undergone considerable transformation: "We are now maintaining an air defense posture to provide surveillance and warning—this differs from the earlier air defense posture that was oriented to defending against a manned bomber attack." [48]

The Air Force had begun to move toward the air defense position described by Brown as early as 1954 with the decision to build the DEW Line. In earlier years, respective commanders of ADC/NORAD usually objected to attempts to deemphasize the active defense mission. The shift was evidenced by comments made by NORAD's commander, General Lucius Clay, Jr., in February 1974, addressing the issue of Soviet options for attack using either ICBMs or strategic bombers:

> If you leave one open, why not leave the other open . . . .
> For the past twenty years we have subscribed to an equation that deterrence is the sum of strategic offense and strategic defense . . . . Perhaps the equation should now read deterrence is the sum of strategic offense plus strategic warning. I think it should. [49]

Judging from comments made by its Chief of Staff and commander of the air defenses, the Air Force in the mid-1970s seemed on the verge of abandoning even the pretense of an active defense capability against the manned bomber.

Administrative and organizational changes in the late 1970s and early 1980s reinforced this trend. ADC (known since January 1968 as the Aerospace Defense Command) gradually lost interceptors, radars, bases, and personnel to TAC. ADC staff officers argued for the continued separate existence of a fighter element with its unique expertise and corporate knowledge in their command. Air Force Headquarters, unable to countenance the existence of two fighter commands, ordered the creation of a new subunit of the Tactical Air Command called Air Defense–TAC (ADTAC) and planned to move it to TAC Headquarters at Langley Air Force Base, Virginia. ADTAC stayed in Colorado Springs from October 1979 to June 1981. ADC, no longer a major command, retained its status as a JCS-specified command for U.S. air defense forces.[50]

In the early 1980s, several events signaled prospects for the first major improvements in air defense in more than two decades. First the Soviets decided to upgrade their strategic bomber force.[51] In addition, the development in 1983 of President Ronald Reagan administration's Strategic Defense Initiative focused attention within the Air Force on requirements for both ballistic missile and bomber defense. Said General Robert T. Herres, head of NORAD in 1985, "It doesn't make any sense to build a house with a roof over our heads—such as ballistic missile defense—while we forget to put walls around the sides," referring to the need for bomber defense.[52]

Planned improvements in the air defenses included replacing the 1950-era interceptor force with modern F–15 and F–16 fighters, modernizing the radar components in the far north and continental United States, and extending the use of AWACS in home air defense operations.* The fates of many of these programs remain uncertain. The future of homeland bomber defense will be decided in the context of

---

* The Air Force fought long and hard for AWACS, a Boeing E–3 that combined functions of surveillance, early warning, and command and control. AWACS's predecessor, the propeller-driven EC–121 Warning Star which saw much service in Southeast Asia, provided early warning and fighter direction against medium- and high-flying planes, but it had problems detecting low-flying aircraft over land. Radar returns generated by beams reflecting off the terrain (ground clutter) made detection of aircraft over land virtually impossible. In the early 1960s, however, the Air Force started in earnest to investigate means to solve this problem. The solution was a radar capable of distinguishing moving objects from the ground below them by using the doppler effect—the apparent change in frequency of vibrations, as of sound, light, or radar, when the observed and the observer are moving relative to one another. According to one Air Staff appraisal, "the radar, not the airframe, is the critical component in the AWACS program" [Lawrence R. Benson, *Sentries Over Europe: First Decade of the E–3 Airborne Warning and Control System in Europe* (Office of History, H.Q., U.S. Air Forces in Europe, Feb 1983); Space Command/ ADCOM Hist, 1983].

overall U.S. nuclear strategy. That strategy has been overwhelmingly dominated, with the exception of the years from 1954 to 1960, by concepts of deterrence that emphasize offensive forces. A shift in policy awarding equal importance to offensive and defensive systems would mark a fundamental change in U.S. strategy.

Appendices

Appendix 1. Milestones in U.S. Air Defense to 1960 *

1921

Maj. Gen. Mason M. Patrick, Chief, Army Air Service, and Brig. Gen. William Mitchell, Assistant Chief, Army Air Service, declared the Army air arm should be responsible for frontier and coastal defense.

1922

Civilian scientists working with the Naval Aircraft Radio Laboratory made the first radar observations when they used radio signals to detect a steamer on the Potomac River.

1925

Scientists at the Carnegie Institution in Washington, D.C., first employed the pulse-technique of radio signal emissions.

1929

The Air Corps experimented with a rudimentary early-warning network at Aberdeen Proving Ground, Maryland.

1933

In the wake of a joint Air Corps–Antiaircraft Artillery Corps exercise at Fort Knox, Kentucky, Capt. Claire L. Chennault, Air Corps Tactical School, wrote "The Role of Defensive Pursuit." The paper claimed that fighters could successfully intercept bombers if equipped with an effective warning system. The Drum Board discounted the possibility of an air attack against the United States.

1934

The Baker Board supported the Drum Board's findings.

---

* Primary source: *A Chronology of Air Defense, 1914–1972* (ADC Hist Study 19, 1973).

1935

A ground control interception (GCI) system was experimented with in the United States for the first time in GHQ Air Force exercises conducted in southern Florida.

1936

The Signal Corps performed the first experiments in radar detection.

1937

In GHQ Air Force maneuvers at Muroc Lake, California, military personnel arranged with the Southern California Edison Company to use its employees as civilian early warning observers.

1938

A joint Air Corps–Antiaircraft Artillery exercise in North Carolina involved 302 observation posts—the most extensive early-warning experiments in the United States to that time.

1940

The War Department created Air Defense Command (ADC) under the command of Brig. Gen. James C. Chaney at Mitchel Field, New York, to study air defense problems. Assigned to the command as plans officer was Capt. Gordon Saville.

General Chaney and Captain Saville reported enthusiastically on British air defenses after returning from an observation trip in England.

1941

A War Department directive gave the peacetime air defense mission to GHQ Air Force.

Major Saville published the first substantive manual on air defense doctrine.

When Pearl Harbor was attacked, eight early-warning stations operated in the United States. Six were in California, one was in Maine, and one in New Jersey. Most available fighters were P–39s and P–40s, neither of which possessed target-seeking radar, making them nearly useless in darkness or bad weather.

1942

An experimental P–61 interceptor, designed specifically for all-weather air defense use, made its first flight.

Fifteen early warning radar stations were completed on the west coast, providing coverage of industrial areas from Maine to Virginia.

1943

The Ground Observer Corps (GOC) reached its peak World War II strength, with approximately 1.5 million volunteers. Seventy-six radar stations were fully operational by June.

The first active GCI site was established at Hicksville, Long Island.

The War Department published FM 100–20, "Command and Employment of Air Power," which stated that the normal composition of an air force included an air defense command.

1944

The GOC and the Aircraft Warning Corps were inactivated. Fighter wings and regions disbanded as the United States deemphasized continental air defense.

1945

Bell Laboratories received the contract to develop a surface-to-air missile for air defense. The project was named NIKE.

The last U.S. early-warning radar stations were inactivated.

The Army Air Forces (AAF) authorized procurement of P–82s as all-weather interceptors. Air Materiel Command asked manufacturers to submit design proposals for a new all-weather interceptor. Proposals led to the F–89.

1946

Boeing began design studies and field tests on the project that developed the BOMARC surface-to-air missile.

The AAF awarded a contract to study ballistic missile defense.

Lt. Gen. George E. Stratemeyer assumed command of ADC established at Mitchel Field, New York.

The Army Antiaircraft and Guided Missile Center activated at Fort Bliss, Texas.

1947

Air Force Chief of Staff General Carl Spaatz approved the Radar Fence Plan (Plan SUPREMACY) which called for the construction of an elaborate air defense radar network.

Headquarters USAF granted ADC the authority to use fighter and radar forces of the Strategic Air Command, the Tactical Air Command, and the Air National Guard in an emergency. The Guard constituted the major source of air defense augmentation units.

1948

The Air Force directed that radars in the northwest be placed on twenty-four-hour-a-day operations because of international tension caused by Soviet aggression in eastern Europe.

The Key West agreement formally invested the Air Force with primary responsibility for the air defense mission.

General Muir S. Fairchild became Air Force Vice Chief of Staff. He called Maj. Gen. Gordon Saville to Washington to identify air defense requirements and to take necessary action to begin work on temporary systems.

Saville presented to Secretary of Defense James Forrestal an interim plan that provided for the "permanent" air defense network.

The Air Force Board of Officers recommended a design competition for a new all-weather interceptor to be available in 1954. From this recommendation came the F–102 and the F–106.

Continental Air Command (CONAC) was created. CONAC was assigned all air defense units and given the mission of air defense. General Stratemeyer became CONAC Commander. ADC remained a planning agency under General Saville.

1949

Upon Saville's recommendation, the Air Force Board of Officers recommended development of a single-seat all-weather interceptor, resulting in the F–86D.

Lt. Gen. Ennis C. Whitehead succeeded Stratemeyer as CONAC Commander.

Congress passed Public Law 30 authorizing construction in Alaska and the continental United States of a radar net costing $85.5 million.

Operation BLACKJACK, the first major air defense exercise in the postwar era, took place in the northeast.

Saville was relieved as ADC Commander and transferred to Headquarters USAF.

The first production model of the E–1 fire control system was installed in the F–94A. This was the first postwar improvement over the wartime SCR–270.

CONAC controlled twenty manned and equipped interceptor squadrons. Fifteen possessed jets—F–80s, F–84s, and F–86s—whereas five had F–82s.

1950

Fairchild and Saville's invitation to electronic firms to submit bids for a fire control system for the 1954 interceptor marked the beginning of the weapons systems approach to procurement.

Construction of the Permanent Radar System began.

The Lashup radar network of forty-four stations was completed. The network operated with World War II–type equipment until the permanent system was constructed.

The Korean War started. Around-the-clock air defense operations began in United States.

The three services issued regulations establishing Air Defense Identification Zones.

An agreement between Generals J. Lawton Collins and Hoyt S. Vandenberg, the Army and Air Force chiefs of staff, gave Air Force air defense commanders operational control of Army antiaircraft artillery units.

The Air Force asked MIT to study the general problem of air defense. Study became Project CHARLES.

General Fairchild died.

1951

ADC was reestablished. Under General Ennis Whitehead, it moved from Mitchel AFB to Ent AFB, Colorado Springs, Colorado. The Army's Antiaircraft Artillery Command also moved from Mitchel to Ent.

The three services agreed to create Project LINCOLN, a military-supported, MIT-managed study of the air defense program.

Project CHARLES submitted its report.

The United States and Canada ratified an agreement for construction of the Pinetree radar net in Canada.

Lt. Gen. Benjamin W. Chidlaw succeeded General Whitehead as ADC commander.

Development of a data link, a method for presenting data on a radarscope instead of through voice communications, began. The system came into use in the semiautomatic ground environment (SAGE) in 1956.

General Saville retired.

1952

Maj. Gen. Frederic H. Smith became Vice Commander of ADC. He continued in that position until 1956.

For the first time on the basis of reported "unknowns," ADC declared the command-wide condition Air Defense Readiness.

A group of scientists, representing MIT's Lincoln Laboratory and other organizations, convened to discuss technical difficulties in air defense. The committee became known as the Summer Study Group.

Operation SKYWATCH, a twenty-four-hour-a-day operation of the GOC in selected areas, began.

The Air Force approved a two-base concept for airborne early-warning and control aircraft, selecting for the bases Otis AFB, Massachusetts, and McClellan AFB, California.

Project EAST RIVER was completed. Its report concluded that civil defense was essentially useless without a strong, active air defense.

The Kelly Committee was established to study air defense requirements.

President Truman approved a National Security Council statement calling for strengthened air defenses.

1953

The Joint Air Defense Board of the Joint Chiefs of Staff (JCS) concluded that nuclear weapons should be developed for air defense.

The Air Force decided to adopt the Lincoln Transition System, later designated SAGE.

The Continental Defense Committee, under Maj. Gen. Harold R. Bull, reported air defense inadequacies.

The National Security Council approved most of the Summer Study Group's proposals, including its recommendation for the Distant Early-Warning (DEW) Line.

The first Falcon missile was fired from an airborne platform—the F–89D.

The Canadian-U.S. Military Study Group recommended establishment of Mid-Canada Line for early warning along the 55th parallel.

General Nathan F. Twining, Air Force Chief of Staff, and Admiral Robert Carney, Chief of Naval Operations, agreed that the Air Force would provide early-warning aircraft and the Navy would provide picket ships and lighter-than-air craft for air defense.

1954

The Air Force approved construction of five Texas Towers (only three were built).

The JCS agreed to establish a joint service command for air defense, Continental Air Defense (CONAD).

The JCS approved the use of nuclear warheads in air-to-air rockets.

The Soviet Union displayed a jet bomber for the first time.

The last conventional-type interceptor aircraft was removed from ADC inventory.

Airborne early-warning operations began off the United States' west coast.

CONAD activated in Colorado Springs.

1955

The Air Force approved development of the F–101 as an interceptor, designated the F–101B.

The Air Force regular force was, for the first time, completely equipped with all-weather fighter-interceptors.

MIT's Project LAMPLIGHT report recommended that frequency-agility radars be installed in the air defense system.

ADC submitted the first SAGE operational plan to Headquarters USAF.

General Chidlaw retired. General Frederic H. Smith served as acting commander pending arrival of Chidlaw's successor, General Earle E. Partridge.

The 4620th Air Defense Wing (experimental SAGE) was established at Lincoln Laboratory. Its primary mission was computer programming.

General Operational Requirement (GOR) 96, *A Ballistic Missile Detection Support System,* outlined the requirement for three northern warning radar sites capable of detecting and tracking ICBMs launched from the Soviet Union.

1956

The 327th Fighter Interceptor Squadron at George AFB, California, received the first F–102A delivered to ADC. The F–102A, while in development, was redesignated the F–106.

CONAD and ADC formally separated. General Partridge was relieved as head of CONAD. Lt. Gen. Joseph H. Atkinson assumed command of ADC.

The first airborne test firing of an MB–1 rocket, fired from an F–89D, occurred at Holloman AFB, New Mexico. Also at Holloman, a GAR–2A (infrared guidance) Falcon missile fired successfully.

1957

The first fully automatic tactical launch of BOMARC occurred.

The Atlantic DEW Line sea barrier became fully operational.

ADC assumed control of Tyndall AFB as a weapons employment center.

The DEW Line from Cape Dyer, Canada, to Cape Lisburne, Alaska, was declared technically ready.

The Air Force fired its first and only armed air-to-air nuclear defense rocket, the MB–1 Genie, from an F–89J over Yucca Flats, Nevada.

NORAD was established at Ent AFB, Colorado.

In July, the DEW Line was declared technically complete; in August the Air Force took formal possession of it from Western Electric, the prime contractor.

The Soviet Union launched Sputnik I.

GOR 156, "Ballistic Missile Defense System," proposed a three-station radar complex combined with computing, communications, and display facilities to generate at least a fifteen-minute warning of a missile attack.

1958

All twenty-four-hour-a-day–staffed GOC posts and filter centers were reduced to Ready Reserve status.

The Mid-Canada Line became fully operational.

The Office of the Secretary of Defense authorized the Air Force to proceed immediately with development of a ballistic missile early-warning system (BMEWS).

Denmark approved extending the DEW Line into Greenland.

The Air Force approved inactivation of the GOC effective January 1, 1959.

A BOMARC missile successfully launched from Cape Canveral, Florida, on signal from SAGE Control Center, Kingston, New York.

SAGE Combat Center No. 1, on Hancock Field, New York, 26th Air Division, became operational.

The U.S. Air Force, in conjunction with the Royal Canadian Air Force, embarked on a program called Continental Air Defense Integration, North (CADIN) to integrate U.S. and Canadian air defense systems.

1959

All ground observer units were discontinued.

Texas Tower No. 4 became operational, completing the Texas Tower program.

The Department of Defense Master Air Defense Plan reduced BOMARC deployment to eighteen sites, two in Canada. Manned interceptor units dropped to forty-four squadrons.

General Lawrence S. Kuter replaced General Partridge as Commander in Chief of the CONAD and the North American Air Defense commands.

The Air Force canceled deployment of the F–108 long-range interceptor.

The 46th Air Defense Missile Squadron on McGuire AFB, New Jersey—the first BOMARC squadron—became operational.

1960

USAF Chief of Staff General Thomas D. White, testifying before the House Appropriations Committee, agreed with compromise solutions in the Master Air Defense Plan of 1959 that cut, among other things, BOMARC and SAGE programs.

BMEWS Site I, at Thule, Greenland, reached initial operational capability. This was the first operation of the BMEWS system.

The Air Force transition to century series all-weather interceptors (F–101B, F–102A, and F–106A) was completed.

Appendix 2. ADC Assigned Personnel Strength and Commanders, to 1960

Date	Personnel strength			
	Officers	Airmen	Civilians	Total
Mar 31, 1946	1,546	5,672	NA	NA
Dec 31, 1946	3,541	22,365	NA	NA
Dec 31, 1947	3,963	25,124	NA	NA
Jun 30, 1948	3,857	20,974	7,349	32,180
Jan 1951	3,913	33,713	4,863	42,489
Dec 31, 1951	8,237	56,992	5,874	71,103
Dec 31, 1952	7,818	54,137	9,070	71,025
Dec 31, 1953	8,163	57,883	8,519	74,565
Dec 31, 1954	9,641	63,442	9,264	82,347
Dec 31, 1955	10,394	65,711	10,397	86,502
Dec 31, 1956	10,832	77,836	11,817	99,485
Dec 31, 1957	12,908	92,543	11,466	116,917
Dec 31, 1958	13,553	92,042	11,703	117,298
Dec 31, 1959	12,663	83,511	NA	NA
Dec 31, 1960	12,432	79,426	NA	NA

Appendix 3. ADC Commanders

Name	Dates
Lt. Gen. George E. Stratemeyer	Mar 27, 1946–Nov 30, 1948
Maj. Gen. Gordon P. Saville	Dec 1, 1948–Sep 1949
Lt. Gen. Ennis C. Whitehead	Jan 8, 1951–Aug 24, 1951
General Benjamin W. Chidlaw	Aug 25, 1951–May 31, 1955
Maj. Gen. Frederic H. Smith	Jun 1, 1955–July 1955 (acting)
General Earle E. Partridge	Jul 20, 1955–Sep 16, 1956
Lt. Gen. Joseph H. Atkinson	Sep 17, 1956–Feb 28, 1961

Notes

Chapter 1. Genesis of the Air Defense Mission

1. Basil Collier, *A History of Air Power* (New York, 1974), p 7; Denys Volan, "Air Defense," undated manuscript in AF/CHO; Ian V. Hogg, *Anti-Aircraft: A History of Air Defence* (London, 1978), pp 11–12.

2. F. S. Haydon, *Aeronautics in the Union and Confederate Armies* (Baltimore, 1941), *passim*.

3. John R. Cuneo, *Winged Mars: The German Air Weapon, 1870–1914* (Harrisburg, Pa., 1942), Vol I, *The German Air Weapon*, p 5; Hogg, *Anti-Aircraft*, pp 13–14.

4. Gavin Hall, "Marshal of the Royal Air Force, the Viscount Trenchard," in Michael Carver, ed, *The War Lords: Military Commanders of the Twentieth Century*, (London, 1976), p 179; Sholto Douglass, *Combat and Command: The Story of an Airman in Two World Wars* (New York, 1966), pp 87, 91–92; Richard P. Hallion, *Rise of the Fighter Aircraft, 1914–1918* (Annapolis, Md., 1984), pp 14–26.

5. Andrew Boyle, *Trenchard* (New York, 1962), p 156.

6. Hall, "Viscount Trenchard," pp 180, 187; Harry M. Ransom, "Lord Trenchard, Architect of Air Power," *The Airpower Historian* 8 (Sep 1956).

7. Alfred Gollin, "Anticipating Air Attack, in Defence of Great Britain," *Aerospace Historian* 23, no. 4 (winter/Dec 1976): 197–201.

8. For example, H. G. Wells, *The War in the Air* (London, 1908).

9. Winston Churchill, "Air Defence Memorandum of 1914," cited in Churchill, *The World Crisis, 1911–1914* (New York, 1928), pp 328–34.

10. Hallion, *Rise of the Fighter*, p 119.

11. Barry D. Powers, *Strategy Without Slide-Rule: British Air Strategy, 1914–1939* (London, 1976), pp 28–30; John Bushby, *Air Defence of Great Britain* (London, 1973), p 22.

12. E. B. Ashmore, *Air Defence* (London, 1929), p 11; Hallion, *Rise of the Fighter*, p 119.

13. Hogg, *Anti-Aircraft*, p 52.

14. Bushby, *Air Defence of Great Britain*, p 28.

15. Hallion, *Rise of the Fighter*, p 121.

16. Malcolm Smith, *British Air Strategy Between the Wars* (Oxford, 1984), p 17.

17. Raymond J. Fredette, *The Sky on Fire: The First Battle of Britain, 1917–1918, and the Birth of the Royal Air Force* (New York, 1976), pp 37–38.

18. *Ibid*.

19. Ashmore, *Air Defence*, pp 92–94; Powers, *Strategy Without Slide-Rule*, p 68; Hallion, *Rise of the Fighter*, pp 122–25; Hogg, *Anti-Aircraft*, pp 53–63.

20. Collier, *History of Air Power*, pp 70–71; Powers, *Strategy Without Slide-Rule*, p 68.

21. Fredette, *Sky on Fire*, p 8.

22. Smith, *British Air Strategy*, p 54; Ashmore, *Air Defence*, pp 168–73.

23. Alexander Graham Bell, "Preparedness for Aerial Defense," in Eugene M. Emme, ed, *The Impact of Air Power: National Security and World Politics* (Princeton, N.J., 1959), pp 30–33.

24. William Mitchell, *Memoirs of World War I: From Start to Finish of Our Greatest War* (New York, 1960), p 218.

25. Robert F. Futrell, *Ideas, Concepts, Doctrine: A History of Basic Thinking in the United States Air Force, 1907–1964* (USAF Hist Study 139, 1971), pp 44–92.

26. Cited in Alfred F. Hurley, *Billy Mitchell: Crusader for Air Power* (Bloomington, Ind., 1975), p 26.

27. Thomas H. Greer, *The Development of Air Doctrine in the Army Air Arm, 1917–1941* (USAF Hist Study 89, 1953), pp 33–36. Hurley's *Billy Mitchell* is the best biography. See also Isaac D. Levine, *Mitchell, Pioneer of Air Power*, rev. ed. (New York, 1972). An outspoken advocate for the bomber, Mitchell never lost sight of the need for a balanced air force. He maintained that fighters would be needed to control the skies to ensure successful bombardment.

28. Sherman's early death cost the air arm the services of one of its most profound theorists, probably at least on the scale of Mitchell [William C. Sherman, *Air Warfare* (New York, 1926)].

29. Futrell, *Ideas, Concepts, Doctrine*, pp 28–29.

30. Wesley Frank Craven and James Lea Cate, eds, *The Army Air Forces in World War II* [hereafter cited as *AAF in WW II*] (Chicago, 1948; Washington, D.C., 1983), Vol I, *Plans and Early Operations: January 1939 to August 1942,* p 62.

31. *Ibid.*; Martin Claussen, "Alleged 100-Mile Limitation in Army Aviation in Coast Defense, 1931–1939," undated manuscript in USAFHRC.

32. Craven and Cate, *AAF in WW II*, Vol I, p 62.

33. *Annual Report of the Chief of the Air Corps,* Aug 17, 1934.

34. *Final Report of the War Department Special Committee on Army Air Corps* (Washington, D.C., Jul 18, 1934) [hereafter cited as *Baker Board*], p 15. The best appraisal of the Air Corps' role in coast defense is John F. Shiner's *Foulois and the U.S. Army Air Corps, 1931–1935* [(Washington, D.C., 1983), esp pp 54–56, 228, 262–63].

35. *Baker Board*, p 15; Ltr, AGO to CG, First Army, subj: Antiaircraft Defense of the Continental U.S. [n.d.], USAFHRC microfilm.

36. *The Joint Board, Joint Action of the Army and Navy* (Washington, D.C., 1935); Alan Bliss, "Air Defense of the Continental United States, 1935–1942" [hereafter cited as "Continental Air Defense"], draft manuscript in AF/CHO, ch II, pp 60–81; see also Shiner, *Foulois*, pp 54–56, 228, 262–63.

37. *Baker Board*, p 15; Shiner, *Foulois*, pp 54–56, 228, 262–63; Ltr, AGO to CG [n.d.].

38. Raymond Richard Flugel, "United States Air Power Doctrine: A Study of the Influence of William Mitchell and Giulio Douhet at the Air Corps Tactical School, 1921–1935" (Ph.D. dissertation, University of Oklahoma, 1965); Robert T. Finney, *History of the Air Corps Tactical School, 1920–1940* (USAF Hist Study 100, 1955), p 27; Perry M. Smith, "Douhet and Mitchell: Some Reappraisals," *Air University Review* 18 (Sep–Oct 1967): 97–101. Historians differ on the extent of Douhet's influence in ACTS. Although few Air Corps officers apparently read Douhet's works, most were familiar with his ideas.

39. Giulio Douhet, *The Command of the Air*, translated by Dino Ferrari and edited by Richard H. Kohn and Joseph P. Harahan (New York, 1942; Washington, D.C., 1983), esp "Book Two: The Probable Aspects of the War of the Future," pp 143–208, 235–43; Edward Warner, "Douhet, Mitchell, Seversky: Theorists of Air Warfare," in Edward Mead Earle, ed, *Makers of Modern Strategy: Military Thought from Machiavelli to Hitler* (Princeton, N.J., 1943), p 485; Bernard Brodie, *Strategy in the Missile Age* (Princeton, N.J., 1959), p 85.

40. Craven and Cate, *AAF in WW II*, Vol I, p 58.

41. Lloyd S. Jones, *U.S. Fighters* (Fallbrook, Calif., 1975), pp 68–70.

42. *Ibid.*

43. Irving Brinton Holley, Jr., *Buying Aircraft: Materiel Procurement for the Army Air Forces* (Washington, D.C., 1964), p 20; Martin P. Claussen, *Comparative History of Research and Development Policies Affecting Air Materiel, 1915–1944* (USAF Hist Study 20, 1945).

44. Technical advances in commercial and military aircraft in the period can be followed in Ronald E. Miller and David Sawers's *The Technical Development of Modern Aviation* (New York, 1970), Roger E. Bilstein's *Flight in America, 1900–1983: From the Wrights to the Astronauts* (Baltimore, 1984), Thomas Foxworth's *The Speed Seekers* (New York, 1976), Douglas J. Ingell's *The Plane That Changed the World: A Biography of the DC-3* (Fallbrook, Calif., 1966), and Kenneth G. Munson's *Airliners Between the Wars, 1919–1939* (New York, 1972) and his *Bombers Between the Wars, 1919–1939* (New York, 1970).

45. Robert F. Futrell, "Commentary," in Lt Col William Geffen, ed, *Command and Commanders in Modern Warfare* (Proceedings of the Second Military History Symposium, USAF Academy, May 23, 1968) (Washington, D.C., 1969), p 278.

46. Finney, *History of the Tactical School*, pp 31–32.

47. *The Coast Artillery Journal* 80 (1930): 299–301.

48. Capt Claire L. Chennault, "The Role of Defensive Pursuit," 1933, copy in AF/CHO, pp 24–29.

49. Rept, Lt Col H. H. Arnold to Brig Gen B. D. Foulois, March Field Exercises, Nov 26, 1934, AAF Central Decimal Files, 1917–1938, Bulky File 321.9 Box 485, RG 18, NA.

50. Jones, *U.S. Fighters*, pp 85–99.

51. Mike Spick, *Fighter Pilot Tactics: The Techniques of Daylight Air Combat* (New York, 1983), p 41.

52. Capt John R. Lovell, "Antiaircraft Preparedness," *The Coast Artillery Journal* 82 (Jul–Aug 1939): 340.

53. Intvw, Thomas A. Sturm with Maj Gen Gordon P. Saville (USAF, ret), Sun City, Ariz., Mar 26–30, 1973; *Biographical Study of USAF General Officers, 1917–1952*, (USAF Hist Study 91, 1953); Kenneth Schaffel, "A Minority of One: Major General Gordon P. Saville," *American Aviation Historical Society Journal* 32, no. 2 (summer 1987):104–09.

54. "Selfridge Planes Return from Miami," *Air Corps News Letter* [hereafter cited as *ACNL*] 19 (Jan 1, 1936): 15; untitled news item on Lt Col Ralph Royce, *ACNL* 19 (Jan 1, 1936), 22; "The GHQ Air Force Concentration in Florida," *ACNL* 19 (Jan 15, 1936), 11–15; "Barksdale Field Personnel in Florida Maneuvers," *ACNL* 19 (Jan 15, 1936), 22; "The Work of the 59th Service Squadron in the Florida Maneuvers," *ACNL* 19 (Feb 1, 1936), 19–22.

55. Saville intvw; Brig Gen Henry C. Pratt, "Comments on G.H.Q. Air Force Exercise, December 12, 1935," in Conference rept on the Florida maneuvers, Dec 12–13, 1935, HQ AFCC, 1935–1942, Reports, Studies, Manuals, AG Section, Box 8, Entry 248, RG 18, NA; Thomas A. Sturm, "Henry Conger Pratt: First Air Corps Permanent General Officer," *Aerospace Historian* 22 (Jun 1975): 22.

56. Pratt, "Comments on G.H.Q. Air Force Exercise."

57. Maj Gen Gordon P. Saville, Comments on "The GHQ Air Force Concentration in Florida" [*ca.* Apr 1, 1973].

58. Bliss, "Continental Air Defense," ch 2, pp 15–16.

59. Final Rept, Joint Antiaircraft–Air Corps Exercises, Fort Bragg, N.C., 1938, Anx 2, "Pursuit Aviation," Box 1, RG 18, NA; Col J. B. Bennett, "The Joint AA–Air Corps Exercise," *The Coast Artillery Journal,* no. 6 (Nov–Dec 1938): 442–46. In 1940 approximately 1 of every 2,500 artillery shots would hit an aircraft. World War II meant increased funding for antiaircraft artillery, and research and development pro-

duced superior guns, fire control, and tracking devices [Constance McLaughlin Green, Harry C. Thomson, and Peter C. Roots, *The Ordnance Department: Planning Munitions for War* (Washington, D.C., 1955), pp 401–21]. For a brief historical overview of the organization of Coast Artillery and its evolving mission, see Larry H. Addington's "The U.S. Coast Artillery and the Problem of Artillery Organization, 1907–1954" [*Military Affairs* 40, no. 1 (1976): 1–6].

60. Maj Muir S. Fairchild, "Foreign Developments in Antiaircraft Defense" (Lecture at ACTS), Nov 8, 1939, Fairchild Papers, Box 5, LC.

61. Bliss, "Continental Air Defense," ch 2, pp 15–16.

62. Gen Haywood S. Hansell, Jr., "The Historical Perspective of Air Power" (Lecture at Air Command and General Staff College), 1976, USAFHRC microfilm.

63. Ltr, Maj Gen Frank M. Andrews, CG, GHQ Air Force, to AG, subj: Report of Annual Tactical Inspection, G.H.Q. Air Force (May 12–18, 1938), Sep 29, 1938, USAFHRC microfilm.

64. Memo, Lt Col Carl A. Spaatz, Air Corps Plans Branch, to CAC, subj: Aviation in National Defense, Mar 30, 1939, AAF Central Decimal Files, 1939–1942, Bulky File 334.7, RG 18, NA.

65. Memo, Maj Gen H. H. Arnold, CAC, to Maj Gen Delos C. Emmons, CG, GHQ Air Force, subj: Pursuit Training and Pursuit Plane Tactical Development, Nov 14, 1939, quoted in Bernard L. Boylan, *Development of the Long-Range Escort Fighter* (USAF Hist Study 136, 1955), pp 30, 255 n. 119.

66. Hearings before the Committee on Military Affairs, House of Representatives, *Air Defense Base Hearings*, 74th Cong, 1st sess (Washington, D.C., 1935), p 55; Victor B. Anthony, "Congress and the Concept of Strategic Aerial Warfare, 1919–1939" (M.A. thesis, Duke University, 1964), p 127.

Chapter 2. Air Defense in World War II

1. J. D. Scott, "The Development of Radar," in M. M. Postan, *et al*, eds, *Design and Development of Weapons: Studies in Government and Industrial Organization* (London, 1964), part 3, ch 15, pp 373–74; Robert M. Page, *The Origins of Radar* (Garden City, N.Y., 1962); Ronald W.

Clark, *The Rise of the Boffins* (London, 1962); Ronald W. Clark, *Tizard* (Cambridge, Mass., 1965); Sir Robert Watson-Watt, *Three Steps to Victory* (London, 1957).

2. Scott, "Development of Radar"; Page, *Origins of Radar*; Clark, *Rise of the Boffins*; Clark, *Tizard*; Watson-Watt, *Three*

Steps to Victory. Accessible explanations of how radar systems work are in Lt Col John B. McKinney's "Radar: A Case History of an Invention" (Term report, Research Center in Technological Innovation, Harvard Business School, Jan 16, 1961).

3. Scott, "Development of Radar"; Page, *Origins of Radar*; Clark, *Rise of the Boffins*; Clark, *Tizard*; Watson-Watt, *Three Steps to Victory*; McKinney, "Radar: Case History of an Invention."

4. Barry R. Posen, *The Sources of Military Doctrine: France, Britain, and Germany Between Two World Wars* (Ithaca, 1984), pp 160–78.

5. Robert W. Ackerman, "The Use of Radio and Radar Equipment by the AAF, 1939-1945," May 1949, USAFHRC microfilm; Dulany Terrett, *The Signal Corps: The Emergency (to December 1941)* (Washington, D.C., 1956), pp 35–38; Futrell, *Ideas, Concepts, Doctrine*, p 54; David Kite Allison, *New Eye for the Navy: The Origin of Radar at the Naval Research Laboratory* (Washington, D.C., 1981).

6. Maj F. W. Hopkins, "Foreign Developments in Antiaircraft Defense" (Lecture at ACTS), *ca.* 1939, Papers of Lt Col Fenton C. Epling, Entry 273, RG 18, NA.

7. Haywood S. Hansell, "Pre-World War II Evaluation of the Air Weapon" (Lecture at Air War College), Nov 16, 1953, cited in Futrell, *Ideas, Concepts, Doctrine*, p 54.

8. Ltr, Maj Gen Muir S. Fairchild to Dr. Bruce Hopper, Sep 26, 1946, Fairchild Collection, USAFHRC microfilm.

9. Saville intvw; *Biographical Study, General Officers.*

10. Craven and Cate, *AAF in WW II*, Vol VI, *Men and Planes*, p 84; Saville intvw.

11. Saville intvw. An Air Corps study conducted in August 1939, however, concluded that an air attack against either the east or west coast was extremely unlikely [War Plans Division Rept, WPD–4078–11, Guiding Principles for Study of Basic AA Requirements for Installations and Metropolitan Areas in the U.S., Aug 1939, Env 23, RG 18, NA].

12. Craven and Cate, *AAF in WW II*, Vol VI, p 84; Saville intvw.

13. Hist, ADC, Feb 26–Jun 2, 1940; Saville intvw.

14. Ltr, AG to CG of Armies, Corps Areas, and Departments *et al*, subj: Creation of Air Defense Command, Feb 26, 1940; Hist, ADC, Feb 26–Jun 2, 1940, App 8; *Biographical Study, General Officers*; Saville intvw.

15. Hist, ADC, Feb 26–Jun 2, 1940.

16. *Ibid.*

17. Terrett, *Signal Corps: Emergency*, p 125; "Outline of Continental U.S. Air Defense in World War II" (ADC Comd Hist, 1945).

18. Hist, ADC, Feb 26–Jun 2, 1940, App I; Ltr, ADC to CG, First Army Aircraft Warning Service, CONUS, May 23, 1940.

19. Saville intvw.

20. Hist, ADC, Feb 26–Jun 2, 1940.

21. *Ibid*, App II; Brig Gen J. E. Chaney, "Final Report on Participation in First Army Maneuvers," Aug 26, 1940, Fiscal Env, Entry 273, RG 18, NA.

22. Hist, ADC, Feb 26–Jun 2, 1940, App II; Chaney, "Final Report."

23. Clark, *Tizard*, pp 248–71.

24. Henry H. Arnold, *Global Mission* (New York, 1949), p 219.

25. Rept, ADC Comdrs, Observations on Trip to England, Dec 15, 1940, Env 23, Box 4, Entry 245, RG 18, NA; Saville intvw.

26. Rept ADC Comdrs, Dec 15, 1940; Saville intvw.

27. Terrett, *Signal Corps: Emergency*, pp 151–74.

28. Saville intvw; Hist, ADC, Feb 26–Jun 2, 1940.

29. Rept, Air Defense Exercise in the Test Sector, Jan 21–24, 1941, Box 5, Entry 270, RG 18, NA (copy also in Box 185, Entry 293B, RG 18, NA).

30. "Conclusions," in Air Defense Exercise rept.

31. Craven and Cate, *AAF in WW II*, Vol I, p 151.

32. Kent Roberts Greenfield, Robert R. Palmer, and Bell I. Wiley, *The Organization of Ground Combat Troops* (Washington, D.C., 1947), pp 150–51.

33. *Ibid.*

34. *Ibid*, p 117.

35. WD Order, Mar 17, 1941, cited in *ibid*, pp 117–18, 122.

36. Memo, Maj Gen William Bryden, DCS, to AC/S, WPD, subj: Defense Commands and Air Defense Set-up, Feb 28, 1941; AG320.2, subj: Air Defense, Mar 7, 1941, both in AG Central Decimal Files, RG 407, NA.

37. "Defense Plans and Operations in the Fourth Air Force Through 1941" (4AF Hist Study), Vol I, p 7, USAFHRC microfilm.

38. Hist, ADC, Feb 26–Jun 2, 1940.

39. Bliss, "Continental Air Defense," ch 2, pp 81–82, and ch 3, p 1; Col Crawford, Air Defense Records, Entries 269–75, RG 18, NA.

40. Craven and Cate, *AAF in WW II*, Vol VI, p 87.

41. Emmons was not happy about the new name for his command. He feared his relief as Commanding General, Air Force Combat Command, would prevent his serving the full four-year tour as Commanding General, GHQ Air Force, prescribed by statute for retirement in his temporary three-star grade [Ltr, Lt Gen Delos C. Emmons to CAC, Jun 24, 1941, Chief of the Air Corps and Adjutant General Folder, Box 3, Entry 241A, RG 18, NA].

42. Craven and Cate, *AAF in WW II*, Vol VI, p 771.

43. Hist, ADC, 1940–1941; Ltr, GHQ Air Force to AG, subj: Inactivation of Headquarters and Headquarters Detachment, ADC, Jun 2, 1941.

44. Terrett, *Signal Corps: Emergency*, p 270.

45. *Ibid*, pp 286–92; George Raynor Thompson, Dixie R. Harris, Pauline M. Oakes, and Dulaney Terrett, *The Signal Corps: The Test (December 1941 to July 1943)* (Washington, D.C., 1957), pp 23–24, 54.

46. Richard F. McMullen, *Aircraft in Air Defense, 1946–1960* (ADC Hist Study 12, 1960).

47. "Defense Plans and Operations" (4AF Hist Study), Vol I, pp 125–27; Bliss, "Continental Air Defense," ch 3, pp 98–112.

48. Gordon P. Saville, "Air Defense Doctrine" (Draft manual), Oct 27, 1941, AAF Central Decimal Files, 1939–1942, Bulky Box 181, Entry 293B, RG 18, NA. This manuscript was eventually published as FM 1–25, Air Defense, Dec 24, 1942.

49. Ltr, Lt Gen H. H. Arnold to Col William E. Kepner, subj: Directive for Board of Officers on the Study of Air Defense Problems, Oct 30, 1940, Box 183, Entry 293B, RG 18, NA.

50. Saville, "Air Defense Doctrine." See also FM 1–25, Dec 24, 1942.

51. Saville, "Air Defense Doctrine"; FM 1–25, Dec. 24, 1942; Saville intv; Gordon P. Saville, "Orientation Concerning Controlled Interception" (Lecture), in document volume, "History of Fighter Command School, March 28–November 5, 1942"; "Air Force Antiaircraft Defense"

(ACTS text), Oct 15, 1938, pp 13–14, Box 2, Entry 248, RG 18, NA.

52. Maj Gen Kenneth P. Bergquist (Historical documentation), Oct 1965, copy in AF/CHO.

53. Gordon W. Prange, *At Dawn We Slept: The Untold Story of Pearl Harbor* (New York, 1981), pp 499–501.

54. Bergquist documentation; Col Flint O. DuPre, *U.S. Air Force Biographical Dictionary* (New York, 1965), p 17.

55. Intvw, Hugh N. Ahmann and Thomas A. Sturm with Maj Gen Howard C. Davidson, Tulip Hill, Md, Dec 5–8, 1974, p 442.

56. Prange, *At Dawn We Slept*, pp 730–31.

57. Craven and Cate, *AAF in WW II*, Vol I, p 198. See also Roberta Wohlstetter, *Pearl Harbor: Warning and Decision* (Stanford, Calif., 1962); Stetson Conn, Rose C. Engelman, and Byron Fairchild, *Guarding the United States and Its Outposts* (Washington, D.C., 1964), pp 174–96; Richard K. Betts, *Surprise Attack: Lessons for Defense Planning* (Washington, D.C., 1982), pp 42–50. In the Philippines, 7 radar sets were available in the islands but only 2 were in operation at the time of the attack. As was the case in Hawaii, there was no way of telling friend from foe. Providing air defense in the Philippines were 107 P–40E fighters and 16 obsolete P–26As and 52 P–35As. On duty in Hawaii were 138 P–40Bs, P–40Cs, and P–40Es along with 14 P–36A fighters. Details of the air defense situation in the Philippines are given in Louis Morton's *The Fall of the Philippines* [(Washington, D.C., 1953), pp 37–45].

58. Immediately after Pearl Harbor, and for a few months thereafter, tensions ran high as major American cities on the east and west coasts readied (with blackouts in such unlikely targets as Kansas) for enemy air attacks. Some often chaotic situations resulted when false alerts were reported. Perhaps the extreme example of phantom attack was the so-called Battle of Los Angeles that occurred during the night of February 24–25, 1942. Faulty information and disorganized reporting procedures led many panicky citizens and military forces to believe the city was being attacked by bombers. Antiaircraft artillery was expended at the rate of 1,440 rounds on reported sightings of enemy aircraft. Reports indicated that four enemy planes had been downed; one was said to have landed in flames in a Hollywood intersection [Craven

and Cate, *AAF in WW II*, Vol I, pp 283–84].

59. Craven and Cate, *AAF in WW II*, Vol I, p 42, and Vol VI, pp 78–79.

60. *Ibid.*; Memo, Arnold [*ca.* Dec 10, 1941]. (Arnold wrote the memo before Marshall activated theaters of operation on the east and west coasts.)

61. Ltr, Maj Gen M. F. Harmon to Lt Gen H. H. Arnold, subj: Change of Mission of Air Force Combat Command, Dec 23, 1941, Chief of AAF (DC/S for Air) Folder, Box 4, Entry 241A, RG 18, NA. (Harmon personally delivered the letter to Arnold.)

62. Conn *et al*, *Guarding the United States*, pp 35–36.

63. Craven and Cate, *AAF in WW II*, Vol VI, pp 92–93; Bliss, "Continental Air Defense," ch 6, pp 55–56.

64. Craven and Cate, *AAF in WW II*, Vol VI, pp 26–30.

65. Saville intvw.

66. Rept, R. A. Watson-Watt, Report on the Air Defense System of the Pacific Coast of the United States, Jan 1942, H. H. Arnold Papers, Box 112, LC.

67. Saville intvw.

68. Conn *et al*, *Guarding the United States*, pp 26–44, 80–105.

69. Ltr, AG to CG, AAF, and Comdr, 3AF, subj: Establishment of the Fighter Command School, USAFHRC microfilm; Craven and Cate, *AAF in WW II*, Vol VI, pp 72–74.

70. Ltr, Lt Gen H. H. Arnold, CG, AAF, to All Volunteers, Aircraft Warning Service, Sep 24, 1943, USAFHRC microfilm; Intvw, Dr. Murray Green with Maj Gen Barney M. Giles, San Antonio, Tex., May 12–13, 1970, transcript in AF/CHO

(Giles was Chief of the Air Staff under Gen Arnold).

71. Air Defense Wing Folder, AAF–CDF 1939–1942, Box 651, RG 18, NA; Saville intvw.

72. Craven and Cate, *AAF in WW II*, Vol VI, pp 92–94; Saville intvw.

73. Memo, Maj Gen Follet Bradley, Air Inspector, to Arnold, subj: Proposed Decrease in Air Defense Establishments, Apr 2, 1943, AAF-CDF Oct 1942–May 1944, 322, Observations-Miscellaneous, RG 18, NA.

74. Note, Gen Arnold to Col Jacob E. Smart, Apr 5, 1943, AAF-CDF 1942–1944, 322, Observations-Miscellaneous, RG 18, NA (Smart was a member of the Advisory Council to the CG, AAF).

75. Memo, Maj Gen Barney M. Giles, C/AS, to C/S, subj: Elimination of Practice Air Raid Alerts, Dec 15, 1943, with attached report by the Joint Intelligence Staff, AAF-CDF 1939–1942, 384, 5B, Aerial Attacks and Raids, RG 18, NA.

76. Robert C. Mikesh, *Balloon Bomb Attacks on North America: Japan's World War II Assaults* (Fallbrook, Calif., 1982); Craven and Cate, *AAF in WW II*, Vol VI, pp 116–18.

77. Intvw, Thomas A. Sturm and Dr. Murray Green with Brig Gen Hume Peabody, Chaptico, Md., Nov 16, 1972; Joseph R. Reither, *The Development of Tactical Doctrines at AAFSAT and AAFTAC* (USAF Hist Study 13, 1944).

78. Clement L. Grant, *AAF Air Defense Activities in the Mediterranean, 1942–20 September, 1944* (USAF Hist Study 66, 1954), pp 50–52; Richard H. Kohn and Joseph P. Harahan, eds, *Condensed Analysis of the Ninth Air Force in the European Theater of Operations* (Washington, D.C., 1946; 1984), pp 76–79.

Chapter 3. Planning for Air Defense in the Postwar Era

1. WD FM 100–20, *Command and Employment of Air Power*, Jul 21, 1943; Craven and Cate, *AAF in WW II*, Vol VII, *Services Around the World*, pp 548–54.

2. Herman S. Wolk, *Planning and Organizing the Postwar Air Force, 1943–1947* (Washington, D.C., 1984), pp 46–47, 50–51, 100–103; Perry M. Smith, *The Air Force Plans for Peace, 1943–1945* (Baltimore and London, 1970), pp 5–14.

3. George R. Thompson and Dixie R. Harris, *The Signal Corps: The Outcome (mid-1943 Through 1945)* (Washington, D.C., 1966), pp 449–57.

4. Maj Gen Francis L. Ankenbrandt, Presentation at USAF Commanders' Conference, Maxwell AFB, Ala., Dec 6–8, 1948, transcript in "Operation Dualism," Vol III, pp 384–85, USAFHRC.

5. WD FM 100–20, Jul 21, 1943; Craven and Cate, *AAF in WW II,* Vol VII, pp 548–54.

6. Ltr, Lt Gen Carl A. Spaatz to Gen H. H. Arnold, Dec 3, 1944, Spaatz Papers, Box 58, LC.

7. Memo, Maj Gen H. R. Oldfield, AAF Sp Asst for AAA, subj: Assignment of Antiaircraft Units to the Air Forces in Defense of the Philippine Islands, May 30, 1945, cited in Futrell, *Ideas, Concepts, Doctrine,* pp 102, 447 n. 48.

8. Ltr, Gen H. H. Arnold to WDGS, subj: Integration of the AAA into the AAF, Aug 4, 1945, AAG Central Decimal File 381, Box 189, RG 18, NA; Chase C. Mooney and Edward C. Williamson, *Organization of the Army Air Arm, 1935–1945* (USAF Hist Study 10, 1956), pp 55–56.

9. Memo, Lt Gen Barney M. Giles, Dep Comdr and C/AS, to Air Staff, subj: Principles for Future AAF Action, Jan 28, 1945, cited in Hist, Continental Air Forces, Dec 15, 1944–Mar 21, 1946.

10. Ltr, Arnold to WDGS, Aug 4, 1945; Mooney and Williamson, *Organization of the Army Air Arm,* pp 55–56.

11. Routing and Referral Slip, Maj Gen Earle E. Partridge, AC/AS–3, to AC/AS–5, subj: AAF Policy As to the Organization of AAA If Integrated into the AAF, Feb 1, 1946. The incumbent of the Air Staff post referred to by Partridge would serve as "a friend at court who would look after . . . the interests of the AA" [Partridge Collection, USAFHRC].

12. Intvw, Col George S. Walborn with Lt Gen Harold W. Grant, 1959, transcript in AF/CHO.

13. AAF 20–9, Activation of HQ Continental Air Forces, Dec 16, 1944; Hist, Continental Air Forces, Dec 15, 1944–Mar 21, 1946. In effect, Arnold returned to the organizational structure he had discarded in early 1942 when he abolished the Air Force Combat Command (formerly GHQ Air Force).

14. Intvw, T. A. Sturm and H. S. Wolk with Lt Gen Ira C. Eaker, Washington, D.C., Nov 27, 1972.

15. Ltr, Maj Gen Samuel E. Anderson, C/S, CAF, to CG, AAF, subj: Interim Air Force, Jun 20, 1945, USAFHRC.

16. Memo, Maj Gen L. S. Kuter to Gen H. H. Arnold, subj: Status of Plans for the Postwar Air Force, Jan 17, 1945, AAG Central File, Box 189, RG 18, NA.

17. Eaker intvw.

18. Rept, Special War Department Committee on the Permanent Military Establishment (Bessell Committee), subj: Interim Plan for the Permanent Military Establishment of the United States, Sep 1945.

19. Ray S. Cline, *The War Department, Washington Command Post: The Operations Division* (Washington, D.C., 1951), p 353.

20. Memo, Col Joseph J. Ladd, Ch, Org Div, to Lt Gen H. S. Vandenberg, AC/AS–3, HQ AAF, subj: Bessell Committee Recommends 165,000 Post War AAF Troop Basis, Nov 7, 1945, USAFHRC.

21. MR, Col Jacob E. Smart, S/AS, subj: Decision Reached at Staff Meeting in Gen Eaker's Office, Aug 29, 1945, cited in Futrell, *Ideas, Concepts, Doctrine,* p 458 n. 58; Eaker intvw; Wolk, *Planning the Postwar Air Force,* pp 101–02; Intvw, T. A. Sturm with Gen Jacob E. Smart, Washington, D.C., Feb 16, 1973.

22. Memo, Brig Gen Glen C. Jamison, Dep AC/AS–5, to Maj Gen Lauris Norstad, subj: The Simpson Board Recommendation for the Reorganization of the War Department, May 3, 1946 [the Patch Board had become the Simpson Board]; Memo, Brig Gen Henry I. Hodes, Asst DC/S, to WD, subj: Statement of Approved Policies to Effect Increased Autonomy of the AAF Within the War Department Structure, Apr 4, 1946; Cline, *Washington Command Post,* pp 353–56.

23. Intvw, William R. Perretto with Lt Gen Barney M. Giles, San Antonio, Tex., Oct 1966, copy of transcript in AF/CHO.

24. Rept, Board of Officers on Organization of the War Department (Patch Board), Dec 28, 1945.

25. Memo, Brig Gen Henry I. Hodes, Asst DC/S, to WD Agencies, Jan 23, 1946.

26. Giles intvw.

27. WD Cir 138, Reorganization of the War Department, May 14, 1946; Hist, ADC, Mar 1946–Jun 1947; Cline, *Washington Command Post,* p 359.

28. ADC was constituted March 21, 1946, activated March 27, and organized effective May 1 [Hist, ADC, Mar 1946–Jun 1947, with appended supporting document HQ ADC GO 1, Mar 27, 1946]. On March 31 ADC had a personnel strength of approximately 7,000 compared to 26,000 for TAC and 84,231 for SAC.

29. WD AG 322, Establishment of Air Defense Strategic Air and Tactical Air Commands, Redesignation of HQ Continental Air Command, Mar 21, 1946.

30. DuPre, *Biographical Dictionary*, pp 225–26; *Biographical Study, General Officers*.

31. Ltr, Gen Carl A. Spaatz, CG, AAF, to CG, ADC, subj: Interim Mission, Mar 12, 1946; Ltr, Maj Gen C. C. Chauncey, DC/AS, to CG, ADC, subj: Interim Mission, Jun 5, 1946; Ltr, HQ ADC to CG, AAF, subj: Mission of ADC, Jul 31, 1946; Ltr, Lt Gen George E. Stratemeyer, CG, ADC, to Lt Gen Ira C. Eaker, Dep Comdr, AAF, subj: Mission of ADC, Nov 13, 1946, all in USAFHRC.

32. Intvw, Alfred Goldberg with Gen Carl A. Spaatz, Washington ,D.C., 1945.

33. Hist, ADC, Mar 1946–Jun 1947.

34. Ltr, Gen Spaatz to Lt Gen Ennis C. Whitehead, Mar 21, 1946; Memo, Stuart Symington, Asst SecWar/Air, to Spaatz, Aug 10, 1946; Memo, Spaatz to Symington, Aug 14, 1946, all in Spaatz Papers, Box 126, LC. See also the Stratemeyer speech to the Aviation Writer's Association [*New York Times*, Jul 11, 1946] in which he said that the AAF could not "push our way out of a wet paper bag." Symington was upset because he feared such remarks would hurt efforts to create an independent Air Force. Spaatz counseled Stratemeyer that "our public relations emphasis must be on the rate of buildup and our eventual plans for the future."

35. Lt Gen Eaker, "The AAF: Its Status, Plans, and Policies" (Remarks made while representing Gen Spaatz at the National War College), Jun 5, 1947, transcript in USAFHRC.

36. Memo, Lt Gen Eaker to Gen Spaatz, subj: Fighter Group for ADC, Jul 19, 1946, Spaatz Papers, Box 262, LC.

37. Air Intel Rept 100–45–34, An Analysis of the Soviet Air Force, Jun 1946, Spaatz Papers, Box 21, LC.

38. *Ibid.*; Joseph B. Mastro, "The Lessons of World War II and the Cold War," in Robin Higham and Jacob W. Kipp, eds, *Soviet Aviation and Air Power: A Historical View* (Boulder, Colo., 1977), p 197.

39. John C. Baker, "The Long-Range Bomber in Soviet Military Planning," and Norman Friedman, "The Soviet Bomber Force: Two Revolutions in Military Affairs," in Paul J. Murphy, ed, *The Soviet Air Forces* (London, 1984), pp 177–87 and 157–76, respectively.

40. *Ibid.*

41. Alexander Boyd, *The Soviet Air Force Since 1918* (New York, 1977), pp 215–16.

42. Stuart Symington, "We've Scuttled Our Air Defense," *American Magazine* 45, no. 2 (Feb 1948): 56.

43. Ltr, Gen Spaatz to All Commands, subj: Current AAF Plans and Programs, Oct 24, 1946, Spaatz Papers, Box 262, LC.

44. Memo, Col Charles R. Bond, AC/AS–3, to Air Staff, Mar 12, 1946, AAG Central File 322, Box 605, RG 18, NA. (This memo summarizes Air Staff planning begun in early February on direction of General Eaker.)

45. Stanley W. Dziuban, *Military Relations Between the United States and Canada: 1939–1945* (Washington, D.C., 1959), p 336. The committee was established in Feb 1946, composed of representatives of service departments, the Departments of State and External Affairs, and the Secretary of the Canadian Defence Committee.

46. Gen Spaatz, Presentation at War Council meeting in OSW, Feb 21, 1946, Spaatz Papers, Box 25, LC.

47. Ltr, HQ ADC to Numbered AF Comdrs, Jul 18, 1946, USAFHRC.

48. Memo, Ch, GMs and Air Def Div, to AC/AS–3, HQ AAF, subj: Status of Air Defense, Jan 15, 1947, USAFHRC.

49. *Ibid.*

50. Hist, 1AF, Mar–Dec 1947.

51. Hist, 4AF, Jan–Jun 1947.

52. Hist, 505th Aircraft Control and Warning Gp, Jul–Dec 1947.

53. Ltr, Gen Spaatz to Lt Gen Stratemeyer, subj: Interim Mission, Mar 12, 1946, USAFHRC.

54. Spaatz, Testimony in *House Hearings on the Military Establishment Appropriations Bill for Fiscal Year 1947*, p 414.

55. Ltr, Lt Gen Eaker on behalf of Gen Spaatz to CG, ADC, subj: Investment of Command Responsibilities of the Land, Sea, and Air Forces in Event of Air Invasion, USAFHRC. On the Guard's role in air defense, see Charles Joseph Gross's *Prelude to the Total Force: The Air National Guard, 1943–1969* (Washington, D.C., 1985) [hereafter cited as *Air National Guard*], Richard F. McMullen's *The Air National Guard in Air Defense, 1946–1971* (ADC Hist Study 38, 1971), and Thomas W. Ray's *The Air National Guard Manned Interceptor Force, 1946–1964* (ADC Hist Study 23, 1964).

56. Ltr, Eaker to CG, ADC.

57. *Ibid.*; Gross, *Air National Guard*; McMullen, *Air Defense and National Policy*;

McMullen, *Air National Guard in Air Defense*; Ray, *Air National Guard Manned Interceptor Force*.

58. HQ ADC A-5, Presentation at AF Comdrs meeting, Brooks Field, Tex., Mar 11, 1947, USAFHRC microfilm.

59. HQ AAF issued new mission statements to SAC and TAC on Oct 10, 1946, replacing the interim statements of Mar 1946. Spaatz recognized that Stratemeyer also wanted to have an updated and more comprehensive statement of the ADC mission, but he felt that "in view of present budget discussions and the possibility of some reorganization in the near future, it would be the better course to withhold action at this time" [Ltr, Spaatz to Stratemeyer, Mar 14, 1947, USAFHRC microfilm]. The U.S. stockpile included only 13 nuclear weapons in Jul 1947 and 50 in 1948. These weapons were large and heavy, and none were assembled [David A. Rosenberg, "The Origins of Overkill: Nuclear Weapons and American Strategy, 1945–1960," *International Security* 7 (spring 1983), p 14].

60. Hist, ADC, Mar 1946–Jun 1947.

61. HQ ADC, Plan for the Air Defense of the Continental U.S. (Short Term), Oct 18, 1946, USAFHRC microfilm.

62. Memo, Col Jacob E. Smart, Dep, Ops ADC, subj: Summary of Actions to Effect Establishment of Air Defense of the United States, Jun 16, 1949, Whitehead Collection, USAFHRC microfilm.

63. Ltr, Gen Stratemeyer to Gen Spaatz, subj: Establishment of an Air Defense in Being, Nov 22, 1946, USAFHRC microfilm.

64. Ltr, Gen Stratemeyer to Gen Spaatz, subj: Air Defense Plan (Long Term), Apr 8, 1947; Intvw, T. A. Sturm with Maj Gen John B. Cary, Washington, D.C., Jan 15, 1972.

65. ADC, Air Defense Plan (Long Term), Apr 8, 1947.

66. Ltr, Stratemeyer to Spaatz, Apr 8, 1947.

67. *Ibid.*

68. *Ibid.*

69. Memo, Ch, GMs and Air Def Div, to AC/AS-3, HQ AAF, Jan 15, 1947, USAFHRC microfilm.

70. Ltr, CG, ADC, to CSAF, subj: Air Defense of the Continental U.S., Jun 2, 1947, USAFHRC microfilm.

71. Memo, AC/AS-3 to AC/AS-4, HQ AAF, subj: Proposed Air Defense Policy, Mar 13, 1947, USAFHRC microfilm.

72. Memo, AC/AS-5 to AC/AS-3, HQ AAF, subj: Proposed Air Defense Policy, Mar 17, 1947, USAFHRC microfilm. On Weyland's support of Patton in World War II, see Alan F. Witt's "Coming of Age: XIX TAC's Role During the 1944 Dash Across France" [*Air University Review* 36, no. 3 (Mar–Apr 1985), pp 71–87].

73. Rept, Air Def Policy Panel to CSAF, Aug 14, 1947, USAFHRC microfilm.

74. Memo, Maj Gen Earle E. Partridge to Lt Gen Eaker, subj: Mission of ADC, Aug 24, 1946, USAFHRC microfilm.

75. Memo, Stuart Symington to Gen Carl Spaatz, n.d. [*ca.* Sep 18, 1946], Spaatz Papers, Box 256, LC.

76. Ltr, Gen Spaatz to Dr. Theodore von Karman, Dec 17, 1946, USAFHRC microfilm.

77. Preliminary RAND Report, subj: Active Defense of the United States Against Air Attack, Jul 10, 1947 (revised and reissued Feb 5, 1948).

78. Ltr, CSAF to ADC, subj: Active Defense of the United States Against Air Attack (comments on RAND Report), Oct 22, 1947, USAFHRC microfilm.

79. Ltr, Gen Spaatz to Comdr, APGC, subj: Evaluation of Potential Air Defense Capabilities of the AAF, Jun 24, 1947, AAF Central Files 381, War Plans Miscellaneous, National Defense 1946–1947, Vol I, Box 642, RG 18, NA.

80. Ltr, David E. Lilienthal to SecWar, Jun 4, 1947, AAF Central Files 381, Box 642, RG 18, NA.

81. Ltr, SecWar Robert P. Patterson to Lilienthal, Jun 18, 1947, AAF Central Files 381, Box 642, RG 18, NA.

82. DuPre, *Biographical Dictionary*, pp 179–80; Biographical information, in Norstad Papers, NA (microfilm copies in AF/CHO).

83. Memo, Maj Gen Norstad to Gen Spaatz, subj: Security of Atomic Energy Commission Facilities, Jul 8, 1947, AAF Central Files 381, Box 642, RG 18, NA.

84. EO 9877, Jul 26, 1947.

85. Letter of Appointment, Pres Harry S. Truman to Thomas K. Finletter, Jul 18, 1947, cited in Air Policy Commission, *Survival in the Air Age* (Washington, D.C., Jan 1, 1948) [hereafter cited as Finletter Commission Rept].

86. Intvw, T. A. Sturm with Maj Gen Francis L. Ankenbrandt, Naples, Fla., Apr 17, 1973.

87. Maj Gen Ankenbrandt, Opening remarks at presentation of Aircraft Control and Warning System for Alaska and the United States, Nov 19, 1947, transcript in USAFHRC microfilm.

88. Memo, Maj Gen Ankenbrandt to Gen Carl Spaatz, subj: Aircraft Control and Warning Plan for Alaska and the Continental U.S. [n.d.], USAFHRC microfilm.

89. Ltr, Gen Hoyt S. Vandenberg to Dr. Vannevar Bush, Chmn, R&D Bd, Dec 9, 1947, Vandenberg Papers, LC.

90. Memo, Ankenbrandt to Spaatz [n.d.].

91. Hoyt S. Vandenberg, "A Progress Report" (Script presentation to House Armed Services Committee), USAFHRC microfilm.

92. Ltr, Gen Vandenberg to Lt Gen Stratemeyer, subj: Aircraft Control and Warning for the U.S., Jan 19, 1948.

93. Ltr, Symington to Gen George C. Kenney, CG, SAC, May 30, 1947, Spaatz Papers, Box 28, LC. Symington told SAC to ease up on B-50 mock bombing and long-distance missions until unification was achieved. "Hundreds of thousands of Americans," he noted, "opposed . . . dropping atomic bombs . . . from a humanitarian standpoint."

94. Tpcon, Gen Vandenberg to Lt Gen Stratemeyer, Nov 13, 1947, rec con in Vandenberg Papers, Box 1, LC; Ltr, DAF to CG, ADC, Dec 14, 1947, subj: Reorganization of ADC, USAFHRC microfilm.

95. Lt Gen Stratemeyer, "Requirements for an Air Defense of the U.S." (Presentation to Secy Symington and Gen Spaatz), Oct 23, 1947, transcript in Vandenberg Papers, Box 32, LC.

96. Ltr, Gen Spaatz to Comdr, APG, subj: Evaluation of Potential Air Defense Capabilities of the AAF [n.d.], AAF Central Files 381, Box 642, RG 18, NA.

97. *Ibid.*

98. Finletter Commission Rept.

99. Hearings before the Committee on Appropriations, House of Representatives, Testimony by Maj Gen Hoyt S. Vandenberg, Mar 18, 1948, transcript in Vandenberg Papers, Box 48, LC.

100. Spaatz, Testimony before Committee on Civilian Components (the Gray Board). This panel, chaired by Assistant Secretary of the Army Gordon Gray, sought "to make a comprehensive, objective, and impartial study of the type and character of civilian components that should be maintained [in the new military establishment] . . . ." [*First Report of the Secretary of Defense* (Washington, 1948), pp 23, 45, 154].

101. AFR 20-13 (advance copy), Organization of ADC, Dec 19, 1947.

102. Memo, Gen Muir S. Fairchild to AS, subj: Mission of the Air National Guard, Nov 16, 1949, Fairchild Papers, Box 2, LC.

103. Ltr, Lt Gen Stratemeyer to Maj Gen Partridge, subj: Current Status and Organization of the Air National Guard and Air Reserve, Nov 20, 1947, Spaatz Papers, Box 265, LC.

104. Ltr, Gen Spaatz to Lt Gen Stratemeyer, Mar 12, 1946, subj: Interim Mission, USAFHRC microfilm.

105. Ltr, Lt Gen Stratemeyer to Maj Gen Butler B. Miltonberger, CNGB, Apr 15, 1946, cited in Hist, ADC, Mar 1946–Jun 1947.

106. Ltr, HQ ADC to CGs, All Air Forces, subj: Mission of ADC, Jun 11, 1946, USAFHRC microfilm.

107. Ltr, Lt Gen Stratemeyer to Gen Spaatz, Sep 25, 1946, cited in Hist, ADC, Mar 1946–Jun 1947.

108. Ltr, Brig Gen John P. McConnell to Maj Gen Partridge, Jun 9, 1949, Partridge Collection, USAFHRC microfilm; Gross, *Air National Guard*, ch 1.

109. Stratemeyer presentation, Oct 23, 1947.

110. AFR 20-13.

111. Ltr, DAF to CG, ADC, Dec 17, 1947, subj: Air Defense, USAFHRC microfilm.

112. Ltr, Lt Gen Stratemeyer to All ADC AF Comdrs, Dec 17, 1947, USAFHRC microfilm.

113. Finletter Commission Rept, p 10.

114. *Ibid.*, p 20.

115. Hist, 4AF, Jan–Nov 1948.

116. Hist, 505th Aircraft Control and Warning Group, Jul–Dec 1947; *ibid.*, Jan–Mar 1948; Hist, 4AF, Jan–Nov 1948.

117. Hist, 1AF, Jan–Jun 1948.

118. Hist, 505th Aircraft Control and Warning Group, Jan–Mar 1948.

119. Hist, 1AF, Jan–Jun 1948.

120. HQ USAF Interstaff Memo, Brig Gen Edward J. Timberlake to Maj Gen Samuel E. Anderson, Mar 25, 1948, USAFHRC microfilm.

121. *Ibid.*

122. Msg, CG, ADC, to 4AF, Mar 27, 1948; Ltr, HQ ADC to CG, 4AF, Mar 31, 1948, subj: Air Defense System, USAFHRC microfilm.

123. Memo, Timberlake to Anderson, Mar 25, 1948.

124. Ltr, Lt Gen Ennis C. Whitehead, CG, FEAF, to Gen Spaatz, Dec 9, 1947, Spaatz Papers, Box 28, LC.

125. Msg, Gen Lucius D. Clay to Lt Gen Stephen J. Chamberlain, Mar 5, 1948, cited in Jean Edward Smith, ed, *The Papers of General Lucius D. Clay: Germany, 1945–1949* (Bloomington, Ind., 1974), Vol II, p 568.

126. Daniel H. Yergin, *Shattered Peace: The Origins of the Cold War and the National Security State* (Boston, 1977), pp 350–53; Walter Millis, ed, *The Forrestal Diaries* (New York, 1951), p 387.

127. AF Bul 1, *Functions of the Armed Forces and the Joint Chiefs of Staff*, May 21, 1948, p 8.

128. Robert J. Watson, *History of the Joint Chiefs of Staff* (Washington, D.C., 1986), Vol V, *The Joint Chiefs of Staff and National Policy, 1953–1954*, [hereafter cited as *JCS and National Policy*], p 208.

129. 1AF Interstaff Memo, Col G. G. Gibbs to C/S, subj: Aircraft Control and Warning Groups, Mar 30, 1948, in Hist, 1AF, Jan–Jun 1948, App A–1; Ltr, Lt Gen Stratemeyer to CG, 1AF, subj: Air Defense Activities, Apr 6, 1948; AS Summary Sheet, Maj Gen S. E. Anderson for CSAF, subj: Withdrawal of Personnel from the 530th Aircraft Control and Warning Group, May 19, 1948, AAF Central Files 322, Box 800, RG 18, NA.

130. Ltr, Stratemeyer to CG, 1AF, Apr 6, 1948.

131. Hist, 505th Aircraft Control and Warning Group, Mar–Jun 1948; HQ ADC Ltr, Mar 31, 1948.

132. Memo, Gen Vandenberg to Secy Symington, subj: Comments on the Forrestal Memo to the JCS, Jul 1, 1948, with App A, Status of Air Warning and Control Screen for Alaska and U.S., Jul 30, 1948, USAFHRC microfilm.

133. Msg, HQ USAF to Joint Brazil-U.S. Military Commission, Apr 30, 1948, Saville Collection, USAFHRC microfilm.

Chapter 4. Saville Takes Charge

1. Richard F. Haynes, *The Awesome Power: Harry S. Truman as Commander in Chief* (Baton Rouge, La., 1973), p 137.

2. Harry R. Borowski, *A Hollow Threat: Strategic Air Power and Containment Before Korea* (Westport, Conn., 1982); Stephen M. Millett, "The Capabilities of the American Nuclear Deterrent, 1945–1950," *Aerospace Historian* (Mar 1980); Rosenberg, "Origins of Overkill"; Gregg Herken, *The Winning Weapon: The Atomic Bomb in the Cold War, 1945–1950* (New York, 1980), pp 196–97; Walton S. Moody, "Building a Strategic Air Force, 1945–1953," (draft manuscript in AF/CHO), chaps 2–5.

3. John Prados, *The Soviet Estimate: U.S. Intelligence Analysis and Russian Military Strength* (New York, 1982), p 39.

4. Ltr, Maj Gen Saville to Gen Fairchild, Jun 1, 1948, Fairchild Papers, Box 2, LC.

5. Intvw, Lt Col Vaughn H. Gallacher with Gen Bruce K. Holloway, Orlando, Fla., Aug 16–18, 1977.

6. Cline, *Washington Command Post*, p 173; Mark A. Stoler, "From Continentalism to Globalism: General Stanley D. Embick, the Joint Strategic Survey Committee, and the Military View of American National Policy During the Second World War," *Diplomatic History* 6, no. 3 (summer 1982): 303–21; Ronald Schaffer, "Stanley D. Embick: Military Dissenter," *Military Affairs* 37, no. 3 (Oct 1973): 89–95.

7. Kenneth Schaffel, "General Muir S. Fairchild: Philosopher of Air Power," *Aerospace Historian* 33, no. 3 (fall/Sep 1986): 165–71.

8. Saville intvw.

9. HQ ADC SO 150, Aug 2, 1948, Saville Collection, USAFHRC microfilm; Saville intvw.

10. Hist, 505th Aircraft Control and Warning Group, Mar–Jan 1948.

11. Hist, 4AF, Jan 1–Nov 30, 1948; Ltr, Maj Gen John E. Upston, CG, 4AF, to CG, ADC, subj: Report of Maneuvers, May 27, 1948; HQ 505th Aircraft Control and Warning Group Analysis of Maneuvers Conducted in the Northwest Air Defense Area, Mar 28–May 17, 1948 (App to Hist, 4AF, Jan 1–Nov 30, 1948); Hist, 505th Aircraft Control and Warning Group, Mar–Jan 1948.

12. Clement L. Grant, *Development of Continental Air Defense to 1 September 1954*

(USAF Hist Study 126, 1957), pp 12–13; Saville intvw.

13. Memo, Bur Budget to OSD, subj: USAF Radar Fence Program, May 24, 1948, USAFHRC microfilm.

14. Memo, Barrow to Forrestal, May 28, 1948, USAFHRC microfilm.

15. Memo, Pres Harry S. Truman to Forrestal, Jun 3, 1948, Vandenberg Papers, Box 40, LC.

16. Memo, Forrestal to JCS, Jul 1, 1948, USAFHRC microfilm.

17. Saville intvw.

18. Saville, "Interim Program for Aircraft Control and Warning System in the Continental U.S. and Alaska" (Presentation to Forrestal), Sep 9, 1948, USAFHRC microfilm.

19. Saville intvw.

20. Saville presentation, Sep 9, 1948.

21. *Ibid.*; Vandenberg, Journal, Aug 24, 1948, Vandenberg Papers, Box 3, LC.

22. Memo, Dr. Vannevar Bush to Vandenberg, subj: Air Defense System, May 18, 1948, USAFHRC microfilm.

23. Ltr, Charles A. Lindbergh to Symington, Aug 2, 1948; Ltr, Symington to Lindbergh, Aug 26, 1948, USAFHRC microfilm.

24. Ltr, HQ USAF to CG, ADC, subj: Interim Program for the Employment of Aircraft Control and Warning Radar; Ltr, Saville to CSAF, Jan 26, 1949, USAFHRC microfilm.

25. HQ USAF Interstaff Memo, Maj Gen S. E. Anderson to Gen Lauris Norstad, subj: Proposed Aircraft Control and Warning Systems, May 17, 1949, USAFHRC microfilm.

26. Ltr, Anderson to CG, ADC, subj: Implementation of Emergency Aircraft Control and Warning System in the Northeastern U.S., USAFHRC microfilm.

27. "Operation Dualism."

28. Stratemeyer presentation, in "Operation Dualism"; EO 10007, Oct 15, 1948.

29. HQ CONAC, Press Release, Feb 1, 1949; AFR 23–1, Organization of Continental Air Command, Jan 11, 1949; CONAC Reg 25–1, Organization and Mission of ADC, Jan 31, 1949, USAFHRC microfilm.

30. Hist, CONAC, Dec 1, 1948–Dec 31, 1949; Saville intvw.

31. Rept of Air Def Ex BLACKJACK, Jan 1–30, 1949 (in Apps, Hist, ADC, Jan–Jun 1951).

32. Saville presentation, Sep 9, 1948.

33. Denys Volan, *The History of the Ground Observer Corps* (ADC Hist Study 36, 1968) [hereafter cited as *GOC*], pp 100–102.

34. Hearings before a Subcommittee of the Committee on Armed Services, House of Representatives, 81st Cong, 1st sess, 1949, pp 329, 333–34.

35. Armed Services Committee, House of Representatives, Feb 10–12, 1949, cited in Grant, *Continental Air Defense*, p 25.

36. Holloway intvw.

37. Col Keith K. Compton, Presentation, in "Operation Dualism."

38. HQ USAF Interstaff Memo, Brig Gen Jack W. Wood to Compt, subj: Pending Inspection Visit to Eglin Field, Jun 3, 1948, Fairchild Papers, Box 2, LC; Compton presentation, in "Operation Dualism"; Col Bruce K. Holloway, Presentation, in *ibid.*

39. Holloway presentation, in "Operation Dualism"; Saville presentation, in *ibid*; Lt Col Edwin F. Carey, HQ ADC, Presentation at Air Command and Staff College, Maxwell AFB, Ala., Mar 25, 1949.

40. *Case History of the F-89 All-Weather Fighter Airplane* (HQ AMC Hist Study 37), appended docs 1, 8, and 9.

41. Richard F. McMullen, *History of Air Defense Weapons, 1946–1962* (ADC Hist Study 14, 1962), pp 38–40. For specifications on the F–87, F–89, and F–94, see Marcelle Size Knaack's *Encyclopedia of U.S. Air Force Aircraft and Missile Systems* (Washington, D.C., 1978), Vol I, *Post-World War II Fighters, 1945–1973* [hereafter cited as *Post-WW II Fighters*], pp 82–111.

42. Memo, Gen Joseph T. McNarney to SAF, subj: Final Report of Board of Officers, Jan 1949, OSAF 334, RG 340, NA.

43. *Ibid.*

44. Fairchild, Remarks at Air Force–Industry Conference, May 20, 1949, Fairchild Papers, Box 4, LC.

45. Hist, ARDC, Jan 1–Dec 31, 1953; McMullen, *Aircraft in Air Defense*, pp 50–55; Knaack, *Post-WW II Fighters*, p 159; Grant, *Continental Air Defense*, p 53.

46. Ltr, Maj Gen Earle E. Partridge, CG, 5AF, to Maj Gen William E. Kepner, CG, APG, Mar 31, 1949, Partridge Collection, USAFHRC microfilm; Ltr, Brig Gen John P. McConnell, Dep Sp Asst for Reserve Forces, HQ USAF, to Partridge, Mar 11, 1949, Partridge Collection, USAFHRC microfilm; DuPre, *Biographical Dictionary*, pp 259–60.

47. HQ CONAC GO 94, Aug 31, 1949, cited in Hist, Western Air Defense

Force, Sep–Dec 1949, App; Hist, Eastern Air Defense Force, Sep–Dec 1949.

48. Intvw, Dr. James C. Hasdorff with Lt Gen Herbert B. Thatcher, Central Harbor, N.H., Aug 9–10, 1977; Saville intvw.

49. Memo, Col J. E. Smart, Dep Ops, AS, to Lt Gen Whitehead, subj: Reorganization of CONAC, Jan 21, 1949, Whitehead Collection, USAFHRC microfilm.

50. Saville intvw.

Chapter 5. Broadening Dimensions: Air Defense as a Public Issue

1. Memo, Maj Gen Thomas D. White, Dir, Leg Liaison, HQ USAF, to Symington, Aug 22, 1949, USAFHRC microfilm.

2. Memo, Vandenberg to Symington, Aug 22, 1949, Vandenberg Papers, Box 34, LC.

3. Ernest Gruening, *Many Battles: The Autobiography of Ernest Gruening* (New York, 1973), p 361.

4. Paul Y. Hammond, "Super Carriers and B–36 Bombers: Appropriations, Strategy, and Politics," in Harold Stein, ed, *American Civil-Military Decisions: A Book of Case Studies* (Tuscaloosa, Ala., 1963), p 516. An informative discussion of the B–36 controversy is in Steven L. Rearden's *The Formative Years, 1947–1950* [(Washington, D.C., 1984), Vol I in *History of the Office of the Secretary of Defense, pp 410–22*].

5. Dean C. Allard, "An Era of Transition, 1945–1953," in Kenneth J. Hagen, ed, *In Peace and War: Interpretations of American Naval History, 1775–1978* (Westport, Conn., 1978), pp 290–303.

6. Stephen Jurika, Jr., ed. *From Pearl Harbor to Vietnam: The Memoirs of Admiral Arthur W. Radford* (Stanford, Calif., 1980) [hereafter cited as *Memoirs of Admiral Radford*], pp 189–90; *Semiannual Report of the Secretary of the Air Force*, Jul–Dec 1949, pp 230–31; Hammond, "Super Carriers," p 517.

7. Hearings before the Committee on Armed Services, House of Representatives, *U.S. Congress National Defense Program: Unification and Strategy*, 81st Cong, 1st sess (Washington, D.C., 1949), pp 2–3.

8. Hammond, "Super Carriers," p 517; *Memoirs of Admiral Radford*, p 187.

9. Paolo E. Coletta, *The United States Navy and Defense Unification, 1947–1953* (Newark, Del., 1981), p 66; Lydus H. Buss, *Seaward Extension of Radar, 1946–1956* (ADC Hist Study 10, 1956), *passim*; Thomas W. Ray, *The ADC Airborne Early Warning and Control Program, 1946–1964* (ADC Hist Study 28, 1965), p 2.

10. Ltr, Dr. Bruce Hopper to Lt Gen Lauris Norstad, Apr 1949, Norstad Papers, NA, microfilm in AF/CHO.

11. Richard G. Hewlett and Francis Duncan, *Atomic Shield, 1947–1952* (Penn State University Press, 1962), Vol II, p 362; Harry S. Truman, *Memoirs* (Garden City, N.Y., 1956), Vol II, *Years of Trial and Hope*, pp 306–08; Margaret Truman, *Harry S. Truman* (New York, 1973), pp 415–16.

12. *Public Papers of the Presidents: Harry S. Truman, 1949* (Washington, D.C., 1964), p 485; Beverly Smith, "This Way Lies Peace," *The Saturday Evening Post*, Oct 13, 1949.

13. Ltr, Warren Magnuson to Symington, Oct 11, 1950, Vandenberg Papers, Box 60, LC; Richard F. McMullen, *Radar Programs for Air Defense, 1946–1966* (ADC Hist Study 34, 1966), pp 23–24.

14. Memo, Fairchild to DCS/P, subj: Senior Officer Assignments, Nov 16, 1949, Fairchild Papers, Box 2, LC.

15. MR, subj: Conference Held to Discuss the Announcement of the Russian Atomic Bomb Explosion, Sep 30, 1949, Fairchild Papers, Box 1, LC.

16. Memo, Symington to Johnson, subj: Atomic Explosion in Russia and Factors Bearing on the Problem, OSAF Special Interest File 9, 1949, Box 36, RG 340, NA.

17. Cited in Futrell, *Ideas, Concepts, Doctrine*, pp 257–58.

18. Ltr, Symington to Magnuson, Nov 28, 1949, Vandenberg Papers, Box 60, LC.

19. MR, Fairchild, Sep 30, 1949; Memo, Fairchild to Vandenberg, Sep 30, 1949, Fairchild Papers, Box 1, LC.

20. MR, Fairchild, Sep 30, 1949; Memo, Fairchild to Vandenberg, Sep 30, 1949.

21. Hist, Directorate of Plans and Ops, HQ USAF, Jul 1949–Jan 1950; Robert

D. Little, *Organizing for Strategic Planning, 1945–1950* (HQ USAF Hist Div Liaison Ofc, Apr 1964), p 61.

22. Gen Cabell, Presentation at Ramey Commanders' Conference, Apr 25–27, 1950; "Attainment and Maintenance of an Operational Air Defense System in the Continental U.S. and Alaska" (USAF presentation to JCS), Mar 2, 1950, Numerical Subject File 1950, War Plans, OSAF, RG 340, NA.

23. Gen S. E. Anderson, Presentation at Ramey Conference.

24. PL 434, 81st Cong, Oct 29, 1949; *Semiannual Report of the Secretary of the Air Force*, Jul–Dec 1949, p 193; Memo, Symington to Vandenberg, Oct 31, 1949; HQ CONAC, Brief Fiscal History of the Aircraft Control and Warning Facilities Construction Program, Jun 26, 1950.

25. Anderson presentation, Ramey Conference.

26. Blue Book Plan, p 11; Memo, Whitehead to Brig Gen Herbert B. Thatcher, DCS/O, HQ CONAC, subj: Number of Combat Crews Required in Fighter Squadrons for Air Defense Mission, Feb 17, 1950; Memo, Col Joseph D. Lee, Ch, Rqrs Div, HQ CONAC, to Whitehead, subj: The Efficient Employment of Combat Aircraft in Air Defense [*ca.* Feb 25, 1950]; Air Defense Briefing, Jan 1, 1951, Vandenberg Papers, Box 88, LC.

27. Anderson presentation, Ramey Conference.

28. Ltr, HQ CONAC to CG, EADF, Oct 10, 1950.

29. Anderson presentation, Ramey Conference.

30. Roy S. Barnard, *The History of ARADCOM* (Washington, D.C., 1972), Vol I, *The Gun Era, 1950–1955* [hereafter cited as *ARADCOM: The Gun Era*], p 37.

31. Robert L. Kelley, *Army Antiaircraft in Air Defense, 1946–1954* (ADC Hist Study 4, 1954), pp 3–17; Barnard, *ARADCOM: The Gun Era*, pp 18–21.

32. McMullen, *History of Air Defense Weapons*, pp 47–52, 89–91; Barnard, *ARADCOM: The Gun Era*, pp 25–28. The BOMARC program is explained in further detail in Chapter 8.

33. Kelley, *Army Antiaircraft in Air Defense*, pp 15–20; Barnard, *ARADCOM: The Gun Era*, pp 44–46, 50–54.

34. AF Bul 1, May 21, 1948; Saville intvw.

35. Memo, Vandenberg to JCS, subj: Air Defense of the U.S., Fairchild Papers, Box 1, LC.

36. NSC–68, *United States Objectives and Programs for National Security*, Apr 7, 1950; Joseph M. Siracusa, "NSC 68: A Reappraisal," *Naval War College Review* 33, no. 6 (Nov–Dec 1980): 4–14; Samuel J. Wells, Jr., "Sounding the Tocsin: NSC–68 and the Soviet Threat," *International Security* 4, no. 2 (fall, 1979): 116–58.

37. Ltr, Ch Nav Ops to Maj Nav Comds and Marine Corps, subj: Responsibilities and Functions of Naval Commanders with Regard to Air Defense of the Continental U.S., Feb 16, 1950, USAFHRC microfilm; Maj George H. Lowes, "Double Decade of Air Defence," [Canadian Forces] *Sentinel*, Jun 1951; *Seventeen Years of Air Defense* (HQ NORAD Hist Ref Paper 9), pp 1–5.

38. *New York Times*, Oct 13, 1949; *Time*, Oct 3, 1949; Ltr, Vannevar Bush to Gen Omar Bradley, Apr 13, 1950, Vandenberg Papers, Box 83, LC; Memo, unsigned to Vandenberg, Mar 20, 1950, Vandenberg Papers, Box 53, LC.

39. Ltr, Carl Vinson to Symington, Feb 13, 1950, USAFHRC microfilm.

40. Hist, ADC, thru Jan 1951.

41. Volan, *GOC*, pp 102–10; Hist, ADC, thru June 1951; Herbert B. Thatcher, Presentation at Ramey Conference.

42. Hist, Directorate of Plans, HQ USAF, Jul–Dec 1950.

43. Memo, Maj Gen Roger Ramey, HQ USAF, to DCS/O, subj: Status of the Aircraft Control and Warning Program, Jan 5, 1952, OSAF, RG 340, NA; Lowes, "Double Decade of Air Defense"; *Seventeen Years of Air Defense*, p 2; Hist, ADC, thru June 1951.

44. Memo, von Karman to Fairchild, subj: Air Defense of the U.S., Nov 29, 1949; Ltr, Fairchild to Whitehead, subj: Air Defense System Engineering Committee, Jan 27, 1950, Fairchild Papers, Box 1, LC; Thomas A. Sturm, *The USAF Scientific Advisory Board: Its First Twenty Years, 1944–1964* (Washington, D.C., 1967), pp 39–40.

45. Alfred Goldberg and Robert D. Little, *History of Headquarters USAF, 1 July 1949 to 30 June 1950* (USAF Hist Study, Dec 1954), p 25. The Air Research and Development Command was established under Maj Gen David M. Schlatter on Jan 23, 1950. Instrumental in the command's establishment were Ridenour's suggestions, seconded by an Air University study headed by Maj Gen Orvil A. Anderson. Anderson's group believed that technology would prove crucial in the future if the United

States was to maintain an edge over the Soviet Union.

46. Ivan A. Getting, "Recollections of the USAF in 1950–1951," copy in AF/CHO

47. Futrell, *Ideas, Concepts, Doctrine,* pp 142–43.

48. Thatcher intvw.

49. Intvw, Lt Col Vaughn H. Gallacher and Dr. James C. Hasdorff with Maj Gen Hugh A. Parker, San Antonio, Tex., Jun 21, 1972.

50. MR, Fairchild, Sep 30, 1949; Memo, Fairchild to Vandenberg, Sep 30, 1949; Thatcher intvw.

51. Hist, CONAC, Vol III, Jan–Jun 1950; Hist, ADC, thru Jan 1951; Memo, Fairchild to Norstad, subj: Acceleration of Air Defense Programs, Nov 19, 1949, Fairchild Papers, Box 1, LC.

52. Thatcher inteviw; Hist, ADC, thru Jun 1951.

53. Hist, ADC, thru Jun 1951.

54. Sp rept, HQ USAF, Observation on Exercise DRUMMER BOY (Nov 4–14), Dec 2, 1949; HQ ADC, *A Decade of Continental Air Defense, 1946–1956* (1956).

55. Observation on Exercise DRUMMER BOY; *Decade of Continental Air Defense.*

56. Observation on Exercise DRUMMER BOY; *Decade of Continental Air Defense.*

57. Hist, 25th Air Div, Apr–Jun 1950.

58. Rept, HQ 25th Air Div, Exercise WHIPSTOCK, Jun 18–24, 1950, cited in 25th Air Div Hist, Apps.

59. Ops analysis rept 3, HQ CONAC, Outcome of Northwest Air Defense Exercise (Jun 18–24, 1950), Sep 20, 1950, USAFHRC microfilm.

60. Col George S. Brown, Presentation at Ramey Conference.

Chapter 6. Continental Air Defense in the Korean War Period

1. Msg, Vandenberg to Twining, Jun 25, 1950, Twining Papers, Box 19, LC; Msg, Vandenberg to Whitehead, Jun 26, 1950, cited in Hist, Directorate of Plans, HQ USAF, Jul–Dec 1950; Hist, 26th Air Div, Apr–Jun 1950; Unidentified news clipping, Twining Papers, Box 19, LC.

2. The Air Force's worldwide response to the start of the Korean crisis is explained in detail in Robert F. Futrell's *The United States Air Force in Korea, 1950–1953* [rev ed (Washington, D.C., 1983), pp 1–37].

3. Dr. Edward Barlow, "Development Objective: Air Defense" (Lecture at Air War College), Apr 1, 1952.

4. Gordon P. Saville, "The Philosophy of Air Defense" (Lecture at Air War College), Jun 7, 1950.

5. Col L. A. Hall, "The Aircraft Industry of the USSR" (Lecture at Air War College) [*ca.* 1950].

6. John Prados, *The Soviet Estimate: U.S. Intelligence Analysis and Russian Military Strength* (New York, 1982), pp 24–26; Ernest Volkman, *Warriors of the Night: Spies, Soldiers, and the American Military* (New York, 1985), chaps 2–4 (uncorrected proofs).

7. Mark E. Miller, *Soviet Strategic Power and Doctrine: The Quest for Superiority* (Miami, Fla., 1982), p 16; Thomas W.

Wolfe, *Soviet Power and Europe, 1945–1970* (Baltimore, 1970), *passim*.

8. NSC 68, printed in *Naval War College Review* 27, no. 6 (May–Jun 1975). Wells gives an excellent analysis of NSC 68 in his "Sounding the Tocsin." Wells points out that the Soviets possessed more military power than they needed to protect their own territory and consolidate their gains in Eastern Europe. They did not, in the early 1950s, use their land forces to annex Western territory or demand concessions.

9. Jack H. Nunn, *The Soviet First Strike Threat: The U.S. Perspective* (New York, 1982), pp 95–96; "Attainment and Maintenance of an Operational Air Defense System in the Continental U.S. and Alaska" (USAF presentation to JCS), Numerical Subject File 1950, War Plans, OSAF, RG 340, NA; Joint Intelligence Committee report JCS 208111, Implications of Soviet Possession of Atomic Weapons, Encl B, Nov 8, 1948, RG 218, NA.

10. Cases for and against preemptive and preventive war are presented in Brodie's insightful *Strategy in the Missile Age* (pp 223–63), Rosenberg's "Origins of Overkill" (pp 25–26), and Moody's "Building a Strategic Air Force" (ch 7).

11. Nunn, *Soviet First Strike Threat*, p 96; Moody, "Building a Strategic Air Force," ch 7.

12. Ltr, HQ CONAC to 1AF, subj: F-82 Maintenance Spares, Feb 28, 1950, USAFHRC microfilm.

13. Ltr, Maj Gen Frank A. Armstrong to Vandenberg, Aug 4, 1950, Vandenberg Papers, Box 33, LC; Thomas A. Sturm, *Air Defense of Alaska, 1940–1957* (NORAD Hist Ref Paper, 1957), pp 12–14.

14. McMullen, *Aircraft in Air Defense*, pp 32–40; Bill Gunston, *Fighters of the Fifties* (Cambridge, England, 1981), pp 116–20.

15. Rept, HQ AAC, Exercise STOP-GAP, Nov 25–27, 1950.

16. Hist, CONAC, Jul–Dec 1950.

17. *Ibid.*

18. Hist, 26th Air Div, Jul–Aug 1950.

19. Ltr, 52d FW Gp CO to 52d FW CO, subj: Authentication and Identification, Nov 6, 1950, USAFHRC microfilm.

20. Hist, Directorate of Plans, HQ USAF, Jul–Dec 1950.

21. Hist, ADC, thru Jan 1951.

22. *Ibid.*

23. Memo, Vandenberg to SecDef, n.d. [*ca*. Aug 20, 1950], Box 33, Vandenberg Papers, LC; Hist, Directorate of Plans, HQ USAF, Jul–Dec 1950.

24. Barnard, *ARADCOM: The Gun Era*, Vol I, pp 50–52.

25. Memo of Agreement, Vandenberg and Collins, Aug 1, 1950, USAFHRC microfilm.

26. Barnard, *ARADCOM: The Gun Era*, Vol I, pp 63–66.

27. McMullen, *Radar Programs*, pp 28–29, 39; Futrell, *Ideas, Concepts, Doctrine*, pp 278–79. The Korean War proved an enormous impetus to increasing military programs, especially those of the Air Force. In fiscal year 1952 the Air Force received a third more funds (in a total defense budget of $43.9 billion) than the Army or Navy. In 2 years SAC doubled its personnel and aircraft; its bases increased from 19 to 30 in the CONUS, and from 1 to 11 overseas.

28. Carl Spaatz, "Air Defense Measures Are Urgent," *Newsweek*, Aug 21, 1950.

29. Saville intvw.

30. Biographical information in Twining Papers, LC.

31. On Finletter's views, see Thomas K. Finletter's *Power and Policy: U.S. Foreign Power and Policy in the Hydrogen Age* [(New York, 1954), pp 206–11, 214–18].

32. Memo, Lt Gen Edwin M. Rawlings, Compt, to DCS/M, HQ USAF, subj: Expediting Completion of the Radar Fence, Jul 27, 1950; Memo, Dir Comms, HQ USAF, to CSAF, subj: Acceleration of Construction Program for First 24 Aircraft

Control and Warning Sites of CONAC, Aug 16, 1950; Note, n.d., Vandenberg Papers, Box 88, LC; Ltr, OSAF to Lt Gen Benjamin Chidlaw, CG, AMC, subj: Size and Composition of USAF, 1950, Aug 28, 1950, Box 12, RG 340, NA.

33. Ltr, Rawlings to ASAF Eugene M. Zuckert, subj: Progress of the Permanent Radar Net, Oct 2, 1950, USAFHRC microfilm.

34. Memo, Lt Col A. J. Evans, AExO, to Vandenberg, subj: Permanent Radar Net, Vandenberg Papers, Box 53, LC; HQ CONAC, Min stf mtg, Dec 6, 1950, USAFHRC microfilm.

35. Memo, Col Wallace C. Barnett, Directorate of Plans, to Asst for Progs, HQ USAF, subj: Replanning for Aircraft Control and Warning Gap Filler Program, Mar 11, 1952; MR, DCS/O, HQ USAF, Sep 21, 1950, Twining Papers, Box 55, LC; Memo, Maj Gen Ramey, Dir Ops, HQ USAF, subj: Status of the Aircraft Control and Warning and Tactical Group Programs, Jan 5, 1952, Box 1031, RG 340, NA.

36. Ltr, HQ CONAC to HQ WADF, subj: Canadian Long Range Early Warning, Oct 16, 1950.

37. Air def briefing, n.d., Vandenberg Papers, Box 88, LC.

38. Rept, Eastern Air Defense Force Exercise, Nov 4–5, 1950, USAFHRC microfilm.

39. Futrell, *Ideas, Concepts, Doctrine*, pp 159–60.

40. Ltr, HQ CONAC to CSAF, subj: Establishment of a Central Air Defense Force, Jul 27, 1950; Ltr, Whitehead to Vandenberg, Sep 12, 1950; Ltr, HQ USAF to CG CONAC, subj: Establishment of a Central Air Defense Force, Oct 5, 1950, with 1st Ind, HQ CONAC to CSAF, Oct 11, 1950, all in USAFHRC microfilm.

41. Ltr, HQ USAF to CGs, CONAC, TAC, and ADC, subj: Designation of Tactical Air Command and Air Defense Command as Major Commands, Nov 10, 1950; Ltr, Whitehead to Vandenberg, Oct 24, 1950, USAFHRC microfilm.

42. Msg, Vandenberg to Cannon, Sep 28, 1950, Vandenberg Papers, Box 68, LC; Ltr, HQ USAF to CGs, CONAC, TAC, and ADC, Nov 10, 1950.

43. Memo, Col James F. Whisenand, Asst Dep Dir Plans, HQ USAF, to Maj Gen Thomas D. White, DCS/Plans, subj: Data on 95-Wing and 143 Programs, Feb 4, 1950, Box 423, RG 341, NA; Little, *Organizing for Strategic Planning*, p 63.

44. *Public Papers of the Presidents: Harry S. Truman, 1950* (Washington, D.C., 1965), p 741.

45. Msg, Vandenberg to All USAF Comdrs, Dec 6, 1950, Vandenberg Papers, Box 86, LC.

46. *Ibid.*

47. Edward A. Kolodziej, *The Uncommon Defense and Congress, 1945–1963* (Columbus, Ohio, 1963), pp 140–50.

48. EO 10197, Dec 20, 1950; CAA Regs, pt 620, Dec 27, 1950; U.S. Dept Commerce, "Flight Plans to Be Mandatory in Defense Identification Zones" (Press release), Dec 21, 1950; Hist, ADC, thru Jun 1951.

49. PL 920, 81st Cong, Jan 12, 1951.

50. Memo, Finletter to Vandenberg, subj: Offensive and Defensive Plans for War, 1951, Mar 23, 1951, Box 16, RG 340, NA.

51. Ltr, Whitehead to Twining, Jan 10, 1951, USAFHRC microfilm.

52. Memo, Twining to Ch, NGB, Jan 22, 1951, USAFHRC microfilm.

53. Memo, Finletter to Vandenberg, Mar 23, 1951, USAFHRC microfilm.

54. Memo, Lt Col A. J. Evans, AExO, to CSAF, subj: Permanent Radar Net, Dec 6, 1950, Vandenberg Papers, Box 53, LC.

55. Memo, Lt Gen Idwal H. Edwards, DCS/O, HQ USAF, to Whitehead, subj: Aircraft Control and Warning System Within the Zone of the Interior, Dec 15, 1950, USAFHRC microfilm.

56. McMullen, *Radar Programs*, p 37.

57. Ltr, John A. McCone to Carl Vinson, Chmn, House Comm Armed Services, Dec 14, 1950, Box 641, RG 340, NA.

58. *Congressional Record*, 82d Cong, 1st sess, Apr 30, 1951, pp 4521–24.

59. Maj Gen Hoyt S. Vandenberg, Statement before the Committee on Appropriations, Third Supplemental Estimates, FY 1951, Vandenberg Papers, Box 41, LC.

60. Hoyt S. Vandenberg, "The Truth About Our Air Power," *The Saturday Evening Post*, Feb 17, 1951.

61. Qtr prog rept, Lincoln Laboratory, Memo on Activities of the Air Defense System Engineering Committee, Jun 1952, with Encl for Apr 7, 1950; Rept, AD Secy, Air Defense System, Oct 24, 1950, appended to HQ ARDC Case Hist, Project LINCOLN, Dec 10, 1952.

62. Robert D. Little, *A History of the Air Force Atomic Energy Program, 1943–1953* (HQ USAF Hist Div Liaison Office, 1959), Vol III, *Building an Atomic Air Force, 1949–1953*, pt 1, p 216; HQ ARDC Case Hist, Project LINCOLN.

63. Ltr, Ivan A. Getting, Pres, Aerospace Corp, to John L. McLucas, SAF, subj: Recollections of USAF, 1950–1951, Mar 12, 1974, copy in AF/CHO.

64. James R. Killian, Jr., Pres, MIT, Statement on the Lincoln Laboratory, Oct 16, 1953.

65. Lt Col O. T. Halley, HQ ADC Liaison Off, Lincoln Lab, Briefing presented to Gen Chidlaw, Jan 23, 1953, written record in USAFHRC microfilm.

66. Ltr, Vandenberg to Killian, Dec 15, 1950, RG 340, NA.

67. Ltr, Twining to Whitehead, Jan 13, 1951, Twining Papers, Box 54, LC; Thomas A. Sturm, *Organization and Responsibility for Air Defense, 1946–1955* (ADC Hist Study 9, 1963), pp 45–46.

68. Barnard, *ARADCOM: The Gun Era*, Vol 1, pp 67, 74–75.

69. Sturm, *Organization for Air Defense*, pp 50–53.

70. Ltr, Whitehead to Vandenberg, subj: Proper Utilization of Resources, Jul 24, 1951, USAFHRC microfilm.

71. *Biographical Study, General Officers*; DuPre, *Biographical Dictionary*, pp 39–40.

72. USAF Commanders' Conference, Colorado Springs, Colo., Oct 30–Nov 1, 1951.

73. RAND Stf Rept F–225 (Air Defense Study), appended to Ltr, Brownlee Haydon, RAND Corp., to Col R. H. Marshall, Mil Exec to USofAF, Oct 12, 1951, RG 340, NA.

74. Final Rept, Project CHARLES, Aug 1, 1951, RG 340, NA; Project LINCOLN.

75. Ltr, Loomis to Killian, Dec 21, 1951, RG 340, NA.

76. Quotes in Clyde R. Littlefield, "History of the Semiautomated Ground Environment" [hereafter cited as "History of SAGE"], unpublished draft manuscript in AF/CHO, p 12; Richard F. McMullen, *The Birth of SAGE, 1951–1958* (ADC Hist Study 33, 1965), *passim*.

77. Littlefield, "History of SAGE," pp 5–6.

78. *Ibid.*, pp 8–9; Thomas M. Smith, "Project WHIRLWIND: An Unorthodox Development Project," *Technology and Culture* 17, no. 3 (Jul 1976): 447–64. Navy support was eventually reduced, and WHIRLWIND became, in effect, an Air Force project.

305

79. Ltr, Finletter to Killian, Feb 5, 1952.

80. McMullen, *Radar Programs, passim*; Mildred Wiley, *Statistical Data Book*, Vol III, *Radar, 1946–1973* (HQ ADC Hist Office, 1973).

81. Grant, *Continental Air Defense*, pp 40–41.

82. McMullen, *Radar Programs, passim*; Wiley, *Statistical Data Book*, Vol III.

83. Memo, USAF Compt to DCS/O, HQ USAF, subj: Air Force Actions in Connection with Air Defense, Feb 10, 1953, USAFHRC microfilm.

84. MR, DCS/O, HQ USAF, Sep 21, 1955, Twining Papers, Box 55, LC.

85. Ltr, Chidlaw to Maj Gen George R. Anderson, CG, CADF, subj: Site Surveys for Additional Aircraft Control and Warning Stations, Jul 11, 1951; Ltr, DCS/M, HQ USAF, to Chidlaw, subj: Site Requirements for Semi-Permanent but Movable Installations, Jul 30, 1951, with 1st Ind, Chidlaw to Dir Instls, HQ USAF, Aug 22, 1951, USAFHRC microfilm.

86. Ltr, Maj Gen Frederic H. Smith to Twining, May 22, 1953, subj: Study of Aircraft Control and Warning Functions, May 22, 1953, USAFHRC microfilm.

87. 1st Ind, Ramey to Chidlaw, Mar 21, 1952, to Ltr, Chidlaw to DCS/O, HQ USAF, Jan 19, 1952; Hist, Plans, HQ USAF.

88. Ltr, HQ ADC to DCS/O, HQ USAF, subj: Third Phase Radar Program, Oct 20, 1953; Ltr, DCS/O, HQ USAF, to Chidlaw, subj: Third Phase Radar Program, Jan 11, 1954; McMullen, *Radar Programs*, p 45.

89. Ltr, Maj Gen Smith to Dir Rqrs, HQ USAF, with 1st Ind, HQ USAF to HQ ADC, Mar 17, 1953; Ltr, HQ ADC to DCS/O, HQ USAF, subj: Small, Automatic Radar Program, Sep 4, 1953, USAFHRC microfilm.

90. Ltr, Whitehead to Twining, subj: Radar Picket Vessel Utilization in Air Defense, Dec 13, 1950.

91. Memo, DCS/O, HQ USAF, Oct 1, 1951; Ltr, Dir Rqrs, HQ USAF, to Chidlaw, subj: Picket Vessels, Oct 29, 1951; Ltr, Ch Nav Ops to All Concerned, subj: Naval Picket Forces, Atlantic and Pacific, Sep 23, 1952, USAFHRC microfilm.

92. Memo, Maj Gen Morris R. Nelson, Dir Rqrs, HQ USAF, to Twining, subj: Airborne Early Warning and Control Equipment, May 2, 1951, Twining Papers, Box 54, LC; Ray, *Early Warning*.

93. Ltr, Whitehead to Twining, subj: Requirement for Airborne Early Warning and Control Equipment, Apr 9, 1951, Twining Papers, Box 54, LC; Ray, *Early Warning*, pp 8–9.

94. Ray, *Early Warning*, pp 19–20, 27.

95. Volan, *GOC*, pp 119–22.

96. Rept, HQ EADF, Air def ex, Jun 22–24, 1951.

97. Final Rept, Project CHARLES, Vol I, pp 76–86, 131–32; Memo, J. Parker Van Zandt, Dep Civ Avn, OSAF, to DCS/O, HQ USAF, subj: Ground Observer Corps, Oct 16, 1951, and reply, Brig Gen John K. Gerhart, Dep Dir Ops, HQ USAF, to Van Zandt, Oct 26, 1951, RG 340, NA.

98. ADC Commanders' Conference, Colorado Springs, Colo., Oct 15–16, 1951, proceedings cited in Volan, *GOC*, pp 132–34.

99. Ltr, Smith to Chidlaw, subj: Activation of the Ground Observer Corps, Dec 3, 1951, USAFHRC microfilm.

100. *Ibid.*

101. Ltr, Chidlaw to Ramey, Nov 20, 1951; Ltr, Ramey to Chidlaw, Dec 5, 1951, USAFHRC microfilm.

102. Ltr, HQ ADC to HQ USAF, subj: 24-Hour Operation of Ground Observer Corps, Jan 22, 1952, USAFHRC microfilm.

103. Ltr, Gen Thomas D. White, DCS/O, HQ USAF, to Chidlaw, subj: 24-Hour Operation of Ground Observer Corps, Mar 28, 1952, USAFHRC microfilm.

104. Msg, HQ ADC to Air Def Forces, Apr 24, 1952, USAFHRC microfilm.

105. Memo, Col John F. Fletcher, Dir, Civ Air Def, to Maj Gen Kenneth P. Bergquist, HQ ADC, subj: Resolution by State Civil Defense Officials, May 2, 1952, USAFHRC microfilm.

106. Millard Caldwell, Remarks at the Conference of State Civil Defense Directors on the Ground Observer Corps, Pentagon, Jun 16, 1953, transcript in USAFHRC microfilm.

107. DOD Press Release, "Air Defense Ground Observers Start 24-Hour Duty July 14," Jun 17, 1952.

108. Ltr, Twining to Prog Dir, subj: Suggested Spot Radio Announcements, Sep 21, 1953, Twining Papers, Box 62, LC.

109. Memo, Finletter to Twining, Jul 16, 1952, Box 1011, RG 340, NA.

110. Quoted in Lydus H. Buss, *Fifteen Years of Air Defense, 1946–1961*, NORAD Hist Ref Paper 3, 1960), p 16.

111. *Ibid.*; Lydus H. Buss, *U.S. Air Defense in the Northeast, 1940–1957* (ADC Hist Study 37, 1957).

112. Hist, ADC, thru 1951; Memo, Maj Gen Raymond C. Maude, Dir Comms, HQ USAF, to CSAF, subj: Authority for Establishment of a Joint USAF-Canadian Project Office, Sep 23, 1952, with Encl, subj: Discussion of Project Pinetree Office, Box 10, RG 340, NA.

113. Lowes, "Double Decade of Air Defense," pp 6–7.

114. Hist, Directorate of Plans, HQ USAF, Jan–Jun 1951; Canadian Emb Note 454, Hume J. Wrong, Canadian Amb to U.S., to Dean Acheson, U.S. SecState, Aug 1, 1951; Memo, Maj Gen Roger M. Ramey, to DCS/O, HQ USAF, subj: Status of the Aircraft Control and Warning Tactical Control Group Program, Jan 5, 1952, Box 1031, RG 340, NA.

115. Ltr, HQ USAF, to HQ ADC, subj: Terms of Reference for the USAF Section of the Project Pinetree Office, Jun 13, 1952, USAFHRC microfilm.

116. Hist, Directorate of Plans, HQ USAF, Jan–Jun 1951; MR, OSAF, Nov 5, 1951, Box 937, RG 340, NA; Hist, Directorate of Ops, HQ USAF, Jan–Jun 1951; Air Stf Summary Sheet, Ramey to DCS/D, Jan 5, 1952.

117. Intvw, Denys Volan, Dir Comd Hist, HQ ADC, with Lt Gen Arthur C. Agan, Comdr, ADC, Colorado Springs, Colo., Nov 2, 1970, transcript p 32.

118. McMullen, *Aircraft in Air Defense*, pp 38–40; McMullen, *Air Defense Weapons*, pp 110–12.

119. McMullen, *Aircraft in Air Defense*, pp 8–27.

120. *Ibid.*; Knaack, *Post–WW II Fighters*, pp 83–100.

121. McMullen, *Aircraft in Air Defense*, pp 8–27; Knaack, *Post–WW II Fighters*, pp 83–100; Hist, AMC, Jan–Jun 1953; Agan intvw, p 32.

122. Gunston, *Fighters of the Fifties*, p 9; Thomas W. Ray, *Nuclear Armament: Its Acquisition, Control, and Application to Manned Interceptors, 1951–1963* (ADC Hist Study 20, 1963), *passim*.

123. Gunston, *Fighters of the Fifties*, p 5.

124. *Ibid.*, p 184.

125. Ltr, Chidlaw to Vandenberg, May 5, 1952, USAFHRC microfilm.

126. General Daniel James, Jr., "Keeping Up Our Defenses Against Aerospace Attacks," *Grumman Aerospace Horizons* 12, no. 4, p 3.

127. Ltr, Chidlaw to White, Aug 25, 1953, Twining Papers, Box 61, LC.

128. Ltr, Gen Earle E. Partridge, CG, ADC, to Twining, Nov 7, 1955, Twining Papers Box 75, LC.

Chapter 7. An Integrated, Efficient, Highly Potent Air Defense System

1. Ltr, Col Barney Oldfield (USAF, ret), to the author, Jun 12, 1985.

2. Information on the April 1952 incident came from Chidlaw's letter and its enclosure to Vandenberg [subj: Next to the Real Thing (rept on Apr 17 Air Defense Exercise), Box 1001, RG 340, NA] and Oldfield's letter (cited above).

3. Interim Rept, Project EAST RIVER, Apr 7, 1952, SAF File, RG 341, NA.

4. Ltr, Robert A. Lovett to Maj Gen Otto L. Nelson, Dir Proj EAST RIVER, May 14, 1952, USAFHRC microfilm.

5. Ltr, HQ ADC to Dir Ops, HQ USAF, subj: Project EAST RIVER Interim Report, Military Measures Precedent to a Manageable Civil Defense, Nov 28, 1952, USAFHRC microfilm.

6. "Night Fighters Over New York," *The Saturday Evening Post*, Feb 2, 1952; Hist, ADC, Jan–Jun 1952.

7. Con, author with Joseph Alsop, Washington, D.C., Jan 17, 1984.

8. Joseph and Stewart Alsop, "Matter of Fact: Air Defense Ignored in Political Shuffle," *Washington Post*, May 9, 1952.

9. *Ibid.*

10. James R. Killian, Jr., Pres, MIT, "Statement on the Lincoln Laboratory," Oct 16, 1953, RG 340, 000.8-12926-50, NA; Memo, Maj Gen Joseph F. Carroll, Dep IG, to DCS/D, HQ USAF, subj: Lincoln Summer Study Group, Jan 16, 1953, RG 340, 000.8-12926-50, NA.

11. Ltr, Lt Gen Laurence C. Craigie, DCS/D, to Chidlaw, Jul 23, 1952, USAFHRC microfilm.

12. Ltr, Dr. Albert G. Hill, Dir Lincoln Lab, to Brig Gen Kenneth P. Bergquist, HQ ADC, Jul 31, 1952, USAFHRC microfilm.

13. Operational Rsch Memo 22, Dept National Def, Canada, subj: An Operational Assessment of a Northern Radar Alerting Chain Employing Equipment Now in Process of Development, Aug 1952.

14. Memo, Carroll to DCS/D, Jan 16, 1953.

15. Final Rept, Summer Study Group, Feb 1, 1953, copy in AF/CHO.

16. *Ibid.*

17. *Ibid.*

18. *Ibid.*

19. Philip M. Stern, *The Oppenheimer Case: Security on Trial* (New York, 1969), p 194. The evolution of Air Force thought on the need for a distant early-warning line is traced in Thomas W. Ray's *A History of the DEW Line, 1946–1964* (ADC Hist Study 31, 1965).

20. NSC, *Public Policies of the Government of the United States Relating to National Security*, RG 341, OPD 381.02, NA.

21. Joseph T. Jockel, "No Boundaries Upstairs: Canada and North American Air Defense," draft manuscript, ch 4, p 18. [Later published as *No Boundaries Upstairs: Canada, the United States and the Origins of North American Air Defence, 1945–1958* (University of British Columbia Press, Vancouver, 1987).]

22. Zacharias's testimony, in *In the Matter of J. Robert Oppenheimer: Transcript of Hearings Before Personnel Security Board* (Washington, D.C., Apr 12–May 6, 1954) [hereafter cited as *Oppenheimer Hearings*].

23. Griggs's testimony, in *Oppenheimer Hearings*; James W. Kuneta, *Oppenheimer: The Years of Risk* (Englewood Cliffs, N.J., 1982), p 182; Gregg Herken, *Counsels of War* (New York, 1985), pp 65–67.

24. Griggs's testimony, in *Oppenheimer Hearings*; Kuneta, *Years of Risk*, pp 184, 350.

25. Wilson's testimony, in *Oppenheimer Hearings*.

26. Joseph and Stewart Alsop, "We Accuse," *Harper's Magazine*, Oct 1954, pp 25–45.

27. Ltr, Whitehead to White, Dec 14, 1953, White Papers, Box 1, LC.

28. "See It Now," TV broadcast of Oct 5, 1952, transcript in Vandenberg Papers, Box 91, LC.

29. Vandenberg, Remarks before Bd Dir, Advertising Council of America, Jan 15, 1953, transcript in Vandenberg Papers, Box 91, LC.

30. Saville intvw.

31. Gordon P. Saville, "The Air Defense Dilemma," *Air Force Magazine* 36, no. 3 (Mar 1953).

32. Ltr, Whitehead to White, Oct 6, 1953, White Papers, Box 1, LC.

33. *History of Strategic Arms Competition: USAF Supporting Studies First Interim Report, 1945–1950*, AF/CHO.

34. Vandenberg remarks, Jan 15, 1953.

35. A. J. Wohlstetter, F. S. Hoffman, R. J. Lutz, and H. S. Rowen, *Selection and Use of Strategic Air Bases* (RAND Study, Apr 1954); A. J. Wohlstetter, F. S. Hoffman, H. S. Rowen, *Protecting U.S. Power to Strike Back in the 1950's and 1960's* (RAND Study, Sep 1956); E. J. Barlow, *Distant Early Warning in the Defense of the United States* (RAND Study, Nov 1952); Herken, *Counsels of War*, pp 88–101; Bernard Brodie, "The Development of Nuclear Strategy," *International Security* 2, no. 4 (spring 1978).

36. "The Hidden Struggle for the H-Bomb: The Story of Dr. Oppenheimer's Persistent Campaign to Reverse U.S. Military Strategy," *Fortune*, May 1953.

37. Griggs's testimony, in *Oppenheimer Hearings*.

38. J. Robert Oppenheimer, "Atomic Weapons and American Policy," *Foreign Affairs*, Jul 1953.

39. Brodie, "Development of Nuclear Strategy"; Herken, *Counsels of War*, pp 88–101. Many of the civilian analysts at RAND did not share the Air Force belief that a completely unexpected Soviet attack was unlikely; they believed the Air Force was not doing enough to protect and shelter SAC bombers. In 1959, Brodie [*Strategy in the Missile Age*, p 185] wrote,

A conspicuous inability or unreadiness to defend our retaliatory force must tend to provoke the opponent to destroy it; in other words, it tempts him to an aggression he might not otherwise contemplate. How can he permit our SAC to live and constantly threaten his existence, if he believes he can destroy it with impunity?

The strongest case for a Soviet surprise attack was made by Albert Wohlstetter in "The Delicate Balance of Terror" [*Foreign Affairs* (Jan 1959)]. By then, the development of the ICBM had made the strategic situation more perilous. By 1978 Brodie had come to support the Air Force position "that some kind of political warning will always be available," although the Air Force did not necessarily hold that position anymore ["Development of Nuclear Strategy," pp 68–69]. Said Brodie:

> Attack out of the blue, which is to say without a condition of crisis, is one of those worst-case fantasies that we have to cope with as a starting point for our security planning, but there are very good reasons why it has never happened historically, at least in modern times, and for comparable reasons, I regard it as so improbable for a nuclear age as to approach virtual certainty that it will not happen, which is to say it is not a possibility worth spending much money on.

The change in Brodie's thought is explained in Lt Col Barry D. Watts's *The Foundations of U.S. Air Doctrine: The Problem of Friction in War* [(Maxwell AFB, Ala., 1984), pp 89–93].

40. Hist, Directorate of Plans, HQ USAF, Jun–Dec 1952; NSC, *Public Policies of the Government of the United States Relating to National Security.*

41. Hist, DCS/D, HQ USAF, Jul–Dec 1952.

42. Ltr, Lovett to C. F. Craig, Pres, AT&T, Dec 1, 1952, RG 340, 676–9–11323, NA.

43. DOD Public Information Release, Jan 3, 1953, Vandenberg Papers, Box 48, LC; Ltr, Finletter to Killian, Jan 15, 1953, RG 340, 000.8–12926–50, NA.

44. E. J. Barlow, *Distant Early Warning in the Defense of the U.S.* (RAND, Santa Monica, Calif., Nov 1952).

45. Chidlaw, Presentation to AF Comdrs, Eglin AFB, Fla., Oct 15–17, 1952, transcript in USAFHRC microfilm.

46. Memo, Brig Gen John K. Gerhart, Dep Dir Ops, HQ USAF, Nov 5, 1952, quoted in Richard F. McMullen, *Air Defense and National Policy, 1951–1957* (ADC Hist Study 24, 1964), p 25.

47. Memo, JCS to SecDef, subj: An Early Warning System, Dec 19, 1952, USAFHRC microfilm.

48. NSC–141, *A Report to NSC by the Secretaries of Defense and State and the Di-*rector for Mutual Security Reexaminations of U.S. Programs for National Security, Jan 1953, RG 341, OPD 381.02, NA.

49. Memo, JCS to SecDef, subj: Status of U.S. Programs for National Security as of Dec 31, 1952, Feb 12, 1953, cited in Watson, *JCS and National Policy*, p 213.

50. Hist, Directorate of Plans, HQ USAF, Jan–Jun 1953, pp 20–22; Grant, *Continental Air Defense*, p 66.

51. Grant, *Continental Air Defense*, p 67.

52. Memo, Twining to DCS/O and DCS/D, HQ USAF, subj: Objective Plan for Air Defense of the U.S., Mar 17, 1953, USAFHRC microfilm.

53. *Ibid.*

54. Hist, Directorate of Plans, Jan–Jun 1953.

55. Air Force plan for defense of the CONUS against air attack, Jun 8, 1953, cited in Watson, *JCS and National Policy*, pp 122–23.

56. *Ibid.*

57. Getting, "Recollections."

58. Ray, *Nuclear Armament*; Air Force Plan, in Watson, *JCS and National Policy*, pp 122–23.

59. Ltr, Maj Gen Robert W. Burns, Actg Asst VCS, USAF, to DCS/O, HQ USAF, Apr 30, 1953, USAFHRC microfilm.

60. Memo, Army C/S, subj: Department of the Army Plan for Defense of the CONUS, Jan 16, 1955, cited in Watson, *JCS and National Policy*, p 226.

61. Memo, Chief Nav Ops, subj: U.S. Naval Basic Defense Plans for CONUS, Mar 30, 1953, cited in *ibid.*, p 226.

62. Memo, JCS to SecDef, subj: Service Divergencies with Respect to the Joint Outline Plan for Early Warning, Jul 29, 1953, cited in *ibid.*, p 232.

63. Stewart and Joseph Alsop, *New York Herald Tribune*, May 29, 1953.

64. Charles J. V. Murphy, "Kelly Versus the Summer Study Group," *Fortune*, July 1953.

65. DOD Ad Hoc Study Gp, "A Report on the Defense of North America Against Atomic or Other Airborne Attack" [hereafter cited as Kelly Rept], May 11, 1953, Files of the OSD; Office of Public Information, Press release, Vandenberg Papers, Box 48, LC; Watson, *JCS and National Policy*, pp 221–22.

66. Kelly Rept.

67. Memo, Maj Gen Herbert B. Thatcher, Dir Plans, DCS/O, HQ USAF,

to SAF, subj: Continental Defense, Feb 15, 1954, RG 341, OPD 667, NA.

68. NSC Paper 153/1, Jan 1, 1953, RG 341, OPD 381.02, NA. On Eisenhower's defense initiatives and policies see Douglas Kinnard's *President Eisenhower and Strategy Management: A Study in Defense Politics* (Lexington, Ky., 1977) and Richard A. Aliano's *American Defense Policy from Eisenhower to Kennedy* (Athens, Ohio, 1975).

69. James E. Hewes, Jr., *From Root to McNamara: Army Organization and Administration, 1900–1963* (Washington, D.C., 1975), p 223.

70. Ltr, Twining to Lt Gen Ira C. Eaker (USAF, ret), Jan 17, 1953, Twining Papers, Box 21, LC; Matthew B. Ridgway, *Soldier: The Memoirs of Matthew B. Ridgway* (New York, 1956), pp 266–67.

71. Ltr, Eisenhower to Wilson, Aug 6, 1953, Vandenberg Papers, Box 31, LC.

72. NSC 159, Jul 22, 1953, as amended in NSC 159/4, Sep 25, 1953, RG 341, OPD 667, NA.

73. *Ibid.*

74. Memo, JCS to SecDef, subj: Continental Defense, Aug 28, 1953, cited in Watson, *JCS and National Policy*, p 239.

75. *The Collected Writings of Arthur W. Radford; Chairman, Joint Chiefs of Staff,* 2 vols (Washington, D.C., 1957), Vol I, *The First Term, 15 August 1953 to 15 August 1955,* p 221; David Holloway, "Soviet Thermonuclear Development," *International Security* 4, no. 3 (winter 1979–1980).

76. NSC 159, Jul 22, 1953, as amended in NSC 159/4, Sep 25, 1953.

77. Ltr, HQ USAF to Chidlaw, subj: Planning Guide for the Third Phase Augmentation Radar Program, Apr 5, 1954; Memo, Thomas D. White, USAF VC/S, to USofAF, subj: Lincoln Transition System, Nov 18, 1953, RG 341, OPD 667, NA.

78. Ltr, HQ USAF to Chidlaw, Apr 5, 1954.

79. Ltr, HQ ADC to Comdrs, WADF and CADF, subj: Siting Directive

for Third Phase Semi-Mobile Radar Program, Apr 1954, USAFHRC microfilm.

80. Memo, Lyle S. Garlock, ASAF, to Asst Compt, OSD, subj: Apportionment Request for Texas Towers, Nov 1, 1954, USAFHRC microfilm.

81. Memo, John W. Abrams and Charles M. Motley, Chmn, Canadian and U.S. Scientific Advisory teams, to Chmn, Mil Study Gp, subj: Report on Canada-U.S. Scientific Advisory Team Evaluation of the Mid-Canada Segment of an Early Warning System, n.d., RG 341, OPD 667, NA.

82. Memo, Brig Gen Joe W. Kelly, HQ USAF, to Harold E. Talbott, SAF, subj: Cooperation Between Canada and the U.S. on an Early Warning Line for North American Air Defense, May 5, 1954, RG 340, 311–2074–52, NA.

83. Memo, Arthur W. Radford, Chmn, JCS, to SecDef, subj: Military Strategy and Posture, Dec 9, 1953, RG 340, OPD 381.02, NA. Continental defense was not treated extensively in NSC 162/2 because it was the subject of NSC 159/4.

84. Lawrence Freedman, *The Evolution of Nuclear Strategy* (London, 1981), pp 88–90.

85. Rosenberg, "Origins of Overkill."

86. Quoted in *Memoirs of Admiral Radford*, p 318.

87. Gen Thomas D. White, "The Scope of United States Air Strategy," *The Annals of the American Academy of Political and Social Science* 299 (May 1955): 25–26 (reprint for the Air Force entitled *Air Power and National Security*).

88. Memo, SecDef to JCS, Aug 13, 1954.

89. Watson, *JCS and National Policy*, p 246.

90. MR, Col Woodward B. Carpenter, HQ USAF, subj: Evaluation of Our Actual and Potential Military Power in Relation to Current Military Committments, Apr 16, 1954, RG 341, OPD 381.02, NA.

91. Ltr, Maj Gen Frederic H. Smith to Lt Gen Laurence Kuter, CG, Air University, Mar 1, 1954, USAFHRC microfilm.

Chapter 8. Defensive Systems Become Operational

1. William P. Vogel, "SAGE: Electronic Sentinel," *The Air Force Blue Book* (Military Publications Institute, 1959).

2. John B. Jacobs, "SAGE Over-

view," *Annals of the History of Computing* 5, no. 4 (Oct 1983).

3. Qtr Prog Rept, Lincoln Laboratory, Jun 1952.

4. *Ibid.*

5. *Ibid.*

6. Briefing, Lt Col O. T. Halley, HQ ADC, to Gen Chidlaw, Jan 23, 1953; McMullen, *Birth of SAGE.*

7. Ltr, Whitehead to Dir Rqr, HQ USAF, subj: British Comprehensive Display System, Jul 22, 1950, USAFHRC microfilm.

8. Briefing, Halley to Chidlaw, Jan 23, 1953; Ltr, Maj Gen Morris R. Nelson to HQ ADC, subj: Employment of an American Version of CDS, Jun 12, 1950, USAFHRC microfilm.

9. Lincoln Laboratory Tech Memo, subj: A Proposal for Air Defense System Evolution: The Transition Phase, Jun 2, 1953.

10. Ltr, Chidlaw to Vandenberg, Oct 13, 1952, USAFHRC microfilm.

11. Ltr, Twining to Chidlaw, Nov 13, 1952, USAFHRC microfilm.

12. Ltr, Lloyd A. Young, Ch, Elct Div, RAND, to Maj Gen F. H. Smith, subj: Discussion of Relationship Between Lincoln Laboratory's Proposed Transition System and the Willow Run Research Center's Air Defense Integrated System, Feb 10, 1953.

13. *Ibid.*

14. Ltr, Killian to Finletter, Jan 9, 1953, RG 340, SAF 000.8-12926-50, Vol III, NA.

15. Getting, "Recollections."

16. Ltr, Finletter to Killian, Jan 9, 1953, RG 340, SAF 000.8-12926-50, Vol III, NA.

17. Ltr, Partridge to Killian, Jan 28, 1953, USAFHRC microfilm.

18. Ltr, Partridge to Chidlaw, Feb 11, 1953, USAFHRC microfilm.

19. Ltr, Col Gilbert L. Myers, Dep Dir Rqr, HQ USAF, to Chidlaw, subj: Lincoln Laboratory Technical Memorandum no 20, Aug 4, 1953, UASFHRC microfilm.

20. Ltr, Albert G. Hill, Dir, Lincoln Lab, to Trevor Gardner, Apr 6, 1953, RG 340, SAF 000.8-12926-50, Vol III, NA.

21. Memo, Gen Earle E. Partridge, Comdr, ARDC, subj: Visit to the University of Michigan, Mar 13, 1953, USAFHRC microfilm.

22. Ltr, Smith to Dir Rqr, HQ USAF, subj: Improvements for the Ground Environment of the CONUS Air Defense Systems, Sep 5, 1953, with Encl, subj: Operational Improvements for ADC Needed by 1956, USAFHRC microfilm.

23. Ltr, Partridge to Killian, May 6, 1953, USAFHRC microfilm.

24. Robert R. Everett, in "Perspectives on SAGE: Discussion," *Annals of Computing,* p 384. Said one Air Force officer [Lt Col Peter J. Schenk, "Problems in Air Defense," *Air University Quarterly Review* 5, no. 2 (spring 1952): 39–53] who worked closely with the scientists:

> We must violate the deepest prejudices of the "military mind" by giving this group of civilian scientists complete access to our problems and weaknesses and letting them eventually prescribe a cure. We must by-pass and violate normal channels of all sorts by allowing unheard-of liberties in accounting and dealing with public property. In giving inordinary support and credit to our select group of experts [the scientists] we must expect to alienate established technical groups [military?] charged with the drab and thankless task of maintaining the existing systems and making small improvements in them. Private industry has recognized this principle long ago and pays seemingly exorbitant fees for expert consultants, but they find the results well worth the costs.

25. Morton M. Astrahan and John F. Jacobs, "History of the Design of the SAGE Computer, the AN-FSQ-7," *Annals of Computing,* p 341; Kent C. Richmond and Thomas M. Smith, *Project Whirlwind: The History of a Pioneer Computer* (Bedford, Mass., 1980).

26. "SAGE: The New Aerial Defense System of the United States," *The Military Engineer* (Mar–Apr 1956), pp 115–16; "The Emerging Shield: The Air Defense Ground Environment," *Air University Quarterly Review* 8, no. 2 (spring 1956): 49–69.

27. C. Robert Wieser, "The Cape Cod System," *Annals of Computing,* pp 362–69.

28. McMullen, *Birth of SAGE,* p 35.

29. Clyde A. Littlefield, "The History of SAGE," draft manuscript in AF/CHO, p 101; C. Baum, *The Systems Builders: The Story of SDC* (Santa Monica, Calif., 1981), pp 23–24.

30. Memo, HQ ARAACOM to HQ CONAD, subj: Integration of SAGE into CONAD Operation, Dec 20, 1955, cited in McMullen, *Birth of SAGE,* pp 44–45.

31. ARAACOM Comd Hist, Jul–Dec 1957.

32. Cited in McMullen, *Birth of SAGE,* p 47.

33. *Ibid.*, p 52.

34. *Ibid.*, p 57.

35. N. F. Kristy, *Man in a Large Information-Processing Center: His Changing Role in SAGE* (RM–3206–PR, Santa Monica, Feb 1963).

36. *Ibid.*

37. On Canadian-American cooperation in early warning and other aspects of air defense see Jockel's *No Boundaries Upstairs*, Melvin Conant's *The Long Polar Watch: Canada and the Defense of North America* (New York, 1962), and Jon B. McLin's *Canada's Changing Defense Policy, 1957–1963: The Problem of a Middle Power in Alliance* (Baltimore, 1967).

38. Ray, *DEW Line*, p 13.

39. ADC DEW Line Sys Ofc, *The DEW System* (brochure), pp 13–17; Richard Morenus, *DEW Line* (New York, 1957), ch 3; Ray, *DEW Line*, pp 12–28.

40. ADC DEW Line Sys Ofc, *DEW System*, pp 13–17; Morenus, *DEW Line*, ch 3; Ray, *DEW Line*, pp 12–28.

41. Memo, Kelly to Talbott, May 5, 1954.

42. Memo, Maj Gen Richard C. Lindsay, Dir Plans, HQ USAF, to DCS/O, HQ USAF, subj: Proposed Non-Agenda Item for Operations Deputies Meeting, Jan 30, 1950, RG 341, OPD 667, NA; Ltr, Chrmn, Canadian Chiefs of Staff, to Chrmn, JCS, Jun 30, 1954, cited in Watson, *JCS and National Policy*, p 266.

43. Brian Cuthbertson, *Canadian Military Independence in the Age of the Superpowers* (Toronto, 1977), p 45.

44. Jockel, "No Boundaries Upstairs," ch 3, pp 41–45.

45. First Rept, Location Study Gp, Nov 12, 1954, cited in Watson, *JCS and National Policy*, p 269.

46. Memo, SecDef to SAF, subj: Distant Early Warning System for CONUS, Oct 5, 1954, RG 340, SAF 676.9–11323–49, NA.

47. Memo, Lyle S. Garlock, ASAF, subj: Revision of Charter for Air Force Management Fund Project Account no. 8, Distant Early Warning System, n.d., RG 340, SAF 676.9–11323–49, NA.

48. Hearings before the Subcommittee on the Air Force of the Committee on Armed Services, Senate, Testimony of Maj Gen Partridge, 84th Cong, 2d sess, pt 3.

49. Ltr, HQ USAF to HQ ADC, subj: Implementation of the DEW Line, Jan 21, 1955; Hist, ADC, Jul–Dec 1954.

50. Ltr, HQ USAF to HQ ADC, Jan 21, 1955; Hist, ADC, Jul–Dec 1954.

51. Conant, *Long Polar Watch*, p 40.

52. Ray, *DEW Line*, p 30.

53. *Ibid.*, pp 33–34.

54. Thomas W. Ray, *A History of Texas Towers in Air Defense, 1952–1964* (ADC Hist Study 29, 1965), pp 1–2.

55. *Ibid.*; Hist, ADC, Jan–Jun 1955.

56. Ray, *Texas Towers*, pp 21–22; Hist, ADC, Jul–Dec 1955; Hist, EADF, Jul–Dec 1956.

57. Rept, Preparedness Investigating Subcom, Com Armed Services, Senate, The Collapse of Texas Tower no. 4, Jun 15, 1961; Hist, ADC, Jul–Dec 1960; Ray, *Texas Towers*, pp 27–28.

58. Ray, *Early Warning*, pp 5–6.

59. Hist, ADC, Jan–Jun 1951; Hist, ADC, Jul–Dec 1951; Hist, WADF, Jul–Dec 1951; Ray, *Early Warning*, pp 8–9.

60. Hist, ADC, Jul–Dec 1951; Hist, ADC, Jan–Jun 1952; Frederick G. Swanborough and Peter Bowers, *United States Military Aircraft Since 1909* (New York, 1963), pp 298–301; Ray, *Early Warning*, pp 10–11.

61. Hist, ADC, Jul–Dec 1956; Hist, WADF, Jul–Dec 1956; Ray, *Early Warning*, pp 32–33.

62. Hist, ADC, Jan–Jun 1956; Hist, ADC, 1958; Ray, *Early Warning*, pp 47–48.

63. Quote in Volan, *GOC*, p 243.

64. Ltr, HQ ADC to HQ USAF, subj: Deactivation of the Ground Observer Corps, Mar 17, 1958; Volan, *GOC*, p 245.

65. Hist, ADC, Jun-Dec 1957.

66. Final Rept, Project LAMPLIGHT, 1955, copy in AF/CHO; McMullen, *Radar Programs*, p 101.

67. Ltr, Lt Gen J. H. Atkinson, HQ ADC, to CSAF, subj: Vulnerability of Our Ground Environment System to ECM, Jan 22, 1957; Ltr, HQ ADC to HQ USAF, subj: Proposed Electronic Countermeasure Fixes for ADC Radars, Jul 15, 1957; Hist, ADC, 1958; McMullen, *Radar Programs*, pp 105–06.

68. McMullen, *Radar Programs*, p 228.

69. Hist, ADC, 1958; George H. Quester, *Deterrence Before Hiroshima: The Airpower Background of Modern Strategy* (New York, 1966), p 132.

70. CIA NIE 11–3–55, Soviet Capabilities and Probable Courses of Action Through 1960, May 17, 1950; John Prados, *The Soviet Estimate: U.S. Intelligence Analysis and Russian Military Strength* (New York, 1982), pp 38–50.

71. Charles A. Cannon, "The Politics of Interest and Ideology: The Senate Air-power Hearings of 1956," *Armed Forces and Society* 3, no. 4 (Aug 1977): 595–605.

72. McMullen, *Aircraft in Air Defense.*

73. Ltr, Chidlaw to Gen Thomas Power, CG, ARDC, Aug 19, 1954, cited in Hist, CONAD-ADC, Jul–Dec 1954.

74. McMullen, *Air Defense Weapons,* pp 250–51; Knaack, *Post-WW II Fighters,* pp 159–73.

75. Bruce Robertson, *U.S. Army and Air Force Fighters 1916–1961* (London, 1961), pp 120–21; Richard P. Hallion, *On the Frontier: Flight Research at Dryden, 1946–1981* (NASA Hist Series, 1984), pp 202–07; Jones, *U.S. Fighters,* pp 273–74; Futrell, *Ideas, Concepts, Doctrine,* pp 268–69; McMullen, *Aircraft in Air Defense,* pp 63–65; Knaack, *Post-WW II Fighters,* p 159.

76. Jones, *U.S. Fighters,* p 285; McMullen, *Aircraft in Air Defense,* p 92; Knaack, *Post-WW II Fighters,* pp 209–21.

77. McMullen, *Aircraft in Air Defense,* pp 75–84; Futrell, *Ideas, Concepts, Doctrine,* p 269; Knaack, *Post-WW II Fighters,* pp 179–80.

78. McMullen, *Aircraft in Air Defense,* pp 84–91; Knaack, *Post-WW II Fighters,* pp 135–57.

79. McMullen, *Aircraft in Air Defense,* pp 99–122.

80. Knaack, *Post-WW II Fighters,* pp 330–31; Futrell, *Ideas, Concepts, Doctrine,* p 272.

81. Quoted in Futrell, *Ideas, Concepts, Doctrine,* p 273.

82. McMullen, *Air Defense Weapons,* p 277.

83. *Ibid,* pp 157–58.

84. Ray, *Nuclear Armament,* pp 3–4.

85. *Ibid,* pp 4–5.

86. Arthur K. Marmor, *The Search for New USAF Weapons, 1958–1959* (USAF Hist Div Liaison Off., 1961), pp 15–20; George H. Quester, *Nuclear Diplomacy: The First Twenty-Five Years* (New York, 1970), p 183. During the July 1957 test, five officers and a cameraman stood directly under the detonation as a public reassurance act. The officers were Col Sydney Bruce, Lt Col Frank Ball, and Majors Norman Bodinger, John Hughes, and Don Luttrell. They contributed to the ease with which nuclear weapons were accommodated on bases with no public outcry [Ltr, Col Barney Oldfield (USAF, ret) to the author, Jun 12, 1985].

87. Hist, ADC, Jul–Dec 1953.

88. *Ibid.*

89. *Ibid.*

90. Cited in *ibid.*

91. Richard F. McMullen, *Interceptor Missiles in Air Defense* (ADC Hist Study 30, 1965), pp 2–3.

92. *Ibid,* p 17.

93. McMullen, *Air Defense Weapons,* p 326.

94. McMullen, *Interceptor Missiles,* pp 125–26.

Chapter 9. Organizing to Meet the Threat

1. Ltr, HQ USAF to HQ ADC, subj: Army Air Force Agreements Concerning Air Defense, May 10, 1951; Memo, Maj Gen T. D. White, Act DCS/O, to Gen Twining, Jul 17, 1951, Twining Papers, Box 55, LC.

2. Ltr, HQ USAF to HQ ADC, May 10, 1951; Memo, White to Twining, Jul 17, 1951.

3. ARDC Case Hist, Project LINCOLN, p 6; DuPre, *Biographical Dictionary,* pp 81–82.

4. "Reports of Boards and Committees," Feb 16–Sep 30, 1952, OSAF 334, Joint Air Defense Board, Box 1011, RG 340, NA; Hist, Directorate of Plans, HQ USAF, Jan–Jun 1953.

5. JCS Paper 1899/89, Dec 16, 1953.

6. Watson, *JCS and National Policy,* p 259.

7. Cited in *ibid.*

8. *Ibid.*

9. Memo, Lt Gen Partridge, DCS/O, to Directorate of Plans, HQ USAF, subj: Continental Air Defense, Jan 11, 1954, OPD 667, RG 341, NA; Ltr, HQ USAF to HQ ADC, subj: Command Arrangements for Air Defense of the U.S., Apr 7, 1954, US- AFHRC microfilm.

10. Ltr, Chidlaw to Twining, subj: Command Arrangements for the Air Defense of the U.S., May 11, 1954, USAFHRC microfilm.

11. *Ibid.*

12. *Ibid.*

13. Memo, HQ ARAACOM, subj: Command Arrangements for the Air De-

fense of the U.S., May 10, 1954, cited in Barnard, *ARADCOM: The Gun Era*, Vol I, pp 159–62.

14. Memo, SecDef Wilson to SA, SN, SAF, and JCS, subj: New Command for Continental Air Defense, Jul 30, 1954, Box 1490, RG 340, NA.

15. HQ CONAD GO 1, Sep 1, 1954. The Air Force mission regulations for ADC (AFR 23–9) were not revised until August 24, 1955. Whereas former editions of the directive stated "The Air Defense Command is organized primarily to provide for and conduct the air defense of the United States. . . ," the new one read ". . . is organized primarily to discharge Air Force responsibilities for the air defense of the United States."

16. Hearings before the Subcommittee on the Air Force of the Committee on Armed Services, Senate, Testimony of General Partridge, 84th Cong, 2d sess, Apr 30–May 1, 1956, pt 3, p 306.

17. Futrell, *Ideas, Concepts, Doctrine*, pp 203–06.

18. *Seventeen Years of Air Defense*, pp 53–54.

19. Ltr, Lt Gen S. R. Mickelsen to Partridge, subj: Proposed Reorganization of CONAD Headquarters, Apr 11, 1956.

20. NORAD Hist Summary, Jan–Jun 1958.

21. Gen Charles Foulkes, "Canadian Defence Policy in a Nuclear Age," *Behind the Headlines* 21 (May 1961).

22. Jockel, "No Boundaries Upstairs," ch 3, pp 48–49, ch 5, pp 2–5.

23. Lt Col P. J. Goodspeed, ed, *The Armed Forces of Canada, 1867–1967* (Ottawa, 1967), pp 219–29.

24. For the decision to equip the Arrow with the most up-todate missile and fire control systems, see Murray Penden's "Fall of the Arrow" [*Wings* 9, no. 1 (Feb 1979)].

25. Quoted in McLin, *Canada's Changing Defense Policy*, p 45.

26. Bill Gunston, *Early Supersonic Fighters of the West* (New York, 1975), pp 120–37. See James Dow's *The Arrow* (Toronto, 1979) for the engineering history of the plane and the political controversy its development engendered in Canada.

27. CSAF Rept CSAFM 336–55 to JCS, Combined Canada-U.S. North American Air Defense Command, Dec 1, 1955, OPD 667, Box 669, RG 341, NA; Jockel, "No Boundaries Upstairs," ch 5, p 9.

28. Jockel, "No Boundaries Upstairs," ch 5, p 11; McLin, *Canada's Changing Defense Policy*, pp 54–57. The Canada-U.S. Regional Planning Group was recognized by NATO to have responsibility for defense of North America, but it had no assigned forces nor command functions as did geographical divisions in NATO.

29. Canadian House of Commons Debate, Jul 18, 1956, p 6135, cited in Jockel, "No Boundaries Upstairs," ch 4, p 50.

30. NORAD Hist Summary, Jan–Jun 1958. The best overview for the Canadian decision to enter NORAD is Jockel's "No Boundaries Upstairs"; also excellent are McLin's *Canada's Changing Defense Policy*, Cuthbertson's *Canadian Military Independence*, and James Eayres's *In Defence of Canada: Growing Up Allied* (Toronto, 1980).

31. McLin, *Canada's Changing Defense Policy*, pp 45–47.

32. *Ibid.*

33. NORAD Hist Summary, Jan–Jun 1958.

34. Intvws, Author with Gen Partridge, Lt Gen Marshall S. Carter, and Air Marshal C. R. Slemon, Colorado Springs, Colo., Apr 15, 1973, personal files.

35. *Ibid.*

36. Cuthbertson, *Canadian Military Independence*, pp 50–51.

37. *The Air Defense Command in the Cuban Crisis, October–December 1962* (ADC Hist Study 15, 1962), pp 163–66.

38. McLin, *Canada's Changing Defense Policy*, p 156; Jockel, "No Boundaries Upstairs," ch 5.

Chapter 10. Epilogue: Impact of a New Threat

1. Sputnik was probably launched by an intermediate-range ballistic missile, generally designated "T–2" [Wernher von Braun and Frederick I. Ordway III, *History of Rocketry and Space Travel*, 3d rev ed (New York, 1975), p 158, and Prados, *Soviet Estimate*, pp 56–57]. For the American reaction to Sputnik see Walter A. McDougall's . . . *The Heavens and the Earth: A Political History of the Space Age* (New York,

1985), James R. Killian's *Sputniks, Scientists, and Eisenhower: A Memoir of the First Special Assistant to the President for Science and Technology* (Cambridge, Mass., 1977), Kinnard's *President Eisenhower and Strategy Management*, and Stephen E. Ambrose's *Ike's Spies: Eisenhower and the Espionage Establishment* (New York, 1981). On the development of Soviet missile technology, McDougall's *Heavens and Earth* (esp pp 20–40) is superb. See also Bruce Parrot's *Politics and Technology in the Soviet Union* (Cambridge, Mass., 1983), Kendall E. Bailes's *Technology and Science Under Lenin and Stalin: Origins of the Soviet Technical Intelligensia, 1917–1941* (Princeton, N.J., 1978), and G. A. Tokaty's "Soviet Rocket Technology" [*Technology and Culture* (fall 1963), pp 516–17].

2. 1st Ind, HQ AAF to CG, Air Tech Serv Comd, Feb 14, 1946, USAFHRC microfilm.

3. R&R, AC/AS-3, GMs Div, to AC/AS-4, R&E Div, subj: Military Characteristics of an Air Defense System, DRB 381, War Plans Miscellaneous, National Defense, 1946–1947, NA.

4. AMC Case Hist, Aircraft Control and Warning Systems, doc 29; Memo, AC/AS-3, GMs and Air Def Div, to AC/AS-4, R&E Div, subj: Development of Radar Equipment for Detecting and Countering Missiles of the German A-4 type, Dec 27, 1946, USAFHRC microfilm.

5. Futrell, *Ideas, Concepts, Doctrine*, p 238.

6. Ltr, DAC/AS-3 to CG, Air Univ, subj: Preparation of AAF Concept and Outline Strategy for War, Apr, 11, 1947, DRB 381, War Plans Miscellaneous, National Defense, 1946–1947, NA.

7. Futrell, *Ideas, Concepts, Doctrine*, p 251.

8. Ernest J. Yanarella, *The Missile Defense Controversy: Strategy, Technology, and Politics, 1955–1972* (Lexington, Ky., 1972), *passim*.

9. *The Active Air Defense of the United States, 1954–1960* (RAND Study R-250, Santa Monica, Calif., Dec 1953), pp 7–8.

10. Memo, HQ CONAD to CSAF as Exec Agt for JCS, subj: Assignment of ICBM and IRBM Defense Responsibility in CONAD, Apr 3, 1956, USAFHRC microfilm.

11. Memo, Gen Partridge, CINCCONAD, to Comdr ADC, Apr 3, 1956, USAFHRC microfilm.

12. Futrell, *Ideas, Concepts, Doctrine*, p 251.

13. Hist, CONAD, 1956–1957.

14. Cited in Benson D. Adams, *Ballistic Missile Defense* (New York, 1971), p 27.

15. *Ibid.*, p 33; *NORAD's Quest for Nike-Zeus and a Long-Range Interceptor* (NORAD Hist Ref Paper 6, 1962).

16. Hist, ADC, 1971.

17. Thomas W. Ray, *History of BMEWS, 1957–1964* (ADC Hist Study 32, 1965); Thomas W. Ray, *Interceptor Dispersal, 1961–1964* (ADC Hist Study 25, 1964).

18. Ray, *BMEWS*.

19. *Ibid.*; "Samos . . . was a Polaroid wonder that developed its own film, scanned it electronically, and radioed the pictures to ground stations" [McDougall, *Heavens and Earth*, p 329]. MIDAS was designed to watch for Soviet first-strike missile attacks. Both satellites were instrumental in dispelling the missile-gap myth. A good account of programs leading to SAMOS and MIDAS is in David Baker's *The Shape of Wars to Come* [(New York, 1984), pp 45–55].

20. Hist, ADC, Jan–Jun 1959.

21. *Ibid.*

22. Hearings on DOD appropriations for FY 1961, House of Representatives, pt 1, Jan 1960, p 54; Richard F. McMullen, *The Aerospace Defense Command and Anti-Bomber Defense, 1946–1972* (ADC Hist Study 39, 1973).

23. Ltr, CINCNORAD (Kuter) to JCS, subj: Defense of Northern Perimeter and ICBM sites, Apr 16, 1962, USAFHRC microfilm.

24. *NORAD's Underground Combat Operations Center, 1956–1966* (NORAD Hist Ref Paper 12, 1966), pp 3–6.

25. NORAD Hist Summary, 1958.

26. *NORAD's Underground COC*, p 18.

27. *Ibid.*, pp 22–23.

28. Thomas A. Sturm, *Command and Control for North American Air Defense, 1959–1963* (USAF Hist Div Liaison Ofc, Jan 1965), pp 11–15.

29. *Ibid.*, pp 14–17.

30. *Ibid.*

31. Richard F. McMullen, *Command and Control Planning, 1958–1965* (ADC Hist Study 35, 1965), pp 1–12.

32. *Ibid.*; Baum, *Systems Builders*, p 77.

33. McMullen, *Command and Control*, pp 59–63.

34. Freedman, *Evolution of Nuclear Strategy*, p 216; James E. Dornan, Jr., "Strategic Rocket Forces," in Ray Bonds, ed,

The Soviet War Machine: An Encyclopedia of Russian Military Equipment and Strategy (New York, 1976), pp 204–08.

35. Soviet priorities in Europe are explained in Thomas Wolfe's *Soviet Power and Europe, 1945–1970.* (Baltimore, 1970) and in RM–3506–PR.

36. Wolfe, *Soviet Power and Europe*; RM–3506–PR; Harriet Fast Scott and William F. Scott, *The Soviet Art of War: Doctrine, Strategy, and Tactics* (Boulder, Colo., 1982), pp 123–27.

37. RM–3506–PR.

38. *Ibid.*

39. R. D. M. Furlong, "NORAD—A Study in Evolution," *International Defense Review* 7, no. 3 (Jun 1974): 317–19.

40. McMullen, *Anti-Bomber Defense*, p 140.

41. A good discussion of MAD's implications for overall U.S. defense strategy is in Freedman's *Evolution of Nuclear Strategy* (pp 245–46).

42. Owen E. Jensen, "Air Defense of North America, Historical Imperatives for Change" (thesis, Naval Postgraduate School, Monterey, Calif., Dec 1982), p 116.

43. Quoted in Freedman, *Evolution of Nuclear Strategy*, p 258.

44. Hist, ADC, 1973–1974; Jensen, "Air Defense of North America," p 169.

45. Hist, ADC, 1973–1974.

46. McMullen, *Anti-Bomber Defense*, pp 221–22.

47. John L. Frisbee, "Air Defense—The Forgotten Front," *Air Force* 53, no. 7 (July 1970).

48. Hist, ADC, 1973–1974.

49. *Ibid.*

50. Lloyd H. Cornett, Jr., and Mildred W. Johnson, *A Handbook of Aerospace Defense Command Organization, 1946–1980*, rev ed (ADC Hist Ofc, Dec 1980), pp 15–16; Jensen, "Air Defense of North America," pp 184–85; Hist, ADC, 1979.

51. *Soviet Military Power* (Washington, D.C., 1984), p 29.

52. Quoted in Lt Col Richard S. Cammarota, "Defensive Watch," *Air Force* 68, no. 2 (Feb 1985), p 84; Lt Col Donald D. Carson, "New Look in Air Defense," *Air Force* 67, no. 6 (Jun 1984): 80–82; Marilyn Silcox, "Southeast ROCC Marks Beginning of New Air Defense Era," *National Defense* 69, no. 399 (Jul–Aug 1984): 42–46; Rick Atkinson, "Air Defense for Continental U.S. Is Coming Back into Vogue," *Washington Post*, Aug 25, 1984; Space Command/ADCOM Hist, 1983.

Glossary

of Abbreviations and Acronyms

AAA	antiaircraft artillery
AAF	Army Air Forces
AAG	Air Adjutant General
ABM	antiballistic missile
AC/AS	Assistant Chief, Air Staff
AC/S	Assistant Chief of Staff
act	acting
ACTS	Air Corps Tactical School
ADC	Air Defense Command (now the Aerospace Defense Command)
ADES	Air Defense Engineering Service
ADIS	Air Defense Integrated System
ADTAC	Air Defense–Tactical Air Command
AEC	Atomic Energy Commission
AEF	American Expeditionary Forces
AExO	Assistant Executive Officer
1AF, 2AF, etc.	First Air Force, Second Air Force, etc.
AFB	Air Force Base
AFCC	Air Force Combat Command
AF/CHO	Office of Air Force History, Bolling AFB, Washington, D.C.
AFR	Air Force Regulation
AG	Adjutant General
AGF	Army Ground Forces
AGO	Adjutant General's Office
agt	agent
Amb	Ambassador
AMC	Air Materiel Command
Anx	annex
APG	Air Proving Ground
APGC	Air Proving Ground Command
App	appendix
ARADCOM	Army Air Defense Command
ARDC	Air Research and Development Command
AS	Air Staff

ASA	Assistant Secretary of the Army
ASAF	Assistant Secretary of the Air Force
Asst	Assistant
AWACS	Airborne Warning and Control System
Bd	Board
BMEWS	Ballistic Missile Early-Warning System
BOMARC	Boeing–Michigan Aeronautical Research Center
BUIC	Backup Interceptor Control
Bul	bulletin
Bur	Bureau
CAA	Civil Aeronautics Administration (formerly Civil Aeronautics Authority)
CAC	Chief of Air Corps
CADF	Central Air Defense Force
CADIN	Continental Air Defense Integration, North
CAF	Continental Air Forces
C/AS	Chief, Air Staff
CDS	comprehensive display system
CG	Commanding General
Ch	Chief [of]
Chmn	chairman/chairmen
CIA	Central Intelligence Agency
CINCCONAD	Commander in Chief, Continental Air Defense
CINCNORAD	Commander in Chief, North American Air Defense Command
Cir	Circular
CNGB	Chief, National Guard Bureau
CO	Commanding Officer
COC	Combat Operations Center
com	committee
Comd	Command
Comdr	Commander
Comm	communication
Compt	Comptroller
con	conversation
CONAC	Continental Air Command
CONAD	Continental Air Defense Command
Cong	Congress
CONUS	continental United States
C/S	Chief of Staff
CSAF	Chief of Staff, Air Force

DAF	Department of the Air Force
DBA	Soviet long-range aviation command
DC/AS	Deputy Chief, Air Staff
DC/S	Deputy Chief of Staff
DCS/D, /M, /O, /P, /Plans	Deputy Chief of Staff, Development; Materiel; Operations; Personnel; and Plans, respectively
Def	Defense
Dep	Deputy [for]
DEW	Distant Early Warning
Dir	Director/Directors
Div	Division
doc	document
DOD	Department of Defense
EADF	Eastern Air Defense Force
ECM	electronic countermeasure
elct	electronics
Emb	Embassy
env	envelope
EO	Executive Order
Ex	exercise
exec	executive
FEAF	Far East Air Forces
FFAR	folding-fin air-to-air rocket
FM	Field Manual
FW	Fighter Wing
FY	fiscal year
GAPA	ground-to-air pilotless aircraft
GCI	ground-controlled interception
GHQ	General Headquarters
GM	guided missile
GO	General Order
GOC	Ground Observer Corps
GOR	General Operational Requirement
Gp	group
Hist	History/Historical
HQ	Headquarters
IBM	International Business Machines Corporation
ICBM	intercontinental ballistic missile
IFF	identification, friend or foe
IG	Inspector General

Instl	installation
Intvw	interview
IRBM	intermediate-range ballistic missiles
JCS	Joint Chiefs of Staff
JSS	Joint Strategic Survey
KISS	"keep it simple, stupid"
Lab	Laboratory
LADA	London Air Defense Area
LC	Library of Congress, Washington, D.C.
Leg	legislative
Ltr	letter
MAD	mutual assured destruction
Memo	memorandum
MIDAS	Missile Defense Alarm System
min	minutes
MIT	Massachusetts Institute of Technology
MR	memo for the record
MRBM	medium-range ballistic missile
Msg	message
mtg	meeting
n.	note
NA	National Archives, Washington, D.C.
NACA	National Advisory Committee for Aeronautics
NASA	National Air and Space Administration
NATO	North Atlantic Treaty Organization
Nav	Naval
NGB	National Guard Bureau
NIE	national intelligence estimate
no.	number
NORAD	North American Air Defense Command
NSC	National Security Council
ofc	office
off	officer
Ops	Operations
Org	Organization
OSAF	Office of the Secretary of the Air Force
OSD	Office of the Secretary of Defense
OSW	Office of the Secretary of War
PL	Public Law

Pres	President
prog	program/progress
proj	project
pt	part
qtr	quarterly
R&E	research and engineering
rec	record
Ref	reference
Reg	Regulation
Rept	report
RG	Record Group
Rqrs	requirements
R&R	routing and record set
rsch	research
SA	Secretary of the Army
SAC	Strategic Air Command
SAF	Secretary of the Air Force
SAGE	semiautomatic ground environment
SAMOS	Satellite and Missile Observation System
S/AS	Secretary, Air Staff
SDC	Systems Development Corporation
SecDef	Secretary of Defense
SecState	Secretary of State
SecWar	Secretary of War
SecWar/Air	Secretary of War for Air
Secy	Secretary
serv	service
sess	session
SN	Secretary of the Navy
SO	Special Order
Sp	special
Stavka	Supreme High Command (U.S.S.R.)
stf	staff
subcom	subcommittee
sys	system
TAC	Tactical Air Command
tech	technical
Tp	telephone
TV	television
UHF	ultrahigh frequency

USAFHRC	USAF Historical Research Center, Maxwell AFB, Montgomery, Ala.
USofAF	Undersecretary of the Air Force
VC/S	Vice Chief of Staff
Vol	volume
WADF	Western Air Defense Force
WD	War Department
WDGS	War Department General Staff
WPD	War Plans Division
WSEG	Weapons Systems Evaluation Group
ZORC	Informal group of civilian scientists (Jerrold R. Zacharias, J Robert Oppenheimer, Isidor I. Rabi, and Charles Lauritsen)

Bibliographic Note

Governmental Sources

Documents contained in the Air Force's Historical Research Center (USAFHRC), Maxwell AFB, Alabama, offer a wealth of information on matters dealing with air defense from the 1930s to the present. Most of the documents in Maxwell are reproduced on microfilm available in the Office of Air Force History (AF/CHO), Bolling AFB, Washington, D.C. Other Air Force air defense documents are stored in the USAF Space Command History Office, Colorado Springs, Colorado.

Also available at USAFHRC are a number of important interviews. Thomas A. Sturm's interview with Maj. Gen. Gordon P. Saville, dated March 26–30, 1973, is of immense importance. Saville's reminiscences add much information to the store of knowledge in continental air defense and open new vistas and paths for further research. Other valuable interviews include those with Generals Earle E. Partridge, Bruce K. Holloway, Laurence S. Kuter, Samuel E. Anderson, Frederic H. Smith, Arthur C. Agan, and Herbert Thatcher.

Governmental holdings used in air defense history include those at the National Archives (NA) in Washington, D.C., and the Library of Congress (LC), also in Washington. Especially useful NA holdings are Record Group (RG) 18, Records of HQ, Army Air Forces; RG 218, Records of the Joint Chiefs of Staff; RG 340, Records of the Office of the Secretary of the Air Force; and RG 341, Records of HQ USAF.

The papers of the Air Force Chiefs of Staff are collected in the Library of Congress. Collections used in this study include those of Generals Muir S. Fairchild, H. H. Arnold, Carl A. Spaatz, Hoyt S. Vandenberg, Nathan N. Twining, and Thomas D. White.

Books

Allison, David Kite. *New Eye for the Navy: The Origin of Radar at the Naval Research Laboratory*. Washington: Naval Research Laboratory, 1981.

Barnard, Roy S. *The History of ARADCOM*. Vol 1, *The Gun Era, 1950–1955*. Washington: Army Air Defense Command, 1972.

Cline, Ray S. *Washington Command Post: The Operations Division* [U.S. Army in World War II: The War Department]. Washington: Office of the Chief of Military History, Department of the Army, 1951.

Conn, Stetson, Rose C. Engelman, and Byron Fairchild. *Guarding the United States and Its Outposts* [U.S. Army in World War II: The Western Hemisphere]. Washington: Office of Military History, 1964.

Cooling, B. Franklin. *The Army Support of Civil Defense, 1945–1966: Plans and Policy.* Washington: Office of the Chief of Military History, 1967.

Craven, Wesley Frank, and James Lea Cate, eds. *The Army Air Forces in World War II.* 7 vols. Chicago: The University of Chicago Press, 1948–1958; Washington: Office of Air Force History, 1983. Vol I: *Plans and Early Operations: January 1939 to August 1942.* Vol VI: *Men and Planes.* Vol VII: *Services Around the World.*

Douhet, Giulio. *The Command of the Air* [USAF Warrior Studies]. Translated by Dino Ferrari and edited by Richard H. Kohn and Joseph P. Harahan. New York: Coward-McCann, 1942; Washington: Office of Air Force History, 1983.

Dziuban, Stanley·W. *Military Relations Between the United States and Canada: 1939–1945* [U.S. Army in World War II: Special Studies]. Washington: Office of the Chief of Military History, 1959.

Futrell, Robert F. *The United States Air Force in Korea, 1950–1953.* Rev. ed. Washington: Office of Air Force History, 1983.

Goodspeed, Lt. Col. P. J., ed. *The Armed Forces of Canada, 1867–1967.* Ottawa: Directorate of History, Canadian Forces Headquarters, 1967.

Green, Constance McLaughlin, Harry C. Thomson, and Peter C. Roots. *The Ordnance Department: Planning Munitions for War* [U.S. Army in World War II: The Technical Services]. Washington: Office of the Chief of Military History, 1955.

Greenfield, Kent Roberts, Robert R. Palmer, and Bell I. Wiley. *The Organization of Ground Combat Troops* [U.S. Army in World War II: The Army Ground Forces]. Washington: Office of Military History, 1947.

Gross, Charles Joseph. *Prelude to the Total Force: The Air National Guard, 1943–1969.* Washington: Office of Air Force History, 1985.

Hallion, Richard P. *On the Frontier: Flight Research at Dryden, 1946–1981* [NASA History Series]. Washington: NASA, 1984.

Hewes, James E., Jr. *From Root to McNamara: Army Organization and Administration, 1900–1963* [Special Studies Series]. Washington: United States Army Center of Military History, 1975.

Holley, Irving Brinton, Jr. *Buying Aircraft: Materiel Procurement for the Army Air Forces* [U.S. Army in World War II: Special Studies]. Washington: Office of the Chief of Military History, Department of the Army, 1964.

Knaack, Marcelle Size. *Post–World War II Fighters, 1945–1973.* Vol I of *Encyclopedia of U.S. Air Force Aircraft and Missile Systems.* Washington: Office of Air Force History, 1978.

Kohn, Richard H., and Joseph P. Harahan, eds. *Condensed Analysis of the Ninth Air Force in the European Theater of Operations* [USAF Warrior Studies]. Washington: HQ AAF Office of the Assistant Chief of Air Staff, 1946; Washington: Office of Air Force History, 1984.

Morton, Louis. *The Fall of the Philippines* [U.S. Army in World War II: The War in the Pacific]. Washington: Office of Military History, 1953.

Public Papers of the Presidents of the United States: Harry S. Truman. Washington: Government Printing Office, 1961–.

Rearden, Steven L. *The Formative Years, 1947–1950.* Vol I of *History of the Office of the Secretary of Defense.* Washington: History Office, Secretary of Defense, 1984.

Shiner, John F. *Foulois and the U.S. Army Air Corps, 1931–1935.* Washington: Office of Air Force History, 1983.

Terrett, Dulaney. *The Signal Corps: The Emergency (to December 1941)* [U.S. Army in World War II: The Technical Services]. Washington: Office of the Chief of Military History, 1956.

Thompson, George Raynor, and Dixie R. Harris. *The Signal Corps: The Outcome (mid-1943 Through 1945)* [U.S. Army in World War II: The Technical Services]. Washington: Office of the Chief of Military History, 1966.

Thompson, George Raynor, et al. *The Signal Corps: The Test (December 1941 to July 1943)* [U.S. Army in World War II: The Technical Services]. Washington: Office of the Chief of Military History, 1957.

Watson, Robert J. *The Joint Chiefs of Staff and National Policy, 1953–1954.* Vol V of *History of the Joint Chiefs of Staff.* Washington: Historical Division, Joint Chiefs of Staff, 1986.

Watts, Lt Col Barry D. *The Foundations of U.S. Air Doctrine: The Problem of Friction in War.* Maxwell AFB, Ala., 1984.
Wolk, Herman S. *Planning and Organizing the Postwar Air Force, 1943–1947.* Washington: Office of Air Force History, 1984.

Air Force Literature

The Air Defense Command in the Cuban Crisis, October–December 1962. ADC Hist Study 15, 1962.
Biographical Study of USAF General Officers, 1917–1952. USAF Hist Study 91, 1953.
Boylan, Bernard L. *Development of the Long-Range Escort Fighter.* USAF Hist Study 136, 1955.
Buss, Lydus H. *Fifteen Years of Air Defense, 1946–1961.* NORAD Hist Ref Paper 3, 1960.
——————. *Seaward Extension of Radar, 1946–1956.* ADC Hist Study 10, 1956.
——————. *Seventeen Years of Air Defense, 1946–1963.* NORAD Hist Ref Paper 9, 1963.
——————. *U.S. Air Defense in the Northeast, 1940–1957.* ADC Hist Study 37, 1957.
Case History of the F–89 All-Weather Fighter Airplane. HQ AMC Hist Study 37.
Claussen, Martin P. *Comparative History of Research and Development Policies Affecting Air Materiel, 1915–1944.* USAF Hist Study 20, 1945.
Cornett, Lloyd H., Jr., and Mildred W. Johnson. *A Handbook of Aerospace Defense Command Organization, 1946–1980.* rev ed. ADC Hist Ofc, Dec 1980.
A Decade of Continental Air Defense, 1946–1956. ADC Hist Study, 1956.
Finney, Robert T. *History of the Air Corps Tactical School, 1920–1940.* USAF Hist Study 100, 1955.
Futrell, Robert F. *Ideas, Concepts, Doctrine: A History of Basic Thinking in the United States Air Force, 1907–1964.* USAF Hist Study 139, 1971.
Goldberg, Alfred, and Robert D. Little. *History of Headquarters USAF, 1 July 1949 to 30 June 1950.* USAF Hist Study, Dec 1954.
Grant, Clement L. *AAF Air Defense Activities in the Mediterranean, 1942–20 September, 1944.* USAF Hist Study 66, 1954.
——————. *Development of Continental Air Defense to 1 September 1954.* USAF Hist Study 126, 1957.
Greer, Thomas H. *The Development of Air Doctrine in the Army Air Arm, 1917–1941.* USAF Hist Study 89, 1953.
Kelley, Robert L. *Army Antiaircraft in Air Defense, 1946–1954.* ADC Hist Study 4, 1954.
Little, Robert D. *A History of the Air Force Atomic Energy Program, 1943–1953.* HQ USAF Hist Div Liaison Office, 1959. Vol III, *Building an Atomic Air Force, 1949–1953.*
——————. *Organizing for Strategic Planning, 1945–1950, the National System and the Air Force.* HQ USAF Hist Div Liaison Office, Apr 1964.
Marmor, Arthur K. *The Search for New USAF Weapons, 1958–1959.* USAF Hist Div Liaison Office, 1961.
McMullen, Richard F. *The Aerospace Defense Anti-Bomber Defense, 1946–1972.* ADC Hist Study 39, 1973.
——————. *Air Defense and National Policy, 1951–1957.* ADC Hist Study 24, 1964.
——————. *The Air National Guard in Air Defense, 1946–1971.* ADC Hist Study 38, 1971.
——————. *Aircraft in Air Defense, 1946–1960.* ADC Hist Study 12, 1960.
——————. *The Birth of SAGE, 1951–1958.* ADC Hist Study 33, 1965.
——————. *Command and Control Planning, 1958–1965.* ADC Hist Study 35, 1965.
——————. *History of Air Defense Weapons, 1946–1962.* ADC Hist Study 14, 1962.
——————. *Interceptor Missiles in Air Defense.* ADC Hist Study 30, 1965.
——————. *Radar Programs for Air Defense, 1946–1966.* ADC Hist Study 34, 1966.
Mooney, Chase C., and Edward C. Williamson, *Organization of the Army Air Arm, 1935–1945.* USAF Hist Study 10, 1956.
NORAD's Quest for Nike-Zeus and a Long-Range Interceptor. NORAD Hist Ref Paper 6, 1962.

NORAD's Underground Combat Operations Center, 1956–1966. NORAD Hist Ref Paper 12, 1966.

Ray, Thomas W. *The ADC Airborne Early Warning and Control Program, 1946–1964.* ADC Hist Study 28, 1965.

——————. *The Air National Guard Manned Interceptor Force, 1946–1964.* ADC Hist Study 23, 1964.

——————. *History of BMEWS, 1957–1964.* ADC Hist Study 32, 1965.

——————. *A History of the DEW Line, 1946–1964.* ADC Hist Study 31, 1965.

——————. *A History of Texas Towers in Air Defense, 1952–1964.* ADC Hist Study 29, 1965.

——————. *Interceptor Dispersal, 1961–1964.* ADC Hist Study 25, 1964.

——————. *Nuclear Armament: Its Acquisition, Control, and Application to Manned Interceptors, 1951–1963.* ADC Hist Study 20, 1963.

Reither, Joseph R. *The Development of Tactical Doctrines at AAFSAT and AAFTAC.* USAF Hist Study 13, 1944.

Sturm, Thomas A. *Air Defense of Alaska, 1940–1957.* NORAD Hist Ref Paper, 1957.

——————. *Command and Control for North American Air Defense, 1959–1963.* USAF Hist Div Liaison Ofc, Jan 1965.

——————. *Organization and Responsibility for Air Defense, 1946–1955.* ADC Hist Study 9, 1963.

——————. *The USAF Scientific Advisory Board: Its First Twenty Years, 1944–1964.* USAF Hist Study, 1967.

Volan, Denys. *The History of the Ground Observer Corps.* ADC Hist Study 36, 1968.

Wiley, Mildred. *Statistical Data Book.* Vol III, *Radar, 1946–1973.* HQ ADC Hist Office, 1973.

Manuscript Histories

Indispensible to this study have been the historical monographs produced by the major Air Force commands, especially the histories produced by the Air Defense Command (ADC) and by the Continental Air Defense (CONAD) and the North American Air Defense (NORAD) commands. Especially insightful were works written by ADC historians Thomas A. Sturm, Richard F. McMullen, Denys Volan, and Thomas W. Ray. In addition, wing and interceptor command histories offer vivid portrayals of duties performed by air defense forces "on the line" and add perspective to that of the command histories.

Nongovernmental Sources

Because many of the primary documents dealing with air defense remain classified, the publications cited here will be those easily accessible to the interested reader.

The best general accounts of American military history that to some degree access the U.S. military's preference for offensive warfare are Russell F. Weigley, *Towards an American Army: Military Thought from Washington to Marshall* (New York, 1962); Walter Millis, *Arms and Men: A Study in American Military History* (New York, 1956); Robert S. Browning III, *Two If by Sea: The Development of American Coastal De-*

fense Policy (Westport, Conn. 1983); Allan R. Millett and Peter Maslowski, *For the Common Defense: A Military History of the United States of America* (London, 1984); and Weigley, *The American Way of War: A History of United States Military Strategy and Policy* (New York, 1973). Millett and Maslowski's study is judicious and comprehensive. Weigley's works are most insightful and provocative.

General and special studies in the development of nuclear strategy are legion, and the list of books, articles, and special reports is growing. Cited below are works that are particularly helpful in fitting air defense into the context and evolution of post–World War II strategy.

An excellent survey is Lawrence Freedman, *The Evolution of Nuclear Strategy* (London, 1981); also see Bernard Brodie, *Strategy in the Missile Age* (Princeton, 1959), and "The Development of Nuclear Strategy" [*International Security* (spring 1978)]; George H. Quester, *Deterrence Before Hiroshima: The Airpower Background of Modern Strategy* (New York, 1966); Gregg Herken, *The Winning Weapon: The Atomic Bomb in the Cold War, 1945–1950* (New York, 1980), and *Counsels of War* (New York, 1985) (Herken interviewed many of the scientists who participated in air defense studies and laboratory experiments in the early 1950s); Aaron L. Friedberg, "A History of the U.S. Strategic Doctrine, 1945 to 1980" [*Journal of Strategic Studies* (Dec 1980)]; David A. Rosenberg (who produced the ground-breaking work in the field of early postwar American plans and capabilities for nuclear war), "American Atomic Strategy and the Hydrogen Bomb Decision" [*Journal of American History* (May 1979)], "The Origins of Overkill: Nuclear Weapons and American Strategy, 1945–1960" [*International Security* (spring 1983)], and "A Smoking, Radiating Ruin at the End of Two Hours: Documents on American War Plans for Nuclear War with the Soviet Union, 1954–1955" [*International Security* (winter 1981/1982)]; Samuel F. Wells, Jr., "Sounding the Tocsin: NSC–68 and the Soviet Threat" [*International Security* (fall 1979)], and "The Origins of Massive Retaliation" [*Political Science Quarterly* (spring 1981)]; and Robert Jervis, "Deterrence and Perception" [*International Security* (winter 1982/1983)]. These citations can only serve as a small, although important, sample of books and articles published on strategic issues with overtones for air defense.

Threat assessment and air defense are closely related issues. See Jack H. Nunn, *The Soviet First Strike Threat: The U.S. Perspective* (New York, 1982); Mark E. Miller, *Soviet Strategic Power and Doctrine: The Quest for Superiority* (Miami, Fla., 1982); John Prados, *The Soviet Estimate: U.S. Intelligence Analysis and Russian Military Strength* (New York, 1982); and Jonathan S. Lockwood, *The Soviet View of U.S. Strategic Doctrine: Implications for Decision Making* (London, 1983).

Background on why military institutions favor offensive doctrines and on advantages and disadvantages of the strategic defensive are touched on in Barry R. Posen, *The Sources of Military Doctrine: France, Britain, and Germany Between Two Wars* (Ithaca, 1984) (Posen's section on the British decision to move ahead in air defense in the 1930s is especially valuable); see also George H. Quester, *Offense and Defense in the International System* (New York, 1977); Jack Snyder, "Civil-Military Relations and the Cult of the Offensive, 1914 and 1984" [*International Security* (summer 1984)]; Charles L. Glaser, "Why Even Good Defenses May Be Bad" [*International Security* (fall 1984)] (Glaser's article is not historical, but nevertheless invites comparisons between the decision to build an extensive air defense network in the 1950s and the debates of the 1960s and 1980s on missile defense); and Maj. Owen E. Jensen, "Classical Military Strategy and Ballistic Missile Defense" [*Air University Review*, (May–June 1984)].

Daniel H. Yergin, *Shattered Peace: The Origins of the Cold War and the National Security State* (Boston, 1977), and John Lewis Gaddis, *Strategies of Containment: A Critical Appraisal of Postwar American National Security Policy* (New York, 1982), present the national security backdrop to the years covered in this book.

Books

Adams, Benson D. *Ballistic Missile Defense*. New York: American Elsevier, 1971.

Aliano, Richard A. *American Defense Policy from Eisenhower to Kennedy*. Athens: Ohio University Press, 1975.

Ambrose, Stephen E. *Ike's Spies: Eisenhower and the Espionage Establishment*. New York: Doubleday, 1981.

Arnold, Henry H. *Global Mission*. New York: Harper & Bros., 1949.

Ashmore, E. B. *Air Defence*. London: Longmans, Green & Co., 1929.

Bailes, Kendall E. *Technology and Science Under Lenin and Stalin: Origins of the Soviet Technical Intelligensia, 1917–1941*. Princeton, N.J.: Princeton University Press, 1978.

Baker, David. *The Shape of Wars to Come*. New York: Stein & Day, 1984.

Betts, Richard K. *Surprise Attack: Lessons for Defense Planning*. Washington: Brookings Institution, 1982.

Bilstein, Roger E. *Flight in America, 1900–1983: From the Wrights to the Astronauts*. Baltimore: Johns Hopkins University Press, 1984.

Bonds, Ray, ed. *The Soviet War Machine: An Encyclopedia of Russian Military Equipment and Strategy*. New York: Hamlyn, 1976.

Borowski, Harry R. *A Hollow Threat: Strategic Air Power and Containment Before Korea*. Westport, Conn.: Greenwood, 1982.

Boyd, Alexander. *The Soviet Air Force Since 1918*. New York, 1977.

Boyle, Andrew. *Trenchard*. New York: Norton, 1962.

Braun, Wernher von, and Frederick I. Ordway III. *History of Rocketry and Space Travel*. 3d rev ed. New York: Crowell, 1975.

Brodie, Bernard. *Strategy in the Missile Age*. Princeton, N.J.: Princeton University Press, 1959.

Browing, Robert S., III. *Two If by Sea: The Development of American Coastal Defense Policy*. Westport, Conn.: Greenwood, 1983.

Bushby, John. *Air Defence of Great Britain*. London: Allan, 1973.

Carver, Michael, ed. *The War Lords: Military Commanders of the Twentieth Century*. London: Weidenfeld & Nicolson, 1976.

Churchill, Winston. *The World Crisis, 1911–1914.* New York: Scribner, 1928.

Clark, Ronald W. *The Rise of the Boffins.* London: Phoenix House, 1962.

————. *Tizard.* Cambridge, Mass.: MIT Press, 1965.

Clausewitz, Carl von. *On War.* Edited and translated by Michael Howard and Peter Paret. Princeton, N.J.: Princeton University Press, 1976.

Coletta, Paolo E. *The United States Navy and Defense Unification, 1947–1953.* Newark: University of Delaware Press, 1981.

Collier, Basil. *A History of Air Power.* New York: Macmillan, 1974.

Collins, John M. *Grand Strategy: Principles and Practices.* Annapolis, Md.: Naval Institute Press, 1973.

Conant, Melvin. *The Long Polar Watch: Canada and the Defense of North America.* New York: Published for the Council on Foreign Relations by Harper, 1962.

Cuneo, John R. *Winged Mars: The German Air Weapon, 1870–1914.* Harrisburg, Pa: Military Service Pub. Co., 1942. Vol I: *The German Air Weapon.*

Cuthbertson, Brian. *Canadian Military Independence in the Age of the Superpowers.* Toronto: Fitzhenry & Whiteside, 1977.

Douglass, Sholto. *Combat and Command, The Story of an Airman in Two World Wars.* New York: Simon & Schuster, 1966.

Dow, James. *The Arrow.* Toronto: J. Lorimer, 1979.

DuPre, Col Flint O. *U.S. Air Force Biographical Dictionary.* New York: Franklin Watts, Inc., 1965.

Earle, Edward Mead, ed. *Makers of Modern Strategy: Military Thought from Machiavelli to Hitler.* Princeton, N.J.: Princeton University Press, 1943.

Eayres, James. *In Defence of Canada: Growing Up Allied.* Toronto: University of Toronto Press, 1980.

Emme, Eugene M., ed. *The Impact of Air Power: National Security and World Politics.* Princeton, N.J.: Van Nostrand, 1959.

Finletter, Thomas K. *Power and Policy: U.S. Foreign Policy and Military Power in the Hydrogen Age.* New York: Harcourt, Brace, 1954.

Forrestal, James. *The Forrestal Diaries.* Edited by Walter Millis. New York: Viking, 1951.

Foxworth, Thomas. *The Speed Seekers.* New York: Doubleday, 1976.

Fredette, Raymond H. *The Sky on Fire: The First Battle of Britain, 1917–1918, and the Birth of the Royal Air Force.* New York: Harcourt, Brace, Jovanovich, 1976.

Freedman, Lawrence. *The Evolution of Nuclear Strategy.* London: Macmillan, 1981.

Gaddis, John Lewis. *Strategies of Containment: A Critical Appraisal of Postwar American National Security Policy.* New York: Oxford University Press, 1982.

Garthoff, Raymond L. *Soviet Strategy in the Nuclear Age.* New York: Praeger, 1960.

Gruening, Ernest. *Many Battles: The Autobiography of Ernest Gruening.* New York: Liveright, 1973.

Gunston, Bill. *Fighters of the Fifties.* Osceola, Wis.: Speciality Press, 1981.

————. *Early Supersonic Fighters of the West.* New York: Scribner, 1975.

Hagen, Kenneth J., ed. *In Peace and War: Interpretations of American Naval History, 1775–1978.* Westport, Conn: Greenwood Press, 1978.

Hallion, Richard P. *Rise of the Fighter Aircraft, 1914–1918.* Annapolis, Md.: Nautical & Aviation Pub. Co. of America, 1984.

Haydon, F. S. *Aeronautics in the Union and Confederate Armies.* Baltimore: Johns Hopkins Press, 1941.

Haynes, Richard F. *The Awesome Power: Harry S. Truman as Commander in Chief.* Baton Rouge: Louisiana State Univeristy Press, 1973.

Herken, Gregg H. *Counsels of War.* New York: Distributed by Random House, 1985.

————. *The Winning Weapon: The Atomic Bomb in the Cold War, 1945–1950.* New York: Knopf, 1980.

Hewlett, Richard G., and Francis Duncan. *Atomic Shield, 1947–1952.* Vol II in *A History of the United States Atomic Energy Commission.* University Park: Pennsylvania State University Press, 1969.

Higham, Robin, and Jacob W. Kipp, eds. *Soviet Aviation and Air Power: A Historical View.* Boulder, Colo.: Westview Press, 1977.

Hogg, Ian V. *Anti-Aircraft: A History of Air Defence.* London: Macdonald & Jane's, 1978.

Hurley, Alfred F. *Billy Mitchell: Crusader for Air Power*. Bloomington: Indiana University Press, 1975.

Ingell, Douglas J. *The Plane That Changed the World: A Biography of the DC–3*. Fallbrook, Calif.: Aero Publishers, 1966.

Jockel, Joseph T. *No Boundaries Upstairs: Canada, the United States, and the Origins of North American Air Defence, 1945–1958* [Foreign Policy and Military History]. Vancouver, Canada: The University of British Columbia Press, 1987.

Jones, Lloyd S. *U.S. Fighters*. Fallbrook, Calif.: Aero Publishers, 1975.

Killian, James R., Jr. *Sputnik, Scientists, and Eisenhower: A Memoir of the First Special Assistant to the President for Science and Technology*. Cambridge, Mass.: MIT Press, 1977.

Kinnard, Douglas. *President Eisenhower and Strategy Management: A Study in Defense Politics*. Lexington: University Press of Kentucky, 1977.

Kolodziej, Edward A. *The Uncommon Defense and Congress, 1945–1963*. Columbus: Ohio State University Press, 1963.

Kuneta, James W. *Oppenheimer: The Years of Risk*. Englewood Cliffs, N.J.: Prentice Hall, 1982.

Levine, Isaac D. *Mitchell, Pioneer of Air Power*. Rev. ed. New York: Arno Press, 1972.

Lockwood, Jonathan S. *The Soviet View of U.S. Strategic Doctrine: Implications for Decision Making*. New Brunswick, N.J.: Transaction Books, 1983.

McLin, Jon B. *Canada's Changing Defense Policy, 1957–1963: The Problem of a Middle Power in Alliance*. Baltimore: Johns Hopkins Press, 1967.

McDougall, Walter A. *. . . The Heavens and the Earth: A Political History of the Space Age*. New York: Basic Books, 1985.

Mikesh, Robert C. *Balloon Bomb Attacks on North America: Japan's World War II Assaults*. Fallbrook, Calif.: Aero Publishers, 1982.

Miller, Mark E. *Soviet Strategic Power and Doctrine: The Quest for Superiority*. Miami, Fla.: Advanced International Studies Institute, 1982.

Miller, Ronald E., and David Sawers. *The Technical Development of Modern Aviation*. New York: Praeger, 1970.

Millett, Allan R., and Peter Maslowski. *For the Common Defense: A Military History of the United States of America*. London: Collier Macmillan, 1984.

Millis, Walter. *Arms and Men: A Study in American Military History*. New York: Putnam, 1956.

Mitchell, William. *Memoirs of World War I: From Start to Finish of Our Greatest War*. New York: Random House, 1960.

Morenus, Richard. *DEW Line: Distant Early Warning, the Miracle of America's First Line of Defense*. New York: Rand-McNally, 1957.

Munson, Kenneth G. *Airliners Between the Wars, 1919–1939*. New York: Macmillan, 1972.
——————. *Bombers Between the Wars, 1919–1939*. New York: Macmillan, 1970.

Murphy, Paul J., ed. *The Soviet Air Forces*. London: McFarland, 1984.

Nunn, Jack H. *The Soviet First Strike Threat: The U.S. Perspective*. New York: Praeger, 1982.

Page, Robert M. *The Origins of Radar*. Garden City, N.Y.: Anchor Books, 1962.

Parrot, Bruce. *Politics and Technology in the Soviet Union*. Cambridge, Mass.: MIT Press, 1983.

Posen, Barry R. *The Sources of Military Doctrine: France, Britain, and Germany Between Two Wars*. Ithaca: Cornell University Press, 1984.

Postan, M. M., et al, eds. *Design and Development of Weapons: Studies in Government and Industrial Organization*. London: Her Majesty's Stationery Office, 1964.

Powers, Barry D. *Strategy Without Slide-Rule: British Air Strategy, 1914–1939*. London: Croom Helm, 1976.

Prados, John. *The Soviet Estimate: U.S. Intelligence Analysis and Russian Military Strength*. New York: Dial, 1982.

Prange, Gordon W. *At Dawn We Slept: The Untold Story of Pearl Harbor*. New York: McGraw-Hill, 1981.

Quester, George H. *Deterrence Before Hiroshima: The Airpower Background of Modern Strategy*. New York: Wiley, 1966.
——————. *Nuclear Diplomacy: The First Twenty-Five Years*. New York, Dunellen Co., 1970.

————. *Offense and Defense in the International System.* New York: Wiley, 1977.

Radford, Adm Arthur W. *The Collected Writings of Arthur W. Radford; Chairman, Joint Chiefs of Staff.* 2 vols. Washington, D.C., 1975.

————. *From Pearl Harbor to Vietnam: The Memoirs of Admiral Arthur W. Radford.* Edited by Stephen Jurika, Jr. Stanford, Calif.: Hoover Institution Press, 1980.

Redmond, Kent C., and Thomas M. Smith. *Project Whirlwind: The History of a Pioneer Computer.* Bedford, Mass.: Digital Press, 1980.

Ridgway, Matthew B. *Soldier: The Memoirs of Matthew B. Ridgway.* New York: Harper, 1956.

Robertson, Bruce, ed. *U.S. Army and Air Force Fighters, 1916–1961.* Fallbrook, Calif.: Aero Publishers, 1961.

Scott, Harriet Fast, and William F. Scott. *The Soviet Art of War: Doctrine, Strategy, and Tactics.* Boulder, Colo.: Westview Press, 1982.

Sherman, William C. *Air Warfare.* New York: Ronald Press Co., 1926.

Smith, Jean Edward, ed. *The Papers of General Lucius D. Clay: Germany, 1945–1949.* Bloomington: Indiana University Press, 1974.

Smith, Malcolm. *British Air Strategy Between the Wars.* Oxford: Clarendon Press, 1984.

Smith, Perry M. *The Air Force Plans for Peace, 1943–1945.* Baltimore and London, 1970.

Spick, Mike. *Fighter Pilot Tactics: The Techniques of Daylight Air Combat.* New York: Stein & Day, 1983.

Stein, Harold. *American Civil-Military Decisions: A Book of Case Studies.* Tuscaloosa: University of Alabama Press, 1963.

Stern, Philip M. *The Oppenheimer Case: Security on Trial.* New York: Harper & Row, 1969.

Swanborough, Frederick G., and Peter Bowers. *United States Military Aircraft Since 1909.* London and New York: G. P. Putnam's Sons, 1963.

Truman, Harry S. *Memoirs.* Vol II, *Years of Trial and Hope.* Garden City, N.Y.: Doubleday, 1956.

Truman, Margaret. *Harry S. Truman.* New York: Morrow, 1973.

Volkman, Ernest. *Warriors of the Night: Spies, Soldiers, and the American Military.* New York: Morrow, 1985.

Watson-Watt, Sir Robert. *Three Steps to Victory.* London: Oldhams Press, 1957.

Weigley, Russell F. *The American Way of War: A History of United States Military Strategy and Policy.* New York: Macmillan 1973.

————. *Towards an American Army: Military Thought from Washington to Marshall.* New York: Columbia University Press, 1962.

Wells, H. G. *The War in the Air.* London: Macmillan, 1908.

Wohlstetter, Roberta. *Pearl Harbor: Warning and Decision.* Stanford, Calif.: Stanford University Press, 1962.

Wolfe, Thomas W. *Soviet Power and Europe, 1945–1970.* Baltimore: Johns Hopkins University Press, 1970.

Yanarella, Ernest J. *The Missile Defense-Controversy: Strategy, Technology, and Politics, 1955–1972.* Lexington,: University Press of Kentucky, 1972.

Yergin, Daniel H. *Shattered Peace: The Origins of the Cold War and the National Security State.* Boston: Houghton Mifflin,1977.

Periodicals

Addington, Larry H. "The U.S. Coast Artillery and the Problem of Artillery Organization, 1907–1954." *Military Affairs* 40 (1976).

Air Corps News Letter 19 (Jan 1, 1936).

Alsop, Joseph, and Stewart Alsop. "Matter of Fact: Air Defense Ignored in Political Shuffle." *Washington Post* (May 9, 1952).

————. "We Accuse." *Harper's* (Oct 1954).

Bennett, Col J. B. "The Joint AA–Air Corps Exercise." *The Coast Artillery Journal* (Nov–Dec 1938).

Brodie, Bernard. "The Development of Nuclear Strategy." *International Security* 2 (spring 1978).

Cammarota, Lt Col Richard S. "Defensive Watch." *Air Force* 68 (Feb 1985).

Cannon, Charles A. "The Politics of Interest and Ideology: The Senate Airpower Hearings of 1956." *Armed Forces and Society* 3 (Aug 1977).

Carson, Lt Col Donald D. "New Look in Air Defense." *Air Force* 67 (Jun 1984).

The Coast Artillery Journal 80 (1930).

"The Emerging Shield: The Air Defense Ground Environment." *Air University Quarterly Review* 8 (spring 1956).

Foulkes, Gen Charles. "Canadian Defence Policy in a Nuclear Age." *Behind the Headlines* 21 (May 1961).

Friedberg, Aaron L. "A History of the U.S. Strategic 'Doctrine'—1945 to 1980." *Journal of Strategic Studies* 3, no. 3 (Dec 1980).

Frisbee, John L. "Air Defense—The Forgotten Front." *Air Force* 53 (Jul 1970).

Furlong, R. D. M. "NORAD—A Study in Evolution." *International Defense Review* 7 (Jun 1974).

Glaser, Charles L. "Why Even Good Defenses May Be Bad." *International Security* 9 (fall 1984).

Gollin, Alfred. "Anticipating Air Attack, in Defence of Great Britain." *Aerospace Historian* 23 (winter/Dec 1976).

Holloway, David. "Soviet Thermonuclear Development." *International Security* 4 (winter 1979–1980).

Jacobs, John B. "SAGE Overview." *Annals of the History of Computing* 5 (Oct 1983).

James, Gen Daniel, Jr. "Keeping Up Our Defenses Against Aerospace Attacks." *Grumman Aerospace Horizons* 12.

Jensen, Maj Owen E. "Classical Military Strategy and Ballistic Missile Defense." *Air University Review* (May–June 1984).

Jervis, Robert. "Deterrence and Perception." *International Security* 7 (winter 1982/83).

Lovell, Capt John R. "Antiaircraft Preparedness." *The Coast Artillery Journal* 82 (Jul–Aug 1939).

Lowes, Maj George H. "Double Decade of Air Defense." [Canadian Forces] *Sentinel* (Jun 1951).

Millett, Stephen M. "The Capabilities of the American Nuclear Deterrent, 1945–1950." *Aerospace Historian* (Mar 1980).

Murphy, Charles J. V. "Kelly versus the Summer Study Group." *Fortune* (July 1953).

Naval War College Review 27 (May–Jun 1975).

"Night Fighter Over New York." *The Saturday Evening Post* (Feb 2, 1952).

Oppenheimer, J. Robert. "Atomic Weapons and American Policy." *Foreign Affairs* (July 1953).

Penden, Murray. "Fall of the Arrow." *Wings* 9 (Feb 1979).

Ransom, Harry M. "Lord Trenchard, Architect of Air Power." *The Air Power Historian* 8.

Rosenberg, David A. "American Atomic Strategy and the Hydrogen Bomb Decision." *Journal of American History* (May 1979).

——————."The Origins of Overkill: Nuclear Weapons and American Strategy, 1945–1960." *International Security* 7 (spring 1983).

——————. "A Smoking, Radiating Ruin at the End of Two Hours: Documents on American War Plans for Nuclear War with the Soviet Union, 1954–1955." *International Security* 6 (winter 1981/1982).

"SAGE: The New Aerial Defense System of the United States." *The Military Engineer* (Mar–Apr 1956).

Saville, Gordon P. "The Air Defense Dilemma." *Air Force Magazine* 36 (Mar 1953).

Schaffel, Kenneth. "General Muir S. Fairchild: Philosopher of Air Power." *Aerospace Historian* 33 (fall/Sep 1986).

——————. "A Minority of One: Major General Gordon P. Saville." *American Aviation Historical Society Journal* 32, no. 2 (summer 1987).

Schaffer, Ronald. "Stanley D. Embick: Military Dissenter." *Military Affairs* 37 (Oct 1973).

Schenk, Lt Col Peter J. "Problems in Air Defense." *Air University Quarterly Review* 5 (spring 1952).

Silcox, Marilyn. "Southeast ROCC Marks Beginning of New Air Defense Era." *National Defense* 69 (Jul–Aug 1984).

Siracusa, Joseph M. "NSC 68: A Reappraisal." *Naval War College Review* 33 (Nov–Dec 1980).

Smith, Beverly. "This Way Lies Peace." *Saturday Evening Post* (Oct 13, 1949).

Smith, Perry M. "Douhet and Mitchell: Some Reappraisals." *Air University Review* 18 (Sep–Oct 1967).

Smith, Thomas M. "Project Whirlwind: An Unorthodox Development Project." *Technology and Culture* 17 (Jul 1976).

Snyder, Jack. "Civil-Military Relations and the Cult of the Offensive, 1914 and 1984." *International Security* 9 (summer 1984).

Stoler, Mark A. "From Continentalism to Globalism: General Stanley D. Embick, the Joint Strategic Survey Committee, and the Military View of American National Policy During the Second World War." *Diplomatic History* 6 (summer 1982).

Sturm, Thomas A. "Henry Conger Pratt: First Air Corps Permanent General Officer." *Aerospace Historian* 22 (Jun 1975).

Symington, Stuart. "We've Scuttled Our Air Defense." *American Magazine* 45 (Feb 1948).

Wells, Samuel F., Jr. "The Origins of Massive Retaliation." *Political Science Quarterly* (spring 1981).

──────. "Sounding the Tocsin: NSC–68 and the Soviet Threat." *International Security* 4 (fall 1979).

White, Gen Thomas D. "The Scope of United States Air Strategy." *The Annals of the American Academy of Political and Social Science* 299 (May 1955). Reprinted for the Air Force as *Air Power and National Security*.

Witt, Alan F. "Coming of Age: XIX TAC's Role During the 1944 Dash Across France." *Air University Review* 36 (Mar–Apr 1985).

Wohlstetter, Albert. "The Delicate Balance of Terror." *Foreign Affairs* (Jan 1959).

Index

Air Force Directorate of Requirements: 199
Air Force Magazine: 180–81, 273
Air Force Operations Staff: 133
Air Force Scientific Advisory Board: 121
Air Forces (numbered)
First: 33, 39, 54, 77–78, 89, 97
Second: 39–40, 54
Third: 40, 42, 54
Fourth: 48, 54, 56, 76–77, 89
Fifth: 103
Tenth: 54, 89
Eleventh: 54
Fourteenth: 54, 89
Twentieth: 50
Air Materiel Command
all-weather interceptor studies: 99–101
on developing all-weather fighters: 161
evaluates SAGE: 203
seeks long-range supersonic missile: 236–37
studies missile defense system: 256
Air National Guard
on air defense duties: 113, 126, 268
called to active duty, Korea: 141–42
control of by regular forces: 76–77
participation in exercises: 77
training for active duty: 60–61
transfer of aircraft to: 131–32, 230
Air Policy Commission: 137
appointed by Truman: 69
Air Proving Ground Command: 68, 73, 199
and early warning aircraft: 155
in emergency posture: 170
in tests for improved interceptor: 99
Air Research and Development Command (ARDC): 199, 262
on assignment of interceptors: 229
in emergency posture: 170
established: 121
evaluates SAGE: 203
Air Reserve: 54–55
on active duty, Korea: 141–42
under CONAC: 140
training for active duty: 60–61, 72–73
Air Service: *See* United States Air Service
Airships: 4, 7
Air Staff (*See also* Eaker, Ira C.; United States Air Force): 43, 52, 107
Air Defense Division of: 86
on atomic weapons: 178
augments Lashup stations: 123–25
Budget Advisory Committee of: 193
and civilian consultants: 152
on control of aircraft artillery: 48
defines Air Reserve functions: 55
delays in completing radar system: 142

Deputy Chief of Staff for Development: 121–22
Directorate of Plans: 187
on distant early warning: 185
in emergency contingency: 79–80, 170–71
Personnel Advisory Council: 50
Post War Division: 50–51
reacts to grounding Scorpions: 161
reviews USAF posture: 113–15
role in air defense: 61–73, 91, 112
Special Projects Office: 50
Air Training Command: 161
electronic graduates of: 126
in emergency posture: 170
expands scholarships for radar training: 142
Air Transport Command: 78, 84
Air War College: 73, 129
Alaska: 211
aircraft control centers in: 92
defense of: 63–64, 116, 129, 131
and DEW Line: 211
early-warning network zones in: 176, 212
emergency air plan for: 77–78
ground-based radar in: 132, 188
and Mid-Canada Line: 188
SAGE facilities in: 264
Soviet threat to: 107–8
strategic position of: 58–59
Alaskan Air Command
and aircraft warning: 59, 78
on air defense needs: 67
squadrons in: 161
Albuquerque, N. Mex.: 95, 134, 139
Aleutian Islands: 108
Alsop, Joseph
as aide to Chennault: 173
on air defense: 173–74, 187, 189
on Oppenheimer: 179
Alsop, Stewart
on air defense: 173–74, 187, 189
on Oppenheimer: 179
American Telephone and Telegraph Co.: 207
The American Way of War: xii–xiii
Anderson, Samuel E.: 86
on goals for Lashup: 95
on revising U.S. defenses: 113–15
Andrews, Frank M.: 18, 21
as Commander, Army forces in Panama: 29
as Commander, GHQ Air Force: 15
Ankenbrandt, Francis L.: 86
prepares air defense plans: 69–71
on training cadre: 87

INDEX

Wings (numbered)
    2d: 15
    14th Pursuit: 36
    52d: 133
WIZARD research program: 256, 258
Wolfe, Kenneth B.: 99–100
World War I
    air-to-air combat in: 2–3
    balloons in: 1
    combat formations in: 16–17
    Soviet weapons of: 65
World War II: 116, 117, 134, 151, 155, 173
    aerial photography of Soviet industry during: 130
    air defense in: 21–45, 64–65, 115
    air defenses dismantled: 47
    atomic bomb in: 118
    Canadian bases obtained in: 159–60
    defense strategy in: 21
    defensive ties with Canada during: 58–59
    doctrine in: 19, 21–24
    equipment for defense in: 65–66
    Japanese suicide attacks in: 109
    radars during: 92, 95, 142–43
    Soviet air power in: 57
    strategic and tactical units in: 74
Wright brothers: 2
Wrong, Hume: 160
Wurtsmith Air Force Base, Mich.: 234

"Yellow" attack code: 134

Zacharias, Jerrold R.
    as Director, Summer Study Group: 174, 176, 178
    supports air defense buildup: 183
Zeppelin balloons: 3–5
ZORC, predecessor to Summer Study Group: 183–84
Zuckert, Eugene M.: 138

356